Flights of Angels

A novel by
Doug James

Foreword by Ed McMahon

ISBN 0-9651695-1-0

Cover art provided courtesy of Naval Historical Center— "Wind Her Up!" by Georges Schreiber, 1943. Gift of Abbott Laboratories

Also by Doug James

Walter Cronkite: His Life and Times

Gucci: A Puppy's Tale

Available in limited quantities from Amazon.com

Now cracks a noble heart.
Good night, sweet prince.
And flights of angels sing thee
to thy rest.

—William Shakespeare,
Hamlet V, ii.

FOREWORD

*F*lights of Angels takes me back to that unforgettable day when I was accepted as a V-5 pilot. World War II was on and I wanted very much to be a Marine fighter pilot and fly the famous Marine fighter, the Corsair. I'm sure anybody who ever watched *The Tonight Show* with Johnny Carson knows how proud I am to be a Marine.

The avenue to my goal of becoming a Marine pilot depended on being accepted into the Navy's V-5 program, but that was not an easy avenue to get onto.

The battery of tests to determine if we had the intelligence to become military pilots was only one phase of the indoctrination process.

The second phase determined if we were as close to physically perfect as possible. The physical examinations were so thorough they took three full days to complete. The eye

Ed McMahon

examination alone took an entire day, because if you were going to be landing on a carrier, your eyes had to be in absolutely perfect condition.

You can understand why passing the physicals and being accepted into the program were very special for me. I'll never forget the day I was notified that I had passed with flying colors and was a V-5 flight cadet.

Like Billy Benson, the protagonist of *Flights of Angels*, I, too, went through pre-flight training in Athens, Georgia, intermediate in Pensacola, Florida, and I received my gold wings "Under the Oaks" in Pensacola.

After I received my wings, I became a fighter pilot, flying the beloved Corsair. I was also a flight instructor, teaching, among other things, carrier landings. What a thrill that was! From the air, the deck of a carrier looks no larger than a playing card. That was when all that flight training paid off.

Flights of Angels brings all these wonderful memories rushing back to me. It's a wonderful read for anybody who ever looked to the skies and yearned to fly.

By the way, Bob Hawthorne's summation of Pre-Flight School at the end of Chapter One ("I wouldn't go through pre-flight school again for a million dollars, but I wouldn't trade the experience for ten million dollars!") was actually said by me. I'm honored to have even a small part in anything that pays tribute to my Navy and Marine pilot buddies in that exciting chapter of my life.

Cordially,

Ed McMahon

(Editor's note: Ed McMahon was recalled to duty during the Korean Conflict where he flew 85 reconnaissance missions in an unarmed plane. He retired as a highly decorated full colonel.)

Lynwood Glazier
1922-1942

Marcy Darnall
1912-1945

INTRODUCTION AND DEDICATION

I was eight years old when Lynwood Glazier, a first lieutenant in the Army Air Corps, was shot down somewhere in the Pacific in 1942. He was 20 years old and his body was never recovered.

I didn't know Lynwood, but his house on Hawthorne Street was only one block over from my Florence, Alabama, home. I was especially intrigued by the story that circulated around the neighborhood that, after his disappearance, his mother closed the door to his room and left it as it was.

Shortly thereafter, Marcy Darnall brought his wife and three children to stay with his parents, our neighbors, when he went off to fly for the Navy. He was killed September 1, 1945, literally the last day of World War II, a few days short of his 33rd birthday.

Both those events remained lodged in the back of my brain for the better part of 60 years. In 2000, I decided the time was right to pay tribute to these two neighbors and to the thousands of ordinary men and women who went off to defend their homeland, never to return.

My original plan was to track the naval career of Marcy, but use Lynwood's home as the setting for the early years of my protagonist, Billy Benson.

I began the chapters on Billy's early life, letting my imagination guide me through the Glazier's house and, importantly, to Lynwood's room.

Before my next trip to Florence, I called Marie Shanks, long-time resident of Hawthorne Street, for the name of the present owner of the house to arrange for a visit.

The downstairs of the California bungalow was very close to what I had imagined, but "Billy's" room was the important feature I needed to experience. I had felt strongly that Lynwood's room would be on the second floor, which turned out to be a correct assumption.

The Frank Armstrongs let me climb the stairs alone. As I approached the door to Lynwood's room—and hesitated there—I became aware of the increased beating of my heart. When I opened the door, I got goose bumps over my arms. I was frankly amazed that the room was nearly identical to my descriptions in the book. I found out later that Lynwood had hung his model airplanes from the ceiling as Billy had.

I am indebted to Lynwood's only sibling, Sylvia Bernstein, of Arlington, Virginia, for providing photographs of her older brother, one of which was used in this dedication. When the prints arrived, I didn't immediately rip open the envelope. After all, I had heard about this young man's death over 50 years earlier. Too, I had visited his home and gone to his room, and now, at last, I was going to see what he looked like. Once more, my heart rate accelerated as I pulled the carefully and lovingly wrapped photos from the parcel. Sylvia had written me a note: "His beautiful countenance should be an inspiration."

She was right.

I looked...I wept...and was inspired.

I began the novel by creating the life of Billy Benson before his entry into naval flight training. I wonder now if I would have completed the project had I begun the other way round, for the more I researched, investigated and interviewed former WWII V-5 pilots,

I realized what an intense and involved program it was and how much work it would take to do the job right.

I need to interrupt here to explain the absence of Billy's early years in *Flights of Angels*. By the time I completed the novel, it was far too long and I was convinced it needed to be cut. Rather than just throw away a wonderful life, I made two books out of one. A sequel to be called *Billy Benson* will be published in 2007 and will clear up the mystery I feel certain you will want explained after you read *Flights of Angels.*

One of the strongest sources of support for the research project was provided by Ken Snyder, former V-5 pilot and now a volunteer in the Emil Buehler Naval Aviation Library at the National Museum of Naval Aviation, in Pensacola, Florida. Ken never failed to deliver with each request via telephone or visit to the museum's library. I appreciate very much his considerable contributions.

And then one day, out of the blue, I received a call from one George Harris, who lives in Baldwin County, over the bay from Mobile. George had read a letter I had written to the editor of the *Mobile Register* and called to compliment me on it. As we chatted, he revealed that he had been a Navy pilot during WWII. When I inquired if he had been a V-5 pilot, he informed me he had. Furthermore, he had been a flight instructor, as were Marcy and my protagonist and, better yet, he had instructed at nearby Barin Field, where Billy Benson was to complete his flight training.

George, his lovely wife Lana and I have spent many hours over wonderful meals (many prepared by George), discussing the Navy and flight training, as well as side trips into politics and religion.

Two of the scenarios I used in Billy Benson's flight training (one fatal, the other, nearly so) were from the various experiences Ken and George shared with me.

On my visit to Barin Field, in south Baldwin County, I purchased a reunion publication that told the story of the lost airplane cranks I incorporated into Chapter Four, which details Billy's advanced training. The author of the piece had accused his back seat pilot of dropping a replacement crank at the wrong time and place. When I told George that anecdote, his expression changed and he said, "Let me see that!" He took the publication, read it quickly and declared emphatically, "That is not the way it happened! I dropped the crank when and where he told me!" How is that for irony?

George served as my technical flight adviser, simplifying tactical maneuvers and technical material for my non-technical brain. He was the first to read the manuscript and I appreciate his comments and enthusiastic endorsement of my efforts.

Too, it was George and Lana who inspired Billy and Suzanne's stay at Mrs. McCauhey's Tea Room (now the Hopkins House) in Pensacola, as honeymooners, as George and Lana had done.

I am grateful to Mrs. Winnie Smith, former owner of the Hopkins House restaurant, who shared the story of Wallis Simpson's residency at the Tea Room.

When I visited the naval base in Millington, Tennessee, in 2001, I was hosted by John Williams, who had been assigned there when it was an air station during WWII. Interestingly, the civilians I had telephoned before I located John knew nothing of the role the site played in flight training, since the base is now the location for the Navy Bureau of Personnel, or NavBuPers, in Navy-ese. John kindly drove me around the base and provided photographs of the way things looked during the war years.

Dick Pace and Jim Constantine, both V-5 pilots and volunteers at the Pensacola Museum of Naval Aviation were, likewise, most helpful in my research.

Bill Flanagan, former V-5 pilot, whose wife also lived on Hawthorne Street in Florence, shared stories about the program and generously lent me his copy of Slipstream, a Corpus Christi flight-training yearbook.

Another yearbook, The Flight Jacket, was graciously lent me by another former V-5 pilot, Mike Wilson of Pensacola.

On each trip back to Florence, I visit Marcy's widow, Elizabeth Darnall Gerber, still beautiful, gracious and vivacious. When I am lucky, her children, Didi, Betty or Brad are there and visiting with them is always a bonus. It was Betty who provided the photograph of her father for the dedication.

I told Elizabeth on one of my visits that I remembered that Marcy had grown a mustache when I saw him before he shipped out to his last duty station in the Philippines. I further said I thought he looked like actor Robert Taylor, also a naval primary fight instructor. Elizabeth said other people thought so, too: so much so, when she was visiting him for the last time in California, she told me several people came by their restaurant table for autographs.

Following WWII, the original NAS New Orleans was relocated to nearby Belle Chase, Louisiana, and the old base was given to the city of New Orleans. It is now where the University of New Orleans is located. Despite several attempts to locate information about the naval instructors' school on the shores of Lake Pontchatrain, I kept running into walls. One of the enlisted journalists at Belle Chase confided to me that everything from the old base had simply been thrown away when the base was closed. A real shame, we felt. I was eventually able to locate 22 base newspapers at the D-Day Museum, fortunately, and a pictorial publication at the Williams Research Center in the French Quarter of New Orleans.

I learned of a group of WWII veterans that meets Saturday mornings at the Lakefront Airport, next to the former site of NAS New Orleans. I drove over early one Saturday morning and was provided several anecdotes about WWII New Orleans by the men who had gathered for breakfast. Bill Rheams, a WWII Army pilot, prodded his buddies for me and kindly provided me with an air anthology in which he recounted highlights of his military flight career.

And it was at the breakfast I learned about the popular New Orleans madam, Norma Wallace, who worked her way briefly into protagonist Billy Benson's life.

Despite these successes, however, I was unable to locate any specifics on the methodology the Navy employed to teach WWII naval flight instructors to teach primary training.

I eventually located an Internet source that offered a fragment of hope, at the U.S. Naval Institute in Annapolis, Maryland. Only the address was provided—no e-mail address, no fax number, no telephone number. The site warned that precise questions must be asked and only those precise requests would be addressed. Along with the two-page response, however, came a note that a July 1, 1945, issue of *Naval Aviation News* was available if I wanted to see it. A telephone number and contact person were included. I called and was promised that the magazine would be sent to me electronically. When the document arrived on my Spring Hill College computer only minutes later, I was unable to retrieve it. I called Tim Jenkins at academic computing for help. I provided my password and waited on the telephone as he performed his magic. I'll never forget his response: "Doug, it's huge!" And huge it was—52 pages! It took four hours to download and print out. But what a treasure it turned out to be! Virtually everything I needed to know about training primary flight instructors was included in that publication. Perseverance had paid off royally.

I certainly cannot end this foreword without effusive thanks to English teacher friend Peggy Harbin, who read the manuscript for grammatical and syntactical errors. I appreciate her energy, candor and expertise, not to mention her great love of literature.

My biggest regret insofar as research was concerned, was my failure to interview Madame Chiang Kai-shek, who was still living while I was working on the book. (She lived to be 105.) I made inquiries via the Taiwanese Consulate in Atlanta and, despite several encouraging telephone calls from one of its representatives, was unable to make contact.

Another diversion: "gage" is the preferred spelling of "gauge" in the world of aviation.

The three years spent writing *Flights of Angels* was a remarkable, fulfilling adventure for me. To a large degree, it was a powerful reminder of a time when ordinary, yet incredible young men— literally hometown, teenage kids—performed uncommon deeds. Neighbors and boys down the street who were on the front lines of battle only one short year after graduating from high school.

Looking through the pages and pages of photographs of thousands of those young aviators, I have an admiration and appreciation for them that by far transcend the words on these pages.

My greatest desire in writing this book was to honor the memories of Lynwood and Marcy and their fallen comrades, and to somehow remind living generations that we owe these warriors a tremendous, incalculable debt: our freedom.

Therefore, to all veterans, living or deceased, my most humble and sincere thanks for putting your lives on the line at such a critical time in the world's history and it is to Lynwood and Marcy and their brothers-in-arms that this book is dedicated.

And it is my fervent desire that the WWII pilots who are still with us—whether Navy, Marine, or Army—who read of Billy Benson's adventures will see themselves once again in open-cockpit planes, thundering through the clouds with their buddies: young, strong, confident, and the least bit cocky, performing heart-stopping acrobatics and doing best what they were predestined to do:

They were born to fly.

—Doug James
Mobile, Alabama
2006
james@shc.edu

"End of Pre-Flight Training," Don Freeman, 1943, Navy Art Collection

CHAPTER ONE
PRE-FLIGHT
ATHENS, GEORGIA, 1943

IN THE DARKNESS OF AN EARLY WINTER MORNING, a two-door Model A Ford sedan clattered up the driveway that ran along the side of a two-story house, and screeched to a stop behind the house. A man and woman stepped from the car and quickly made their way across the yard, climbed the wooden steps, and entered the back door without knocking.

"Good morning, Edna," the man said cheerfully as he entered the warmth of the kitchen.

"Good morning, John," the dark-haired woman replied.

"Is Billy all ready to go?" the woman visitor asked.

"Yes," the dark-haired woman answered. "I'm not sure that I am, though."

She pulled a small, lace-trimmed handkerchief from her apron pocket and pressed it to her eyes.

The man walked to his sister and embraced her gently.

"It's going to be all right, Edna. You can't let this get you down."

"I know it, John. I hate this war and I wish…"

"I know," John said."But we're in it and somebody has to stop it."

A man wearing dark, pin-striped trousers with matching vest, white shirt, and dark tie entered the kitchen.

"Good morning, Grace," he called to his sister-in-law.

"'Morning, Jim," she said.

"'Morning, Jim," John said.

"Is Billy ready to come down?" John asked.

Jim nodded. "Any minute now."

"We need to get on to the curb market."

"I'll see if I can speed him up," Jim said, turning to walk to the foot of the stairs in the living room.

"Billy, Uncle John and Aunt Grace are here," he called. "They need to get to the curb market."

The reply of "Coming, Dad," was followed by the thudding sound of his rapid descent of the wooden stairs. A red Irish setter was close behind.

Billy was wearing woolen trousers and a dark, wool coat, white shirt, and dark tie.

"We wanted to say goodbye before we head down to the curb market," his uncle said.

"Thanks."

His aunt hugged him.

"We'll miss you."

"Thanks. I'll miss you, too."

"Excuse us a minute," his uncle said, taking Billy by the elbow and steering him toward the living room.

The two stood in the center of the room, John's hand resting lightly on his nephew's upper arm. The two were a study in contrasts: Billy, tall, lean and blond, his uncle, dark, muscular and sturdy in build.

"We're proud of you, Billy, and we know you'll be a good Navy pilot."

"Thank you, Uncle John."

"The next few months will probably be pretty tough. You'll miss civilian life and being home, but I promise you, if you take it just one day at a time, it'll work out."

Billy nodded agreement.

"It'll probably help, too, if you concentrate on your training more than how much you'd rather be here. I guess I'm saying, 'Forget about us while you're in pre-flight.' "

Billy nodded again.

"But remember that we love you and we'll be thinking about you every day."

"Okay."

His uncle put his arms around his nephew and hugged him tightly.

"I love you, Billy."

Billy responded by embracing his uncle.

"I love you, too, Uncle John."

"We need to be heading to the train station, Billy," his father called from the kitchen.

"Okay, Dad."

*   *   *

In 1941, immediately after and because of the urgency created by the Japanese attack on Pearl Harbor. the U.S. Navy introduced its highly successful V-5 flight program, which allowed young men to attend flight school directly out of high school.

Chief of U.S. Naval Training, Captain Arthur W. Radford, had asked Lieutenant Commander Thomas J. Hamilton, naval pilot and former Naval Academy football coach, to develop a demanding, toughening program that would produce the strongest, most daring, best prepared, and most determined airmen in the world.

To complement the rigid, compressed flight training program, Hamilton called on legendary American boxer Gene Tunney to help lay out the new fitness regimen. Coaches from across the country and spectrum of sports were commissioned for the venture.

Football, soccer, basketball, boxing, swimming, track, wrestling, gymnastics, tumbling, and hand-to-hand combat were determined to be the sports that would best develop the men's natural agility and strength, as well as a spirit of competition and, yes, aggression.

In early 1942, Secretary of the Navy Frank Knox announced plans for creating five regional induction centers, to be known as pre-flight schools and considered legitimate extensions of the U.S. Naval Academy: the University of Iowa, in Iowa City; St. Mary's College, in Moraga, California; the University of North Carolina, in Chapel Hill: the Del Monte Hotel, in Monterey, California; and the University of Georgia, in Athens. Each of the campuses would be thought of as an "Annapolis of the Air." Other campuses were added as the war progressed.

Thirty thousand Navy and Marine cadets a year enrolled and participated in the extremely rigorous program at the pre-flight schools. Those who completed the grueling three-month-long "boot camp" phase qualified for the flight program.

The post-Depression country was still desperately poor. The demands of war would coincide with the needs of men who urgently desired college or vocational training but who lacked the finances to pursue them.

And not only were individuals financially strapped.

There was hardly a single enterprise in the country that had not been adversely affected by the Great Depression. Education was no exception. Following on the heels of that dramatic economic downturn, the worst in the history of the modern world, the heavy indebtedness created by involvement in World War I seriously hampered America's recovery. Money for college and university tuitions from students as well as from state and federal revenues was still in short supply. Enrollment had fallen off drastically as World War II drained the schools of dollars and, of course, male students.

Universities, therefore, competed vigorously for the V-5 flight program that promised millions of federal dollars—literally lifeblood to them—to continue operation.

So it was, on 27 February 1943, that James William Benson Jr., of the United States Naval Reserve, certified Civil Aeronautics Authority-sanctioned pilot and E-base (flight Elimination Base) survivor, boarded a train that would take him to Naval Pre-flight School at the University of Georgia, Athens, Georgia.

* * *

IN THE BRACING AND BRIGHT EARLY MORNING of late February 1943, a steam-driven train of the Louisville and Nashville line lumbered southward through the red clay foothills of the Appalachian Mountains. Blinding, horizontal shafts of sunlight cut across fields and pastures, shimmering this new day with a thin, silver glaze of frost where cattle calmly stood chewing hay in their thoughtful, detached manner, clouds of condensate rolling from their undulating mouths.

The train passed through small towns, stopping briefly at some to pick up or let off passengers and continued noisily down the tracks to Birmingham. There the eastbound cars were attached to a Seaboard Line train and the men resumed their journey eastward through Atlanta, for another stop and on to Athens.

The candidates who had attended and successfully survived naval flight E-Bases and now headed for pre-flight school eagerly sought each other out as each man boarded the train. They gravitated toward one noisy, swaying, ancient car, constructed mostly of wood, reeking of antiquity and outfitted with uninviting, uncomfortable, thin, hard seats, covered with worn mohair. The creaking, bouncing car was immediately dubbed the "stage coach." One window resisted all attempts at closing it, creating a drafty, frigid, meat locker temperature, more or less discouraging other passengers from settling there, permitting the men to engage each other enthusiastically.

Eighteen or 19-year-old boys, not yet men, really—the smooth-skinned, apple-cheeked, dewy-eyed innocents, as well as those wizened ones well into their twenties—from the dusty farms, ranches and oil fields of Oklahoma and Texas, the swampy bayous of Louisiana, and from other Southeastern states; high school and prep school sports heroes; sons of sharecroppers as well as moneyed old Southern families—were on their way to new life-altering adventures in Athens.

Most of the men wore shirts with ties, some, apparently for the first time, jackets or topcoats, low-cut or high-top shoes, Western boots, some scuffed and well worn, others sported carefully shined Brooks Brothers footwear. Changes of clothes and personal items were packed inside new Samsonite luggage or worn cardboard cases or in a few instances, cardboard boxes tied with cord.

The aged few—those who were all of 24 or 25 or the new flight program's maximum age of 26—because of the perceived age differences, would instantly be nicknamed "Pappy" or "Dad" or "Pops," on the trains carrying them to pre-flight.

Home states, also, created the impetus for many monikers: "Gator," for burly Floridians; "Tennessee," for some from the Volunteer State: "Waco" or "Dallas" or just plain "Tex," for citizens of the Lone Star State.

All the men had voluntarily answered the call of their country, whether as a means of escaping the endless, dead-end monotony of plowing tired, dried-up fields, or the likelihood of minimum wage jobs for life, or to seek the romance and status associated with being a Navy pilot as touted in the half-page advertisement in *Life* magazine, which featured a handsome, heavenward-gazing, square-jawed Navy pilot in the cockpit of a fighter plane and the seductive promise of 75 dollars a month, which was, in the post-Depression world of the early 1940's, a virtual king's ransom.

The men moved about the car, introducing themselves to each other, sharing little pleasantries as they expressed their anticipation and excitement at entering the Navy and receiving training as pilots.

Billy had made short train trips to Memphis or Nashville with his mother and sisters when he was younger but not as an adult. Nor had he eaten on one. Friends had spoken so enthusiastically of the food and service on their rail travels, that he was anticipating that experience, too, as the morning wore on.

It was not until the civilian passengers had eaten their noon meal that a black man in a white coat summoned the cadets to the dining car.

White linen tablecloths and napkins, silver, and bud vases with one real flower in each, greeted the men as they entered the car. They took seats at the window-side tables as black men in crisp, white jackets began pouring glasses of water from heavy silver pitchers, into glasses with short stems.

Billy commented that all the Negro waiters were the same size.

"My father says it's easier and cheaper for the railroads to hire waiters who are the same size than it is to buy coats in different sizes," Jay Sanderson, one of Billy's table companions, said.

Normally, menus accompanied by short pencils and paper meal order cards were offered to diners traveling by train. For the men en route to military training, however, there would be no choices.

As soon as the men were in place and their water glasses filled, a waiter walked down the narrow center aisle with a tray filled with rolls and squares of butter on small, white plates and handed each man his bread ration. A few of the men who had never seen butter served in that manner, straight away speared it with their forks and gobbled it up.

Waiters immediately emerged from the small galley with plates of food for each man: a generous grilled hamburger steak, a mound of mashed potatoes and a generous portion of bright, shiny, green peas. A verdant sprig of parsley was placed in the center of the plate.

That they had not been permitted to choose their noon meal was of no consequence to the young men. Like Billy, they were characteristically hungry, many not having eaten since leaving their homes shortly after sunrise that morning.

After he completed his meal, Billy sampled the parsley.

It doesn't taste like food, he decided. *It tastes…it just tastes green.*

As the men finished their entrees, the assembly line of waiters collected their empty plates as others placed small dishes with slices of apple pie before each of them. Empty cups followed, with an offer of hot coffee from another waiter, poured from a heavy silver pot with a Bakelite rod protruding straight out from its side.

The men rose from their tables as they finished eating and returned to their seats where many of them lit up cigarettes. Others, now sated, fell asleep.

When the train arrived in Athens later that afternoon, a young man in khaki uniform—shirt, tie, trousers, fore-and-aft cap—was waiting beside a battleship-gray school-type bus, to transport the candidates to the nearby campus of the University of Georgia.

Once on the bus, the cadet, hanging on to the vertical post beside the entrance, asked for a volunteer to collect the men's records. Barry Dorsey, who was sitting at the front of the bus, raised his hand and jumped up.

"I'll do it," he announced.

"What's your name?"

"Barry Dorsey, sir."

"Rule Number One of military service, Mr. Dorsey," the cadet said, raising his finger and speaking loudly enough for all on the bus to hear, "never be the first, never be the last and never, never, never volunteer for anything."

The men laughed loudly.

"Then I un-volunteer," Dorsey responded, undismayed and smiling broadly.

The men laughed again.

"Too late! You're it!"

Again there was laughter.

"Also, I'm not a 'sir.' Give me ten months or so and you can call me that."

He then faced the other men on the bus.

"Okay, men, Mr. Dorsey, here, will come down the aisle and take your records. Get a good look at him. He has your records. When we get off the bus, stay together."

Dorsey was someone who would be hard to forget. He wore a well-fitting brown tweed jacket, a laundry-fresh, starched and ironed shirt, patterned tie neatly secured with a fashionable four-in-hand knot, fawn colored trousers, polished brown shoes, and a felt hat. He was tanned, handsome and his perfect white teeth emphasized his confident, winning smile. He kept a pipe clenched tightly in his teeth as he walked through the bus, collecting the envelopes holding the men's orders.

*   *   *

THE SITES chosen for the V-5 pre-flight program underwent extreme transformations to accommodate the 1900 or so men assigned to each campus at a time, arriving every two weeks, in groups of about 250.

Although the first centers—four colleges and one hotel—continued operating more or less normally during the war, the large chunks of property staked out by and for military training literally became entities unto themselves.

At the University of Georgia, the Navy took over 19 buildings completely: Baldwin Hall, for example, the university's large demonstration-classroom building was renamed the Operations Building and would centralize all military administrative offices. The six dormitories handed over were given naval names: Ranger, Yorktown, Hornet, Wasp, Lexington and Langley Barracks. Meals were served at the John Paul Jones Mess Hall.

Memorial Hall provided extra dormitory space and contained a recreation center, as well as an auditorium large enough to accommodate the entire cadet population at one time. Films for entertainment were enjoyed in the Fine Arts Auditorium, while Conner Hall provided facilities for showing military films, which encompassed every aspect of naval life from technical subjects to personal hygiene, malaria and prevention of venereal diseases.

The Lucas House contained a barbershop and a ship's store, where toilet articles and snacks, or in Navy jargon, "poagie-bait," were sold. Lucas House also held an eight-booth telephone center where on-site operators placed long-distance calls for the men.

The university's athletic facilities were taken over by the Navy, since the university was now nearly exclusively female. The women's physical education activities were limited essentially to exercising, swimming, tennis, and social dancing.

In addition to the housing facilities that had been appropriated, the Navy constructed four large barracks on Ag Hill: Essex, Saratoga, Enterprise, and Bonne Homme Richard. It took over the existing baseball field and erected a large field house with showers and 600 lockers, four full-sized football fields and a cinder track. Mammoth Farragut Gym contained an indoor swimming pool, a drill hall for military marching maneuvers and indoors sports as well as a firing range.

To complete the massive undertaking of converting a major state university into a literal wartime naval base, an enormous staff of instructors, coaches, medical, dental, religious, and enlisted support personnel were assembled on each campus. Uniforms, military issue beds, blankets, books, compasses, local and war maps, athletic equipment, weapons, munitions, and tons of food had to be provided and replaced as they were consumed or wore out.

* * *

THE CADET standing at the front of the bus answered eager questions about the pre-flight program as the bus made its way along campus streets. When it screeched to a halt near a large, white-columned brick building with a long, broad flight of steps leading up to the pair of front doors, he ducked his head to look out the bus window.

"All right, men, here we are. Put out your smokes." He then quickly added, "Not on the deck and not out the windows. That's a serious violation of regs here or at any military installation. Crush them out and put them in one of your pockets or field strip them.

Crush them, sprinkle the tobacco on the ground and put the paper in your pocket.

"Fall in outside the bus here, lining up in three rows, facing away from the bus."

He jumped from the bus and took a position a few yards from where the men were lining up.

"Mr. Dorsey, fall in beside me, please."

Barry gathered up the stack of envelopes, slipped his pipe into a pocket of his jacket and walked quickly to the side of the cadet.

As the driver of the bus pulled away, the cadet cheerfully waved his hand at it. "Wave goodbye to the bus, men. That's the last time you'll be in a vehicle until you leave this place.

"Transfer your bags to your left hand. Never, repeat, never carry anything in your right hand. That hand is reserved for saluting officers.

"Do any of you know military drill commands?"

Billy and a few of the men raised their hands.

"Very well. When I give the command, 'A-ten-HUT!' Come to attention.

"A-ten-HUT!"

The men straightened.

"Now, when I say, 'Left face!' all of you will turn smartly to your left and stand fast. 'Standing fast' means you hold that position.

"Ready?

"Comp'ny! Lay-uft face!"

The men turned.

"Very good. You all turned in the same direction. You show promise.

"Mr. Dorsey, take your place in front of the men, facing me."

Barry walked quickly to the head of the formation.

The cadet moved to stand in front of Barry, facing the men.

"When I give the order to move out, lead with your left foot. I'll call cadence. Stay in step. Don't look like a bunch of farmers."

"We are a bunch of farmers," one of the men on the back row volunteered, drawing laughter from the men.

"You may have been in the civilian world, but there are no farms in the Navy."

He turned his back to the men and called over his shoulder:

"Forward, march!

"Ah-left! Ah-left! Ah-left, right, left!"

He led the men across the broad, grassy expanse to the Operations Building.

"Comp'ny, halt!"

He turned and walked to the side of the men.

"Ri-i-i-ght face!"

The men turned to face him.

"Very good.

"Mr. Dorsey and I are going inside. While we're in there, you will remain in formation. Do not talk. Do not move about. Do you understand?"

The men nodded their heads and mumbled that they understood.

"When you understand a question or order, you say 'Aye, Aye!'

"Not only that, you say it forcefully."

The cadet repeated his question but much louder:

"Do you understand?"

Aye, Aye!

"Very good!"

"To an officer, of course, you would say, 'Aye, aye, sir!' and what that means is 'I heard the order, I understand the order, I will carry out the order.'

"Now, on my command, place your bags on the ground. You will remain in the bent-over position until I give you the command, 'Ready, two!'

"Does everybody understand?"

Aye, Aye!

"Ready...ground bags!

The men complied.

"Ready, two!"

The men stood straight.

The cadet separated his feet and locked his hands behind his back.

"This is parade rest, gentlemen. When I give the command, you do the same."

He came to attention.

"Pa-ra-a-ade rest!"

"Welcome to the Navy's pre-flight school and to Athens, Georgia. I am Cadet Thompson and I'm here to get you through the first couple of days. We'll name a squad leader who will take over after that.

"Gentlemen, as long as you are in flight training—not just here but in primary, intermediate, final squadron, all the way until you receive your wings—you will march everywhere you go. You will not be permitted to drive an automobile. You will go everywhere together, which is to say, as a unit, virtually joined at the hip. You eat together, you will go to class together, you will exercise together, you will shower together, and make head calls together.

"You will do everything as a team. Teamwork in the service is essential. Think of teamwork this way: It gives the enemy somebody else to shoot at.

"If two of you go somewhere, you will march together, side by side, in step. One of you will call cadence. You will salute smartly every officer you see, even if he—or she —is across the street.

"If you're going to sick call, have a chit in your left hand and march to the sick bay, even if you go alone.

"When you get liberty, you will march to town, in uniform and in step.

"You're going to be just like those nuns you used to see at your hometown A and P—always two of them together.

"Now, as I said, Mr. Dorsey and I are going inside to get everything ready for your check in.

"While we're inside, remember to remain perfectly still. No talking, no moving, no pocket pool. If an officer should pass by or come to your formation, you," he pointed at Billy, who was standing on Thompson's right at the end of the front row, "What's your name?"

"Benson!"

"Mr. Benson will call you to attention.

"If an officer comes by, do not salute. You are not in uniform. You do not salute in the Navy if you are out of uniform or if you are uncovered—that is, not wearing a hat—or indoors. Mr. Benson, if an officer comes by, call your men to attention and address the officer as 'Sir!' Respond to his questions with 'Aye, aye, sir,' or 'No, sir!'

"And that includes women. Females who are naval officers are gentlemen by an act of Congress. You will say 'Aye, aye, sir,' to male or female naval officers. After he—or she—leaves, you may put your company at parade rest. Do you understand?"

"Aye, aye!" Billy responded forcefully.

"Wrong, Mr. Benson. You are at parade rest. You cannot speak in formation unless you are at attention."

But I just did and you didn't say it was wrong, Billy thought. *This is like 'May I?,'* a game he played as a child.

He quickly considered several options he felt would satisfy the cadet.

"Comp'ny! A-ten-chun!" he called.

The men snapped to attention.

"Very good, Mr. Benson, except we say, 'A-ten-HUT!'"

Billy called a strong, visceral, "A-ten-HUT!"

"Wrong, Mr. Benson. Your men are already at attention. You cannot call them to attention if they are already at attention, can you? Put them at parade rest first and then bring them to attention."

May I?

"Comp'ny! Pa-ra-a-de rest!" Billy commanded.

"Good. Now call them to attention."

"Comp'ny, A-ten-HUT!"

"Now, do you understand what you're to do if an officer comes by?"

"Aye, aye!"

"Very well. Put your men back at parade rest."

"Comp'ny, parade rest!"

"Welcome to the Navy, Mr. Benson," Cadet Thompson said with a smile and a wink.

Later, when all the men were permitted to climb the steps and enter the administration building, they proceeded to a row of wooden desks set up in the lobby and passageways. Unsmiling men in the traditional blue "Cracker Jack" enlisted naval uniforms sat behind the desks. The cadets were registered, had their orders checked and new service records opened. They were also assigned their roommates—four to a room. Billy and Barry were going to share a room with Jay Sanderson and Bob Hawthorne.

When the men introduced themselves, Billy dropped the 'y' from the end of his name, as he had begun to do on the train to Athens. He was now "Bill" to his Navy friends, although he would continue to answer to and identify himself as "Billy" when he telephoned or wrote letters home.

The men were regrouped in front of the Operations Building as Squad B, Company L, Eighteenth Battalion, and marched off across campus. They moved briskly to Cadet Thompson's cadence—*ah-left, ah-right, ah-left, right, left*—by way of the "Burma Road," a gently winding cinder-covered trail through a ravine. At Enterprise Barracks, they were given room assignments and permitted to leave their bags in their rooms. Before they could settle in, however, they were formed up again and marched to chow.

A veritable cornucopia of food—5000 calories per man per day—served cafeteria-style, awaited the men, weary and hungry from their long day: roast beef, mountains of mashed potatoes and gravy, fresh vegetables, breads, desserts, unlimited amounts of fresh, cold milk served in pint glass bottles.

It was obvious that many of the men who had known only Depression scarcities and ramshackle houses or a collection of shacks known as "Hoovervilles" to call home, had not seen servings of food like this in their entire lives. Jokes abounded about "hobo floats," a toothpick in a glass of water. A diet of only beans or turnip greens or cornbread was not unheard of.

"Eat all you want, gentleman!" a wandering Marine with a broad-brimmed campaign hat, held in place by a narrow leather strap on the back of his shaved head, reminded the new men, emphasizing his words by smacking his palm with a swagger stick. "But eat all you take or you'll have me to answer to! There's a war on, gentleman! We don't waste food!"

Billy felt the Marine had nothing to worry about. He was so hungry, his only hope was he could get enough to eat.

After the filling, hasty meal, the men were marched back to Enterprise Barracks.

Cadet Thompson led them to cleaning lockers that held the mops, swabs, dust pans, fox tails (wooden-handled brushes for sweeping litter into the dust pans), toilet brushes, window cleaner, rags, and detergent for a thorough Navy field day, a procedure that would be rigorously carried out each Thursday night during their flight training.

Thompson then escorted the men to the basement to draw their bed linens and gathered them in groups in various individual rooms to demonstrate the military way to make beds: tight hospital corners on the bottom sheet, tight top sheet with hospital corners at the foot, but the top neatly folded back six inches from the top of the bed and tucked in precisely and without wrinkles along both sides. The pillow was placed carefully on the top sheet, with the loose material of the case smoothed out of sight at the top, away from the inspecting officer. The scratchy, gray, wool blanket was folded into a perfect square at the foot with one corner carefully turned back as a triangle.

"If a quarter won't bounce off your rack, it isn't tight enough," Cadet Thompson announced. "Let's see how this one does."

He pulled a quarter from his pocket and flipped it with his thumb a few feet into the air. When it hit the taut sheets of the bed, it bounced and the men cheered and applauded.

"You have to strip your rack every morning for fifteen minutes, to air it out. If you were planning on sleeping on top of the sheets so you won't mess up your rack, forget it," he added.

"Your laundry bags will be tied to these end rails on the top racks, two to a rack. Secure them with square knots. Secure everything with square knots. I'll show you how. Watch this."

As he proceeded to loop the two ends of the pull strings onto the bed, he added, "You have to keep something in this bag at all times for inspection. Oh, free laundry service is provided, by the way. Everything has to be folded and stowed in your lockers the Navy way. You'll learn there are three ways of doing anything: the right way, the wrong way and the Navy way. But I'll show you how to do that after you are issued your uniforms tomorrow.

"All right, guys," Cadet Thompson told the assembled men in the passageway, "take the rest of the night to get your racks made and your gear squared away. Reveille goes at oh-six-hundred. Meet me out front at oh-six-fifteen. We have to be at the chow hall at oh-six-twenty-three.

"You may have noticed you didn't have much time to eat last night. You will have precisely twenty-six minutes for every meal. Get in and get out. Don't forget what that gy-rine told you about wasting food. When you go by him in the scullery, he'll check your tray. If there's any food on it, he'll make you eat it there and may try to make you eat the tray as well.

"Since you won't have much time between reveille and breakfast formation, I recommend that you shower before you turn in tonight. Shave after breakfast, when we come back. You'll have about forty-five minutes after breakfast every morning to get your rooms squared away.

"Okay?"

"Lights out at twenty-two hundred. That's ten o'clock."

"Does somebody come around and wake us up?" one of the men asked.

Thompson laughed. "Sure. One of the co-eds tip-toes to each bed and wakes you up with a big, wet kiss."

The men laughed.

"No, I'm afraid it won't be anything so gentle. That bitch-box up there will tell you everything you need to know: tattoo at twenty-one-fifty—meaning you have ten minutes to get ready for lights out at twenty-two hundred—reveille at oh-six-hundred and on and on."

He turned, waved and called over his shoulder, "See you in the morning."

The men went to their rooms and began making their beds and getting ready to turn in.

"Do you guys mind if I open the windows?" Jay Sanderson asked.

None of the men objected.

Jay's face always seemed flushed, as if he were constantly in a stage of embarrassment.

"I'm so hot natured, my family says I should live at the North Pole."

"Where do you live?" Billy asked.

"I grew up in Southern California," he said, "but I've lived in Texas for the past two years."

"Not exactly known for cool weather," Barry remarked.

"Where are you from?" Jay asked Barry.

"Born in Atlanta, but I've been living in Augusta since thirty-nine."

"Augusta?" Bob Hawthorne asked. "Where the Masters are played?"

Barry nodded.

"You play golf?" Billy asked.

"Every chance I get," Barry said.

"Do you know Bobby Jones?" Bob asked.

"As a matter of fact, I caddied for him when I was big enough to carry his bag. That's when I moved to Augusta. I learned a lot that way and now I give lessons."

"And that's why you're so tan?" Billy asked.

"I guess so. I'm outside on the links just about every day it isn't raining or snowing."

"And how about you, Bill?" Barry asked. "What are you running from?"

"Nothing as exciting as caddying for Bobby Jones. I attended college last year, got CPT flight certified and worked at a little grocery store. Not much, really."

"And you, Bob. How about you?"

Bob Hawthorne seemed always to have a smile on his face. His eyes, highlighted by thick, dark lashes, squinted nearly shut whenever he grinned.

"I grew up in an orphanage in Spring Hill, Tennessee," he replied. "When I hit eighteen, I felt it was time to stop free-loading and get out and see the world."

"From the air?" Jay asked.

"I think the view would be better," he said. His smile was emphasized by one dimple on the left side of his face. "Better than from a foxhole."

The men finished making their beds.

"This rack looks so good, I hate to mess it up by sleeping in it," Bob said.

"Well, I'm going to hit the showers and then my rack, to give my feet a rest," Jay said. "All this walking isn't my idea of fun."

"I think we've gotten just a taste today of what's in store for us the twelve weeks we're here," Billy prophesied.

At 2150, an amplified voice emanating from the wooden speaker boxes announced Tattoo. Lights out was called ten minutes later.

For the rest of their naval careers, the men's schedules would be controlled by a disembodied voice telling them what to do, when and where to do it, always preceded by a slow, forceful, *Now hear this!* From the mundane: *Sweepers, sweepers, man your brooms. Commence with a clean sweep-down of all berthing spaces* or calls to colors, to the life threatening: *This is not a drill! This is not a drill! Man your battle stations! Man your battle stations!*

At lights out, all rooms were plunged into darkness and silence. The men slipped between their sheets and sank peacefully into the sound, deep sleep that is the exclusive domain of the young, to be roused from their slumber at 0500, when the voice in the box would indifferently and coldly announce, *Now hear this: reveille, reveille, reveille!* to begin another day in the Navy.

*   *   *

On their second day in the Navy, Billy and members of the new class returned to the Operations Building, where they were ordered to strip to their shorts to receive complete flight physical examinations over a course of three days and begin their immunizations. A medical record to be maintained separately from the service record by specialized flight surgeons and flight corpsmen was begun on each of the men. For many of the men, the Navy introduced the first professional medical care they had ever received.

Their chest measurements were taken and a dental officer made sure they had at least eight properly spaced teeth.

Restricted cockpit size of planes placed limits on height and weight: from 64 to 76 inches in height and between one 124 and 200 pounds in weight.

Nearly a full day was devoted to series of eye tests—to ascertain that the candidates had perfect vision, depth, and color perception. Their hearing was tested individually in soundproof chambers.

Flexibility, strength, alertness, and agility were noted. While wearing a heavy backpack, each man was subjected to a timed test up and down a step, for durability and heart and breathing recovery rates.

At clothing issue, the petty officer who gave them instructions for the procedure, concluded his comments by telling the men: "We have only two sizes of uniforms—too small and too large."

The cadets were issued three sets of undress, or everyday, uniforms each and then sent to a dressing area where they stenciled their uniforms, removed their civilian shorts and dressed from head to toe in Navy issue: khaki fore-and-aft caps—with matching sewn-on patch, embroidered with a shield over an anchor and the initials U.S., identifying them as V-5 pre-flight cadets—khaki shirt, khaki tie, khaki webbed belt, khaki trousers, and matching socks. High-topped, black leather field shoes, or "boondockers," completed the everyday uniform.

Name tags to be worn on their left shirt pockets would be provided later.

The issued athletic gear consisted of khaki tee shirts, khaki shorts, an athletic supporter, thick, white socks, and high-topped black gym shoes with white laces.

Additionally, the men were measured for one Navy blue dress uniform each: a double-breasted jacket with brass buttons and trousers, to be tailored and distributed later, but they received the black webbed belt, black socks and black dress shoes to be worn with the dress uniform.

"One more stop, men," Cadet Thompson announced. "Leave your new issue here and line up in the passageway. It's time to take care of that long, civilian hair."

The men gave each other looks of mock dread.

Thompson led the men to a barbershop with three chairs and a thick carpet of human hair from the sections who had been just been shorn. Each man was in and out of the chair in less than 30 seconds.

Billy's hand instinctively went to his bare head as he stepped down from the chair. He could feel the stubble only if he ran his hand backward over his scalp.

"And this is your last free Navy haircut. You'll have to shell out 25 cents for the rest from now on," their cadet leader informed them.

Back at the changing room, Thompson called each man's name and presented him with a pair of dog tags—oblong metal with rolled edges and notched at the ends opposite the chain holes—to be attached to a long, beaded, metal necklace.

"You're Navy issue from stem to stern," he said. Now you know the true meaning of 'uniform.' The only way we can tell you apart is by the name on your dog tags and name tags."

The men looked at each other. He was right. They all looked the same: bald and khaki from head to toe.

"What's the notch in the dog tags for?" one of the men asked Thompson.

"You don't want to know," he said.

"Sure I do. What's it for?" the man persisted.

"For identification. The notch is driven in between your top incisors when you're killed in action."

The man looked at the notch and said, "Oh."

He wasn't satisfied yet.

"How is it driven in?"

"Rifle butt. Heel of a hand. Heel of a boot. Anything. It doesn't matter. You'll be dead. You won't care."

"You know? You were right. I really didn't want to know."

The cadets bundled up their civilian clothes and military issue before marching back to their barracks.

"Before we go to noon chow, guys," their cadet leader told them as they stood in formation in front of their dormitory, "go to your rooms, repack your civilian bags with everything you brought with you, except Bibles, prayer books, toilet articles, or small personal items that can fit inside your shaving kit on inspection days. I'll come around to your rooms and give you a box and an address label so you can send it all back home. Your civilian days are over."

When they entered the chow hall, the men who were already eating began to point and laugh at the new men's uniforms and especially their shorn heads.

Fresh meat, men!

Oooooo! I'm scared!

Tojo, you better watch out for these Jap-killers!

The men at one table hissed at them.

One man jumped up, faced them, grabbed his crotch with one hand and shook it as he yelled, "Hey, you skinheads! I got more hair on my balls than all of you got on your heads!"

Billy and his squad tried to ignore the taunts, but found it difficult not to feel humiliated.

*   *   *

TWO MIMEOGRAPHED SCHEDULES were distributed to each of the men in Billy's squad: one was a detailed daily schedule of classes by periods, for the first two weeks of training; the other was a daily schedule of military training, physical education and special events that would be followed throughout the three-month long pre-flight school.

During the week, each day's schedule was divided evenly into three parts: academics, military orientation and sports, beginning at six in the morning and ending at ten at night, with only minutes of free time throughout the day. There would be no let up for the first two weeks.

Barry was named squad leader. Each morning, the squads comprising Company L, Eighteenth Battalion, mustered in the large field across from their barracks, across from the dairy science and forestry buildings. With a cadet commander calling out the orders, each squad leader reported to him the number of men present before colors—the raising of the flag. Afterward, the student commander gave out the general orders for the day.

During the morning inspection that followed, a cadet clerk with a clip board walked behind the inspecting cadet, recording gigs, or demerits, for such indiscretions as "Irish pennants," or loose threads, missing buttons, poorly shined shoes or a misaligned "gig line," in which the center vertical edge of the shirt did not line up perfectly with the edges of the belt, buckle and trouser fly.

Classroom decorum was the same as practiced at Annapolis: when the students entered their classrooms, they stood beside their wooden desks, assigned by the men's last names, until the squad leader gave the command, *Be seated*, at which time the men sat at attention. When the officer instructor entered, the first man to spot him jumped to his feet and called out *Attention on deck!* The men stood smartly at attention until the officer gave the command, *At ease.*

Any man who was called on to respond to a question or had a question to ask, stood at attention, announced his name: *Cadet Benson, Sir!* before continuing.

At the end of the class when the officer dismissed the men, the squad leader sounded *Attention on deck!* as the men stood rigidly until the instructor left the room, or space.

Additionally, any time an instructor met a cadet in the passageways, the cadet "braced the bulkhead," snapping to rigid attention, his back to the bulkhead, or wall.

Academics consisted of hefty portions of mathematics and physics, which, for many of the cadets, was a continuation of high school courses. Also covered were principles of flight, engines, celestial air navigation, meteorology, altitude, azimuth calculations, vectographs, and plotting boards. The class in communications involved radio protocol, learning to read and use Morse code, signal flags, semaphore, and blinker lights.

Nomenclature and recognition of air and sea craft were particularly stressful on the students, who were required to be able to identify every plane and every ship of every nation involved in the war. The men were shown photographs, drawings, slides, and models to study. Testing was accomplished by flashing a picture of the craft on a screen, with the occasional flashing of a nude woman, which broke the tension for some, while irritating others with what they believed was misplaced frivolity. At first, the cadets were permitted three seconds or so to mark their answers for each craft shown, but the time was progressively shortened to a second or even a fraction of a second.

The cadets' favorite course was probably Essentials of Naval Service, taught by Mr. Sanderson, an ensign barely older than some of the students. He was less formal than the senior officers and made his lectures on Navy history, lore, philosophies, tactics, and hardware especially interesting. He also presented stimulating lectures on patriotism and was successful in focusing and intensifying the repugnance the men already held for Hitler, Mussolini and Tojo, their war machines and their motherlands.

"Now 'scuttlebutt' can be one of two things, men," Mr. Sanderson revealed in one lecture. "It can be the water fountain or the gossip or rumors that float around, probably beginning at the water barrel in the days of sailing vessels. Civilians often call it 'the grapevine.'

"Don't ask me how we arrived at the word 'head' for the bathroom, 'bulkheads,' or 'decks' for the components of rooms, or, as we call them, 'compartments,' or 'spaces.' I think 'overhead' and 'passageway' are self-explanatory.

"When you're on a ship or a base, you say you're 'aboard.' When you leave same, you're 'ashore,' even if it's just the bar across the street from the base."

He always ended his lectures with one piece of advice that was a humorous fact of warfare, invariably raising his index finger and prefacing the statement with, "Remember!"

Remember:

"Incoming fire always has the right of way,"

or

"It is highly recommended that you do not bail out of your plane over an area you have just bombed."

or

"Don't draw fire. It irritates the people around you,"

or

"When in doubt, empty the magazine,"

or

"If the enemy is in range, so are you."

Muscular, leather-lunged Marine drill instructors were responsible for teaching the basics of military drill.

The spring rains turned the Georgia red clay into thick mud, but military drill went on, regardless of climatic conditions. The more inhospitable the conditions, the more the Marines seemed to flourish, calling cadences with even more volume as the environment worsened:

I don' know but I've been told,
(I don' know but I've told,)
Georgia girls are mighty cold,
(Georgia girls are mighty cold,)
Sound off!
(One-two)
Sound off!
(Three-four)

The Marines also taught basic military operations, instructing the cadets how to effectively use bayonets and fire, clean and properly store their M-1 rifles.

Rifles, the men were told by Gunny Sergeant Wyatt, could also be called "pieces," but never "guns."

"This is my rifle," he recited, pointing to the rifle,

"This is my gun," he said, pointing to his crotch.

Then in the same manner, "This one's for shooting, this one's for fun."

"And if I hear any of you calling your piece a gun, you'll sleep with it! See how much fun that is," he threatened.

They made the Double 'V' and Navy 'N' formations with their bodies and especially enjoyed performing the kneeling, thrusting, standing, Queen Anne's Salute and the precise slapping, rapping, rhythmic nine-count manual with their rifles.

On Saturdays, those cadets who had accrued gigs or demerits for uniform or room inspection, or other infractions, met a Marine in "the Bullpen," where their sins would be purged by performing hours of marching, regardless of the temperature or rain or snow.

The coaching staff joined the Marine drill instructors to oversee the exhausting obstacle, or "confidence," course, at the corner of the campus called Camp Wilkins. The obstacles which had been constructed of unfinished, bark-covered wood had a natural, Civilian Conservation Corps look to them. Dressed only in their black sneakers, socks, jocks and shorts, the increasingly fit and tanned men were timed as they snaked through the course, over and under logs, a rope climb, followed by a leap over water, hand-over-hand maneuvers down long logs 10 feet from the ground, another rope climb up the side of a 20-foot-high wall, as well as a climb up and a run down a towering A-frame log barrier.

And then there was the dreaded "nutcracker:" a long, rough, natural tree trunk, elevated over a water hazard, that the men, with only their thin cotton shorts and supporters to protect their genitals, straddled and scooted down as rapidly as possible.

The obstacle course was not a one-time affair, rather it was visited over and over, with each man's time to be shortened with every run.

Much time was spent outside the classroom, learning about the poisonous, nonpoisonous and beneficial tropical plants, fish, animals, and insects a downed pilot should be familiar with.

On their three-day, 20-mile survival hike, the men carried 50-pound packs on their backs, led by indefatigable Marines in pith helmets and fatigues.

Instructions for constructing lean-to shelters were given, using materials available if shot down in the Pacific. Fire starting, fresh water collection, raft building, rock climbing, quicksand avoidance, and swimming in heavy seas were important components of the course. The men ate without utensils, learned to boil water in folded leaves and fabricated beds raised high off the ground with posts made from tree limbs and branches.

Organized team sports like baseball, football, track, tumbling, wrestling, boxing, swimming, and basketball—to inspire aggressiveness—were interspersed with hours of calisthenics: push-ups, push-ups, push-ups, and more push-ups, chin-ups, sit-ups, and rope-climbing. The university's tennis courts were paved over and converted to handball courts.

Lieutenant Paul 'Bear' Bryant and the other officers recruited from the ranks of college coaches drove them ruthlessly.

During the season of football and basketball and baseball, teams were formed to compete with each other. The teams performed so well, in fact, that the cadets tried to convince their coaches to let them play against college teams in the area, but travel restrictions and gas rationing prevented the practice. In an accidental meeting between cadet (later Rear Admiral) Thomas Hamilton and First Lady Eleanor Roosevelt in the early days of the V-5 program, Hamilton mentioned to the first lady the cadets' disappointment over the ruling. Within the week, an executive order from President Roosevelt removed all travel restrictions from the athletic program and competitive games with smaller colleges were initiated for football and basketball, but not baseball. The games became the most popular form of entertainment for the cadets.

Many hours were devoted to instruction in man-overboard maneuvers at the pool, which included participation in a four-mile swim, learning to swim blindfolded and treading water fully clothed. Also in that particular exercise, the cadets were taught how to remove their trousers and make life preservers from them by tying knots in the ends of the legs and flapping air into them. The men were additionally taught how to jump from a 20-foot platform and swim through or under burning oil sticks.

A combat team very often depends on its feet for transportation and the condition of the troops' feet is critical in warfare. The Navy recognized this fact and took precautions to prevent serious foot problems among its V-5 cadets. As the men broke in their field shoes, many developed blisters or painful circles around the ankles, where the tops of the stiff leather shoes chaffed from the miles of marching. The constant walking and increased and intense physical activities resulted in sore feet, blisters and pulled muscles. The men could receive permission to visit sickbay for treatment to prevent infection or go to a special room in the gym to soak their battered feet or even receive a rubdown for their aching muscles.

To balance the conventional exercise program, there were the occasional, so-named "hard labor" activities, like sawing logs or chopping wood. A victory garden was planted and maintained by the cadets, who also used their chopping skills to dispatch their own Thanksgiving turkeys.

The cadets constructed a ship's store where snacks, toiletries and magazines were sold.

The concrete floors of old university poultry houses were broken up with sledgehammers and hauled away by the cadets. Campus landscaping was performed with picks, shovels and wheelbarrows.

When the mayor of Athens asked the school's commanding officer if the cadets could remove more than 11 miles of trolley tracks that ran through the town, teams were sent out to perform the task, building good relations with the city in the doing.

The men seemed to stay wet all day: from perspiration caused by the constant marching and their vigorous physical training classes and from the frequent showers that left puddles in the Georgia clay. The military-issue raincoats rarely dried out completely overnight.

But the heavy daily doses of physical activity paid off dramatically and handsomely for the cadets. Billy was no exception: he and his classmates were brown from being shirtless and in shorts during the long hours of exercises and he began to notice that his trousers were getting looser in the waist and his shirts tighter. He proudly observed in the mirror the increasing muscularity of his arms and chest.

Not only were he and his classmates in the best physical condition of their young lives, none could argue against the success of the V-5 program: the pilots of the U.S. Navy it produced were the envy of every nation's military force.

The harder the men were worked, the more fuel they consumed. Billy could have never imagined he and his fellow cadets could pack away as much food as they did, three times a day. Not only was there plenty of good and nutritious chow, the choices in a balanced diet were ample: baked chicken, ham, meatloaf, spaghetti and meatballs, tasty vegetables, homemade cakes, pies, and breads. The only consistent complaint the men expressed about their meals was the incessant, omnipresence of the slick, barely-palatable powdered eggs they received for breakfast.

"With all these chickens running around, why do they have to serve these nasty-tasting powered eggs?" the men asked.

One morning meal that had been new to the men, at first intimidating, was a longstanding traditional Blue Jacket breakfast: baked beans—Navy, of course—bacon and cornbread. Since beans of all sorts were favorites of Billy, he looked forward to the combination, primarily for the flavors, but also because it gave the men a break from the abhorrent powered eggs. He wished he had the time to enjoy that breakfast at a leisurely pace.

The downside of large servings of beans at any meal, unfortunately, was the gastric, flatulent, combustive effect the legumes had on the troops, which seemed to intensify after lights out.

Adding to the frustration of having such a short time to enjoy their food, one mess cook was notorious for irritating the men by playing very fast renditions of "The Flight of the Bumblebee" and "After You're Gone," on the chow hall public address system.

Reflecting the sharp, divided sectionalism of the time and heightened by the pressures inherent in the pre-flight program, as well as other aggravations of military life, food fights in the chow halls erupted frequently between Southern and Northern cadets.

One memorable scene in one such culinary confrontation was the meringue profile of "Wrong Way" Carrigan's face, left on a bulkhead behind where he had been sitting as he quickly pushed back in his chair and turned his head to avoid a rapidly approaching, airborne coconut cream pie.

The busy daily schedule, coupled with hours of study at night, two-hour watches, constant field days to keep their rooms and barracks spotless, uniform maintenance, and spit-shining shoes for morning inspections, contributed to sleep deprivation for all. Billy began drinking coffee at breakfast to help keep him awake in class and give his brain an extra jolt, despite warnings from those who claimed to know for a fact that it was into the coffee the mess cooks dumped the infamous, mysterious saltpeter, which was supposed to lower the cadets' libido.

Billy doubted the rumor and for good reasons: if the chemical were being added to any of the food, it seemed to have had no physical effect on him or his roommates, all of whom were at the very zenith of their sexual powers. Upon awakening each morning, the irrepressible, potent, penile turgidity of the robust 19 and 20-year-olds strained against the thin broadcloth of their drawers or protruded proudly from their gaping flies with imperious impunity.

Not one of the men showed any shame nor made any attempt to conceal the engorged phallic phenomenon, the universal, unabashed symbol of proud, self-satisfied masculinity.

*   *   *

AS HAD BEEN PREDICTED by the pre-flight school's commanding officer, Captain Charles Smith, at his welcoming ceremony for the new class, the ranks of students were diminishing. Following the weekly review board meetings, the men in the various squads would return to their rooms to find a rack empty, its bare mattress folded over at the middle, toward the head of the rack.

The school used the Navy's standard four-point grading scale, with two-point-five being the minimum passing grade. Two failures meant "washout," or dismissal and a bus ticket to boot camp or, for prior service cadets, back to the fleet.

Breaking any of the lengthy list of rules and regulations could also result in a disciplinary washout, including: seriously disrespecting an officer, lying, cheating, stealing, intoxication, bringing a woman into the barracks, or other similar violations.

"When you see that empty rack, men," "Skipper" Smith had told them, "go on with your lives. Don't stop to question his disappearance. Don't try to contact him. Don't even talk about him. He isn't there and that is all you need to acknowledge. Forget about him. Don't lose your focus on the purpose for your being here.

"When you graduate from flight school and you're out in the fleet and the rack next to you is suddenly empty, don't stop to question. Don't stop to mourn. Don't lose your focus then, either.

"Death is an all too-real reality in combat. Thousands, even millions may be killed, but I promise you this: There are no atheists in foxholes.

"I suspect there are more genuine, heart-felt prayers from military men on the front lines than from all the cathedrals in the world.

"Don't worry about your fallen comrades. I assure you, if they are worth your concern, they have made their peace with God and are ready to meet Him. They'll be all right. Worry about yourself.

41

Think only of the living and staying alive, or how to send your enemies to their Maker. Those are your responsibilities in the Navy."

Billy and most of the other cadets returned to the same auditorium—Memorial Hall—each Sunday for Protestant Divine Services. Jewish cadets were transported to the Congregation Children of Israel Synagogue Friday evenings and Catholics attended St. Joseph's Catholic Church early Sunday mornings, both houses of worship being located in Athens.

On Sunday mornings in Athens or at any U.S. military base or ship of the line, when the chaplain's pennant—a long, white, sharply-pointed standard with a blue cross down its length—was hoisted (above the American flag at sea; below it ashore), card playing, smoking and loud talking were forbidden until the pennant was lowered and removed at the completion of services.

Cadets, wearing their dress blues when they returned from the tailors, who were neither Catholic nor Jewish, whether believers or not, were nevertheless marched weekly to the worship services, which were based strongly on the Episcopalian order of worship.

Churches services were always a welcome respite for Billy. He appreciated the opportunity to engage in the singing of hymns, participate in responsive readings, listen to a well-delivered, positive sermon, and reflect on his place in the Navy, the school and the world.

He had also become better acquainted with Greg Walker, a tall, dark-haired, muscular Tennessean who had been awarded the sobriquet "Preacher," for the fact that he always kept a thin New Testament in his front shirt pocket and read it anytime the men were standing in line, which was frequent. Billy and the other men respected Walker's spirituality, as opposed to merely being religious, his quiet manner and wise, kind reflections.

The men had a tendency to apologize to Greg whenever they uttered an obscenity or took the name of the Lord in vain.

Billy noticed that Greg would tap his sternum and move his lips when the Deity were profaned.

He asked him about that.

"Catholics have what they call a Holy Name Society," Preacher explained. "Whenever the Lord's name is taken in vain, they say,

'Blessed be the name of the Lord.' I'm not Catholic, but I think that's an appropriate response. I hope it somehow compensates for the disrespectful language.

"I think," he continued in his quiet manner, "whenever somebody calls on the Lord and really doesn't need Him, we sidetrack Him from someone who does need Him. Sort of like crying 'Wolf,' you know. That's why I think we're asked to call on Him only when we need His help."

"I think you're probably going to have a bruised chest before you get out of the Navy," Billy suggested.

Greg smiled.

"You're probably right."

During one of their discussions of why they had volunteered for pre-flight, Billy remarked, "I don't consider warfare romantic or in any way idealistic. I really believe we have to stop the Germans and the Japs before they try to take over the United States."

Preacher agreed.

"Righteousness has to prevail. Love comes from God. Evil comes from the devil, but 'Vengeance is mine, saith the Lord,' won't work. We have to do His work for Him."

"The Eternal God is your refuge," Preacher added, looking like an Old Testament prophet, his index finger raised over his head, "and underneath are the everlasting arms. He will drive out your enemy before you, saying, 'Destroy him!' "

In carrying out their duties to country, life would be short for many of the men around him, Billy realized. Life could be short for him, intensifying his credo of *I shall use my time, and if necessary, I may be called upon to give my life.*

Having faith in something that transcended his prospects for a long, happy life was of great comfort to him and the short chapel services held throughout the week and the extended Divine Services on Sunday strengthened that faith.

*   *   *

AFTER THE FIRST TWO WEEKS of restriction, Billy's class began to receive some weekend base liberty. Since the walk—the march—to downtown Athens was too far from base, considering the limited amount of time the men had, most of them preferred to stay on base. Movies, a visit to the library, to the recreation room on the third floor of Memorial Hall and workouts in the gyms for the athletically addicted, offered moments of relaxation and a chance to drink a soft drink, eat some ice cream, read civilian magazines, listen to the latest songs on a juke box, get caught up on reading the newsy, witty and irreverent base paper, the *Skycracker*, or just do nothing at all.

On special occasions, the women from the university or from other near-by colleges, or the Navy WAVES from Milledgeville, would attend dances and socials held in Dahlgren Hall. Too, the sororities frequently invited some of the men to their houses for parties.

Billy and his roommates were invited to one such party, at the Omicron Alpha Tau sorority house.

Barry had promised Billy that he was going to see to it that he "became a man" that evening, since he was the only admitted virgin of the four who roomed together.

Barry had procured a bottle of particularly poor quality whiskey from a bootlegger he knew in the sheriff's department.

"Now, Bill," Barry told his uninitiated friend, "when we get the two of you relaxed with a couple of drinks, you just take her by the hand and ease on up the stairs to her room. She's done this before— I knew this girl before I came into the Navy—*knew* in the biblical sense—and you won't have to worry about what to do, except to just relax and enjoy it."

"I'm not so sure I want to do this, Barry," Billy said. "Anyway, I've never had any hard liquor."

"Not to worry, Bill. It might even be better that way. We'll just loosen her up and let her take over from there. Trust me. Oh, take this," he said, reaching into his shirt pocket.

He pressed a coin-shaped, gold foil package into Billy's hand.

Billy looked down. His cheeks flushed red when he saw the condom, which he slipped hastily into a trouser pocket.

Barry left the room and soon returned with a smiling, attractive young lady with dark blonde hair and who was wearing a soft, flowing kerchief dress.

"Bill, this is Daisy. Daisy, this is Bill."

The two spoke. Daisy was already unsteady on her feet and Billy could smell liquor on her breath.

Barry poured Daisy another drink from the flask he pulled from his hip pocket and added some Coca-Cola to it.

"Now, you two just sit here and get acquainted," Barry told them, as he took the hand of another young lady standing nearby and left the room.

Daisy turned her glass up and emptied it.

She took a deep breath, blew it out and swallowed. "Boy! That stuff really tastes bad. If it weren't for the Coca-Cola, I couldn't have drunk it. I shouldn't drink, you know. I almost always get sick."

Before Billy could respond, however, Daisy's drink and whatever she had eaten for supper, came up without warning, hitting Billy's midsection in a sudden, horizontal gush.

He jumped back—too late—and looked about for something to clean himself.

"See?" Daisy said, standing and wiping her mouth with the tip of her fingers. She hiccoughed, turned and disappeared up the stairs.

The housemother ran to Billy and showed him to a nearby bathroom to clean off his uniform.

When he emerged with a large, dark, wet stain on his tie, shirt and trousers, he headed for the front door, to return to his barracks.

Barry saw him and walked quickly to him.

Billy looked at his stained shirt and then at Barry.

"Didn't go so well, huh?" Barry asked.

"I always seem to wind up with the wrong dates," he said. "See you guys back at the room. I need a shower."

*   *   *

THE 12-WEEK PRE-FLIGHT SCHOOL came rapidly to a close the last week of May 1943.

Billy had not distinguished himself academically, attaining an overall average of three-point-two, which was only slightly above average. Barry Dorsey, on the other hand, was in the top ten percent of the class.

"I'll be admiral before I'm forty," he promised his roommates.

The men unceremoniously turned in their books, received their medical records, tickets home, and orders to primary flight training at Memphis Naval Air Station, in Tennessee.

They packed their uniforms in the hard-sided, green suitcases they had purchased at the ship's store, and mustered in front of their quarters to board the bus that would take them to the train station for 14 days' leave.

There was no final ceremony: no band, no parade, no farewell to mark their progress. Only the personal satisfaction that each had in accomplishing the requirements necessary to continue their dreams of becoming Navy pilots.

On the bus, the former collection of strangers was now a band of brothers. They would all attend the next phase of their training together, as well as intermediate and advanced training. Their first three months of the demanding program of eating, living, sleeping and working together had already bonded them for life.

Bob Hawthorne, who was sitting with Billy on the bus and who was going to spend his leave time in Riverton with Billy, summed up his feelings about the three-month program: "Bill, I promise you, I wouldn't go through pre-flight school again for a million dollars, but I wouldn't trade the experience for ten million!"

Stearman N2S-3, the "Yellow Peril," flying 9-plane formation

CHAPTER TWO
PRIMARY FLIGHT TRAINING
MEMPHIS, TENNESSEE, NAS

T HE SURVIVORS OF BILLY'S CLASS climbed once again
onto the cars of trains that would take them to their homes in
the Southeast and as far west as Texas and Oklahoma, for a two-
week leave. The men bore little resemblance to the disparate, rag-
tag mixed bag of civilians who had left their homes for naval indoctrination only three months earlier. Shorn of their hair, trim and fit,
dressed in travel uniforms of flattering double-breasted dress blues,
with twin vertical rows of large, shiny, brass buttons, white hats
with black patent-leather brims, and carrying identical olive drab,
hard-sided suitcases, the cadets now resembled each other in dress
and in the way they walked and moved.

Their assimilation into "being uniform" and "being Navy," was
more than an expression: it was a reality.

They walked to waiting rows of upholstered seats and fell weari-
ly into them. Two pairs of padded chairs faced each other to encourage conversation, but the men were less interested in engaging each
other now than they were in catching up on their sleep. For the first
time since leaving their homes three months earlier, they gratefully
indulged in the luxury of covering their faces with their hats and,
with closed eyes, crossed arms, they could sleep the sleep of the
dead without fear of missing a muster, a class, an inspection or a
watch. For two glorious weeks, they could sleep for as long as they
wished, come and go as they pleased, linger over meals with family and friends and put aside the unending demands of the life of a
military cadet.

As the train approached each station, a conductor in a dark uniform with brass buttons and a distinctive, smallish, circular, flat-
topped hat, swayed through the cars calling the name of the stop.
One by one, the men drowsily placed their hats onto their heads,
pulled themselves up, grabbed their suitcases, grunted or waved a

goodbye, and stumbled off the train into the arms of their families or loved ones.

Billy's parents and sisters were waiting at the Jackson's Bluff station to greet him and Bob Hawthorne later that beautiful afternoon in late May. Billy was swallowed up in a loving sea of hugs and embraces.

He introduced Bob to his family before the two cadets placed their suitcases into the trunk of the Hudson and climbed into the back seat, as Billy's sisters squeezed in between them.

Predominant among the comments was how much Billy had changed, which pleased him greatly. He knew he had changed. He felt stronger, bigger, harder, smarter, and more mature, but still, it was good to hear it from others.

"I can hardly wait for your Uncle John to see you," his mother said proudly.

Neither could Billy, for it was Uncle John he wanted to impress most of all.

The 20-minute ride back to Riverton was filled with tales of adventure and anecdotes that thrilled his sisters, Alice and Susie, and his father, but saddened his mother somewhat, who realized her son was no longer the same boy she had seen off mere months earlier.

When the car pulled into the Benson's back yard, his great-aunt Ollie, Velma, the family's live-in maid, and her ward, Robert, and Buddy, Billy's Irish setter, spilled from the house to complete the homecoming. More hugs and kisses followed, accompanied by the nearly uncontrollable barking of Buddy, as he galloped circles around them excitedly.

Billy felt goose bumps rippling over his body as he entered the kitchen, which, he suddenly realized, had always been redolent with the comforting smells of food.

"Ummm, what is that wonderful aroma?" he asked, as he sniffed the air.

"Chicken-fried steak and gravy, mashed potatoes, green beans, and biscuits," Velma proudly announced.

Billy put his arm around her shoulder, squeezed her and kissed her forehead.

"A woman after my own heart. Thanks, Velma."

Once again in the literal heart of his father's house, his mother's kitchen, with Buddy pressed close to his leg, he knew he was home.

He suddenly realized he hadn't been homesick while he was away. He had written a few cards, made occasional telephone calls home, but his days and nights had been so filled with Navy training and military minutia, he had had little time to dwell on anything outside pre-flight training. He had missed all this, but had had no problem in setting it aside to give his full attention to the naval matters that pressed themselves on him.

I used my time, he thought, reflecting on the Jack London credo he had pledged himself to while in high school.

He saw the newspaper page with a map of Europe studded with pushpins, taped to the basement door beside the stove.

"What's this?" he asked.

"My war map," his father said. "So we can keep up with the troops."

"Good for you, Dad," Billy said.

"Grab your suitcase and come on upstairs, Bob. Let's get cleaned up for supper."

The two climbed the stairs, followed by Buddy, and went to Billy's room.

His model airplanes acknowledged their entrance and swung to and fro from their ceiling-mounted wires as a greeting.

The windows were already opened and the spreads looked freshly washed and ironed. It was obvious that the room had been carefully and lovingly prepared for his homecoming.

Again, the ripples of pleasure traversed his body. His mother had surprised him by hanging new draperies that matched the plaid bedspreads. Everything had been dusted and the wooden furniture polished to a shine. Before leaving for the Navy, he had always assumed things more or less kept themselves clean. Having just completed an intensive, crash course in weekly field days, however, he now truly appreciated the neatness of his room and home.

Billy felt the urge to comment on how comforting is the concept of Home, but thought better of it. Bob, an orphan, raised in an orphanage, might not have been able to share his appreciation for it. He could not hide his overt pleasure at being home, however, as he removed his coat, loosened his tie and the top button of his shirt and fell onto his bed by the windows as Buddy cheerfully sat on the floor beside him.

Billy stretched, groaning with pleasure, locked his hands behind his head and looked at his scale model air force hanging overhead.

"Ahh!" he luxuriated. "Just think, Bob, we can stay in bed until tomorrow afternoon, if we want to."

Bob didn't answer. Billy looked over at his friend in the other bed.

He was sound asleep.

* * *

THE NEXT DAY, both cadets were awake at sunrise. "I was afraid this would happen," Billy said, as he swung his feet over the side of his bed.

"Old habits die hard," Bob said. "Maybe we'll be able to sleep later tomorrow."

Their day was full. After a leisurely breakfast of bacon, eggs and biscuits with milk gravy, they walked through the alley to Riverton High, where he had graduated in 1942. They stopped by the principal's office and wandered from room to room, spending time with faculty members and students Billy knew.

All were impressed with his physical improvement and complimented him on how the Navy training had agreed with him, although he received considerable ribbing over his haircut.

"Navy issue," he would say, running his hand over his head.

They walked to Mrs. Watson's house, to whom Billy had delivered groceries and driven to her book club meetings in a LaSalle automobile he and his Uncle John had restored.

"Billy, how nice to see you," Mrs. Watson said. "And how good you look!"

She gave Billy a hug.

"Thanks, Miz Watson. This is one of my classmates, Bob Hawthorne."

"How nice to meet you, Bob. Please come in."

The house seemed unchanged, but for the first time Billy could remember, he smelled food being prepared.

"Umm, what smells so good?" he asked, as Mrs. Watson took them to the parlor.

"Oh, Billy, the most wonderful thing has happened!" she said, as she eased herself into her Belter chair.

"When Willie called to thank me for helping him buy his bus tickets, he told me about his brother. He was concerned about what would happen to him when he moved to Michigan."

"Willie is a colored man I worked with at Riley's Grocery," Billy explained to Bob. "Miz Watson helped him and his family with bus tickets to Detroit."

"I didn't know he had a brother," Billy said to Mrs. Watson.

"Yes, Marcus. Marcus Aurelius. He lived with Willie's family in a tiny little room. He's a cook down at the Riverton Hotel."

She leaned toward her guests and spoke *sotto voce*, even though Marcus was at work. "He stutters severely and really doesn't talk very much at all and doesn't have many friends. Actually, I don't know if he has *any*."

She sat up and spoke at normal volume.

"But Billy, he is the most wonderful cook! Actually, I think of him as a chef. You smell the pot roast he put on early this morning before he went to work. I just turned it off. It just melts in your mouth.

"Anyway, as Willie and I talked, I thought of the little apartment over the garage, where my cook and driver used to live. I suggested that Willie and Marcus come by so I could meet him.

"Well, he was so polite. And you know, with his impediment, I felt he might not find a decent place to live. I'm afraid we aren't as benevolent as we should be with colored people and people with special physical problems. So, I thought, here is an opportunity to help someone and at the same time, maybe have somebody to watch out for me.

"Since he moved in, he has been so helpful, Billy. He even drives me to my club meetings in the LaSalle.

"He cooks, he cleans, he keeps the car washed, and he has cleaned and painted the garage apartment. It's so nice to have someone out there. I just can't say enough about him and the way it worked out.

"And I have you to thank for all this, Billy. Look at how much good has come of that one act of kindness of yours."

"Oh, no, Miz Watson. You're the one who deserves the credit."

"I wouldn't have known about it if you hadn't asked, would I?" she asked.

"No, but I'm really glad it has turned out so well for you."

They left her with a hug and a wave and then walked out to Riley's Grocery, where Billy made home deliveries during his high school years.

After a noon meal with his mother and aunt at the Benson's, the two cadets took long, after-dinner naps.

The next morning, they took off again, walking from one end of the town to the other, visiting friends and making the rounds on Market Street.

The following day, they drove the Hudson to the landing strip at McBreyer Bottom, where they visited with Jim Hayes, who had given Billy his flight lessons.

At breakfast on the fourth morning of his leave, Billy announced, "Mom, Bob and I are going on a forced march out to the farm today to see Uncle John and Aunt Grace."

"But that's eight miles," his mother protested.

"Hah! We probably walked more than eight miles every day at pre-flight. And we don't want to let what we've built up turn to fat," Billy said.

"We'll wear our athletic gear and walk and run out there."

"It's a long way," she reminded them.

"We'll spend the night and maybe get Uncle John to bring us back, in the event we bit off more than we could chew."

"Is that all right with you, Bob?" Edna asked.

"Oh, yes, ma'am. It'll be good for us."

"Well, okay," she said. "I guess you know what you're doing."

Billy and Bob went back to his room to change into shorts, tee shirts, their rubber and canvas sneakers, and slipped their toothbrushes and a few dollar bills into the back pockets of their shorts. Billy hugged his mother, and the two struck out for the tree-lined, two-lane roads of the eastern part of the county.

*   *   *

"IS ALL THIS YOUR UNCLE'S?" Bob asked, as he and Billy, now walking to cool down, approached the house from the road leading to the front of it.

"Actually, the entire family owns it. Uncle John and Aunt Grace live here and work it. And Uncle Kenneth. Do you like it?"

"It's great!" Bob said, admiring the comfortable-looking old house, highlighted perfectly by the whitewashed tree trunks and creeks beside and in front of it.

"It reminds me of one of those Currier and Ives prints," he added. "I've always wanted to live out in the country in a place like this."

"I was born in that front room there," Billy said, pointing. "And I pretty well grew up here. Especially during the summers. It's my second home," Billy said.

"Come on around back. Let's see if Aunt Grace is here."

Rattler, a blue-tick hound, lifted his head as the two passed where he lay coiled in the grass under a tree. Billy spoke to him and scratched his head.

"Rattler isn't much of a watch dog," Billy said unnecessarily.

They surprised Grace, who was in the kitchen when Billy knocked loudly on the back screen door.

"Aunt Grace?" he called.

"Billy!" his aunt said as she unhooked the screen door to let him in. "I wasn't expecting to see you so soon! Come on in!"

Billy hugged his aunt carefully, trying not to get her wet from perspiration from his two hour-long run.

He introduced Bob and the two sat at the kitchen table and emptied two glasses of cold spring water immediately.

"My! How you have filled out, Billy! I almost didn't recognize you when you knocked on the door."

"I think everybody is surprised at what a difference only three months can make.

"Where's Uncle John?" he asked. "I'm anxious for him to see what the Navy has done to us."

"He had to go over to the church to do a little work. He'll be back pretty soon. I know he'll be glad to see you."

"Uncle John was in the Marine Corps," Billy said to Bob. "He thinks only Marines do any exercise."

Billy's Uncle Kenneth came into the kitchen through the back door.

Billy stood and spoke to him. Kenneth, unsmiling, waved, walked on into his room and closed the door.

"Something's wrong with Kenneth," his aunt said softly to Billy.

"He looks bad! Is he sick?" Billy asked in a whisper.

"He won't talk about it and won't let me talk about it, either."

"He's always been a little strange," Billy said quietly, leaning toward Bob.

"Well, anyway," Billy asked his aunt aloud, "Is it okay if Bob and I stay over tonight?"

"Oh, sure, honey, if Bob doesn't mind roughing it."

"Shoot, no!" Bob said enthusiastically."I really like your place and anywhere we sleep is fine with me."

"I'll get some clean sheets and ya'll can go on out to the barn and see if that room in the loft is going to be okay." she said.

"Come on, Bob. Let's do a little reconnoitering," Billy said after his aunt brought their sheets.

The two walked to the barn, which was straight behind the house and up the grade on the other side of a gate beside the outhouse.

"We don't have running water out here. There's the head," Billy said, gesturing as they walked by the privy.

"It won't be my first time," Bob said.

"Here's the barn. Watch your step. Uncle John keeps chickens and cows. There's a ladder inside here up to the loft."

They climbed the ladder to the hayloft where bales of hay were neatly stacked on the wooden floor. Billy opened the door of rough vertical boards that led to a long room.

The tin roof of the room sloped down from the wall that ran down the center of the loft where two mismatched beds were placed. A table between the beds held a kerosene lantern with a green glass shade. Two old overstuffed chairs on either side of a flat-topped trunk topped with a stack of worn magazines completed the décor.

Billy laid the sheets his aunt had given him on one of the beds and pushed open the two large wooden shutters that covered the square holes in the wall that served as windows.

Bob stood in one of the openings and looked out onto the pasture that lay beyond the fence. "Man! This is great!"

He took a deep breath. "I smell something like perfume. Like blossoms. Is there a plum tree nearby?"

Billy looked out the other window. "Oh, there are fruit trees all over the place. There's the apple orchard over there. And the plum trees over here."

"Man! I love this place! Do you think your Uncle John would adopt me?" Bob asked with a quick laugh.

"I wouldn't be surprised. He can always use another hand out here.

"Is this going to be okay?" Billy asked, motioning to the beds.

"Perfect!" Bob answered, testing one of the beds. "I'd like to move right in."

He patted the mattress with his hand. "Good and firm. The way I like it."

Billy laughed and hit his mattress with his palm. "The mattresses are stuffed with straw.

"It might get a little cool tonight. There are some quilts in that trunk if you think you'll need them."

"No, I think the sheet will be fine."

"Come on. I'll steal us some skivvies and clothes from Uncle John's room so we can go down to the creek and get cleaned up," Billy said. "We won't let the Navy know we were out of uniform while we were on leave."

The two were in the deep pool when they heard John calling to them.

"Hey! I heard there are some guys impersonating Marines down here," he said, as he approached them.

"Hey, Uncle John!" Billy called, climbing from the pool.

"Holy smoke!" John said, looking at the trim, muscular, Olympian enthusiastically coming toward him.

"Your Aunt Grace was right! It's hard to believe that the Navy did all that to you and not the Corps!"

Billy took his uncle's extended hand.

"We'll hug after you've put some clothes on," his uncle said. "People might talk about me if I did that to a naked man."

"And here's my friend, Bob Hawthorne," Billy said, as Bob walked toward John.

"Damn! Here's another Charles Atlas! The Navy must be doing something right!"

Bob and Uncle John shook hands.

"We stole some of your clothes," Billy said, pointing to the stack of folded underwear, pants and shirts on the creek bed.

"Aren't you afraid they'll be too small for you?"

$$* \quad * \quad *$$

BILLY, BOB AND UNCLE JOHN were at the table eating peach cobbler as Grace washed dishes at the sink.

"I've really enjoyed being out here today," Bob said. "I told Bill, when we first got here, this is the kind of place where I've always wanted to live."

"Visit us anytime you like, with or without Billy," John replied. "And when you get out of the Navy, come on back. We'll put you to work."

"Are you serious?" Bob asked.

John looked at his sister, who smiled and nodded.

"I'm serious," he said.

A car horn blew out front. John left the kitchen to go to the front door.

"Come on in, folks!" they heard him call.

Billy and Bob stayed at the table as Grace joined her brother in the living room.

The Chambers were new neighbors who sold Watkins products. They had brought by the vanilla extract Grace had ordered. Billy and Bob placed their dessert bowls in the sink and walked into the living room to meet their company.

Uncle John had turned up the Aladdin kerosene lamps, bathing the room in bright, white light.

"And this is our daughter, Molly, who has been off with the rodeo," Mr. Chambers announced proudly.

Molly wore a sleeveless western shirt of faded denim. The tail of the shirt was outside her jeans and tied in front of her waist with a loose knot, affording a tantalizing occasional glance of a tight, flat, muscular abdomen. She wore a pair of snug jeans with a zipper down the front like men's, not on one side, the way women's jeans were made. Her light brown hair was pinned behind her head in two tight braids. It was easy to imagine her strong legs pressed tightly to the sides of a bucking horse, western hat in one hand waving in the air and one well-developed arm securely holding the animal's reins.

Molly smiled broadly when she and her parents were introduced to Billy and Bob.

"Are you two escapees from a chain gang or just out of boot camp?" she asked.

Her perfect teeth and freckles completed her healthy, wholesome look.

"Boot camp," Bob said.

Billy and Bob were impressed with the way she stalked confidently toward them to give them firm handshakes.

If women were permitted in the flight program, this is what they would look like, Billy thought.

"There's a picture of how he looked when he left," John said, pointing to Billy's high school graduation picture on the pump organ.

When Molly turned to look at the photograph, Billy and Bob were immediately attracted to her shapely derriere. Billy's mouth dropped open as he unabashedly admired the way her firm, round buttocks filled the jeans.

Uncle John pressed his jaw shut with the back of his hand as a subtle reminder to Billy that his own was open.

It wasn't long before the three younger members of the group were sitting around the kitchen table, engaged in spirited conversation as Billy's aunt and uncle entertained Molly's parents in the living room.

Billy and Bob kept her laughing as they shared stories about preflight school. Molly told of her adventures in the rodeo, but not all of them were good memories.

"I finally had to leave," she said. "I just didn't like the way they were mistreating the animals. They were doing some really bad things to the broncos and bulls to make them buck and all and I just didn't want to be a part of it anymore.

"But tell me about those haircuts. What do you call them?" she asked.

"Everybody's had something to say about these," Billy said, his hand going automatically to the tuft of hair on the top of his otherwise bare head. "Of course, we really didn't have a choice in the matter. Once a week, every week, just like clockwork, we were herded back into the barber's chair. Uncle John said the Marines call this a 'high and tight.'

"Some call them 'white walls,'" Bob offered.

"Let me rub them," Molly said, leaning over the table to run her palm back and forth over the stubble of their heads.

Aunt Grace came in to make lemonade. She poured them each a glassful and returned to the living room to serve the others.

Uncle John walked through the kitchen nearly immediately afterward on the way to his room, returning with a bottle of sour mash cradled in his arm.

"I think we need to add a little kick to this bug juice," he said softly. "What do you say?"

Billy was quietly surprised and pleased at the proposal. His uncle had never offered him liquor.

John poured a generous amount of bourbon into each of their glasses and then his.

Billy noticed right away how the alcohol improved everybody's wit.

Nearly an hour later, his Aunt Grace returned to the kitchen. "Molly, your folks are ready to leave. Did you want to stay longer or go with them?"

Molly looked across the table at Bob and then at Grace.

"I guess all of you will be needing to get to bed," Molly said.

"We can go out back and talk and won't bother Aunt Grace," Billy suggested.

"Would that be all right?" Molly asked.

"Oh, sure," Grace said with a smile. "I'll tell your folks."

She walked back to the living room.

Mrs. Chambers walked into the kitchen. "Are you boys going to see that Molly gets home safely?"

Billy and Bob stood.

"Yes, ma'am," Billy said. "Where do you live?"

"About a quarter of a mile up the road. At the old Chisholm place," Mrs. Chambers replied.

"Yes, ma'am. We'll walk her home," Billy said.

"Okay, then. We'll see you in the morning, Molly," Mrs. Chambers said. "Goodnight, boys. Nice to have met you."

Thank you.

Good night.

"Let's go on outside," Billy said to Molly and Bob. "Aunt Grace will be wanting to go to bed."

Billy refilled their glasses of lemonade and the three walked to the chairs and hammock under the trees in the back yard.

The Chambers left. Grace finished cleaning up the kitchen and went to bed. John sat at the kitchen table, studying a Burpee's seed catalogue.

Later, Billy quietly entered the kitchen and placed the empty lemonade glasses in the sink.

His uncle looked up from his catalogue.

"Bob and I are going to walk Molly home," he said to his uncle.

"Aren't you tired?" John asked.

"About to drop. I still haven't caught up on my sleep."

"Why don't you let Bob walk Molly home?" his uncle asked.

Billy looked at his uncle.

"You don't think I should go with them?"

"They might prefer to be alone."

"You think so?"

His uncle nodded.

"You don't miss much, do you?" Billy asked.

"Not much," his uncle said. "Especially when it's something so obvious as an old-fashioned game of footsie."

Billy smiled and nodded.

"And why don't you get Bob the flashlight?" his uncle suggested. "We wouldn't want him to get lost taking Molly the long way home."

*   *   *

BILLY WOKE UP THE NEXT MORNING and stretched. He could see the sun coming up through the open windows. He looked over at Bob, who was sound asleep. He was wearing only his tee shirt and lying on his stomach, his right knee nearly to his shoulder, as if he were climbing a mountain. His head was under the pillow.

Jay Sanderson always slept in the buff, back in pre-flight school, but not Bob. He always slept in his shorts. *When did he start this?* Billy wondered.

Billy got dressed, climbed down the ladder, stopped at the outhouse, washed his hands and face on the back porch and went into the kitchen where his aunt was sifting flour at the Hoosier cabinet.

She turned when she heard the back door open.

"Good morning, honey," she said.

"Good morning, Aunt Grace!" he said as he gave her a kiss on the cheek. "That coffee sure smells good."

"Help yourself. Where's Bob?"

"He's still asleep. He walked Molly home and I went on to bed. I don't know what time he got back."

"Are you ready to eat?"

"Is Uncle John up?"

"Oh, sure. He's at the spring house, getting the buttermilk and butter for biscuits."

"I think I'll go down to the creek and get a quick bath first."

"Won't it be too cold?" she asked.

"I'll let you know," he said with a grin.

"I'll take a mug of coffee down with me, if that's okay. I might need it to warm me up."

"Of course, honey."

He poured some coffee into a heavy white mug, took a bar of soap and towel from the washstand on the back porch and walked down to the creek. Steam rose from its surface in the cool morning air.

He dropped his clothes in a heap and tested the water.

He dipped the soap in the water and splashed water over his body to make a lather that he washed off by diving into the pool.

When he left the water, he made a dash for his towel.

As he hurriedly dried himself, his eye spotted something lying on the cream-colored pebbles that made up the creek bed.

He smiled broadly when he recognized the object.

"That son of a gun," he said aloud, walking over to his uncle's boxer shorts that Bob had been wearing the day before.

"That randy little son of a gun!"

*   *   *

Two days before Billy and Bob were to head for Memphis, Bob took a bus to the orphanage in Spring Hill, Tennessee, for a quick visit.

Billy had spent his remaining time at home, helping his father catch up on chores that needed four hands.

On Billy's last evening at home, the Bensons had finished supper, the dishes were washed and put away. His father was reading the newspaper in the living room and his sisters were studying. Billy and his mother were sitting in the back yard swing hung beneath a wooden 'A' frame. Buddy lay beside the swing.

"Your father prays for you at every meal," his mother said.

"I pray for all of you, too," Billy replied.

She patted his knee. "Thank you.

"Are you anxious to leave?" she asked.

"Well, not anxious, but I am ready to start learning to fly Navy planes."

"Will it be dangerous?"

He paused.

"It can be. But not if we do as we're told."

"You're pretty good at that."

He placed his arm around his mother.

"I had good teachers."

"We're all so proud of you, Billy."

"Thanks."

"How much longer will the schools last?"

"The one in Memphis, the primary phase, lasts three months. Intermediate comes after that, down in Pensacola. That one lasts two and a half months. And finally, advanced, or what they call 'final squadron.' That could be in Pensacola or Corpus Christi or Jacksonville. It lasts about three months."

"Are you happy?" she asked.

"With the Navy?" he asked for clarification.

"Yes."

"Happy? Well, there wasn't much time in pre-flight for us to be what you might call happy. But I really like the guys in the program. I liked the training, even though it was pretty tough and we didn't get much sleep or time to ourselves. But these next three phases won't be quite so much like boot camp. We had some good times. So, yeah, I guess maybe I am happy. I'll be happier when I get my wings, of course."

"You'll like Memphis," she said. "Remember how we used to visit the big Sears and Roebuck store and ride the streetcars out to the zoo and the amusement park?"

He laughed.

"I'm afraid I won't be riding many streetcars, Mom."

He had never called his mother "Mom" before he left for preflight training, and she had noticed that Bob called him "Bill," not "Billy." She still wasn't sure she was comfortable with the way her son was no longer her little boy in knickers. She felt the changes had come much too swiftly.

She knew she couldn't hold on to him forever. He would soon be going off, only God knew where and for how long, to fight in the war.

Even though she was settled, secure and content in her home, in her familiar routines surrounded by her family, she could not take total comfort in those domestic comforts. Not with her son being trained as a military pilot.

He, on the contrary, was just beginning to be caught up in the maelstrom of life, of world transformations, eagerly looking forward to the changes he would encounter.

Tomorrow he would be gone from them again and, while everybody in the family would miss his presence, she would feel his absence with an emptiness in the pit of her mother's soul that only a mother could.

She would quietly observe the alterations in her son and in his life, but she would never reveal her apprehensions to anyone.

Yes, she had been aware of the dangers he had faced when he and his friends rode off on their bicycles for a day of exploring the caves along the riverbank or when he and his Boy Scout troop went off for weekend hikes and encampments.

She had always admonished him to "Be careful," and trusted him to exercise the good judgment she and her husband had tried to instill in their children.

She had very early vowed to herself that she would never be one of those parents who would try to smother her children or keep them from reaching and learning. She believed they would never grow if they were not permitted to experience new adventures for themselves or even made mistakes.

So far, things had worked out well for him, but she knew of the risks young pilots faced and she quietly feared for him. She was consoled somewhat in the knowledge that he had rarely given her cause to believe he was careless or reckless.

The two gently pushed the swing back and forth, mother and son, the chains creaking quietly with each push, under a clear, star-filled sky. Many words and feelings would go unspoken. Sitting in the dark on a perfect night in spring, they both knew nothing in their lives or in the world would ever be the same again.

Later that night, as he lay in his bed staring at the gently swaying shadows of his model planes hanging from the ceiling, his arms locked behind his head, his mind pored over the events of the past few days and months of his life since graduating from high school.

The lonely whistle of a train down in East Riverton echoed through the night, adding to the melancholy of his thoughts.

He looked over at the other bed. Buddy had taken his customary place there and was sound asleep. Everything looked so normal, just the way it always had been, but Billy knew he could never go back to the way things were, to who he had been.

He wouldn't want to if he could.

He was ready to move on.

It is the old who prefer to look at life through a rearview mirror, back to the past, to what they knew, to what made them feel happy and secure. The old don't like surprises, especially when life is nearly over.

The young never want to go back. The young anticipate and are anxious for the changes the future brings, for the surprises that the unknown reveals and Billy was young. He was eager to continue with the alterations being wrought in his life. He was looking forward to the adventures primary flight training promised.

He knew tomorrow night he would be in a different bed, in a different state, in a different program.

He could hardly wait for morning.

*   *   *

THE MILLINGTON, TENNESSEE, LOCATION of the military primary flight school north of Memphis had been established during World War I as an aviation school—Park Field—for the Army's Signal Corps. The site had been leased from the 10 civilian owners who farmed it. Because it was already naturally level, it would need only tree and stump removal and paving.

Even though the field had served as an airbase for the primitive cloth and wood planes that evolved from the Wright Brothers' first models, it was deactivated shortly after the November 11, 1918, Armistice was signed and most of the buildings demolished. Some private farming resumed, but the Franklin D. Roosevelt administration set up tent camps in the 1930s for those who had lost their jobs during the Great Depression.

Barely one month after the bombing of Pearl Harbor, however, Secretary of the Navy Frank Knox ordered that the field be re-commissioned, this time as a Naval Reserve Aviation Base.

Hangars, landing fields, repair shop; medical, administrative, housing, messing facilities, gymnasium; and buildings for schools were constructed, originally for 10,000 men, officers and the women reserves known as WAVES. Upwards of 20,000 military and civilian support personnel would populate the base at the height of World War II.

The primary flight training would be conducted on the south side of the Millington-Arlington Road, which split the base in half. Aviation maintenance schools in gargantuan hangars were located the north side of the road.

*   *   *

BILLY AND MEMBERS OF HIS PRE-FLIGHT CLASS held a reunion of sorts on the bus from the train station taking them to the Millington Naval Air Station, some 15 miles north of Memphis. The men worked their way up and down the central aisle, engaging in lively conversation, sharing lies and truths about their sexual conquests and bar time.

There was little to see outside the windows of the bus in the misty, darkening evening. There were few lights from houses or businesses along the way and very little traffic.

"Man! Where are they taking us?" Barry Dorsey wondered aloud, trying to peer through the darkness outside. "The Steppes of Russia?"

Presently, the bus stopped at the brightly lighted main gate with the standard 10-foot high chain link fence with three rows of barbed wire on top, drawing a line between the civilian world and the military. A Navy sentry with his rifle slung over his shoulder and a German shepherd at his side were patrolling the area.

The driver turned on the overhead lights of the bus and pushed the handle that swung the door open. A deadpan young sailor carrying an olive-drab flashlight climbed on board.

"I need to see your ID cards and your orders!" he called. "And I'd appreciate it if you'd put out your smokes and stay quiet while I come around."

The men crushed their cigarettes, put them in their pockets and opened their bags. They removed the brown envelopes that held copies of their orders and pulled wallets from their hip pockets to show identification cards.

The guard walked slowly down the center aisle of the bus.

He completed his inspection, left the bus and waved it through the gate.

The driver drove on in the increasingly foggy night, stopping at a two-storied, wood-frame building and turned on the overhead lights once again.

"Okay, guys," he said, looking at the men through the large, rectangular mirror over his head, "grab your gear and go into that building there to turn in your orders."

About a half hour later, the men trooped up the flight of stairs at the end of a long wooden building to a large open bay that would be their new living quarters. Forty double bunks lined the sides of the room. Tall, gray, metal lockers were lined up back-to-back down the center aisle.

The men who had arrived earlier mingled among them, shaking their hands and welcoming them to their new duty station.

"Take any rack you want to for now," said the young sailor who had led them into the large open bay berthing space. "We'll assign you alphabetically when all your company gets here."

"Draw your bed sheets at the linen locker down there at the other end. When you get your gear stowed, the chow hall is all the way across that grinder there," he said, pointing through the window. "They've saved you some horse cock and other shit to make sandwiches. Be sure you march over as a unit. You're supposed to march everywhere here, just like in pre-flight," he added.

He looked at his wristwatch

"Reveille is at oh-four-thirty. Get showered and shaved and your racks squared away, and report outside for muster at oh-five hundred, to go to chow. Report back to the building, where you just turned in your orders, at oh-five-forty, to start checking in. Any questions?"

He looked around.

"Okay. See you in the morning."

Billy turned to Barry. "Here we go again."

*   *   *

WHEN THE CLAXON HORN SOUNDED REVEILLE and the night watch switched on the overhead lights, some men were already in the head. Those who had still been sleeping crawled from their racks, grabbed their shaving kits, threw towels over their shoulders, and began their early morning ablutions.

Only those cadets who arrived early could expect hot water. Waiting in line, two or three deep, for a cold-water shave and a quick, icy shower, was SOP, or standard operating procedure, for those who stayed in their racks until reveille.

The long enamel-coated iron troughs the Navy used as urinals were placed conspicuously, openly, in the busy passageways and the toilet stalls that lacked doors, too, were on the short side of privacy.

The military discourages secrets in its heads and latrines. Everything was in the open. The men left their open sleeping spaces and entered an open area with facing rows of identical white lavatories under mirrors and single shelves for toilet kits.

Open-bay barracks.

Open showers.

Open heads.

Open.

Everything open.

The military wants no surprises in its open-bay barracks.

As Billy walked back to his bunk to dress, he became aware of the drone of aircraft on the ground beyond the buildings around him and in the air. It was a sound that would rarely cease, even during nighttime hours, except, as was the case the previous night, when fog and light rain had grounded the planes. It was a welcome, comforting, background reassurance to the men on the ground that all was well with their mates in the air.

And after sunset, slow-moving, crisscrossing red and green wingtip lights and fiery engine exhaust stacks wove a magical, intricate tapestry in the dark sky as cadets completed Stage F night training, the final phase in primary flight training.

The men mustered that first morning in their khaki shirts with matching trousers, ties and fore-and-aft caps, to march to breakfast. As they set out across the grinder for morning chow, Billy was reminded of Sunday school classes that told about the wandering Children of Israel in the wilderness.

The cavernous steam-filled chow hall was redolent with the comforting smell of coffee and food. Men on the serving lines—who had been there since four o'clock—shouted for more food or insults to the men they were serving. The animated banter of hundreds of cadets, filled with energy and anticipating a full day of classes or flying, sitting at long rows of tables lined up end-to-end, could be heard above the sounds of clattering dishes and clanging cooking pots.

There was no Marine drill instructor pacing about the chow hall, threatening the men, as there had been at pre-flight, but signs on the bulkheads proclaimed the same message:

Don't waste food.

Eat all you take.

Billy's flight went straight to the serving line to pick up the heavy, compartmented metal trays for their food. That morning it was ground beef cooked in a mysterious creamy sauce, served over toast, known commonly in the fleet as SOS, or "shit on a shingle." Fruit, cereal and milk were available and coffee from huge steaming urns was drunk from large, thick, white glass coffee mugs.

Returning to their quarters as the sun was rising, the new class received its first view of the base: an enormous, absolutely flat, treeless plain, filled with seemingly unending rows of plain, nondescript, two-storied, temporary-looking frame buildings, covered with gray asbestos shingles, and separated by acres of asphalt expanses called "grinders," where close-order drills were performed and ceremonies conducted.

The base could just as well have been on the prairies of the midwest.

The flight students' cluster of barracks was distinguished from the other buildings only by the slightly elevated tract of land where they had been constructed

The company of cadets was broken down into sections, or "wings," which would alternate morning and afternoon training. One wing would be flying while the other attended ground school.

Billy's wing chose Barry Dorsey as its leader again.

Racks were assigned by last name, field day was held, lockers stowed the "Navy way" and primary flight school was underway.

"Ground school," or classroom flight school lectures taught by officers and senior petty officers, picked up virtually where pre-flight school had ended. Naval organization, navigation, theories of aerodynamics, weather, communication, gunnery, physical education, and close-order drill occupied their daylight hours. Additionally, the barracks had to be swept, swabbed and dusted, their beds made and GI cans emptied daily. Thursday evenings were reserved for an all-out, all-hands field day—a thorough cleaning of all spaces for inspections every Friday morning, in which an officer would run his white-gloved hands over window sills, locker tops and any other surface he felt inclined to check.

The men were treated less like "boots" at NAS Memphis and were given evening and weekend liberty if they had no watches or other assigned details.

Technically they were still enlisted men, but not generally considered as such. They weren't commissioned officers, either, although they dressed in officers' uniforms. They were in a nether region, unfortunately, caught between two well-defined entities, only barely tolerated by both, belonging to neither, associating only with each other.

After three weeks of ground school, the wings began flight training at last. That phase of the training was divided into six progressive stages, as dictated by a detailed mimeographed syllabus each man was issued and required to follow:

Stage A, Basic dual flight to solo;

Stage B, Primary Solo, refining pilot skills, for smoothness and precision;

Stage C, Advanced Solo, precision and rapid coordination, or Acrobatics;

Stage D, Final, for qualification to advance to intermediate training;

Stage E, Formation flying, for reaction and adaptability, and, finally, the most feared of all the stages of training, for students as well as instructors,

Stage F, Night Flying, for familiarization and adaptability for night flying.

Billy's wing was marched to one of three enormous, flat-roofed hangars, where each man received flight gear consisting of a one-piece flight suit, a canvas helmet with goggles, leather gloves and a sea bag for stowage. In other flight schools, such as those in Iowa, Illinois, Indiana, Kansas, Massachusetts, Minnesota, and Michigan, where frigid weather was a major concern, the students were issued leather flight attire in the winter. In those climes, however, if the temperature dropped below 10 degrees Fahrenheit, no flying in the open planes was done. Even if the temperature were above that, however, unprotected cheeks and noses sometimes became frost-bitten and flying would sometimes last only 10 or 15 minutes.

Each man was responsible for his own gear, stowed in a seabag which was kept under lock and key in shelves inside one of the hangars. On the days each man would fly, seat pack parachutes were issued

Next came their introduction to the airplane that came to symbolize Army and Navy cadet primary flight training during World War II, the Stearman biplane, developed by Harold Zipp and Jack Clark in 1933. Contemporary sources said it had no unusual characteristics save safety, strength and dependability: perfect, of course, for training purposes.

*   *   *

THE ORIGINAL STEARMAN "KAYDET," as it was known by the U.S. Army, was equipped with the 220 Lycoming R-680 engine ('R' for rotary or radial), produced by E.L. Cord, best known for his innovative and distinctive Auburn, Cord and Duesenberg automobiles.

Even though the engine was under-powered and the little plane's design already outdated when the war began, it was so sturdy, forgiving and reliable for training purposes, it was quickly adopted by the military and manufactured by Boeing, its parent company, in Wichita, Kansas, which produced over 8000 for the United States. The plane was also sold to the governments of Canada, China, the Philippines, Venezuela, Argentina, and Brazil for military use.

In 1940, to avoid a shortage of Lycoming engines, the Army specified alternate engines, the 220 Continental R-670 and the 225-horsepower Jacobs R-755.

The Army's version was known as the PT-13, PT-14 or PT 18, depending on the power plant, while the Navy's version was the N2S. Both planes were identical except for the colors and engines. The fuselage of the Army's plane was painted a medium, or "Air Corps" blue, the wings bright yellow and horizontal red and white stripes on the rudder.

The Navy chose to paint its entire plane a blazing chrome "safety" yellow with a bright red band around the fuselage and two red stripes on the top wing. The predominant yellow color and unpredictable consequences inspired the first cadets to quickly rename it the "Yellow Peril."

In the U.S., each plane was crated and shipped to military airfields where it would be assembled in one designated hangar and pushed onto the flight lines. As many as 300 would be in the air at once at any one of the flight schools, taking off six to eight abreast simultaneously.

*   *   *

LIEUTENANT (JUNIOR GRADE) MARK DABNEY met Billy's wing. He was wearing the uniform of the day for aviation officers: a greenish-brown two-piece suit, khaki shirt, and dark tie, with matching green-brown hat, brown shoes, and khaki socks. He led the cadets to the flight line where hundreds of Stearmans were lined up in two precise rows, wing-tip-to-wing-tip, for nearly as far as the men could see. Enlisted men—plane captains—in dungarees, long-sleeved, light-blue chambray shirts and white "Dixie cup" hats, were busily servicing the little planes. The same aviation mechanic, or "mech," was assigned to perform maintenance on the same planes, to assure quality control.

As he walked with his class toward one of the trainers, Billy thought it looked like an airplane from a cartoon, something that might be featured in a Captain Marvel comic book, with its coat of bright yellow paint, its small size, its pair of over-and-under wings, the top one oddly positioned a half-wing's width forward of the bottom one and all its ribs clearly visible under the glossy fabric covering

If an airplane could look "happy," Billy thought, the Yellow Peril filled the bill.

As had been the case with the Piper "Grasshopper," in which Billy had received his flight training in Riverton, the seats were situated fore and aft in the fuselage. Unlike the Grasshopper, however, there was no canopy. The Stearman had two open cockpits, protected from the elements only by small, V-shaped windshields in front of each seat.

Up close, the plane appeared much larger and the struts and cables and sturdy construction made it appear strong.

"Okay men. Here it is. Your passage to naval aviation," Mr. Dabney said.

"This is the Stearman Kaydet trainer.

"If it looks old-fashioned, it's because it *is* old-fashioned. But it's as tough as a tank. It's small, a wingspan of thirty-two feet and twenty-four feet long and it's slow. It's powered by a two hundred and twenty horsepower engine, with a top speed of one hundred and twenty-four miles an hour."

He pointed to the top wing.

"The center section of the top wing holds forty-six gallons of fuel. That puts a lot of weight up there. Makes it top heavy. And it throws the center of gravity behind the wheels. The landing gear is pretty narrow, as you can see. This means that you will always have to make three-point landings. You'll have to set all three wheels down on the runway at the same time. That's a good practice to get into, anyway, because when you land fighter planes on carriers, you'll need to keep your tail down to grab the arresting cable with your tail hook.

"A top-heavy plane with narrow landing gear like this is an invitation for disaster. You'll have to be aware of the possibility of a ground loop on landing."

He illustrated the landing by pointing his index finger toward the ground and quickly moving it in a circular fashion.

"Too, if you should make a quick stop on the ground, you can flip the plane right over. If that happens, don't panic! Somebody will get out here and rescue you. But whatever you do, do not, repeat, do not unfasten your seat belt. You'll drop out on your head and risk breaking it or your neck. Of course, the enlisted men love to see officer candidates pull dumb stunts like that."

The men laughed as they visualized the spectacle.

"Now, more information about the plane's construction. The wings are made of wood, covered with dope-covered fabric to tighten it up, just like those model planes you used to build when you were kids at home."

He pointed to the wheels.

"A single-leg landing gear."

And then to the body.

"The fuselage is over-built and double-welded. Strong. Tough.

"Like I said, it's slow and old-fashioned. But it's the perfect plane for training cadets. It's reliable and most of all, it's safe.

"Safety. That's the name of the game, gentlemen. That is your number one priority in flight school and in the fleet. Have you ever considered why we say you're 'safe for solo' or whatever the next step is in your training? The Navy doesn't want to see its eleven-thousand-dollar planes smashed up. It doesn't want to send any of you back home in a wooden box. And believe me, your flight instructors sure as hell want to go home every night in one piece."

He pointed as he spoke. "Respect this propeller. Even when the plane seems to be innocently sitting out here unattended. Every now and then, one of these things comes alive for no apparent reason. It cranks itself up enough to turn the propeller over a couple of times and that is certainly enough to get your attention if you're in its way.

"When you do your pre-flight walk about, stay away from the propeller. As you inspect your wings, keep one hand on the leading edge so you won't be tempted to stand so close you get your head cracked by a renegade prop.

"Now hear this! I'd better not ever see any of you trying to get into your plane holding your parachute by the leg straps, thrown over one shoulder. You will always wear a parachute when you fly.

"Always wear it properly. There are a couple of guys here singing soprano, who used to sing bass. They failed to snug their straps up around their legs, the way they were supposed to, and when they bailed out, the jerk of the opening 'chute cracked their nuts."

Some of the men grimaced. As boys, their feet had slipped off the pedals as they were riding their bicycles. They knew only too well the painful occurrence firsthand.

"Not a pleasant experience, I assure you," Mr. Dabney added.

"When you climb into the back seat, you'll sit on your parachute. That's why it's called a 'parachute seat pack.' Fasten your seat belt the first thing. You never know when you might catch a wind current that flips you over or a flying partner who gets a wild hair and decides to fly upside down without any warning.

"Let me tell you a story that I know is true, because it happened to me.

"I had an instructor, a fighter pilot, just returned from the fleet and as hard as nails. He read me the riot act before I even climbed into the cockpit for my first solo flight check. This hard-ass had already made up his mind he was going to give me a down arrow for that session.

"He got into the back seat, but for some weird reason, failed to fasten his seat belt. When I did my first loop, he fell right out of the plane. I saw his 'chute open up and I circled him until he landed to make sure he was all right.

"He gave me the finger all the way down, like it was my fault, and even after he gathered up his chute and lay down on it, he was still giving me the finger."

The men laughed.

"Wait. There's more. I flew back to the airfield and taxied up to my parking spot. My crew chief noticed the back seat was empty. As I was telling him what happened, the base CO drove up. He wanted to know why I was back without my instructor and I told him, too.

"The old man jumped out of his car, took off his coat, climbed into the back seat and flew to where I told him the instructor was.

"When we circled the instructor, he gave me the finger again, not knowing the skipper was flying the plane.

"When the instructor was brought back to the base, he and I had to go up again for my check ride."

"Did you pass it, sir?" Barry asked.

"Of course! He's the one who recommended me for flight instructors' school."

"Are you sure that wasn't his way for getting back at you?" Wrong Way Carrigan asked, to everyone's laughter.

"You might be right, Mr. Carrigan.

"But, getting to where I was, I know it sounds funny to get dumped out of a plane. It sounds funny until it happens to you. If you don't have your seat belt fastened, the law of gravity is no respecter of persons. Even though the fall itself won't kill you, the sudden stop sure as hell will. Always wear your seatbelt, gentle-men and wear your parachute correctly.

"One more thing. Never forget what you're doing. Never let your mind wander, either on the ground or in the air.

"When I was a flight student here, I was the next man to take off. A chief was out on the flight line, not paying attention, and backed into a propeller. People were yelling at him, but he couldn't hear above the noise of the engines. Nobody knew why, but he just got careless.

"We had to fly anyway. His blood and brains were splattered all over the place. I still haven't forgotten that. I doubt if I ever will.

"Never let yourself get sloppy. Never forget safety.

"Now, before we draw parachutes and take off into the wild blue yonder, let me give you a heads up on the parachute.

"When you get airborne and there's a problem with your plane and your instructor tells you to hit the silk, he's not talking about some doll you're about to hump in the back seat of your dad's Oldsmobile. What that means is you're going to have to jump out of the airplane. You do it and pray your parachute opens."

The men looked at each other uneasily.

"Unbuckle your seat belt and go up and over the side of the plane, head first, Australian-style. That way, you'll have a better view of the ground. You can see where you're headed. Do not, I repeat, do not pull your ripcord until you have cleared the plane.

"Guys have gotten their 'chutes snagged by the empennage and dragged down by the plane because they pulled the ripcord too soon. Wait until you're clear, pull the ripcord and make sure your legs don't get caught in the lift webs.

"Everybody understand that?"

The men nodded.

"I didn't hear you," he said, cupping his hand to his ear.

Aye, aye, sir!

"Okay. Much better.

"Now, let me give you a heads up on something you're probably going to hear every time you go up. As soon as you're off the ground, your instructor will ask you, 'Where are you going to put it?'

"You'll never know when your engine will quit on you."

He paused and looked at the men.

"Or," he said, holding up his index finger and waving it, "or when your instructor shuts off your power switch or fuel supply."

The men looked at each other again.

"As soon as your wheels clear the ground, start looking for an emergency landing strip. If your engine quits or your instructor shuts it off for you, never try to return to base. Continue as straight ahead as possible. A clearing is best—a pasture, a cornfield, somebody's back yard—but you may have to settle for a crash landing between some trees.

"Always ask yourself, 'Where am I going to put it?'

"Got that?"

Aye, aye, sir!

"Okay. Let's walk back to the hangar. Get suited up and draw a parachute. Meet me back at the front of the hangar at the flight assignment board, that big blackboard near the front of the hangar. I'll show you how to tell when you're flying and who your instructor is and all that."

There was a certain air of jubilation, of juvenile high spirits, as the men pulled the one-piece green flight suits over their uniforms and zipped them up. They snugged the canvas helmets over their heads and adjusted the chinstraps. A 'Y'-shaped plastic tube hung from the ear holes in the helmet. Their natural-colored, leather gloves had loose cuffs.

After all were dressed and fitted with their parachutes, the men met at the flight assignment board, a large portable blackboard covered with a painted grid that broke down the squadrons by morning or afternoon training periods and rectangles where the planes' numbers, the names of individual men flying them and each man's instructor had been written in chalk.

Since arriving at NAS, Memphis, the scuttlebutt in Billy's barracks had focused on the two types of flight instructors in the V-5 program. One type, Voluntary Reservists (USNR-V) who had been civilian pilots before the war, had volunteered to teach flying. They received commissions and were happy to drive to work each morning and go home to their wives and families each night, just like civilians.

The second category of instructors, however, included the embittered ones, the reservists (USN-R) who had gone through the flight program just as Billy was doing and had anticipated combat duty or something they believed significant to help the war effort. They had anticipated anything but teaching a bunch of teenaged reservists to fly the comical and unromantic Yellow Perils. They would never fly fighters and never see combat. They would see only an unending flow of adolescent cadets they had to train to fight in a war that had left the instructors behind.

Perhaps Navy-recruiting posters showing handsome pilots looking dramatically skyward had inspired the angry instructors, too.

It was because of these intolerant and short-fused instructors that the gosport, the flexible speaking tube from instructor to cadet, was called "the blasphemy tube."

For his first flight, Billy was assigned to Lt. (jg) Jim Wright. Fortunately for Billy, Mr. Wright was from the first ranking of flight instructors, a well-adjusted brownbagger from Memphis, content to be stationed in his hometown.

Billy saluted his instructor, who returned it with a motion that looked as if he were merely brushing a fly from his face.

"Mr. Benson? I'm Mr. Wright."

He extended his hand.

"Good to meet you, sir."

"Where did you learn to fly, Mr. Benson?"

"I was in the Civilian Pilot Training program, sir."

"Oh yes, the CPT. Piper Cub?"

"The L-4."

"Oh, yes. The Grasshopper."

"Aye, sir."

"Okay, Mr. Benson, let's go over to the maintenance office to sign our yellow sheet."

At the Dutch door of the maintenance office, Mr. Wright told the yeoman the number of the plane they were to fly that day. He was shown a detailed list of the maintenance performed on the plane, attesting to the airworthiness of the plane, written on a sheet of yellow paper.

"The mechs and plane captains do some forty-five specific checks on each plane before each flight," Mr. Wright told him. "This yellow sheet is a receipt of what they found."

Mr. Wright signed the yellow sheet and gave it back to the yeoman.

"The log yeoman in there will keep up with your flight hours also. He'll write everything down in your flight log. Check it whenever you want to see how you're doing towards meeting the flight hour requirements.

"You'll be responsible for informing the plane captain of any problems you encounter while you're up. The more information they have, the better they can maintain the plane.

"Let's check out our plane, Mr. Benson. And then we'll take it up and see how it compares with the Grasshopper."

Billy tried to keep up with his instructor's long stride, but his cumbersome parachute, slung loosely under his buttocks, made walking fast awkward.

"You don't have to wear that thing out to the plane for my benefit," Wright said, pointing to Billy's parachute. He was carrying his own over his shoulder. "Just be sure you put it on before you climb in."

"Aye, sir."

When they arrived at the plane, parked on a large round concrete mat or "dumbbell," the aviation mechanic designated the plane captain was wiping his hands on an orange shop rag. He saluted Mr. Wright, who returned the salute in the same nonchalant way he had Billy's.

"All ready for you, Mr. Wright."

"Thanks, Jonesy.

"Okay, Mr. Benson. Let's do our preflight inspection. Even though our plane captains are competent, you're the one who's going to take the plane up. Never assume everything is ready for takeoff until you check it yourself.

"The Marines have a saying: If you assume something, you make an 'ass-a-me.'

"Understand?"

"Aye, sir."

Mr. Wright laid his parachute on the leading edge of the plane's bottom wing and began the walkabout.

Billy followed his instructor around the plane as he conducted a detailed inspection, beginning with the tip of the port, or left, wing and continuing around to the starboard side and back again: wing strength, oil level, movement of the ailerons and flaps on the trailing edges of the wings, the movable elevators on the horizontal sections of the tail and the vertical rudder which helps steer the plane, the same as in water craft. The bolts holding the struts were checked and the luggage compartment cover behind the backseat was opened, inspected and securely closed.

When Mr. Wright removed the cap from the end of the pitot tube, a long, narrow, pipe near the port end of the leading edge of the port wing, he reminded Billy that would be his responsibility when he did his own pre-flight check.

"You won't be about to know how fast you're going if your pee-toe tube is covered, will you?"

"No, sir."

"Everything looks ship-shape. Hop in, Mr. Benson. Be careful, though. Step only on that black catwalk area on the wing near the fuselage and don't lean on the windshield. When you get in, sit on your parachute. There's a handle under your seat to raise or lower it, just like a barber's chair."

Billy grabbed the inside edge of his cockpit and pulled himself up onto the wing and stepped in. He adjusted the seat and fastened the seat belt snugly across his body. He also clipped a pad to his right knee, to make notes in his flight log on everything Mr. Wright said and did.

"Our communication is one-way, Mr. Benson. I can talk to you through this tube from my mouthpiece, to the ear connection in your helmet, but you can't talk to me. It's called a gosport. Your end should be hanging down under the instrument panel."

Billy lifted the hollow tube and inserted it into the 'Y'- shaped tube suspended from his helmet.

His instructor secured what resembled a small feedbag over his mouth, held in place by an elastic strap that passed around the back of his helmet. He pushed a plastic tube into a fitting at the bottom of it.

"Is your seatbelt fastened?" Wright asked through the primitive communication system, looking at Billy through his rearview mirror.

Billy nodded his head and answered, even though he could not be heard.

"You can follow along on the take-off checklist, mounted to the right side of your instrument panel," Mr. Wright said.

Billy located the checklist, looked up and nodded.

"Check your fuel supply up here under the wing," Mr. Wright told him, pointing to a tube above and to his right.

"Ignition switch off...gas on," Mr. Wright said, loudly enough for Jonesy, the mech, to hear.

"Okay, Jonesy."

Jonesy, who was standing in front of the plane, reached up to the propeller and rotated it twice.

"That clears the combustion chambers of oil," Wright said for Billy's benefit.

"Fuel cock control on," Mr. Wright said to his flight captain.

He called out and set other controls as Jonesy retrieved a steel handle with two 90 degree bends, from inside the engine panel. He inserted it into the starter extension hole in the starter panel on the left side of the engine cowl and began to turn the handle.

"He's energizing the inertia starter," Mr. Wright told Billy. "That gets the starter up to speed.

"If I can't get the plane started the first time, Jonesy will have to rewind it again and that makes him very unhappy. It's a lot of work. Watch how he has to lean his entire body into it. He'll do it again for me if the plane doesn't start, because I'm an officer.

"When you're in the front seat, if you don't start it the first time, he'll make *you* crank it, because you're not an officer. It'll make you appreciate what he has to do. Got it?

"Aye, sir."

"All clear," Jonesy called, after energizing the starter and removing the handle.

Mr. Wright turned the ignition switch to *both* and called "Contact!" to Jonesy.

Jonesy primed the engine by turning and then pushing a lever just underneath the starter extension hole before pulling the starter clutch and magneto handle, also in the starter panel.

The engine started on the first try. Wright set the throttle to run between 500 and 700 rpms and tested the foot pedals and rudder.

"The engine has to be warmed up for a minimum of fifteen minutes."

Billy nodded again.

"The magneto check for the Stearman is the same as for the Piper L-4," Mr. Wright continued. "You know about magnetos, don't you?"

Billy nodded as he recalled the definition: *The magneto is a special generator to supply the high voltage necessary for the reciprocating engine of an aircraft.*

Billy watched his tachometer as his instructor added power. When the mag switch was turned left, the rpms dropped to around 75 and when turned back to *both*, the rpms picked back up. A turn to the right tested for another normal drop and back to both.

Satisfied the magnetos were working correctly, and the engine warmed up, Mr. Wright announced, "Okay, here we go."

Billy looked out at Jonesy, who held the lines to the four triangular, wooden wheel chocks in his hands. Each wheel was chocked fore and aft. When Mr. Wright signaled Jonesy with a head nod and a thumbs-up. Jonesy pulled the wheel chocks, retreated to safety and waved the plane off the round mat and onto the taxiway.

Wright monitored the gages on the instrument panel—oil pressure, oil temperature, carburetor, mixture control, and throttle. He unlocked the tail wheel to steer the plane as it taxied on the ground, checked the windsock on the tower and pushed the throttle forward. The plane joined a swarm of other funny little cartoon planes moving slowly into position on the airstrip, zigzagging for better visibility. The procession looked like giant yellow crabs playing a game of follow the leader.

Mr. Wright came to a stop and tested his controls once again.

"That big number up there on the control tower is for the runway we're on.

"Notice the tetrahedrons down there near the tarmac. Always check them and the windsock before taking off.

Billy nodded his head after looking at the delicately mounted, four-sided polygon, with its long, pointed nose swinging freely in response to wind direction.

"Put your gloves on and pull your goggles down."

Billy felt a charge in the pit of his stomach as he lowered his goggles with his gloved hands, a rite of passage for aviators.

The planes ahead of them were cleared one by one for takeoff.

Billy's plane was next.

"Check the wind sock again and keep your eyes on the lights in the tower," Mr. Wright said.

They sat looking at the light gun held by a WAVE in an open window, high up in the control tower. The light was red at the time. Yellow would be 'caution' and a green light would mean 'go.'

The light flashed green.

"Okay, this is it, Mr. Benson!"

The rotary engine roared in response as Mr. Wright pushed his throttle full forward, and the plane began to accelerate down the smooth, paved asphalt runway. Not the bumpity, bumpity, bump on the grassy river bottom field in Riverton, but a flat, even surface, conducive to building more speed for takeoff. When the instructor pulled back on his stick, the plane rose slowly and serenely into the air.

The gasoline exhaust-scented air rushing into Billy's face and around him was deliciously invigorating. He breathed deeply the heavenly ambrosia and let it fill his lungs. He smelled and tasted its magic in his nostrils, on his tongue and in his throat. Watching the ground drop below him without a Plexiglas canopy obstructing his view made him feel it was he who was flying, not the plane. Nearly completely exposed to the elements, with virtually unlimited vision—except dead ahead, which was the back of his instructor's head—up and down and all around, the open cockpit made flying seem almost a religious experience.

Billy was Gabriel the messenger, serenely soaring back to the throne of God; he was Icarus, flying higher and higher over the pure, blue Aegean; he was Merlin, sailing over the flagged turrets of Camelot.

Billy was engaging in the purest form of powered flight man can experience.

But he had to focus on reality.

The nose of the plane remained elevated, pulling them upward until they leveled off at 2000 feet.

"We'll have to remember to keep a sharp eye for bandits and always maintain a respectful distance from other planes," Mr. Wright reminded him. "Crashes in the air kill too many pilots and there's no excuse for not watching where you're going."

Billy looked all around their plane. He could see other yellow specks in the distance, but none close.

"Don't forget that you may have to set it down without notice," Wright continued. "Always look for a landing site. You never know when you might have engine failure, or I might cut off your gas supply."

He made eye contact with Billy through his rearview mirror. Billy nodded and surveyed the ground for clearings conducive to emergency landings.

Mr. Wright began to rock the plane from side to side, watching in his mirror to see how Billy responded.

Billy moved easily and confidently with the plane's motion, making no attempt to remain vertical, as if he were still Earth bound.

"Hold your arms horizontally, out over the sides of the plane, Mr. Benson."

Billy stuck his hands over each side of the plane. The rush of air made it difficult for him to keep his arms straight out.

"Keep them there. We're going to check your seat belt."

Mr. Wright put the plane into a slow roll and remained briefly upside down.

As Billy tried to acclimate himself to this attitude, Mr. Wright righted the plane.

"How was that? Okay?"

Billy nodded his head.

"Take the stick, Mr. Benson. Let me see you do some basic maneuvers."

Billy placed his feet on the pedals and grasped the stick. A jolt of electricity traversed his body as the little plane responded to his controls. He felt he was actually wearing the open plane, holding it to his body by the seatbelt, the way suspenders hold up pants. No, it was more. It was as if he were part of the Stearman, as if he had somehow sprouted two pairs of bright yellow wings.

He had never felt so free, so weightless, so unshackled from gravity.

Convinced of Billy's ability to control the plane, Mr. Wright spoke again through the tube, "Very good, Mr. Benson. Let me see a stall."

When Billy returned from his first flight, he wondered if his feet had descended enough to touch the tarmac. He balled up his gloved right fist and banged it repeatedly into the palm of his left hand, oblivious to the parachute hanging clumsily from his posterior. He could hardly wait to share his euphoria with Bob and Barry and the others in his wing, who, of course, would be equally ecstatic and enthusiastic from their first flights as Billy was.

It was all Barry could do the keep the attention of his excited wing long enough to march them back to their barracks.

When they arrived, he ordered them to stand easy for mail call.

Hawthorne!

Yo!

Benson!

Yo!

Once dismissed from formation, the men again exploded with joy and unabashed enthusiasm, stampeded to their topside sleeping quarters, still noisily expressing exhilaration with their first V-5 training flight, finally, four months after entering the flight program.

Billy sat on his rack amidst the celebratory clamor, to read the letter from his mother.

Dear Son,

I hope this finds you well. Everybody sends their love.

Buddy is doing fine, too.

I won't take too much of your time and feel what I'm about to say won't upset you too terribly, but I felt you needed to know.

Your Uncle Kenneth died in his sleep earlier this week. He had been sick for quite some time, but wouldn't see a doctor.

Kenneth wasn't a very happy man and didn't enjoy life very much. I never understood him, but, well, he was my brother and I did care for his welfare.

We'll bury him in the family plot out at Wesley Chapel tomorrow.

Again, I hope things are going well and that this won't upset you.

Love,

Mother.

Billy folded the letter, slipped it back into the envelope, and reflected on the life of his unsociable uncle.

A wasted life.

A totally wasted life.

How is it that people can live for thirty or forty years or longer and not make any sort of positive impact on the world?

He wondered how his own epitaph would read.

Will I have done anything good, anything lasting, anything positive, that people will remember me for?

Will I have used my time?

Or will I have just selfishly taken up space, air and food, for naught?

He lifted the lock on his locker, a dull, metallic clank, and slipped the letter inside his personal drawer. He didn't know why he saved the letter. He knew he'd never read it again nor would he grieve for his uncle.

A wasted life.

*   *   *

FOR THE REST OF THE WEEK, Billy's wing continued completing Stage A of primary flight school.

For those who were already CPT certified, Stage A was little more than a review of what they had already learned—basic flight maneuvers with instructors, leading to a solo—but the cadets were warned not to show disinterest or to ignore that phase of primary training. The instructors became noticeably irritable if those who were already certified failed to demonstrate appropriate interest in and respect for basic ground school and flight training.

The next time the cadets took to the sky in their Stearmans, however, the constant call for safety seemed to have been ignored by one of the men and a fatality was only narrowly avoided.

All planes in the air were suddenly given a "heads up" by lights flashing dramatically on the flight tower. As Billy returned from his second flight, he and his instructor were met by the cacophony of blaring, raspy warning horns sounding raucously from the flight tower and ear-piercing sirens echoing from the air crash truck and ambulance that were speeding to the farthest end of the field where the runway ended and the trees began.

The enthusiasm and joy that had characterized the wing's first flight were replaced by bewilderment and unanswered questions in the midst of massive confusion on the ground.

"What happened, anyway?" Billy asked Barry Dorsey, as they paused to watch the return of the crash truck and the battleship gray Packard ambulance crossing the landing field, racing in the direction of the base hospital.

"All I know is what our plane captain told me, that one of the cadets fell out of his plane when his instructor did a slow roll. Whoever it was dropped out of the plane and didn't open his 'chute until the very last minute."

"Damn!" Billy said, surprised at his own response. "Do you know who it was?"

"No. Let's see if we can find out."

Inside the hangar, they were told the cadet at the center of all the commotion was Bob Hawthorne.

"Bob Hawthorne?" Billy asked incredulously. "Bob Hawthorne?" he asked again.

"That's hard to believe," Barry said.

"Are you going to the hospital to check on him?" Billy asked Barry.

"Yeah. Right after chow. Do you want to go with me?"

"Yes, I do."

* * *

BOB, WEARING STRIPED NAVY-ISSUE PAJAMAS, was on an open ward, lying in a narrow, white, metal hospital bed when Billy and Barry arrived. The scratches on Bob's face and hands had been painted with Mercurochrome.

"Hey, Bob," Billy said.

"Hey, Billy."

"How ya doin'?" Barry asked.

"Okay, I guess. Nothing's broken."

"What happened?" Billy asked.

"I fell out of my plane."

"Didn't you wear your seat belt?" Barry asked.

"Naw. I must not have snapped it all the way or something."

"I bet you'll check it next time," Billy said with a smile.

Bob laughed quietly. "I sure will."

Neither Billy nor Barry believed their friend had been as careless with his seat belt as he claimed.

Billy had noticed that Bob had not been the same since mail call the day Billy learned his Uncle Kenneth had died. He had become withdrawn and sullen. His aggressive spirit had quieted, his permanent smile was absent. He stopped speaking to his buddies and isolated himself totally.

There were questions Billy wanted to ask, but wouldn't, not until Bob indicated he wanted to answer them.

Billy had wondered about him, but felt he would eventually come around. Besides, everybody's schedule was already full enough without taking on any extra freight.

Bob was released from the hospital the next morning and rejoined his wing just before it left for noon chow. His mood had improved somewhat, but he still chose not to talk about his experience to anyone.

That night, however, after Billy had fallen sleep, he was gently shaken awake.

He opened his eyes. Bob was in his shorts, bending over his bed, shaking his shoulder and calling his name softly.

"Bill?"

"Bill?"

"Huh? Oh, hey, Bob. What is it?" he asked in a husky voice.

"Can I see you out on the ladder?"

"Sure."

Billy swung his feet to the other side of his rack and followed Bob to the stairwell. Bob closed the door quietly and walked over to his friend.

"I gotta talk to somebody, Bill. Okay?"

"Sure, Bob."

Bob began pacing back and forth, hitting his fist into his palm, trying to arrange his thoughts.

"I got a letter from Molly."

"Yeah? I didn't know you two were writing."

Bob stopped pacing and put his hands on his hips.

"We're not. Well, we weren't, until last week."

He began pacing again.

"Yeah, I got a letter from ol' Molly, all right and it wasn't good news for her or for me."

"Yeah?"

Bob leaned against the rail of the stairs.

"When you and I were visiting your Uncle John, you know I walked her back home."

"Right."

"Well, we didn't exactly go straight to her house."

Billy nodded his head. He remembered seeing Bob's shorts at the creek.

"No, we went down to the creek, where you and I had taken a bath that afternoon."

Billy waited.

"It had been nearly four months since I'd been with a girl, Bill, and I was about to explode. I was hornier than a hoot owl, and Molly was hot to trot, too—and so, well, we, you know..."

Billy nodded his head.

"And in that letter I was talking about, Molly said she had missed her period. And that she's coming up here and she wants me to meet her next Saturday afternoon at the Peabody Hotel."

"Are you going to see her?"

"That's what I wanted to talk to you about.

"Man! I don't know why I didn't have some rubbers with me. I mean, I never meant to get her pregnant and, well, listen, will you go with me? I'm going to need some moral support."

"Sure, I'll go with you, Bob. I'm not sure what I can do."

"Just having you there will mean a lot, Bill." He put his hand on Billy's shoulder. "You're my best friend, Bill. I appreciate how you took me home with you and all. And just look at the shitty way I paid you back for being so nice to me, by knocking up your uncle's neighbor's girl."

"You don't owe me an apology, Bob."

"Well, listen, just let me know if there's anything I can ever do for you."

"There is one thing I'd like to know."

"Okay. Shoot."

"Why did you fall out of the plane?"

"Oh, that. Bad move, Bill. I don't think I should say too much, you know, because of the review board hearing that's coming up. I already had an interview with the psychologist at the hospital. I think that went all right.

"But after I got the letter from Molly, I just got so depressed. I started feeling sorry for myself, actually. You know, how I'm an orphan and no family, no home and all that. No education, except for high school. And then this thing with Molly. I just didn't think I'm ready for a family.

"I think you can probably figure everything out for yourself. Do I have to make a full confession to you?"

"No. Of course not."

Billy pointed at his friend's hands and arms. "How did you get so scratched up?"

Bob turned his hands over and looked at them.

"I came down through a bunch of trees.

"This is weird, Bill, but after I fell out of the plane, I was thinking, 'Bob, if you hit the ground, if you don't pull the ripcord, you'll never be able to go back to Uncle John's farm.'"

Billy placed his hand on Bob's shoulder. "I'm glad you pulled the ripcord, Bob."

Bob smiled broadly, his dimple making an appearance for the first time in over a week. "I am too, Bill. Believe me, I am, too."

*   *   *

THE FRIDAY before Billy and Bob were to meet Molly, Billy was scheduled to solo, having completed 13 ½ hours of dual flying with his instructor. He met his check pilot, Mr. Wright, at the flight assignment board.

"I'll ride with you to the east auxiliary field, Mr. Benson. You can let me out there and I'll stay on the ground for your check ride," Wright said. "I prefer not to be in the cockpit when I do flight checks. I might be tempted to help you out."

"Aye, sir."

Billy walked to his plane carrying his parachute under his arm, like a bundle of laundry—the preferred manner—followed by his instructor.

When they arrived at the plane, Mr. Wright stood aside as Billy laid his parachute on the leading edge of the lower wing and began his pre-flight check. He removed the cover from the pitot tube and held it up for Mr. Wright to see. After he had completed his walk around, Mr. Wright climbed onto the wing and got into the front seat. Billy stepped into the back seat, adjusted his seat and snapped his seat belt. Jonesy secured their harnesses.

He tested the ease of motion of the joystick and the pedals. He went through the start-up procedure with Jonesy.

He was relieved that the plane started up with the first try.

After the engine had warmed up, Billy checked the mags. He taxied into position, noting the wind direction as indicated by the wind tetrahedron and the windsock, pulled on his gloves, lowered his goggles, checked his controls again and stared at the lights on the control tower.

He sat waiting, squeezing and relaxing his grip on the top of the control stick.

The light turned green.

He pushed the throttle forward and the propeller revved up, pulling the little yellow cartoon plane down the runway, faster and faster. When he felt the tail lift, he pulled back on the stick to climb smoothly into the air.

They flew to a small field east of the air station used primarily for touch and go's and check rides. He landed and waited for Mr. Wright to climb out onto the wing.

"Do you understand what you're to do today?" he shouted.

"Aye, aye sir,' " Billy shouted back. "I wrote everything down."

He showed his instructor his hand-written list: takeoff, taxi, touch and go, stall, spin, and full-stall landing.

"You really need to pay attention to your landings, Mr. Benson," Mr. Wright shouted above the noise of the engine. "They're still pretty hard. Remember that trick I showed you about the speck on the windshield."

"Aye, sir."

Wright extended his gloved hand.

"Good luck, Mr. Benson."

"Thank you, sir," Billy said, shaking his instructor's hand and saluting smartly.

When Wright was safely out of the plane's way, Billy taxied to the end of the short airstrip.

He checked the windsock and the space on both sides of his plane and looked overhead. There was no control tower at the auxiliary field.

He tested his controls once again.

He waved to his instructor who was standing off to the side of the field and pushed the throttle forward. The plane sped down the runway and Billy was quickly airborne once more.

He adjusted mentally to the weight differential without his instructor in the front seat and climbed to begin his flight checks.

He circled the field for his touch and go. He eased gracefully to the tarmac as lightly and delicately as a butterfly.

The stall and the spin were perfectly executed.

Only the full-stall landing left.

He felt good.

He felt better than good.

He felt like Captain Marvel, Billy Batson, Superman, and Batman, all rolled into one.

He held the stick between his knees and shook his gloved fists triumphantly in the air. He tilted his head back and yelled victoriously at the top of his lungs.

He looked at the scenery below him, the distant air station and the fields beyond the air station, Memphis in the distance and passing alongside the city, the long, dark, flat, winding ribbon that was the Mississippi River.

Shazam! He yelled into the wind. *I am Captain Billy Benson and I am the master of all that I survey!*

I am Captain Billy Benson and I am the master of the air!

Oh, dear God, thank you so much for this wonderful day and this wonderful gift of flight.

He could have flown on forever.

But it was time to return to Earth for the final step of his check ride.

He banked slowly and lined himself up with the airfield again.

Looking through the front windshield, he selected a speck that had earlier been an insect, to line it up against the horizon.

He decreased his speed and altitude.

He watched the approaching ground and the speck against the horizon.

Now, kill the power. Forget about the ground underneath the plane. Line up the speck on the windshield with the horizon.

He eased up on the stick and let the speck drift ever so easily downward.

His wheels dropped slowly and hovered—what he imagined were only micrometers—ever so slightly over the tarmac, before caressing it seamlessly, as gently as a kiss.

Yes! Yes! Perfect! I did it! I greased it! I just...greased the runway!

Grinning broadly, he taxied to the side of the field and waited for Mr. Wright to climb back into his seat.

"Good job, Mr. Benson. Take it on home!"

"Aye, aye, sir."

On the short flight back to the main airfield, Billy could not stop grinning: *Like a mule eatin' briars*, his Aunt Ollie would have said.

He knew he had flown perfectly that day.

His landing at the main air station landing field was perfect.

It's been a perfect flight check.

He unlocked his tail wheel and taxied the plane toward the hangar, where an air crewman waved him to a parking space.

As Billy let the engine idle at a low speed to cool down, Mr. Wright climbed out of the plane and jumped to the tarmac. "Meet me inside, Mr. Benson."

"Aye, aye, sir."

Billy throttled the engine up to 800 rpms and pulled the mixture control back to *full lean*. When the engine began to cut out, he moved the throttle forward slowly and switched off the ignition switch and gas valve. He stared at the spinning propeller as it suddenly stopped with a backward jerk and a quick cough.

He shifted his goggles onto his helmet and sat there for a moment. He took a deep breath and let it out, released his shoulder harness, leaned forward and pressed his forehead against the control panel. He extended his arms over the edges of the cockpit and hugged the plane.

Thank you, my little yellow friend. Thank you.

He jumped from the plane, removed his parachute, gathered it under his arm and strutted proudly back to the hangar.

"Good job, Mr. Benson," Mr. Wright said again, at the door of the hangar.

"Thank you, sir," Billy said, with a snappy salute.

"Come on over to the board with me. I want you to watch me give you an arrow."

"Aye, aye, sir!"

Following each check flight, each man's instructor drew an arrow with a piece of chalk after the student's name on the flight assignment blackboard.

An up arrow ↑ meant the student had flown successfully that session, but a down arrow ↓ meant he had failed and would have to appear before a mandatory review board. If the cadet showed unusual promise or if his explanation for the discrepancy was credible, he could continue in the program after another check flight. Two up arrows were required to remove a down arrow, however.

Billy watched with pride as Mr. Wright drew a larger-than-required up arrow, followed by an exclamation point.

"Your execution of all phases of your assignment was excellent and your landings were perfect, Mr. Benson. Perfect three-point landings."

"Thank you, sir."

*   *   *

"I'VE ALREADY TAKEN THREE SHOWERS today, Bill, and I'm still sweating like an accused man at his own hanging," Bob told Billy as they boarded the base shuttle bus that would take them to downtown Memphis.

The shuttle buses, known to military personnel as "cattle cars," were large, gray, bus-sized trailers, pulled by semi-truck tractors. A back-to-back row of benches ran lengthwise down the center. Those who had to stand maintained their balance by clinging to overhead handles. Openings around the top of the sides let in air and light and the two large entry openings on each side were closed off with horizontal bars when the bus was in motion. Rolled up canvas could be dropped from the outside in cold or rainy weather.

Bob and Billy stood by one of the large, central openings and every so often, Bob lifted his arms to cool off and dry his choker whites, the obligatory liberty uniform for warm weather.

Billy looked about the bus at the other men, excitedly discussing the events of the week, or their plans for liberty. The flight cadets were in their starched and ironed cotton uniforms, with gold buttons leading up the front of the coats, to high, starched collars and accented by black shoulder boards. Each wore a white hat with a thin gold braid over the black patent leather visor, white socks and shoes with white sole edges.

The enlisted men wore starched and ironed cotton jumpers with the distinguishing oversized, square collars down their backs and large black neckerchiefs, tightly rolled and neatly tied in perfect square knots, their notorious, thin cotton trousers, tight at the waist and hips, flaring to bell-shaped bottoms and ending with black socks and spit-shined black shoes.

Billy knew how many of the men would look when they returned from their time "on the beach," as "going ashore" was termed. Their pristine uniforms would be doused with alcohol, soiled, wrinkled and smeared from top to bottom with lipstick and leg paint, worn as badges of honor. He who was most slathered was mentally declared the winner of an outlandish, testostoral, masculine competition.

Both groups of men were careful to wear their uniforms correctly on base, especially at inspections. While on liberty though, the headgear, in particular, was subject to customizing. Instead of wearing their hats parallel to the deck as required, officers' hats were often worn with a "salty" tilt to one side.

The enlisted white hat, however, was open to many more options: cocked to one side, slid down over one eye, with or without "wings," rolled out around the entire circumference, square-blocked or worn so far back on the head as to defy gravity.

Although both uniforms had pockets, the Navy discouraged their use and hands were never to find anchorage there. Enlisted men slid their wallets into one of the two tight front pockets in their trousers. A pocket comb and some change might be slipped into the other front pocket. Liberty and identification cards were kept in one of the top jumper pockets. There were no pockets in the back—and if there had been, they would have been far too tight against the buttocks to accommodate even an identification card.

The officers were provided rear trouser pockets for wallets: "Gigs," or demerits, could be given for overstuffed wallets for officers or the men.

Officers or enlisted men who smoked slid their cigarette packs and matches into their socks, usually "inboard," where they would not show. Zippo lighters, the brand preferred by most military personnel of all branches of service, were carried in a trouser pocket and identifiable audibly by the familiar metallic *zing*! of the top, when flipped opened by the thumb, followed by the rusty sound of a thumb-turned wheel over the flint, that threw a mini-shower of sparks toward the fluid-soaked wick and then the sharp *snap*! when the top was closed.

Women have always seemed to be naturally attracted to men in uniform, especially to sailors. Being young and fit were attractive attributes. Having ready cash and a flair for adventure were, likewise, appealing, not to mention the "one in every port" reputation of Navy men.

The officer candidates would probably be the best long-term choices for women: handsome and romantic as knights in shining white armor in their choker whites, not to mention better education and higher pay scale, however, the less-inhibited, swaggering enlisted men, confident in their revealing bell-bottomed trousers, snug about the buttocks and crotches, that offered previews of each man's potential—especially when boxer shorts were worn—and promised the women good times, *tonight, right now! in the present.*

Those not headed for the flesh pots of Memphis—or any contemporary Sodom anywhere—might go to the movies or to the USO, where they would jitterbug with local girls, eat doughnuts and drink Coca-Colas from straws in the bottles and maybe even be invited to go home with one of the volunteers, meet her family and sit in the front porch swing and talk.

Billy felt the predominance of whiteness all around him gave the cheery, joyful young men the appearance of a band of angels.

Well, maybe to those who couldn't read their minds, he thought after brief reconsideration.

Bob's angelic appearance was beginning to wilt noticeably, however, as his perspiration melted the starch in his collar. And now, he could feel moisture trickling from under his arms.

He sniffed his armpits.

"Do I stink?" he asked.

Billy shook his head.

"I do when I sweat. Maybe if I keep my elbows down to my sides, nobody will smell me if I do.

"Can you see any scratches on my face?"

"Yeah, a couple."

"Maybe she won't notice."

"Thanks again for coming with me, Bill. I really appreciate it."

"Glad to do it, Bob. I needed to get away from the base, anyway."

"Bill, maybe I should just swear off women. What do you think? Just keep it in my pants, you know. Women aren't anything but trouble, anyway."

The shuttle bus passed along sad little post-Depression west Tennessee farms, with their unpainted lap-sided houses and outbuildings, rusty barbed-wire fences strung between decaying handhewn posts, and sway-backed mules wandering lazily around barren dirt pastures. It went by dismal white sharecropper's shacks, past Negro farms, through the ragged suburbs the whites commonly called "nigger town" and it then reached the broad, tree-lined streets of white, urban, segregated Memphis.

"Bill, I can't stay still," Bob announced needlessly. "I'm as nervous as a whore in church."

"Relax. We're almost there." Billy said.

"I know. And the closer we get, the more I sweat."

The bus continued westward down Union Avenue, busy this Saturday with cars, rumbling streetcars and throngs of pedestrians on the sidewalks.

Bob looked at the round Hamilton pilot's watch he had bought at the base exchange.

"She wanted us there before five o'clock. It's going to be close. She said she'd be in the Grand Lobby, by the fountain."

"There it is," Billy said, pointing to the block ahead of them.

The brakes of the bus screeched as it eased to a stop at the curb.

The men stepped off in groups, heading in different directions.

* * *

MEMPHIS DURING WWII was a wide-open, military boomtown. With the enormous air station only a few miles north, the streets were filled with sailors every evening and all day Saturdays and Sundays.

Merchants welcomed the business the sailors brought and offered every possible convenience for them—sacred, profane and everything in between.

The camp followers—the flesh peddlers—set up shop in hotel rooms, motor courts and private residences.

Bootleggers offered their wares at locations known only by word of mouth, primarily in what were politely called the "colored sections" of towns.

Negro sailors from the segregated naval base were confined to the city's segregated back streets, primarily around Beale Street, where jazz, women, liquor (brand name or homemade "shinney"), barbecue "rib joints," catfish restaurants and pool halls offered respite.

At that time, African-American sailors were assigned primarily to duty as mess cooks or stewards (up to that time, there had never been any white stewards), serving meals on starched, white linen tablecloths to white officers in the wardrooms afloat and ashore. (The U.S. Navy wardroom at that time strongly reflected its formal British roots. American naval officers on flag ships—signaling an admiral was on board—were served finger bowls prior to engaging the enemy in the Pacific.)

NAS Memphis, however, due to preferences and influences from President and Mrs. Franklin Roosevelt, opened some of its aviation maintenance classes to blacks during the war. It would not be until 1944, however, that the Navy would permit Negro men to receive commissions, the pioneers being dubbed the "Golden Thirteen." It would be 1946, under President Truman, before the Navy would open all its rates to black sailors.

For the white officers and aviation cadets, the Peabody Hotel was a principal meeting point and watering hole during the war years. A downstairs bar offered drinks and afforded the men an opportunity to meet WAVES, as well as civilian women. The clientele who brought their own liquor could take an elevator up to the Service Club, where setups could be purchased.

*   *   *

BILLY AND BOB pushed through the elegant polished brass and glass doors and paused just inside the hotel's lobby, removed their hats to survey the scene.

Conventions and parties continued during the war. A large banner hanging from between two pillars on the second level read *Welcome Woodmen of the World.* The three-stories-tall Grand Lobby was always filled, as it was this day, with conventioneers, other civilians, as well as military personnel. A Negro man in a dark suit could be heard above the hubbub, playing a black grand piano in the farthest corner: "On the Sunny Side of the Street," a song made popular that year by Judy Garland.

"Grab your coat and get your hat. Leave your worries on the doorstep," Bob recited absently. "Man, wouldn't I love to be able to do that right now."

He spied Molly who was standing at the large travertine fountain to their right, waving at them.

She was the only woman in the lobby not wearing a hat.

"Oh, shit! There she is. Well, come on. Let's get this over with."

Bob smiled bravely and raised his arm to wave back, exposing a large stain under his arm.

"You'd better keep your arms down," Billy said from the corner of his mouth.

"Can you smell me?"

" 'Fraid so."

"Oh, shit!"

Molly was wearing a close-fitting, light-colored, two-piece linen suit that accentuated her firm, athletic figure. She wore orange-colored lipstick and carried a small black purse that matched her low-heeled shoes.

"Damn! Even after all this, she still makes my tongue hard. She's gorgeous, isn't she?" Bob asked.

"Yes, she is," Billy agreed enthusiastically.

Molly walked toward them with her confident stride and gave Bob a hug that he half returned, since he kept his elbows locked firmly to his sides. She then gave Billy a friendly embrace.

"I'm so glad to see you both. How are you?"

Bob pulled his handkerchief from his hip pocket and wiped his face again.

"Fine. How are you?" he asked.

"What happened to your face?"

"Oh, this? Our training gets rough sometimes."

"That rough, huh? Well, come on," she said, positioning herself between the two men and slipping her hands around their arms to lead them to the fountain. "Let's watch the ducks go back to the roof."

"Ducks?" Bob asked.

"Yes. They swim in the fountain all day and then, at five o'clock, they're taken back upstairs. You know what a fool I am over animals."

A crowd had gathered to watch the spectacle.

At exactly five o'clock, the elevator doors opened and a man wearing a costume reminiscent of a ringmaster's exited and rolled out a red carpet from the elevator to a matching carpeted ramp that led down from the ornate, carved-stone fountain. A John Phillip Sousa march began playing over speakers in the Grand Lobby.

Billy recognized the music: *The Stars and Stripes Forever*. He smiled because he got the joke. He and his friends used to bellow the lyrics they had learned at Camp Cherokee:

O, be kind to your web-footed friends,

For a duck may be somebody's mother...

"That's Mr. Pembroke. He's the Duckmaster," Molly said, pointing to the man in the costume.

Bob looked at Billy with a confused look and repeated, "Duckmaster?"

"Yes," Molly explained, "he brings the ducks down in the mornings at eleven and lets them swim in the fountain all day and now he's going to take them back up to their penthouses on the roof."

"Not a bad life," Bob said.

The three joined the hotel guests who had lined up on either side of the red carpet to watch the four celebrity ducks leave the fountain on cue, quacking merrily as they waddled down the carpet and into the waiting elevator.

Everybody applauded, the carpet was rolled up, the doors of the elevator shut and the happy crowd dispersed. The Negro man began playing the piano again.

"Wasn't that sweet?" she asked.

"Oh, sure. Sweet," Bob said.

"Come on over here. Let's sit and talk a little," she said, pointing to a sofa and wing chairs in front of a marble pillar.

Billy stole a glance at Bob, who continued to sweat. The stains under his arms had spread and now the entire back of his coat was soaked with perspiration. Bob wiped his face again.

Molly sat on one of the chairs to the side of the sofa. Bob sat on the end of the sofa nearest Molly. Billy sat on the other side of him.

"I like your lipstick," Bob said, trying hard to be calm and affable.

"It's Tangee," she said. "Every tube is the same color, but it goes on everybody a different color."

Bob nodded. "Um."

"Do you like my hair?" she asked cheerfully, leaning toward them and lifting the ends of her hair and letting them cascade back into place. "I had it cut."

"Yeah, I like it. It's nice," Bob said.

Billy nodded.

"I wanted to get it cut short, like yours," she said.

Bob and Billy smiled politely and nodded again.

"I've joined the Army," she said.

"The Army!" Bob exclaimed, a bit too loudly.

"So I could work with the veterinarians and horses," she said.

"But, you can't go into the Army if you're…if you're going to…" Bob tried to say.

He was confused and almost in a state.

"Oh," she said. "What I wrote you in the letter. It was just late, I guess. I started the day after I mailed the letter."

"You mean, you're not…I'm…"

"No. Everything is fine. I was just late."

"Damn! I wish you'd told me."

"Bob, I just did."

"I mean earlier."

"Well, I wanted to see you, anyway."

Bob moaned and dropped his head to his hands. He shook his head in disbelief or relief, or both.

"Why is your back so wet?" she asked.

He sat up and gestured dramatically with his hands. "Because I've been sweating like a damned pig ever since I got your letter."

She moved from her chair gracefully and slipped in tightly next to him, placing her hand provocatively on his thigh.

"Oh, Bob, I'm sorry. I'd have called you if I'd known how to reach you.

"But you really need to get out of this wet uniform," she said, tugging at the back of his sodden coat with her thumb and forefinger. "I've already checked into a room on the third floor. We could have room service pick up your uniform and they'd wash and iron it for you."

"Are you serious?" Bob asked.

"Sure. And I'll give you a bath. I hate to say it, Bob, but you really do need one, you know. Maybe we can have our supper sent up, too."

He looked at her. She gave him a sweet, Tangee-orange smile and slowly blinked her eyes.

He turned to look at Billy.

"Forget what I said about women, Bill. I guess I'm addicted to them.

"Is there a drug store nearby?" he asked Molly as he suddenly stood. "I need to see if they…I need to pick up something."

She unsnapped her purse and reached inside.

"Is this what you wanted to pick up?" she asked, discreetly displaying a packaged condom.

He looked at the condom and then back at her.

"If I do this right, I'm going to need more than one," he said, turning to leave.

"Wait," she said, patting the sofa. "Sit back down."

He dropped to the sofa obediently.

She opened her purse fully and held it for him to see inside.

"How many do you have in there?" he asked.

"A dozen."

He smiled broadly, his dark eyes squinting nearly shut as he anticipated the sensual pleasure the cache promised.

"That should be just about enough," he said.

"Bill, my good friend," he said, getting to his feet again and extending his hand. "Thank you so much for standing by me today. I hate to be rude, but time's a'wasting. I need to go topside and get out of this wet uniform."

Billy stood and shook his friend's hand. "My pleasure."

"Not as much as we're going to have," Bob said salaciously.

"Thanks, Bill," Molly said, giving him another hug and a kiss on the cheek.

Bob leaned over and said quietly in Billy's ear, "I may not be the 'Duckmaster,' but the spelling is close."

Bill smiled and nodded.

"Don't wait up," Bob said aloud, placing his hand in the small of Molly's back to steer her toward the same elevator the ducks had taken.

He waddled like Charlie Chaplain's Little Tramp.

"Quack! Quack!" he added, looking back at Billy.

"Quack! Quack!"

Billy smiled as the two entered the elevator. He wandered out of the hotel lobby, onto the street and met up with some members of his wing. They found a restaurant where they had dinner of crisp, salty, fried Mississippi River catfish, French-fried potatoes, coleslaw, hushpuppies, washed down by refreshingly bitter Ballentine beer, drunk from steel cans with triangular holes in their tops the waitress punched with a sharp-pointed metal "church key."

Afterward, the others wanted to check out some bars. Billy begged off and took the bus back to the base to catch up on his sleep.

He spent Sunday studying and, before turning in for the night, polished his shoes and prepared his uniform for the next day.

Early Monday morning, he was awakened from a sound sleep by Bob, dressed in freshly ironed whites, again bending over his bed, grinning gleefully.

Billy opened his eyes.

"Come on in to the head with me," he said *sotto voce*. "I gotta tell you about this wonderful night."

"Oh, man, I was about to have a wet dream."

"Sorry, mate. Maybe she'll come back tomorrow night."

"What time is it?"

"Nearly three o'clock. Molly had to take the train back to Riverton early. She's leaving for boot camp this afternoon."

"Ohhhh!" Billy moaned quietly, as he stood.

He climbed slowly from his rack and stumbled toward the head. He stopped by the urinal trough to relieve himself as Bob waited anxiously beside one of the lavatories.

Bob began talking excitedly as Billy washed his hands. His smile was radiant and his eyes narrowed to dark slits as he recounted the night's pleasures.

"Bill, my boy, I cannot begin to tell you how thankful I am that Molly isn't pregnant. And her going away present to me? Wow! Man! *Whew!* Let me tell you, it was the best I ever had. And the best she ever had, too, if you know what I mean.

"Bill, has a woman ever given you a bath?"

Billy shook his head.

"Bill, I promise you, there are places on my body I have touched all my life and never had any idea of what I was missing, until she touched me there. I'm getting hard again, just thinking about it," he added.

"We used half the rubbers she brought. Of course, it took the rest of Saturday night and most of Sunday to do it. I don't think I'll be able to touch myself for a week."

Billy smiled at his exuberant friend as he sang the praises of lust and love.

What a difference a night and good news make, Billy thought.

"Your uniform looks better," Billy said. "I'll bet you're the only member of the liberty party who came back in a clean one."

"I should hope so! I spent a week's pay on room service laundry, Bill! Do you know how much they charge just to wash a pair of socks? And they even starched and ironed my shorts!

"And room service food? Another week's pay!

"And do you know how much it costs to take a taxi back out here?

"But, you know what, Bill? It doesn't matter. I promise you, my friend, it was worth every penny!

"Oh, and we're going to write. As soon as she gets to basic training."

As he listened to Bob's enthusiastic monologue, Billy found himself focusing his attention on his friend's head, first on one side and then the other.

Bob suddenly stopped talking and looked at Billy.

"What? What is it? What are you looking at?" he asked, puzzled.

"Your ears," Billy said.

"My ears? What about my ears?" Bob asked, quickly looking into the mirror, not knowing what to expect.

"You've got leg makeup all inside your ears."

Bob smiled and turned slowly from the mirror to face Billy.

"Yeah," he said proudly, his dark eyes again nearly shut with recalled rapture, "and I'll bet there's a lot of Tangee lipstick some-place else."

*   *   *

AS STAGE B of primary training began, ground school tests continued at a steady pace. The complexity and variety of flight maneuvers increased. As the pressure mounted, tensions and egos swelled exponentially.

Sam Richards got into a cuss-fight with Lieutenant Jack Loper, also known as "Smilin' Jack," after a popular comic strip pilot of the time. Loper had even grown a narrow, neatly trimmed mustache to complete the effect. He was also secretly known as "Jack-Ass Jack," or "the Mad Looper," for his delectation in flying loop after loop after loop. Loper had Richards fly so many loops in succession, his ears bled, which brought on the post-flight altercation, resulting in a captain's mast for Sam. He was angrily unrepentant and continued to rail against his instructor, even at his own hearing and was summarily dropped from the flight program and shipped off to Great Lakes Recruit Training Center, to serve the remainder of his service time as an enlisted man, or "white hat."

Billy's former roommate in pre-flight, Jay Sanderson, was unable to keep his grades up and also dropped from the program. He was upbeat about his dismissal, however: "I'll have to serve only two years in the reserve, instead of the four to six years you commissioned guys have."

Bill Jenkins was washed out of the program, not for poor atti-tude, grades or deficient flying skills, but because he vomited every time he flew. He had tried every medication and technique that members of his wing recommended, including Coca-Cola and Dramamine. (Possessing or taking any unauthorized medications—

even aspirin—was against all the rules for flight cadets.) He even fasted before flights. Nothing worked. He drenched himself with his own vomitus so often, he finally sought medical help at sick call, but to no avail. The flight surgeon declared him physically unfit for the flight program. He received a medical discharge from the program and the Navy.

Aristocratic and stuffy Parker Spencer, who had received "gentlemen's B's" at the University of Kentucky, unable to keep up his ground school grades, was requested to attend a review board meeting. His blue-blood lineage and political connections saved him the embarrassment of being cast ignominiously into the world of the unwashed enlisted ranks, however. (Spencer's father had been aboard Commander—later Admiral—Richard Byrd's plane when he flew over the South Pole.) The younger Spencer was quietly transferred to the lighter-than-air craft (LTA) school at NAS Lakehurst, New Jersey, where he became a dirigible pilot.

Approximately 30 per cent of cadets washed out of the V-5 program overall.

Bob Hawthorne, too, had his day with the review board. After he learned he was not going to be a father, his self-confidence returned so fervently he fairly exuded the poise, credibility and cocky boldness of a combat fighter, as he sat straight-backed in his mandatory starched and sharply ironed choker whites at the hearing:

"No, sir! Fastening my seat belt incorrectly was just an oversight. I was so excited about my second flight, I must have forgotten to secure it properly."

"No, sir! Terminating my life never entered my mind!"

Bob was spared the humiliation of being disenrolled and, after a reconfirming check ride, returned to his wing as a hero.

Stage B training extended to auxiliary fields around Memphis, including Arkansas, just on the other side of the Mississippi River. The cadets continued to review and practice what they had learned in Stage A.

The slow, gentle turns they had learned now became steeply banked at higher speeds. They learned emergency landing procedures, wing-overs (or Chandelles, or "peeling off"), S-turns to circles or slips to banking against the wind to control their landing of the plane.

At the end of each phase of the dual flight training, the men were required to perform the maneuvers with check pilots in the front seats or observing from the ground.

The classroom lectures continued. Recognition of ships and planes was still stressed as well as stressful. Aerology, or weather prediction, was a critical skill to conquer. Dead reckoning navigation courses emphasized the use of electronic instruments. For night flying, celestial navigation was an essential skill in recognizing stars for locating targets and safe returns to home base or ship.

Ironically, the ability to send and receive Morse Code defeated and flunked out more students than any one of the other technical aspects of training.

Military drill was performed on the expansive grinders. In bad weather, the men met in one of the cavernous drill halls, so large, in fact, it was said the personnel at the southern end spoke with Southern drawls and the ones at the northern end spoke with Yankee accents.

Regular physical training was a continuation of what they had begun in pre-flight: hand-to-hand combat; running the obstacle course, participation in team sports and warfare swimming lessons, including abandon ship exercises and lifeboat procedures in what was said to be the largest indoor swimming pool in the world.

The third phase of primary flight training involved aerial acrobatics to teach the men how to control their planes in any contingency, to increase their confidence in themselves and their planes, to literally be one with their flying machines.

During this phase, so many cadets had been killed fleet wide after being caught in an inverted stall, a special checkout was made compulsory for that particular procedure for all primary cadets.

Forming echelons from 'V' formations and back again was especially hazardous and performed with trepidation: Because the top wing of the Stearman interfered with the wingmen's visibility, echelon formations were done stepped upward, as opposed to stairsteps down, the procedure used in single-wing planes. When the formations were changed, the wingmen—those off the port, or left, side of the lead plane—were required to cross *over* the lead plane, as opposed to underneath, as the cadets would do later in Vultees and Texans. As the nearly blind crossovers were performed, with the 225-horsepower engines spinning the propellers like lethal, motorized sabers, each cadet prayed sudden wind gusts or unexpected steering changes by another pilot would not cause a collision.

Once oriented to a growing repertoire of maneuvers and increasing confidence of their capabilities, however, the cadets were constantly warned not to become so full of themselves that they became reckless or careless.

During their intensive primary training at NAS Memphis, the cadets would spend a total of 85 actual hours in the air, including dual, solo and check.

Besides the formal ground school instruction, critiques following air checks, uncounted hours of discussion, or "bull sessions," and individual study periods provided additional insight and understanding of the expansive flight syllabus.

One member of the wing developed his own special private technique for perfecting his flying:

Patrick O'Hara had emigrated to America from Ireland with his family when he was 11. His rosy cheeks, appreciation of a good joke, ability to hold his liquor and the broad remnants of an engaging brogue made him a class favorite. He was fond of telling his Yank friends that he had left a small, but in his father's way of thinking, perfect, village: 400 hard-core Catholics, 34 bars and "neither a Brit nor a Protestant for miles around."

Pat, as he was called, typically spent hours practicing his flight maneuvers while seated on his rack, his technical books lying open on either side of him for quick reference. Oblivious to all that was going on around him in the noisy barracks, he sat there in deep concentration for long periods of time, energetically pulling on an imaginary stick, pushing imaginary pedals and turning imaginary switches, until he got each of the moves down perfectly.

The required Immelman turn, developed by German World War I ace Max Immelman, consisted of a half loop, followed by a slow half roll at the top of the loop. It was a particularly difficult dog-fight maneuver and mastering it took considerable effort for all the cadets.

O'Hara practiced the exercise for long stretches.

At chow one morning, he confessed to his tablemates how, the night before, he dreamed that he rehearsed the Immelman turn over and over as slept.

"Sure and you're right about that, me lad," Wrong Way Carrigan said, with a loud, dirty laugh and in his best Irish brogue. "The night watch said you gave your joystick an extra good workout under your sheet."

The men at the table exploded with laughter. Pat's Irish face turned bright red and tears sprang into his eyes. He was speechless, since he didn't know if Wrong Way was telling the truth or not.

*   *   *

COMPLETION OF STAGE C was an important milestone in the primary flight-training program. The crux of the Stage C check ride was being able to hit three out of five S turns to a perfect three-point landing, inside a 100-foot chalked circle on the ground. Absolutely faultless judgment was required to put the plane down in the center of the circle and bounces didn't count. Coming in too low would put the plane on the tarmac too soon; coming in too high would result in overshooting the target. Side slips to the circle were also required. In both cases, nothing short of perfection was accepted.

When the cadets began Stage D to hone their smooth, accurate, precision flying to near-perfection, they moved to the front seats of their Stearman trainers. From this time on, each man was to think of himself as a Navy pilot and not just a cadet. (When the men soloed from the front seat, a 125-pound weight was strapped securely into the back seat to balance out the weight.)

Stage E was formation flying, in which groups of three planes would practice taking off abreast or in "V" formation, flying together and landing on auxiliary fields together.

In the early days of aviation, radios were not available and pilots devised visual signals that became standard all around the world. As electronic communications improved, radio silence in some operations would still be necessary for security purposes. The

Stearmans had no radios at that time, requiring that the primary flight cadets recognize visual signals on the ground and in the air.

Red, yellow, and green lights were flashed from the tower for takeoffs.

Hand signals, flags, and lights were used by ground crews to assist in landing the Stearmans.

While in the air, the lead pilot issued commands for formations with his hand or with the plane itself.

Moving his hand vertically, back and forth from his nose outward, like a hatchet, the leader indicated that the formation continue in a forward direction.

When the leader wiggled his plane's rudder—the movable vertical control panel on the back of the tail—the planes in the formation fell into a column behind his tail. When he activated the elevators—the movable flaps on the rear horizontal stabilizers—making the plane swoop up and down, the formation would join up, wing-tip to wing-tip.

To bring a wingman forward, the leader could slap the side of his plane repeatedly or simply extend his arm and give a "come on up" motion.

When a wingman wanted to take the lead, he came alongside the leader, patted himself on the head, pointed to himself and pulled ahead.

To recall the planes in the event of an accident or because of worsening weather conditions, flashing lights and a striped flag flown from the control tower or a Stearman with stripes painted around the fuselage would be dispatched to fly around for the airborne planes to see.

As primary training came to a close, the men and their flying machines had become single components. They had arrived at the point in their symbiotic relationship that they were said to be operating on natural instincts, like riding a bicycle or driving a car, or in flight lingo, "flying by the seat of their pants." Being above the ground and in the clouds for many of them was now second nature. The natural-born pilots like Billy were beginning to fly quite literally as easily as they walked.

At this point in their training, the men moved on to more difficult tasks.

Through hours spent in the darkness of the ground school's mechanical Link trainers and under their planes' flying hoods, which kept out all natural light, the men had learned to rely on their instruments and not on their eyes. The horizon can play tricks, they were told, but the instruments rarely lie.

There was only one barrier left for them to hurdle in primary: night flying.

*   *   *

BILLY MET MR. WRIGHT on the flight line, did their walk-around and prepared for the late-night takeoff.

Billy was clearly uneasy about the flight.

"Don't be over-apprehensive, Mr. Benson," Mr. Wright said calmly.

"I'll make sure you do a good job."

"Thank you, sir."

"I think, once you get in the air and get your night vision, you'll even enjoy it. Okay?"

"Aye, sir."

The instruments on the panel were illuminated with a soft green glow. The switches on the control panel were not lighted and had to be located by feel, adding yet another level of difficulty to the operation.

As the men were harnessed in and their seatbelts firmly snapped, Wright spoke again, "We'll move slowly on the mat and taxiway, go up and take a good look-see at what's around us. Okay?"

"Aye, sir."

"We'll just follow the plane ahead of us, taxi down the runway, circle the field and touch and go and do it again."

"Aye, sir."

Billy started his engine, warmed it up, checked his controls and the mags, had Jonesy pull the chocks and joined the roaring, slowly moving procession to the runway.

Each plane had lights on its wingtips: red on the port side, green on the starboard.

Rows of flare pots on both sides of the runway illuminated the field.

When his plane rose into the dark night sky, Billy felt all that he had learned during daylight flying was useless, locked in the cargo space. He felt he had somehow flown into a cave. He was immediately overwhelmed with what seemed to be futile navigation.

"Take your time, Mr. Benson," Mr. Wright said through the gosport. "Be patient. Wait for your eyes to adjust to the night conditions."

In only minutes, the lights on the ground became visible.

The base was spread out below them like a gigantic black mat, pin-pointed with circles of streetlights, crossing and crisscrossing geometrically. The red lights atop the red and white-checkered water tower near the base hangars winked encouragingly at him and he made out the revolving light at the control tower. He observed the orange glow of the flare pots on the runway.

Memphis came into view beyond as a fuzzy, parabolic illumination. He could see the lights across the Mississippi River Bridge and into east Arkansas.

He felt more confident now. It was rather like the exhilaration he used to feel being on a roller coaster or halted on the top of a Ferris wheel.

"Okay," Mr. Wright said, "I'm going to take it in. Keep your eyes on the flare pots with your peripheral vision. There is no exact science to night landings. Just don't panic. When you find your landing spot on the field, make your approach, reduce your power and glide on in.

"Frankly, the pots along the sides interfere with my night vision," he added, "so I prefer to just look straight ahead. That way, I can estimate when I'm about twenty feet off the runway for my landings."

His instructor approached the landing strip and stalled his aircraft enough to perform a touch and go. He then added power and took off. He circled the field and did it a second and then a third time.

"Okay, Mr. Benson, you try it this time."

"A touch and go or a full-stall landing?" he shouted.

"One of each."

"Aye, sir."

Billy swallowed hard as he grasped the stick and placed his feet on the pedals.

He looked out of both sides of the plane and climbed slowly, circled the field and picked his landing site.

When he was lined up between the two rows of lights, he began his approach, dropping, dropping, slower and slower, until he was hovering between the smoky, flickering orange lamps. He kept his eyes straight ahead where the rows nearly converged. He reduced his power as the wheels touched the runway easily and smoothly.

Greased it, he said to himself proudly and with relief.

He pushed the throttle forward to climb again.

"Good job, Mr. Benson. Once more around for another touch and go, circle the field and then land."

"Aye, aye, sir."

Can I do it a second time?

He banked another graceful wide circle around the field and began his second approach.

Come on, Benson. Come on. One more time.

Again, he landed so seamlessly there was barely a feeling of contact when the three wheels delicately stroked the tarmac.

Damn! I did it again!

Billy couldn't stop grinning as he gunned the engine, made another broad circle and set the plane down as well as his instructor had.

"Good job, Mr. Benson."

Billy watched with pride as Mr. Wright gave him his final up arrow at the hangar.

"You're a good pilot, Mr. Benson," he told Billy. "You're a natural. You fly by the seat of your pants. You know that term, don't you?"

"Aye, sir."

"If your test scores for ground school were as good as your check ride scores, you'd be an ace in no time."

Billy laughed softly."Aye, sir. Thank you, sir."

Mr. Wright extended his hand. "It's been a pleasure knowing you, Mr. Benson, and having you as my student."

Billy removed his glove and smiled again as he shook his flight instructor's hand. "Thank you, sir. I appreciate your patience. You're an excellent pilot and teacher."

"Thank you. Good luck in intermediate and advanced."

"Thank you, sir."

"Maybe we'll see you back here as an instructor."

"Thank you, sir. But I hope not."

*   *   *

ON THE MORNING OF 10 JUNE 1943, the last day of flight training, the cadets were mustered on the flight line alongside their planes, instructors and plane captains. The cadets had been assembled to perform their last flight at primary: a massive 'V' formation, made up of 15 smaller formations of three planes each.

On a signal, the men saluted their instructors, climbed into their cockpits—two to a plane—and prepared to taxi into position, beginning with the planes at the farthest end of the flight line.

Lining up in threes, groups of nine planes took off simultaneously with the center formation slightly forward of the groups on either side. The subsequent Stearmans fell in behind the lead group and the formation soon increased to a total of 45 planes, one enormous 'V', their engines droning on hypnotically like the flight of giant yellow bees, the wind singing through the struts and cables of the wings.

Billy was piloting his Stearman with Bob Hawthorne in the front seat as co-pilot, and in the last position on the port side of the formation. Billy wore the non-issue white silk scarf his older sister Alice had sent him. He had arranged it so the long ends would billow behind him over the fuselage. He felt like Captain Marvel, with his cape fluttering in the breeze.

As they soared majestically over the city of Memphis, crossed the Mississippi River and turned back over Memphis, people on the sidewalks below stopped to gaze skyward. Housewives emerged from their homes and shaded their eyes with their hands to behold the spectacle. Motorists craned their necks to peer through their windshields. School children on playgrounds pointed and laughed at the final flight of the primary cadets.

As Billy looked ahead and to his right, he felt chills over his body at the sight of the yellow bi-wing planes, the sun reflecting luminously off their taut, golden skins against a brilliant blue sky.

It looks like...like...a flight of angels, he thought.

A flight of angels.

The men landed, walked quietly to the hangar to return their parachutes and flight gear and marched back to their quarters.

Primary flight school ended on 11 June 1943, as unceremoniously as had pre-flight.

The four phases of their training could be compared to a symphony.

The first two movements were completed, but there would be no applause until all four were concluded.

A bus appeared outside their barracks. The men descended the stairs with their olive-drab suitcases in hand. They held final formation, were dismissed and climbed aboard the cattle car for the ride to the train station.

A week's leave was allotted to the men and then it was on to Pensacola, Florida, "The Cradle of Naval Aviation," to conclude the final movement of their symphony of the air.

Vultee Valiant—"the Vultee Vibrator."

CHAPTER THREE

INTERMEDIATE TRAINING

PENSACOLA

FOR THE CHILDREN OF ISRAEL and the Crusaders of the Middle Ages, the Promised Land was Jerusalem. For devout Muslims, Mecca. For Tibetan Buddhists, Lhasa. For Hindus, Nirvana. For Christians, Heaven.

For candidates of naval aviation, Naval Air Station, Pensacola, Florida.

*   *   *

LONG BEFORE THE HOSTILITIES of World War II began, years before the V-5 flight program, Pensacola Naval Air Station had acquired such a reputation as the very heart and soul of naval aviation, for many young men aspiring to be naval aviators, there could be no higher earthly honor than receiving orders to, and—more importantly—receiving a set of gold Navy wings from that magical, enchanted Eden, that ethereal Camelot: NAS Pensacola.

The Spanish settled Pensacola, first as a military colony during their occupation of Florida in the 17th century. There they tamed the hostile, intimidating, sub-tropical environment and constructed massive and well-fortified Fort Barrancas on the site of what would become, more than a century later, NAS Pensacola, to guard the settlement against invasions by their enemies: pirates, or even worse, the British.

England's victory over France in the French and Indian wars turned the tables, however, when the 1763 Treaty of Paris granted ownership of Florida to Great Britain. The Spanish reluctantly withdrew and Florida was divided: East Florida, with St. Augustine as its capital; and West Florida, which had Pensacola as its capital.

After the American Revolution, Great Britain lost its hold in the New World and ceded Florida to the United States government in 1821. President John Quincy Adams immediately envisioned the outpost as the ideal site for establishing a naval yard to build warships from the area's forests of massive oaks, an infinite source of raw materials. Additionally, easy access to the Gulf of Mexico, the Caribbean and the Atlantic beyond, made it a strategic military location.

The American Gulf Squadron that blockaded the Mexican Coast during the Mexican War and later landed the Army of General Winfield Scott at Vera Cruz, was outfitted at the Pensacola Navy Yard.

During the War for Southern Independence, Confederate forces burned the installation to the ground on May 9, 1862, when they mistakenly feared the Union troops that had captured New Orleans would turn their sights next toward Pensacola.

Ironically, on the following day, the Rebels were surprised by an attack by enemy forces from Fort Pickens, on neighboring Santa Rosa Island, the only fort in the South to remain in Union hands. Under the command of Admiral David Farragut, the Union quickly rehabilitated the yard and used it as a repair and fleet supply base.

Shortly afterward, Farragut achieved his brilliant naval victory against the Confederate navy in nearby Mobile Bay, which provided the impetus for utterance of his famous words: *"Damn the torpedoes! Full speed ahead!"*

The Pensacola Naval Yard was totally rebuilt after the Civil War, but decommissioned and shut down in 1911, during a lull in world conflicts.

When pre-World War I events began heating up in Europe, however, a series of pioneering firsts occurred at Pensacola.

Manila Bay hero Admiral Harris Dewey recommended to Secretary of the Navy Josephus Daniels that Pensacola be reopened as the nation's first Naval Air Station. The advice was wisely taken and the proposal was realized in 1914, when the fledgling flight program, created to prepare the U.S. Navy for very probable involvement in what would be called World War I, was made up of only nine officers, fewer than two dozen enlisted men and nine flying boats.

Of the Navy's first three planes, one was built by the Wright brothers and two by Glenn Curtiss.

T.G. Ellyson, the Navy's first pilot, so designated by his number—Naval Aviator Number One—was taught to fly by Curtiss, and the two others, J.H. Towers and John Rodgers, Naval Aviators Two and Three, respectively, were trained by the Wright brothers.

Barely two years later, in 1916, as the European war caught up the major countries of the world and the advantages that air power could provide in combat were recognized, the rejuvenated air station began training pilots in greater numbers. By war's end, over 1000 men had been taught to fly in Pensacola.

Lighter-than-air craft (LTA), known also as blimps or dirigibles, were first introduced into the Navy at Pensacola in 1916. LTA pilots were trained there until 1921, when the training was relocated to NAS Lakehurst, New Jersey.

The USS *Jupiter*, a collier, or coal ship, was reconfigured to become the Navy's first aircraft carrier and renamed the USS *Langley*, in Norfolk, in 1922. (Following the demise of sailing vessels, all naval vessels were powered by coal until 1913, when oil was used.) The *Langley* was transferred to Pensacola, where several months of experimentation with carrier landings took place, giving the base another distinction: that of becoming the home of carrier-based aviation.

Chevalier Field, named for Godfrey de Couralles Chevalier, Naval Aviator Number Seven, was constructed in 1921, on 25 acres on the eastern side of the base. Ten years later, it was enlarged to include 62 acres.

When hostilities erupted in Europe again in the late 1930s and in the Pacific in the early 1940s, Pensacola Naval Air Base, like a stubborn, unconquerable phoenix, fluttered to life yet again.

The earlier flying boats, especially the glamorous PBYs, or Catalinas, even though retained, were deemed second in importance to land-based airplanes, which dictated new guidelines for all new naval air bases.

It was determined in 1943 that the Naval Air Command, under the Chief of Naval Operations, would be established and headquartered in Pensacola.

To be the seat of all U.S. naval flight activities, NAS Pensacola needed to look the part, therefore, a gigantic building program was initiated to provide housing for the thousands of enlisted personnel, flight students and support personnel, as well as mess halls, administrative offices, athletic facilities, and housing for officers.

The two and three-storied structures erected at Pensacola featured Georgian-style, red-brick architecture, with lavish uses of ornate wooden trim, tall, white wooden columns supporting classic Grecian-style porticos, all aesthetically set among gigantic, ancient Spanish moss-laden oaks, and broad, open expanses of green lawns.

The grand, graceful white houses of Officer's Country and Admiral's Row, with inviting screened porches, were set perfectly and romantically among the profuse oaks trees.

The long stretches of 30-foot high brick walls standing along the bay front, seemingly for no apparent function, remained as mute testimony to the folly of mistaken tactical or medical notions. Some historians and archeologists have written that the walls were constructed by the Spanish to keep out night marauders. Others contend the walls were supposed to hold back the "bad air," or malaria, which blew in from the bay. Still others suggested the walls were erected to keep out the actual carriers of malaria—mosquitoes—since it was believed they could not fly high enough to go over the walls.

Regardless of the reasons for the walls, they contributed to the romance of the picturesque and lush base, which contrasted radically with the unimaginative, temporary-looking frame buildings of NAS Memphis, with its acres of flat asphalt-paved grinders, virtual absence of trees and only occasional, accidental splotches of grass.

Where the Memphis runways were virtually at the center of all base activities, Chevalier Field was laid out and constructed near the water, far off to the side of the main entrance. Outlying fields, or OLFs, for training in Florida's Panhandle and southern Alabama allowed NAS Pensacola to be much more than just one enormous paved surface.

Bronson, Bauer, Choctaw, Harold, Helm, Holley, King, Lyons, Milton, Pace, Santa Rosa, Saufley, Spencer, and Whiting were among the many auxiliary fields in Florida within a 35-mile radius of the main Panhandle base. Other supplementary fields within a 60-mile range of Pensacola, in contiguous Alabama, included Barin, Brewton, Evergreen, Magnolia, Silverhill, and Summerdale.

Where NAS Memphis was noticeably as level, bare and monotonous as a prairie—transitory in appearance and depressing psychologically in its gray monotony—NAS Pensacola was located on gently undulating landscaped topography, permanently green and calming in look and mood.

Naval Air Station Memphis bore all the brutish earmarks of the no-frills Army engineers who designed it, to hastily meet the coarse demands of wartime efficiency. Naval Air Station Pensacola, by sharp comparison, seemed to have been lovingly and thoughtfully conceived by Jeffersonian, artistic, military gentle-men while sitting around a linen-covered wardroom table; sensitive scholars who loved natural and classical beauty as much as they loved flying.

Pensacola was not the only center of aviation activity in Florida, however. By the end of World War II, there were literally hundreds of Army and Navy airfields in the low-lying and clement Sunshine State, permitting year-round training.

Despite the proliferation of other airfields in the state and in the nation, NAS Pensacola resolutely and steadfastly remained and remains the reigning monarch of naval aviation training, graduating 28,562 pilots during World War II, confirming its title, "Cradle of Naval Aviation."

*   *   *

IT WAS A WARM, CLOUDY SEPTEMBER AFTERNOON in 1943, when the train carrying Billy and other members of his squadron returning from leave, puffed slowly and clanking, squeaking, screeching into the Pensacola station, on the east side of the small Southern town heavily infused with Spanish architecture. It stopped in short, jabbing jolts, with screaming brakes and rattling, thudding cars. As the mechanical dragon continued breathing heavily, puffing and spewing noisy flumes of steam from underneath its carriage, the cadets from primary flight training stepped down from the cars onto the concrete platform and walked into the waiting room that had filled with other passengers. They had expected to find at least a representative from the base and a bus waiting to carry them to the next phase of their aviation program.

Barry Dorsey walked through the terminal, pushed through the front doors of the station and stepped onto the sidewalk in hopes of seeing a familiar battleship-gray base bus, along with a uniformed base delegate, but saw neither.

After a short discussion with members of the group, Barry looked up the telephone number of the base and called from a pay phone.

No one he talked to could locate the Officer of the Day, or OOD, but after donations of nickels for several telephone calls from the tired and anxious cadets, Barry located the Chief of the Day who informed him that a bus would be dispatched to pick them up.

The closer the bus got to the base, the more prolific the bars, tattoo parlors, uniform shops, pawnshops, and hamburger stands, creating a less than desirable herald for the naval aviator's Valhalla. All the cadets on Billy's bus stared anxiously ahead for their first glimpse of NAS Pensacola as their bus rounded the curve in Admiral Murray Boulevard / Duncan Highway and the main gate of the base came into view.

The bus rumbled slowly across the heavy, road-level wooden causeway that spanned Bayou Grande—clearly separating civilian territory from the military base. The wooden structure was reminiscent of a medieval drawbridge over a broad shallow moat that, in this case, provided homes to alligators, cranes and other semi-tropical aquatic fauna and flora.

The bus proceeded to the main entrance of the air station, where it stopped under one of a pair of wide porticos that extended from either side of the imposing red brick structure. A Marine sentry climbed on board to check identifications and orders.

Before the sentry completed his rounds, another Marine exited the building, came up the steps of the bus and loudly asked the men, "Are you intermediates?"

Yes.

"Who's in charge?"

"I am," Barry Dorsey responded from his seat near the door of the bus.

"You're supposed to report to Saufley Field."

A groan arose from the men.

"Do you know where that is?" the second Marine asked the driver.

"Sure. But I was instructed to bring them here," the driver said.

"Well, my instructions are to send all intermediate cadets to Ellyson," the second Marine said.

"Oh, great! We've got a clusterf*** even before we get through the gate," O'Hara complained aloud.

"Turn around here and take them to Ellyson," the second Marine told the driver, while shooting O'Hara a dirty look. "You'd better hurry, though. We've got a thunderstorm headed this way."

"The Bobsey Twins, Lost in the Storm," Carrigan wailed from the back of the bus.

"Looks like we won't get to see the cradle of naval aviation today," Billy said to Bob Hawthorne, who shared his seat with him.

The driver drove slowly around the building, through the portico on the other side and headed north, as a shower began.

Half an hour later, the bus stopped at the front gate of Saufley Air Field, the auxiliary facility used for berthing and training intermediate cadets.

A light rain was falling as the ubiquitous Marine guard climbed onto the bus to check the men's orders and identifications.

Afterward, he gave the building number to the driver, pointed the direction he was to proceed and stepped off the bus.

When the driver stopped the bus again and opened the door, the men grabbed their gear, climbed from the bus and dashed through the rain into the two-story brick building that was to be their barracks during intermediate flight training.

After evening chow, the men marched back to their quarters in the rain, removed their soaked raincoats, began stowing their lockers, and making up their racks. A field day followed, ending at around ten o'clock. The men showered, prepared the uniforms they would wear the next day and turned in for the night.

Shortly after midnight, as the storm increased, the men were fairly knocked from their beds by a bolt of lightning that struck the west end of their barracks and set fire to it.

The night watch came running into the open bay, yelling, "Everybody out! Don't take anything with you. Get out! Get out! Head for the gym next door!"

The men jumped from their racks and dashed again through the pelting rain, running through the double doors of the gymnasium, located only yards from their barracks.

Those who had been sleeping in their skivvies were soaked to the skin. Those who had slept in the buff, wandered about aimlessly, dripping wet, in the self-conscious, defenseless manner men exhibit when they are naked in the company of clothed men.

Two station fire trucks arrived with screaming sirens and blaring horns and set about putting out the fire, as the men crowded around windows and doors of the gymnasium to observe.

Shortly after the fire trucks left, a large, gray, four-by-four truck with a throaty diesel engine and an arching canvas top over the bed, resembling a covered wagon, arrived at the gym and backed up to a side door. A sailor jumped from behind the wheel of the truck, leaned through the gym door and called to the men inside to line up for blankets.

The squadron spent the rest of the night in fitful sleep, wrapped in their scratchy Navy issue blankets, on the cold, hard gym floor or on narrow, wooden bleachers.

They were awakened the next morning when an officer snapped on the overhead lights and called, "All right, men! Reveille! Go back to your quarters and pack up your gear. Come back over here and get shaved and showered and go on to chow. We're going to have to find berthing for you someplace else. We should know something by the time you get back from breakfast."

A bus was waiting for the men when they marched back from the chow hall.

The same officer who had held reveille on them had them take their gear and board the waiting bus for a ride back to mainside. He climbed on after the men were seated and stood beside the driver.

"Sorry about all this inconvenience, men. You've all been indoctrinated thoroughly on how important weather is in flight training. It's something to deal with on the ground, too. Down here on the

Gulf Coast, it seems we're always at the mercy of thunderstorms and hurricanes.

"Considerable damage was done to your barracks and it looks like it won't be repaired any time soon. War shortages may hold us up a while. Meanwhile, we're going to send you over to mainside where there's an empty barracks that's available now. It won't be as accommodating as this one was, but it'll be adequate. We'll bus you back and forth for your training.

"There's a good lesson here: Learn to adapt. It's going to be the story of your naval careers. Very few things work out the way you think they should."

He stepped off the bus, but before the driver could close its doors, another officer drove up in a gray Buick.

"Have the driver wait, Carter," the second officer called from his car's open window.

He got out and walked to the first officer. The two talked out of earshot as the men on the bus waited in silence.

The first officer stepped back onto the bus.

"Okay, men. It looks like the change has changed."

A second car arrived and a third officer got out. The three conferred briefly and the first officer returned.

O'Hara laid his forehead on the back of the seat in front of him and shook it slowly, as he moaned audibly, "Oh, shit! Another clusterf***."

"Well, men," the first officer announced, "the changed change has changed, or maybe it hasn't. Anyway, you'll proceed to NAS."

He turned to the driver. "Take them to the old Marine Corps barracks, like I had told you the first time."

He turned to the men. "We'll let you know when and if we get *this* building repaired."

He stepped off the bus, the driver closed the door and drove off again toward NAS Pensacola.

*   *   *

THE BUS SCREECHED TO A STOP before a hulking, two storied, wooden building of undeterminable age. Split and broken wooden shingles covered the sides underneath peeling paint. A large, wooden sign of faded red and yellow paint, near the front entrance, read:

Marine Corps Barracks.
Semper Fidelis

A small marble headstone stood near the sign:

Jack
Our little buddy
1917

The men stepped quietly from their bus into the bright Florida sunshine and looked at the aged structure.

"Splinterville," Bob Hawthorne said absently.

"This is where the Marines were quartered," the bus driver said. "They've got some new barracks. This one is going to be demolished."

"I don't think anybody'll have to do that," Barry suggested. "I think it's going to collapse all by itself.

"Well, come on, guys. Let's see what it looks like inside," he added.

"I told you," Bob said. "Splinterville."

The men walked inside.

"Well, I've seen worse," Barry said.

"Where?" someone asked. "On Tobacco Road?"

Billy dropped his bags beside a metal rack underneath a window in the large open bay. The heads of the double-deck beds were pushed against the bulkheads. A thin, striped mattress covered each and a feather pillow lay at the head. Tall, gray, individual metal lockers placed along the walls separated the beds. Two long tables in the center of the room held stacks of neatly folded sheets, pillowcases and olive-drab wool blankets.

Billy opened the windows near his bunk. Other men from the squadron were doing the same to relieve the stuffy air.

Spanish moss hanging in long, soft, gray strands swayed gently in the branches of the massive oak trees outside their barracks and the fishy smell of the bay drifted through the screened open windows.

Bob Hawthorne began making his bed, next to Billy's.

"Our new home!" Billy said, stretching out on the bare mattress, his head cradled under his hands. "I'm beginning to feel like a gypsy."

"Or a member of a flying circus," Bob suggested.

"Does it ever get cold down here?" Billy asked, resting his feet on the wool blanket.

"Yeah. In late January or early February," Rob Black volunteered as he passed by on his way to the showers. "For three whole days and then it's back to summer."

"Who's over here?" Billy asked, nodding to the bed to his left, where an unfamiliar seabag lay, stenciled with a black globe and anchor next to what appeared to be a case for a musical instrument.

"Dunno. I don't recognize the seabag," Bob replied.

Billy yawned and stretched.

"Think we'll get any more sack time down here?" he asked.

"Man, I hope so," Bob answered. "I'm getting bags under the bags under my eyes. And I sure as hell didn't sleep very much last night, either."

A tall, dark-haired man in an olive-green colored uniform approached, loudly whistling Waltzing Matilda.

Billy turned his head.

"Goo-day, mate!" the stranger called cheerily.

"And goo-day to you, too," Billy responded. "Looks like the Marines have landed."

"T.J. Macintosh," the Marine said, extending his hand.

Billy swung his feet over the side of his bed and stood to shake the man's hand.

"Bill Benson. And this is Bob Hawthorne."

Bob walked to the foot of Billy's bed and shook the Marine's hand.

"Hi."

"Goo-day."

"You're joining our class?" Billy asked.

"Right. I did my preflight at St. Mary's College."

"Where's that?" Billy asked.

"Moraga, California."

"How about primary?" Bob asked.

"Ottumwa, Iowa. The little carrier on the prairie," he added with a laugh.

"We did ours at NAS Memphis," Bob volunteered. "That place was as flat as a prairie, too."

"Welcome," Billy said "It's good to have a Marine on board."

"Thanks," T.J. said, as he put his hand around the handles of his sea bag and the music case.

"Any other Marines in your class?" he asked, looking about the room.

"Nope," Billy replied."You're the only one."

"Do you chaps smoke?" T.J. asked.

"No," Billy said, shaking his head.

"Well, in that case, would you two swabbies care to share a private room with a jarhead?" Macintosh asked.

"Instead of this open bay?" Billy asked rhetorically. "Talk about being in the right place at the right time! You bet! Come on, Bob. Grab your gear."

Bob quickly removed the sheet he had already tucked around his mattress, threw his things together and fell in behind Billy and the Marine.

"Right here, lads," MacIntosh said, turning a battered metal knob and pushing open the brown, paneled wooden door.

"How does this look?" he asked, dropping his bag on the single bed beside the door.

"Like the Waldorf-Astoria!" Billy said, tossing his bag onto the top bunk across from MacIntosh's.

When Bob came in, Billy asked, "Mind if I take the upper?"

"Not at all," Bob answered, looking around the room approvingly.

"How did you find this?" Billy asked.

"Marines never leave one of their own in the field. We stick together. We look out for each other. Semper Fi—Ever Faithful, you know. When I came through the gate this morning, the Marine there told me about the clusterf*** over at Saufley and the change in billeting. So, since this used to be the Marine barracks, he was able to get the key for me."

"How did he know we were going to be quartered here?" Bob asked.

"Easy-peasy. Just about every Navy base has Marine sentries. Right? And every gatehouse has a telephone and every sentry knows all the Navy's switchboard operators. The operators hook everybody up and they kill time at night when things get slow, by shooting the shit. Sentries can listen in on just about any unsecured base telephone conversation they want to."

"There's a lesson there, somewhere," Billy suggested. "'Loose lips sink ships,' and all that."

"But more important for me was finding some place away from the smokers," T.J. said. "I hate bloody cigarette smoke and the way me clothes stink."

"Same here," Billy agreed. "Fortunately, we had to keep all the windows open in Memphis because of the heat and that helped. I was dreading the cooler weather when the windows have to be kept shut."

"Two-thirds of all me mates at home smoke. I'm sure Yanks aren't any better," T.J. said.

"Probably worse," Billy said.

"A desk, three bureaus, two closets, our own lavatory!" Bob said as happily as if it were, indeed, the Waldorf. "This is great! Thanks for letting us bunk with you."

"My pleasure," T.J. said as he used his thumb to move the lever on the base of the heavy duty, wall-mounted, oscillating fan.

"Hope you lads like lots of fresh air," he added, as he opened the pair of windows behind the desk.

"Hah!" Billy said. "Having spent the last three months in open cockpits, I think we're more than used to fresh air by now."

"Are you British?" Bob asked, as he began spreading the bottom sheet on his bunk.

"No. Me Dad was. I was born in Australia, but me Mum's a Yank. After me Dad died, she and I moved to Hawaii. Because she's a Yank, I have dual citizenship."

"Were you in Hawaii during the Jap attack on Pearl?" Bob asked.

"No. The attack was on the island of Oahu. We lived in Hilo, on the island of Hawaii, but we had moved to California by then, anyway."

"You're a Hollywood Marine?" Billy asked.

"Right. San Diego. How'd you know that term?"

"My uncle was a Marine. That's where he did his basic."

"Oh. Well, I completed basic last year. I had had a year of college before I went to basic. Whilst I was in boot camp, I decided that I'd rather have a commission than be enlisted. I requested flight training, and here I am."

"You're a private?" Bob asked.

"Right. Working on me gold bars."

"What does T.J stand for?" Billy asked.

"Thomas Jefferson."

Bob and Billy stopped making their beds and faced T.J.

"As in American President Thomas Jefferson?" Bob asked.

"Right. Me Mum's folks are from Virginia. Me younger brother's name is Robert E. Lee MacIntosh."

"Oh, we're all good old Rebels!" Billy exclaimed.

"You ain't seen nuthin' yet," T.J. responded cheerfully, digging into his seabag.

"Look at this!"

He pulled out a framed photographic print of Robert E. Lee in his general's uniform, seated ramrod-straight on the back of his horse, Traveler.

"Son of a gun!" Bob said.

"Oh, there's more!" T.J. announced gleefully, turning again to his bag to retrieve a large brown envelope.

He pulled a folded cloth from the envelope as Billy and Bob looked on with interest.

T.J. dropped the envelope onto his bed and cheerfully unfolded a flag nearly as large as his bed.

He displayed it proudly by the top corners.

"A Confederate battle flag!" Bob said in amazement.

"Actually, it's a Confederate Navy Jack," he corrected.

"Is it old?" Billy asked reverently.

"Oh, no. Just one a Virginia relative sent me a few years ago."

"Are you going to hang it up?"

"Right-O! It'll have to come down for inspections, of course, but I think it'll look smashing over me bed. What do you think?"

Billy and Bob agreed that it would.

"What else is in your sea bag?" Billy asked.

"No kangaroos. But a few great Hawaiian shirts for beach parties, barbies and such. And I never travel without me trusty ukulele," he said, opening the small instrument case.

"I'm always afraid this will get broken. I have to hand carry it."

He hummed as he tightened and tuned the strings of the ukulele. He strummed a seven-chord introduction and began singing:

Ah-loe-ha O-eeeee,
Ah-loe-ha O-eeeee,
Eke onaona noho ika lipo...

Billy and Bob collapsed with laughter at the spectacle of the muscular Marine accompanying himself on the small, stringed instrument.

T.J. stopped in mid-stroke with a look of pretended hurt on his face.

"You're laughing at me musical talent?"

"No, T.J. Not at all," Billy said, wiping tears from his eyes. "It just took us by surprise, that's all."

"Oh, you'll find I'm full of surprises, you will," he promised.

*   *   *

THEIR BEDS MADE AND GEAR STOWED, field day on their room completed, the three undressed, grabbed their soap, threw towels across their shoulders, and joined the men of the squadron as they moved toward the large, open three-sided, white-tiled shower, already echoing with spraying water and the shouted jokes and gentle jibes of young men who enjoyed each other's company.

"Looks like we all had the same idea at the same time," Billy said as he observed the room filled with cadets.

"The only good thing about this is there won't be any hot water left," he added. "You don't think there's a chance they'll use up the cold water, do you?"

The three men talked casually as they crossed their arms and leaned against the wall to wait for empty shower spaces.

All across the nation and, indeed, around the world, the same sort of scene would be played out at similar military bases in similar barracks. Young men in their prime, torn down and rebuilt into the foremost fighting machines each country's training could produce. Fit, lean and hard of muscle, their minds sharpened and focused for a single role: to kill, to take the lives of the other young men who had been trained for the same purpose.

Loving mother's sons, polite brothers and respectful students, kind and gentle by nature, retrained, reprogrammed from their passive, serene lives of civility to the active, bloody pursuit of aggression, taught to fight and kill and destroy, in a global conflict not of their making, but one requiring their obedience and servitude, nevertheless, and tragically, for too many, their oblation, the ultimate sacrifice.

All of England and the countries of Europe had forfeited an entire generation in "The Great War." And now, less than a quarter of a century later, the same insensate, blood-thirsty dogs of war had insanely been let loose again, to obliterate cities and entire countries, ravage the landscape and lay waste to the innocents.

In some places, however, the lives of far too many warriors would not be wasted on the battlefield, but expended upon the cold, callous and capricious orders of dictatorial despots: Stalin and Hitler, for examples, executed their own senior officers in successful purges intended to secure the total obedience of the surviving junior officers; youthful German paratroopers were ordered to jump to their deaths without parachutes from airplanes with assurances that snow banks would break their fall.

In the same manner, Hitler heartlessly sacrificed his own submarine crews as he turned his attention to the eastern front, pursuing his vendetta against the Russians. Being assigned to a U-boat in the Nazi Navy was a virtual death sentence: the average lifespan of Nazi submariners was only about 60 days and very many submarines and their crews were lost on their first patrols.

Near the close of the war, as numbers of Nazi soldiers diminished, prepubescent boys as young as nine or ten would be given oversized uniforms, weapons and orders to defend indefensible bridges.

In Japan's final desperate hours, the young Kamikaze pilots, the "Divine Wind," would become flying suicide bombers—whether they wanted to or not—in attempts to destroy America's Pacific fleet.

Additionally, another entire generation of Australian warriors would stain the earth with its blood.

The three gentle warriors chatted amiably, waiting their turns in the showers and soon, their places in the world's conflict.

*   *   *

AT 0500 THE NEXT MORNING, the men in the open bay were rudely awakened when the overhead lights were snapped on and the sleep-shattering crash of a GI can rolled loudly down the center of their bay.

A Marine with closely-cropped hair and wearing red and gold shorts and short-sleeved shirt, stretched taut by his huge, muscular, tattooed arms, stood with his hands on his hips, yelling at the top of his leatherneck lungs, "All right, you f***in' maggots! Outta those f***in' racks! Now! Both feet on the f***in' deck! I want you ladies outside in ten minutes in athletic gear! I'm gonna make real men outta you! You're gonna look like Marines! Like me!"

He proceeded down the central aisle, kicking the beds, yelling obscenities at the men.

T.J. and his roommates were awakened by the noise.

As he listened to the clamor in the bay, a smile crossed T.J.'s face.

"Gunny Gillespie! That no-good son of a bitch!"

He threw off his bed sheet, quickly pulled on the pair of shorts hanging from one short corner post of his bed and stepped into the passageway leading to the open bay.

"Who the bloody 'ell is out here making all this bloody noise?" he yelled.

The Marine looked up with a scowl on his face, ready for a fight.

When he saw T.J., his face brightened with a broad smile.

"T.J.! What the f*** are you doing with this bunch of f***in' Navy riff-raff?"

"They're teaching me to fly," T.J. said, enthusiastically pumping the gunny sergeant's large hand. "But what are *you* doing here?" he asked. "I thought you were going to Pendleton."

"No such luck. I'm the new athletic director here. Speaking of which, are you going to run with us like that?" he said, pointing to T.J.'s boxer shorts. "You need to get dressed out."

"Right-o! Be right back."

Outside the barracks, Gunny Sergeant Gillespie announced that the men would have 45 minutes of exercise each morning before morning chow and team sports and drills in the afternoons.

The men groaned.

Gillespie led them through a series of stretching exercises, calisthenics, including sit-ups and push-ups, before taking them on a 30-minute run.

When the men returned to their quarters, the gunny sergeant pulled T.J. aside.

"T.J., why don't I put you in charge of these men for their morning physical training? That way, I won't have to get up at four o'clock. Okay?"

"Right-o."

Before leading their exercise at his first session, T.J. instituted a practice that would continue throughout their intermediate training:

"All right, mates, let's build a bit of espirit d'corps!

"Ready?"

Ready!

"It's all for one!"

"And one for all!" the men shouted back.

*   *   *

AFTER CHOW THAT MORNING, the men were loaded onto a bus and transported to Saufley Field where they would resume ground school classes: Morse code, celestial navigation, ship and plane recognition and other aviation-related topics.

The men were also coincidentally introduced to Maxine, the Saufley elephant, whose initial appearance and later disappearance at the air base were mysteries.

While she was a resident of Saufley Field, it was rumored that the facing end of Maxine determined the success or failure of flights on any particular day, to a busload of cadets heading for the flight line. If Maxine faced the bus, up arrows were in the offing. If her ample derrière faced the bus, disappointment and down arrows might follow.

But more importantly, it was at Saufley that the men would be introduced to the Vultee Valiant, the notorious "Vibrator."

The Vultee BT (for Basic Trainer)-13 airplanes that had been lined up precisely on the tarmac at Saufley Field were awe-inspiring. Billy and his classmates gazed in wonderment at the four rows of shiny, silver-gray planes, seeming to stretch out into infinity. Their low-set, cantilevered wings and aluminum skin, not cloth over wood, appeared aggressive, masculine and military. The Vultees looked like real fighter planes, unlike the cartoon-like, bright yellow, fabric-covered Stearman. Each of the men felt a rush of pride and maturity as a real pilot, anticipating the next step in training: 160 hours of flying the Vultee.

"It's kind of like going from tricycles to motorcycles," Bob commented.

And the Vultees had closed cockpits, even heaters. No more flight cancellations or having to endure the capricious whims of the weather.

Billy viewed the closed cockpits with mixed feelings, however. He had seen the photographs, as well as the Dilbert cartoons, of cigarette-puffing pilots at the controls of the enclosed trainers. He dreaded the prospect of flying with an instructor who chain-smoked in the confines of a closed cockpit.

Even though the Vultee's landing gear was not retractable (it was, in the original airplane, but the military hierarchy felt the intermediate cadets were not yet prepared for that added level of responsibility), the pitch of the propellers was adjustable. Additionally, each plane was equipped with two full sets of flight controls, blind-flying instruments, air-to-ground radios, and an instructor-cadet intercom system, a great improvement over the Yellow Peril's archaic, one-way gosports.

Between September 1939 to the summer of 1944, a total of 1,537 Valiants were built by Vultee Aircraft, in Downey, California, for the Army and the Navy. The Vultee Valiant outnumbered all basic trainers produced by other manufacturers.

The Pratt and Whitney radial, air-cooled, 450-horsepower engines were capable of propelling the planes at cruising speeds of 135 miles per hour and could attain maximum diving speed of 230 miles per hour.

*   *   *

"THEY HAVE A WINGSPAN of forty feet. They're twenty-eight feet, eleven and a half inches long," flight instructor Lt. Jim Foster was telling Billy's classmates as they stood on the flight line beside a Vultee Valiant BT-13.

Mr. Foster wore a thin, chevron-shaped mustache that ran up from the corners of his mouth to just under his nose, like actor Robert Taylor's, who was also a naval aviator.

"They hold one-hundred and twenty gallons of fuel in two wing tanks and have a maximum range of seven-hundred and twenty-five miles. They weigh in at about thirty-four hundred pounds. The Stearman weighs about twenty-seven hundred pounds, so with nearly twice the horsepower and a quarter of a ton more weight in the Valiant, you're going to see a big difference in the way they handle. And you'll be surprised at how little stick and rudder pedals you'll have to use.

"Unfortunately, like the Stearman, the Vultees utilize an inertial starter. Nothing has changed there. Make damned sure your engine starts the first time. You know that story: Keep your plane captain happy. You probably know some of them get pretty cantankerous if they have to crank them a second time, or woe is you, a third time."

The men smiled. They knew firsthand that unpleasant experience with the Stearman and the short fuses of some of the plane captains.

"And, like the Stearman, these planes are sturdy and easy to fly, but they're relatively slow and as noisy as hell.

"Oh, did I tell you they vibrate? They'll shake the fillings right out of your teeth. They vibrate the windows in the tower and buildings all over the base during take-offs and once you're airborne and there's nothing left to rattle on the ground, they'll rattle your canopies. That's why everybody calls them Vultee 'Vibrators.' "

*   *   *

THE CADETS' TRAINING—formation flight, aerobatics, instrument flying and night flying—would be virtually a repetition of their primary training, but with a more complicated aircraft that would have to be dissected, analyzed and absorbed, in graphic detail, from its metal skin to its complex inner workings.

Ground school continued with the study of the steadily increasing intricacies of powered flight, adding concentrated indoctrination of the mechanics, controls and aeronautical characteristics of the BT-13.

The front cockpit instrument panel was arrayed with 29 switches and gages, not including switches on the electrical control panel, and 27 controls on the left and right sides of the cockpit, as compared with the sparse 11-gage instrument panel of the Stearman.

*   *   *

"THE TOPIC TODAY, GENTLEMEN, IS SAFETY, beginning with flathatting," ground school instructor Lt. Fred Simpson began.

"Do any of you know that term?"

Wrong Way Carrigan raised his hand.

"Mr. Carrigan."

Carrigan stood and spoke: "Sir, flathatting is a practice some pilots have of showing out: making low passes at high speeds to impress or scare people on the ground."

"You would never be guilty of such a practice would you, Mr. Carrigan?"

"No, sir!"

"Very well, Mr. Carrigan. Have a seat.

"That is the correct answer to my question, and flathatting, gentlemen, is an unforgivable sin in Navy flying.

"Whether it is to let your girlfriend know you are overhead or you simply just lose control of your senses and fly at fence posts, straight and level three feet off a highway or into a dead end box canyon, let me tell you that flathatting is dangerous and too frequently deadly.

"Even if you don't kill yourself, you're a goner, anyway, because the Navy will arrest you, court martial you, lock you up and throw away the key for the duration of the war.

"One hotshot I knew thought it would be amusing to force a thousand men to the deck during a Saturday morning inspection. Need I tell you he's in the brig right now? The only stick he's going to have in his hand is the business end of a swab.

"A friend from California, Lt. Matt Portz, told me about two pilots who were killed when they plowed up a vineyard outside Livermore while flathatting. Mr. Portz was sent out to settle the property damage done to several rows of choice vines. The owner rightly said that the vines could be replaced, but the lives of the two pilots never could be.

"These are true stories, men. Don't you be the subject of another.

"I want to warn you here and now that the people in this area have been encouraged to report the time, place and number of any plane flying in a non-military manner. In case you haven't noticed, each plane has a different number and so large it can be seen from a great distance.

"Last year, nearly fifteen million hours were flown, not just in training, but fleet-wide. Unfortunately, nearly thirteen thousand major accidents occurred, half of which destroyed an aircraft. That in itself is bad enough. But when you factor in nearly three thousand fatalities, I think you understand that we don't want you trying to kill yourselves. Stay alive. Don't try to kill yourself or people in the air or on the ground.

"Don't be a statistic as a result of flathatting or any other harebrained lapses of sanity."

*   *   *

AFTER MORE HOURS OF FILMS, lectures and tests about the Vultee, each cadet was taken through multiple dry runs in the front seat of the plane until the day he would actually fly it.

When that day arrived, a tall, young enlisted man in blue dungaree trousers, chambray shirt and a white hat, was waiting on the flight line as Billy and his instructor, Lieutenant "Harry" Harris, approached the plane they would fly. The sailor came to attention and saluted the officer.

"Good morning, Mr. Harris. The plane is ready for your inspection."

"Good morning, Barney," Harris replied, returning the salute.

"Barney, this is Mr. Benson. He's going up for his first flight in a Vultee."

Billy extended his hand. "Good morning, Barney."

Barney shook Billy's hand, "Good morning."

Meeting enlisted men was always awkward. The officer instructors were usually formal and addressed each cadet by his last name or with the title "Mister." Enlisted men didn't salute the cadets and didn't call them "Mister" since they weren't yet commissioned officers. The enlisted men frequently didn't use any names when referring to them, unless they had to and then they would include the title 'cadet' before the last name.

"Okay, let's do our walk around, Mr. Benson," Lt. Harris said to Billy, preparatory to his first flight in the BT-13.

They laid their parachutes gently on the port horizontal stabilizer beside the vertical tail section and began their inspection, beginning with the fuselage baggage compartment, proceeding to the cockpits, to look for gear adrift, or items left unsecured. Mr. Harris stepped forward and signaled for Billy to join him on the narrow black catwalk where the wing joined the fuselage. He turned the handle located on the front cockpit enclosure and slid it aft for the inspection before opening the rear canopy.

They knelt on the wing as Mr. Harris opened the fuel cap to check the fuel level of that tank.

"For a crew of two, you'll need a full load of fuel. How much would that be?"

"One hundred and twenty gallons, sir."

"How much in each tank?"

"Sixty gallons, sir."

"Good. And the weight of the baggage carried must not exceed…?"

"One hundred pounds, sir."

"Good. I'm glad you've paid attention."

Jumping off the wing onto the tarmac, they walked along the trailing, or rear edge, of the port wing, looking for defects. They looked on the top surface, underneath and at the end of the wing for wear. They pushed the end of the wing up and down to check for internal structural defects. As a safety reminder to stand clear of the prop, they kept their right hands on the leading edge of the wing as they worked their way to the engine compartment. They opened the cover panel and inspected the engine and checked the oil level. They closed and latched the cover securely. They walked to the front of the plane, standing clear of the capricious propeller, to see if the plane was level, removed the cap protecting the pitot tube, inspected the starboard wing and the fuel supply in its wing tank, checked the landing gear and moved slowly aft, continuing down the fuselage, to the empennage, or tail section, opened and carefully closed the baggage compartment behind the cockpit, and ended up where they started.

Satisfied the plane was safe to fly, the men retrieved their parachutes, slipped them on and returned to the port wing.

"Are you nervous, Mr. Benson?"

"A little, sir."

"I'll keep a close eye on you. Just relax and concentrate on what you've learned and think about what you're doing. I think you're going to do just fine."

"Thank you, sir."

"You go up first, Mr. Benson."

"Aye, sir."

Billy pulled himself onto the wing of the plane with the handgrip on the side of the fuselage.

Mr. Harris climbed onto the wing and stood beside Billy on the black strip beside their cockpits.

"Before we start up the engine, let me give you a review of emergency procedures.

"The emergency exit panel release must be unlocked before take-off.

"See that crossbar there?"

"Yes, sir," Billy said.

"Push it up, so the word 'Locked' is covered."

"Aye, sir."

Billy grasped the 'T' bar and swung it upward.

"If we have to make an emergency exit on the ground, pull the emergency exit panel release handle down. Then, push out on the handle.

"If we have an emergency in flight, turn the enclosure release handle, here, and push the enclosure forward open. If it should jam, use the emergency exit panel release.

"Got that?"

Billy had not seriously considered he would have to leave his plane in an emergency. He tried not to show his apprehension.

He swallowed and said, "Aye, sir."

"Good. Climb in and adjust your seat to assure that you have full rudder movement. We have a cushion in the baggage compartment if you need one."

Billy adjusted his seat and tested the pedals on the deck.

"I have full rudder movement, sir."

"Good."

"We'll leave our canopies open until we're at five hundred feet."

"Aye, sir."

Mr. Harris climbed into the back seat of the plane and called to Barney.

"Okay, Barney. Button us up, please."

Barney climbed nimbly onto the port wing and fastened their shoulder harnesses to the backs of their seats before taking his place on the port side of the engine compartment, to await the order to crank the inertia starter.

Billy rubbed his hands together and wet his lips as he scanned the instrument panel.

"Put on your helmet, Mr. Benson and I'll follow along on the check-off list as you go through your start-up procedure."

"Aye, sir."

Billy stuffed wads of cotton into his ears he had brought from the hangar and pulled on the canvas helmet. It was equipped with earphones, as was his instructor's, enabling him to listen to Mr. Harris's comments, made through a microphone on the starboard side of the rear seat. Billy also had a microphone he could use to talk to Mr. Harris.

"Okay, Barney, rotate the propeller, please," Billy said as he pulled on his gloves.

Barney rotated the propeller twice to clear it of oil.

Billy called out the steps from his check-off list and set the controls, as Mr. Harris monitored.

"Ignition switch on *bat*.

"Carburetor air on *cold*.

"Prop control in *decrease rpm*."

"Be extra careful here, Mr. Benson," Mr. Harris interjected. "Don't make the mistake of confusing the mixture control for the prop control after the engine starts. If you do, you'll cut off the engine. And you know how much that would piss Barney off."

Billy smiled and nodded his head.

"Aye, sir."

Billy resumed the check off:

"Oil cooler in *open* position.

"Fuel selector valve on *reserve tank*.

"Pump fuel pressure to three or four pounds per inch.

"Check the cut-out pressure of the warning lamp.

"Seven to nine strokes of the engine primer, since it's cold.

"Mixture control to *full rich*.

"Set throttle one-tenth open.

"Energize starter.

"Energize the starter, Barney!" Billy called to the plane captain.

Barney reached for the crank he had already inserted into the side of the engine compartment. He leaned forward and began the arduous task of turning the handle of the inertia starter around and around to get the starter to speed.

"Turn ignition switch to *both*, engage starter and operate fuel pump to maintain pressure as engine runs," Billy recited.

As the primed starter began turning the propeller, the plane wobbled with the torque created by the spinning blades. The plane shook faster and faster and the engine grew louder and louder. All the forewarnings regarding the noise level the Vultee produced were not quite accurate. The din was deafening. Until they were airborne and the cockpit canopies were slid shut and locked, normal communication was nearly impossible.

Barney removed the inertia handle and stood clear of the propeller.

"Idle at eight-hundred to one thousand rpms until oil pressure is established," Billy announced into his microphone, hoping he could be heard.

When the oil pressure gage indicated that oil was circulating properly, Billy adjusted the mixture control to *full rich* and opened the throttle wide to test the oil pressure. The needle moved smoothly to 60 pounds.

"Oil pressure sixty pounds," Billy reported.

"Check the oil temperature. We want fifty to seventy degrees Centigrade," Mr. Harris replied on the inter-com.

"Check."

"And now the cylinder-head temperature: Reading two hundred degrees Centigrade."

"Check."

"Check for generator charge."

"Check."

"Check the magnetos. Switch each one separately to see if there's more than a one hundred rpm drop at fifteen hundred rpms."

"Check.

"Check-off complete, sir.

"Very good, Mr. Benson.

"Let's get the chocks pulled and head for the airstrip."

"Aye, sir," Billy answered, with a nod of his head.

Billy signaled to Barney to remove the wheel chocks.

Billy then followed the plane captain's hand signals to taxi from the flight line to the end of the field for take off.

"We need to keep a sharp lookout for other planes or fuel trucks or anything else on the taxiway," Mr. Harris said into his microphone.

"Aye, sir."

"Free the tail wheel to swivel, Mr. Benson. That'll help if we need to make any severe turns while we're taxiing and try not to use your brakes."

"Aye, sir."

They taxied to the northwest runway as Billy steered the plane's tail to swing back and forth to allow a clear view of any obstacles as they proceeded to the runway to await the signal from the tower for take off.

"Set the rudder and elevator trim tabs at *neutral*," Billy read out.

"Set wing flaps at twenty degrees.

"Mixture at *full rich*."

"Mr. Benson," Mr. Harris said into his microphone, "don't forget that the surface controls on this plane are much more sensitive than you were accustomed to in the Stearman. You won't need as much movement of the control stick and the rudder pedal action."

"Aye, sir."

Billy's gloved hand rested on the throttle lever on the port side of his cockpit. When the green light flashed from the tower, he pushed the throttle control forward to send the plane racing, roaring deafeningly down the runway.

When the plane reached 70 miles per hour, he pulled back on the stick and the plane left the runway in a thunderous roar.

He watched the hand of the altimeter as the plane climbed steadily upward: 100 feet, 200, 300. He took a quick look at the ground falling beneath the plane as they steadily rose above the tall, omnipresent pine trees surrounding the airfield and much of the Panhandle region.

At 500 feet, Mr. Harris spoke to Billy through his microphone: "You can close your cockpit canopy now, Mr. Benson."

Billy replied,"Aye, sir," even though he could not be heard without his microphone. He pushed the enclosure forward and locked it.

"Remember to always scout the territory for an emergency landing site," Harris said through the inter-com.

Billy nodded.

The plane continued to gain altitude as Billy steered it in a west by northwesterly direction.

"We'll climb to six thousand feet, Mr. Benson."

"Aye, sir."

Billy had never flown above 2000 feet. He was anxious to see the Gulf of Mexico from over a mile in the air.

The needle on the altimeter continued to move around the dial:
Twelve hundred feet,
Thirteen hundred feet,
Fourteen hundred feet,
…and then, silence.

Wthout warning, the engine quit completely.

Billy's head snapped up sharply from the instrument panel. The propeller had stopped, parallel to the horizon, as if ready for inspection on the flight line.

He automatically checked the fuel supply switch and pushed the stick forward to prevent a stall as he had been taught.

Billy knew instructors routinely and unexpectedly reduced the power, stalling the planes as part of training but he had never known of one to test his response on take-off.

"Did you do that, Mr. Benson?" his instructor asked in the plane, now eerily silent.

"No, sir. I thought you did."

"No. Let me take it from here," Mr. Harris said, taking the stick in the baffling, disquieting stillness of the cockpit.

Billy lifted his hands from the controls quickly, unsure of what to do with them.

Mr. Harris kept the nose down, which, as the plane lost altitude and gained speed, would provide lift for the wings. He quickly shut off the ignition switch and gas supply and looked ahead for a landing site.

Billy looked out of his cockpit, first one side and then the other, as the trees and the farmland grew closer. He would have preferred the unbearable roar of the engine to the sound of wind blowing by the plane and whistling through the canopy.

He wondered how long a plane weighing nearly two tons could stay aloft without power. Was the Vultee like the Avenger, which was jokingly said to fall at an even faster rate than it could fly?

"Never try to turn back to the field you left whenever this happens," Mr. Harris said as he continued to look for a clearing. "Don't raise the flaps. Keep the nose down and glide in the direction you were going, if at all possible."

"There's a pasture up ahead. We're in Alabama. Baldwin County. Fortunately, it's full of pastures and potato fields. I'm going to make a circle and land there, in that pasture and pray the ground is hard enough that we don't go nose over."

Mr. Harris' composure and professional response to the emergency did not go unnoticed by Billy. He hoped he had appeared calm and unruffled, too.

Billy looked intently through the windshield and felt his body stiffen as the plane began to make a wide, 1000-foot circle to the right of the pasture, all the while dropping, dropping, gracefully and silently toward the ground.

"Here's where a three-point landing is critical. Keep the tail down. It'll help us keep the nose out of the cow patties.

"Hang on. Here we go!"

Billy braced himself against the sides of the cockpit as the wheels hovered over the ground and crunched down solidly with the muffled sound of heavy metal straining at all its welds and joints. The plane taxied a short distance and stopped quickly as Mr. Harris applied the brakes.

"Get your canopy open and get out, Mr. Benson," Harris said, as he pulled the lever to release his three-point seat belt and shoulder harness simultaneously, grabbed his fire extinguisher, pushed his enclosure covering forward and stepped forward to help Billy out of his cockpit with his free hand.

They both jumped off the wing onto the ground and ran a safe distance from the plane before looking back at it.

"Sir, did I do something wrong?" Billy asked.

"Not that I could tell. I did smell gas, though."

"Will there be an inquiry?"

"Well, there'll be something. For both of us.

"Let's get out of these parachutes and see if we can find a farmer with a telephone."

"Aye, sir."

They trudged down the road to a farmhouse Mr. Harris had spotted as he was circling for a landing. They walked up the long dirt road to the home, as a bony red dog barked at them from underneath the house. The two men walked up the steps and across the worn, wooden porch. Mr. Harris knocked on the screen door.

A man in faded overalls, followed by his entire family, gathered inside the screen door to see the strange sight: two Navy pilots in flight suits, but no plane. The family had been in the back of the house eating its noon meal and had not seen the plane nor heard it land in the pasture down the road.

The farmer had no telephone, but offered to drive them in his old Ford truck to nearby Barin Field, in Foley, Alabama.

After arriving at Barin, Mr. Harris called the Chief Flight Officer at Saufley, gave him a brief report of the plane's engine failure and requested transportation for a return to Florida.

"Let's see if we can get some chow while we wait," Mr. Harris suggested, to Billy's pleasure. "Smelling the food at that farmer's house made me hungry."

A jeep from Saufley arrived about two hours later and picked up the grounded pilots who had waiting quietly sitting around one of the four hangars. A flatbed salvage truck would be dispatched later to remove the plane's wings and load everything to transport it back to Saufley Field, where it would be examined or disassembled if necessary.

Billy kept replaying the engine failure scenario. His hands and feet were where they were supposed to be; his left hand on the throttle and his right on the stick. His feet were on the rudder pedals and the plane was climbing without complications to 6000 feet.

They reported immediately to Lieutenant Commander Jeff McCorkle, the chief flight officer.

Mr. Harris knocked on the doorframe to McCorkle's office.

"Come on in, Harry," McCorkle said, rising from his chair and extending his hand to Harris.

"You're both okay?"

"Yes, sir. This is Mr. Benson, the cadet who was flying the plane at the time."

The flight officer held out his hand to Billy.

"Mr. Benson. Both of you, have a seat." And then he called out, "Barney, are you still out there?"

Barney, the plane captain, answered from across the passageway, "Aye, sir."

"Bring me the yellow sheet, please."

"Aye, sir."

Barney entered and handed the paper to McCorkle. The yellow sheet would attest to the maintenance done on the downed plane and bore the signatures of Barney, Mr. Harris and Billy.

"Oh, Barney, see if Mr. Thompson can step in and then you come back with him."

"Aye, sir."

Mr. Thompson was the flight maintenance officer.

When all the men were assembled and seated in mismatched chairs around the office, Billy and Mr. Harris reviewed the event as McCorkle took notes.

"We're all glad you're both safe," Commander McCorkle said. "That's number one. Two, we're glad you were able to land the plane safely. BuAer gives me a hard time each time we lose a plane. You wouldn't believe the paper work.

"I'm satisfied this wasn't due to pilot error, Mr. Benson. But you know that we'll bring the plane back here to examine it. Based on Mr. Harris's description of the incident, I think there's no reason you shouldn't continue with your training.

"Too, I've got your training records from primary," he said, lifting a folder. "Based on your good marks there and favorable comments from your instructors, I have every reason to believe the plane malfunctioned and not you.

"If the inspection of the plane indicates the problem was with the plane, then that's that. End of story. If, on the other hand, there's evidence of pilot error, then that'll be something else.

"You understand that, don't you?" he asked Billy.

"Aye, sir."

"We'll wait until all the evidence is in before we cross that bridge, however.

"So, Mr. Benson, let's get you back onto the horse. Harry and Barney, let's try this again tomorrow. Start all over in another plane and let's get Mr. Benson checked out. Okay? And let me know how he does."

Commander McCorkle had a driver take Billy to his quarters at NAS mainside.

The mood was somber at Splinterville. One of their own was missing and the uncertainty caused by the absence of any communication had cast a pall over the wing. The men had returned from the flight line, showered, changed, marched to chow and returned in virtual silence.

When the jeep screeched to a stop outside the barracks and Billy jumped out, however, Preacher Walker saw him through a window and shouted, "Praise the Lord! Bill is back!"

The men jumped to the windows, looked in disbelief, swarmed noisily to the front doors, opened them and pulled Billy into their company with handshakes, pats on the back and shouted words of welcome.

They escorted him into the bay and stood around him.

"All we knew was that your plane was missing," Bob said.

"We didn't know if you had crashed or taken off for Berlin," T.J. added.

"Is there going to be a board?" Barry asked.

"It all depends on what the examination of the plane reveals," Billy said. "They're going to bring it back on a flatbed truck to look at it. Mr. Harris doesn't think I made any errors, though. Neither do I. We'll just have to wait."

"Are you grounded?" Carrigan asked.

"No. I'm supposed to try again tomorrow. Same instructor. Same plane captain. Different plane, of course."

T.J. put his arm around Billy's neck.

"We're glad you're safe, mate," he said.

"Thanks, T.J. So am I.

"Thank you, guys!" Billy said with a hand lifted in gratitude for his homecoming. "It's good to be back to good old Splinterville."

He turned to go into his room followed by his roommates.

T.J. shut the door.

As Billy began removing his flight suit, he cheerfully commented, "Man! I'm about to starve. I hope I'll still be able to get some chow."

He noted the solemn faces of his roommates as he looked from one to the other and fell quiet, waiting for one of the others to speak.

T.J. broke the silence.

"Bill, we were all really concerned about your disappearance today. You know that most of us follow the reports in *Nav News* to see how many of our mates are killed in training exercises. Our wing has been lucky so far and we just didn't know what to expect when we got the word your plane was missing."

Bob spoke up next. "Yeah. When we came back, we all gathered in the bay and Preacher said a prayer for you."

Tears sprang from Billy's eyes. He quickly wiped them.

"We're not supposed to be emotional about this sort of thing," T.J. continued, "but today, I realized I have something to say to you chaps, because of, well, you know, what might happen to one of us. So, I wanted to tell the three of you that I really care for you and, while I have the balls to say it, I love each one of you. There."

"The same goes for me," Barry said. "I love you three and treasure your friendship over anybody I have met in my life, outside my own family."

"Me, too," Bob spoke up. "I never had a family until I came into the Navy. Bill's taken me home with him and his Uncle John and Aunt Grace are the closest things to parents I've ever had. And you guys are the closest things to brothers I have. I love all three of you and consider you my family."

"Thanks, guys, all of you," Billy added. "I guess I never considered that you would be worried about me.

"I love all of you, too, and, for that matter, everybody in our wing. I never thought I would find so many great guys I could care for the way I do. A flight of brothers. Thanks for being concerned about me and praying for me. I really appreciate it."

Billy went to each of them and offered his hand, but each pulled him into a tight embrace.

Billy tried not to be emotional, but tears filled his eyes again, anyway.

T.J. put his hand out. The others stacked their hands and held the hand under theirs.

"All for one," T.J. said quietly.

"And one for all," the others joined him.

* * *

BILLY FLEW THE NEXT DAY. The pre-flight walk around, check off and takeoff were textbook. The climb to 6000 feet went perfectly. When he was straight and level, Mr. Harris spoke to him over the headset.

"Good job, Mr. Benson. Do you feel redeemed?"

"Aye, sir. I do!"

"Good. How are you on wingovers?"

"Pretty good on the Stearman, sir."

"Well, let's see how you can do in the Vultee."

"Aye, sir."

* * *

BILLY WAS EXONERATED. Inspection of his Vultee's engine revealed a defective carburetor and his record was cleared.

Ground school training continued. Billy and the cadets continued to struggle with Morse code and vessel identification, which had not changed since pre-flight in Athens, still requiring split-second, instantaneous recognition.

And flight checks, flight checks, flight checks.

More ground school with more classes and tests.

Morning exercise sessions.

Afternoon team sports and close-order drills.

Study sessions in the room at Splinterville every weeknight.

Military drill, athletics, gunnery classes.

Solo flights, flight checks, instrument training under the flying hood, Link training, flight checks, night flying, acrobatic flying—more loops, turns, spins, inverted spins, wingovers, chandelles and echelons.

In intermediate formations, echelons were different from and easier to perform than had been the case in primary training, because of the Yellow Perils' restricted vision. The low, single-wing Vultee made it possible for intermediate echelon formations to line up, stair steps down, from the port side of the lead plane.

Easier, also, was communicating with members of the wing. Whenever the lead plane wanted to perform a wingover, for example, he could inform the men via his radio—and not with just hand signals—to begin the long, beautiful, graceful arch, followed by the planes in the formation.

Billy never tired of performing or just watching wingovers.

Radio-equipped planes required that the men receive ground school training in the proper use of military transmissions as required by the FAA. The men were tested on the manual as well as given practice sessions in proper protocol for transmission:

Navy Saufley, this is Navy zero-one-six-three-niner, five miles east at five thousand feet. Request permission to enter traffic pattern. Over.

Navy zero-one-six-three-niner, this is Navy Saufley. Cleared into traffic pattern to the right at five hundred feet. Runway four to the northwest. Compass heading three-thirty. Call on base leg. Over.

Navy Saufley, this is Navy zero-one-six-three-niner. Roger that.

Having radios for the first time, however, inspired some of the more frivolous and high-spirited students to violate the strict national and international rules that controlled all radio transmissions.

During one afternoon of seriously unimpressive formation training, the tower heard one of the disheartened cadets exclaim anonymously over his radio, "That has to be the most f***ed up formation I've ever seen."

The tower quickly and angrily responded, "Aircraft making last transmission, identify yourself!"

There was a brief silence and then came the anonymous reply, "We may be f***ed up, but we're not that f***ed up."

*   *   *

ON FRIDAY MORNING, December third, the week after Thanksgiving, the men in Billy's squadron, dressed in shorts, tee-shirts and high-topped sneakers, left their quarters for a six-mile run from their quarters to the lighthouse on the bay and back to Splinterville.

Running along the soft, sandy shoulder of the base road, they passed the just-completed three-story brick naval hospital and trotted along long stretches of the 30-foot high brick walls, past the original multi-level Spanish Fort Barancas, constructed of hand-made brick, long before there was a town called Pensacola.

The men jogged underneath the huge, sturdy, muscular arms of the grand old live oaks, once part of the Federal Government's forest for constructing sailing vessels when the site was a Navy Yard. Their limbs, festooned with dreamy, thick, gray moss, undulated gently in response to the constant breezes blowing in from the bay.

When the men neared the lighthouse, the road guards posted themselves smartly at parade rest on both sides of the formation in the center of the road to stop vehicular traffic. The men changed lanes and directions and headed back to their quarters, running in the same direction of the light vehicular traffic along the side of the road.

T.J. had put Barry at the front of the formation at the lighthouse to set the pace while he dropped back to run alongside Billy to carry on a breezy commentary about the native inhabitants of Australia's outback.

"They're so bleedin' primitive, they don't even wear any clothes. They don't even have bowls to drink the stinkin' water," he was saying, when Billy failed to lift his foot high enough to clear a bulge in the pavement. He pitched forward suddenly onto the street, sliding across the sandy pavement on his left side.

"Watch it, mate!" T.J. called, trying to catch his friend as members of the squadron ran around the two or jumped over them.

"I'll stay with him," T.J. called to Barry.

"Okay, everybody," Barry yelled to his squad, "keep up the pace! Let's take it on home!"

T.J. squatted in the road beside Billy, who rolled onto his back and tried to sit up.

"Hold it, there, mate. Let's see if you broke anything."

"Nothing but me pride and maybe me bleedin' arse," Billy replied, sitting up with effort, looking at his abraded palms.

"I see you haven't lost your sense of humor," T.J. said. "But let me check you out, anyway, " he said, feeling Billy's skinned elbow and leg for broken bones.

"I think I'm okay," he insisted. "Just help me up."

"All right, mate, here we go," T.J. said, pulling him up by his good elbow.

"Do you think you can make it over there to the hospital?" he asked, pointing to the hospital that could seen in the distance through a wide opening between the high brick walls.

"Sure."

T.J. walked slowly alongside Billy as he limped across the road and up the long, narrow street to the hospital.

Billy had difficulty gripping the ink pen with his bloodied hand as he signed in at the nurse's station in the emergency room. He walked slowly to the row of chairs against the wall where T.J. had already taken a seat.

When Billy's name was called, T.J. walked with him into the treatment room and helped him into a metal chair.

It was not long before a doctor with a white coat over his khaki uniform breezed into the room.

Billy painfully pushed himself up from the chair and stood, as he had been indoctrinated, in respect for a commissioned officer.

"What do we have here?" he asked, seeing Billy's skinned hands, knees and elbow.

"I took a fall, sir."

"I'll get a pharmacist's mate in here to help you get out of your running gear so we can take a look at you."

As he started out the door, the doctor spoke to T.J.

"Are you a patient, too?"

"No, sir. I was just helping me mate."

"It would be better if you waited outside."

"Aye, aye, sir," T.J. said cheerfully. "I'll be waiting out here, mate," he said to Billy.

Billy nodded and sat in the chair to wait.

A few minutes later, a young enlisted medic in white cotton jumper and trousers came into the treatment room.

"I'm supposed to help you get out of your clothes so the doctor can look at you."

Billy pushed himself up again from the chair.

"You really messed yourself up, didn't you?" the corpsman asked.

"I'm afraid so."

Billy gingerly took the bottom of his shirt and tried to pull it up.

"Can you help me with this?" Billy asked.

The corpsman pulled it off carefully as Billy slowly lifted his arms.

His side and hip also bore the marks of his skid along the pavement.

"Can you get your shorts off?" the medic asked.

Billy winced as he tried to slide his thumbs inside the waistband to remove the trunks.

"I think they're stuck where the blood has dried," he said.

He made painful another effort.

"I can't do it," Billy said. "See if you can pull it loose over here."

The medic tugged gently at the waistband of the shorts.

Billy cried out.

"*Ow!* Hold it! That isn't going to work. Look out in the waiting room for a man dressed like me. His name is T.J. Ask him to come in here."

The medic disappeared through the door.

Billy tried again to pull the fabric free of his skin.

"What is it, mate?" T.J. asked as he came into the treatment room.

"I can't get these shorts off. The blood's dried and they're stuck."

T.J. raised his index finger.

"Don't go away. I'll be right back."

The medic reentered as T.J. left and the two waited.

Presently T.J. returned and held the door for a sturdy Navy nurse in a stiffly starched, white cotton uniform and a matching cap with two gold stripes across the front of it. She entered the room with the self-assurance and deportment of a boatswain's mate.

Billy immediately came to his feet again.

"Casey, this is me mate, Billy Benson."

"Benson, huh! He looks more like Joe Palooka to me!" she replied.

"What happened to him?"

"He took a fall whilst we were running," T.J. answered. "We need to get those shorts off so the doctor can check him out, but they're stuck."

"Couldn't you get them off, Harry?" she asked the corpsman.

"I really didn't try very hard, Miz Casey. I don't think I want to pull another man's supporter off," Harry replied, smiling.

"Same here. Can you help him, Casey?" T. J. asked.

"Nothing to it," she said, swaggering toward Billy, her extended elbows swinging with each step.

Casey confidently stood behind her target, slipped her thumbs firmly inside his supporter and gave the shorts and jock strap a swift thrust to the floor.

Yee-ow!

Billy yelled so loudly, the patients waiting in sick call looked uncertainly toward the treatment room.

Casey stepped back to admire Billy's derrière.

He was in too much distress to notice.

"Hubba! Hubba!" she said approvingly.

She dusted her hands as a sign of her success and strutted audaciously back to the door where T.J. was standing, a smile on his face.

"I knew ye could do it, Casey, old girl! Good show!"

Casey turned to survey the naked, battered body standing before her, his red-stained shorts down around his feet. She looked into Billy's eye and winked.

"That's the good show," she said, pointing at Billy. "He's four-o! That's a real man, T.J.!"

She then gave Billy a thumbs-up, adding another enthusiastic "Four-o!" and disappeared out the door.

"I'll be waiting," T.J. said to Billy from the door.

"Hubba, hubba, me arse!"

T.J. left just as the doctor returned to look over Billy's abrasions, watching his patient's face as he pressed on his arm, hands and hip.

"I don't think you broke anything. You might want to just sponge yourself off for a day or two, instead of taking a shower.

"Harry, clean him up with some hydrogen peroxide and then paint these abrasions with iodine. Put some bandages on them and give him a few aspirins. Okay?"

"Sir, we're not supposed to take any medications unless the flight surgeon prescribes them," Billy reminded the doctor.

"I can take care of that, cadet. Don't you worry. You'll also need a tetanus booster. I'll send in a nurse. Take it easy this weekend. No physical training until next week. Keep the bandages clean and dry. Don't let anything get infected. Take the aspirins for pain. Come back if you need us to look at it again."

He patted Billy's shoulder and left the room.

Billy stepped out of his shorts and jock. Harry picked them up gingerly between thumb and forefinger and dropped them into the chair as Billy stood at the end of the metal treatment table, facing the door. He watched as Harry dipped several four-inch-by-four-inch squares of gauze into the hydrogen peroxide he had poured into a small metal bowl.

"This is going to be cold," he warned.

They didn't hear the door open, but both were startled when a white enamel emesis basin hit the tile-covered deck with a loud clang.

The patients and medics in the waiting room looked again at the treatment room door.

When Billy and Harry looked up, they saw a young nurse standing just inside the door. She held a syringe firmly, its needle wrapped in a small cotton alcohol sponge. Her mouth was open and she was obviously in a flustered state

"Oh, I'm so sorry," she apologized.

"I'll get that for you, Miss Walker," Harry said, bending over to retrieve the kidney-shaped basin.

"I've got the tetanus booster," she said, absently holding out the syringe, staring, as if in a trance, at the perfect, albeit somewhat battered, specimen of Nordic manhood, standing *au natural* at the end of the treatment table.

Billy smiled warmly at her.

"Hip or arm?" he asked.

"What?" she asked vaguely.

161

Harry was enjoying the breach of commissioned etiquette Miss Walker was displaying.

Billy swung his shoulder toward her. "Do you want to give me that shot in my shoulder?

"Or in my hip?" he asked, as he turned the right side of his body slightly further in her direction.

Miss Walker made an effort to snap out of her trance.

"Oh. Uh…shoulder."

Billy stood with his shoulder toward her.

She walked to him, carefully keeping her eyes fixed on his shoulder.

Billy, still smiling, focused on her face, studying the fine features and smooth skin.

She wiped his deltoid with the alcohol sponge and inserted the needle expertly and quickly. Billy breathed in her faint floral aroma—*was it roses?*—and relished the touch of her soft, warm hands on his arm.

She pulled back on the plunger slightly and then pressed it with her thumb. She removed the needle and wiped his arm again.

"Did that hurt?" she asked.

"No, ma'am," Billy replied pleasantly, looking into her soft, brown eyes. "It felt good. You can give me another one if you want to."

Miss Walker gave him a quick, bewildered look, took the basin Harry handed her and left the room, starring straight ahead.

Harry lifted his eyebrows and smiled at Billy.

"I think you've got a fan."

"What's her name?" Billy asked.

"Ensign Suzanne Walker, Nurse Corps."

*   *   *

THE NEXT AFTERNOON, Saturday, Billy called the information desk at the hospital for Suzanne Walker's schedule.

She'll be on AM's on Ward F, starting Monday.

"She's not there now?"

No, sir.

"Does she stay in the nurses' quarters?"

Yes, sir. As far as I know.

162

"Is it near the hospital?"

Yes, sir. Just a few yards over. You can see it from the hospital.

"Thanks."

Billy limped to the nurses' quarters and removed his soft barracks cap as he entered the lobby. He looked around for a reception desk, but didn't see one.

He could see into the large, adjacent lounge where several women in civilian dress and men in uniforms were seated on the sofas and chairs, in spirited conversation.

He limped over to two women standing beside the door to the lounge.

"Excuse me, but does Suzanne Walker live here?"

The women looked at his face, then at his bandaged hand.

One of them nodded.

"Is she here now?"

"I think so."

"Would you mind asking her if she could come out here?"

The woman who had answered him asked, "Are you the cadet who fell yesterday and skinned himself up?"

Billy was surprised at the question and hesitated a second before answering, "Yes."

The women pulled their heads into their shoulders, pressed their hands to their mouths and giggled like schoolgirls.

"We'll get her," the first woman said, and both of them left quickly.

Billy walked in a small, nervous circle, toying with his cap as he waited.

When Suzanne came through the door and slowly walked up to him, he smiled broadly at her.

She was as beautiful as he had remembered: Only a few inches shorter than he, trim figure, light brown hair hanging loosely at her shoulders and those bright, brown eyes with long, dark lashes. The aroma of roses lingered.

She still seemed shy.

He liked that.

"Hi!" he said.

"Hello," she said, uncertainly.

"I wanted to introduce myself. I'm Bill Benson. One of the V-5 cadets. I'm in Pensacola for flight training. You remember me, don't you?"

She nodded, her face flushing.

"I wanted to thank you for the shot. Like I said, it didn't hurt at all. And I thought I'd like to get to know you better so I came by."

She looked into his face doubtfully, but didn't reply.

"I called the hospital. They said you weren't on duty today so I just walked on over here."

She still didn't respond.

This isn't going too well, he thought.

"I hope you don't mind that I came over, you know, without being introduced or calling or anything."

"Well," she began.

Billy was hopeful.

"Yes?"

"We're not supposed to…Ah, we aren't…"

"You're not supposed to what?" he asked, now in doubt.

"We can't date enlisted men," she said.

"Oh."

She was right. Navy regulations forbade commissioned officers from fraternizing with enlisted personnel. And Billy wouldn't be commissioned for months.

"Well," he said, with good humor, "sometimes rules can be bent a little bit, can't they?"

"I'm just an ensign, you know," she replied. "I don't think I'd want to try to buck the system."

Hmmm.

He continued to look at her as he thought of an alternative.

"Maybe we could see each other somewhere else on base," he suggested optimistically.

"You have to wear your uniform everywhere," she said. "Everybody would know you aren't an officer."

"But if you were in your civvies, nobody would know."

Billy smiled at her and lifted his eyebrows.

She can't refute that.

"No, I-I don't know. No, I think I'd better not."

"You're sure about that?" Billy asked pleasantly.

She nodded.

Billy's smile faded.

"Okay. Thanks. Sorry I bothered you."

He turned and left.

She watched him push through the door, limp down the steps and continue on down the sidewalk.

When she turned to go to her room, the two nurses Billy had asked to fetch her and who had been watching from across the front hall, ran to her.

"What a dreamboat!" the tall one said.

"Are you going to see him?" the other asked.

"No."

"Do you mean to say you let him get away?" the tall one asked her, as if he might be a fish or a deer.

"No. I guess I sent him away," she confessed.

"Sent him away? Why? He's too cute for you to let him get away, Suzanne," the other nurse said. "Casey was right about him. I wish I had been in the treatment room, too."

"I don't think it's professional to talk about patients like that," Suzanne said.

"Well, you saw what Casey saw," the tall one said. "She said he was four-o. Didn't you think he was four-o?"

"'Four-o, fore and aft!' is what she said," the other one added with a laugh.

Suzanne played innocent. "Oh, you two. Ninety-nine percent of these cadets are probably four-o."

"Yeah, but they're not knocking on your door, trying to get in," the tall one said.

Suzanne turned, walked to her room and closed the door.

Why does the Navy have to make everything so complicated?

Before she finished asking herself that question, she knew the answer: *I'm wrong to blame the Navy. I know that. I volunteered for military life and I have to accept it. I'm just being petty because I can't have my way.*

She walked to the window, catching a glimpse of Billy just as he disappeared behind a building.

She regretted the disparity in their stations.

This sounds like H.M.S. Pinafore.

She agreed that he seemed to be the sort of man she would enjoy getting to know better, but as one who believed in following the rules, she would never know.

He was enlisted and she was commissioned and according to the Navy, never should the twain meet.

He's an officer candidate after all, she rationalized. *In only a few months, he'll be an ensign, the same rank I am. Maybe the rules could be bent, the way he suggested.*

But how? I refused him outright. He wouldn't come back to see me after he gets his commission. And when he leaves here, he'll forget me. I don't think I'll forget him very soon, though.

She continued to stand at her window as she sorted through her options.

Well, if he could get my schedule, I can get his.

* * *

THE NEXT AFTERNOON, Monday, Suzanne went straight from the ward to her room to change into a civilian dress and jacket, against the late November chill. She walked to her car on the staff's parking lot and arrived at Billy's quarters just minutes before his Splinterville crew arrived from the flight line in their bus. She watched as the men stepped from the bus and lined up in three ranks.

She remained in her car until the men had been dismissed. As they began walking to their barracks, she stepped out of her car and stood behind the door.

A pretty woman—or virtually any woman at all—at an all-male gathering will always attract the attention of men.

Each cadet passing by looked at her and smiled or nodded, in hopes of receiving any acknowledgement from her, subtle or otherwise.

The look on her face remained pleasant, but not one that offered what could be construed as an invitation.

The men were covered and wearing their flight suits, many nearly the same size and all more or less resembling each other, but she recognized Billy easily by his slow, stiff gait as he, T.J. and Bob slowly walked to their barracks, in animated conversation.

She recognized T.J., having seen him once or twice in the lounge at the nurses' quarters.

When Billy spied her, she smiled uncertainly, lifting her hand at him slightly.

He returned her smile, excused himself and limped toward her.

"Hi," he said.

"Hi."

"I'm surprised to see you here."

"I guess you are. I'm sorry I was so, so…"

"Military?"

"I guess."

"Does this mean we'll be able to see each other?" he asked.

"We can try. I really don't want to get into trouble. Or you, either."

"I know. Thanks."

"But if it doesn't work out…"

"I know."

"Maybe we could go to a movie sometime or something like that," she suggested.

"On base?" he asked.

"It's probably going to be if-y anywhere. You know, if the head nurse or somebody sees us together."

"How about this weekend? Maybe Saturday night." he suggested.

"I have plans for this weekend. Maybe next week?"

"How about next Saturday? That'll be…the eleventh."

"Do you have a car?" she asked.

He laughed. "I'm afraid not."

"Okay. I'll pick you up here," she said. "At seven?"

He breathed her soft, floral perfume again and fought the urge to grab her on the spot and plant a kiss on her inviting, pink lips. Instead, he smiled broadly and placed his hand briefly and lightly over hers, resting on the top of the car's door.

"That sounds good. Thanks for coming over."

He held the door as she got back inside.

She started the engine, smiled and lifted her hand to him in sort of a wave.

He resisted the temptation to throw his cap into the air or shout or turn cartwheels. Instead, he stood calmly as he watched as her car drove away and then returned to the barracks unhurriedly.

Inside Splinterville, members of the squadron, many of whom had been watching from the windows, greeted him as if he were a returning war hero. They called friendly obscenities to him, made wolf calls, rubbed his head, and gave his back friendly pats.

Bob, Barry and T.J. were waiting for him in his room.

"Good show, mate!" T.J. shouted, followed by "All for one and one for all!" for their ceremonial stacking of hands.

When the three friends had his hands firmly in theirs, however, they pulled Billy out the door and dragged him, protesting all the way, toward the showers.

"My uniform! My bandages!" Billy protested.

"Bandages, me arse!" T.J. responded.

The men who were already in the showers laughingly stepped aside as the men pulled Billy under the showerheads, all four becoming saturated in the process.

The next day, the quartet flew in wet shoes and were thankful the Vultees had closed cockpits.

*   *   *

BILLY WAS WAITING outside his barracks when Suzanne pulled up in her Buick sedan.

She slid across the bench seat to let him take the steering wheel.

"Hi!" he said, as he opened the door and sat in the drivers' seat.

"Hi."

He closed the door.

"Buick Roadmaster. The 'doctors' car.'"

"How did you know my dad was a doctor?"

"I didn't. Buicks are called 'the doctors' car,' because so many doctors drive them."

"Oh."

He looked over the heavily chromed instruments and dashboard.

"What's this?" he asked, pointing to a small metal lever on the left side of the steering column.

"That's a turn indicator. Pull it down for left turns and up for right."

"Oh, yeah. I read about these. Little lights outside the car blink off and on to show the direction you're going to turn."

"Right."

"Does it have an automatic transmission, like the Cadillac?"

"No, you'll have to shift gears."

"Three forward gears?"

She nodded.

He turned the key in the ignition and pressed the starter.

He sat a moment listening to the engine running and then opened his door and walked to her door.

She looked at him, confused.

"Cadets aren't allowed to drive."

She slid to the driver's side.

"I just wanted to remember how it feels to be behind the wheel again."

She laughed lightly.

"Okay, now where do we go?" she asked.

"We can stay on base," he suggested. "Let's just drive down to the bay. There are some picnic tables there and we can talk and get acquainted."

"Okay."

Billy was encouraged by Suzanne's change of heart to see him. Their initial meeting in the treatment room had certainly been unique. And their encounter at the nurses' quarters had not been particularly pleasant. Her appearance at his quarters was totally unexpected. Whatever the situation was between them now, he determined that this evening would be controlled and as enjoyable and unthreatening as he could make it.

The thick cumulus cloud layer held the Earth's heat that night. Even though it was November and cool, the night air wasn't cold. She wore a light jacket and he had a long-sleeved, knit cotton sweater underneath his khaki shirt.

The picnic table he had suggested was empty and only a few yards from the main road and the same approximate distance from the bay. It was positioned so the built-on benches ran vertically with the water.

They sat on opposite sides of the table, which gave each a view of the bay.

He opened the dialogue with the standard questions: *Where is your home? Do you have brothers and sisters?*

She was from Texas. Her mother had died when she was 11. Her father died more recently. She had three brothers and one sister. Two of her brothers were also doctors and one was a college professor. Her sister was married to a doctor and lived in Rhode Island. Her brothers got most of the inheritance although she had received the Buick and a small trust fund.

They occasionally fell silent to watch a boat pass or listen to the waves lapping on the shore after the boat had passed. He held her fingers lightly in his across the table as they spoke.

He gave her no reason to mistrust him. He was a perfect gentleman, despite the fact that being so close to her was maddening. Her hair was caught up in the back by braids, pinned close to her head. Women in the military were not permitted to let their hair touch their uniform collars. He wanted to reach across the table and loosen the pins to watch her hair cascade across her shoulders.

She wore little makeup, no jewelry and no nail polish, as dictated by Navy Regs. The bones of her face were stunning in the dim light. Billy found himself studying the way the light reflected off her cheeks, forehead and nose. She spoke softly, in an educated Texas accent, choosing her words carefully. She seemed to be humble.

As he studied her, he liked everything about her, except the fact that she still seemed to view him with caution. He felt she didn't fully trust him.

Is it because I'm a man? In the military? In the Navy? Enlisted? Is it because she was embarrassed by the way she had barged in on me while I was naked? Is it some of these things? All of them? Or something entirely different?

Whatever the cause was, she could not accuse him of anything except absolute gentlemanly propriety that evening.

* * *

IN GROUND SCHOOL NAVIGATION CLASS, the men worked with maneuvering boards and time, rate and distance tables to solve course-plotting problems.

Unlike the Army, which had only one assigned navigator aboard each aircraft, the Navy trained all its officers to be navigators. The mysterious disappearance of the Army's ill-fated B-24, *Lady Be Good*, that crashed in the Libyan Desert in April of that year because of faulty navigation, made a strong case for the Navy's policy.

Mr. Lee, the popular navigation instructor, played Mozart during Practical Works, or what he called P-Works, as the men worked at their charting assignments. He frequently propped his foot on his desk chair as he lectured, exposing short engineer's boots. He had established a reputation for his quick wit as well as his ability to simplify complex technological problems. Typical of his sense of humor was the Monday morning he had hoped to catch T.J. off guard.

"Mr. Macintosh?" he called, straight-faced.

T.J. jumped to his feet quickly and came to a textbook Marine posture of attention, arms stiffly to his sides and his eyes straight ahead.

"Aye, sir?"

"Did I see you in the bar of the San Carlos Hotel over the weekend in civilian clothes and with a female naval officer?" he demanded.

Without hesitation, T.J. replied forcefully, with a straight face, "Sir! I hope not, sir!"

Mr. Lee and the class members roared with laughter.

Actually, T.J. could have pleaded "Not guilty" to part of the charge, since he had escorted *two* female officers to the popular Navy hangout, as well as to a series of other bars along Palafox and Cervantes Streets.

Mr. Lee's ability to impart effective navigation skills would prove to be a lifesaver for many of the men once they were in the fleet.

Flying over trackless expanses of water made thorough knowledge of navigation all the more important. Flying over land, with its familiar roads and landmarks, however, made it possible for pilots to simply follow highways from city to city.

Flight training over the Gulf of Mexico, while thrilling, awe-inspiring and sobering, demanded a solid understanding of all facets of navigation, however.

"Okay, men. Here are some gouges for your test tomorrow. Hit the books. Dismissed."

Attention on deck!

* * *

NUDITY AMONG MEN is a common trait as old as civilization itself. Greek, Celtic and Gallic warriors went to battle totally unclothed and armed only with spears, swords and shields.

Since there is virtually no privacy aboard military land bases and ships of the line, particularly submarines, it is important that male nudity is healthy and totally devoid of sexuality and sensuality.

The amount of nudity at Splinterville was no different, therefore, from any other barracks where military men were quartered.

The men casually walked about naked to and from the showers, their towels thrown over their shoulders. Many slept naked and some, like T.J., disdained shorts under their uniforms.

Hi-jinks in the nude, too, were standard fare and the more outrageous, the more laughable.

Each night, for example, after his shower, tall, lanky Greg Johnson enjoyed running naked at full tilt from the shower to his top bunk, giving an impressive Tarzan yell as he sped between the bunks. He would toss his towel and shaving kit onto his locker top and make a leap for the sprinkler system pipe nearest his rack, grab it and swing into his bunk.

One night while Johnson was in the shower, Pat O'Hara, who slept in the rack below, and some of the men who slept nearby, replaced the frame's springs on Johnson's rack with light string.

The word was passed and Billy, his roommates and most of the men in the bay, waited as casually as they could for Greg to make his appearance.

He emerged from the shower, emitting his jungle yell and made his leap. When he hit his rack, however, the strings snapped and he fell through to O'Hara's bunk.

He lay there for a confused instant, trying to figure what happened.

The uproarious laughter from his wing let him know he had been had.

"It doesn't take much to entertain us, does it?" T.J. asked dryly as he and his roommates turned to go back to their room to resume studying navigation.

Later the discussion turned from studying the helpful navigation notes Mr. Lee had shared, to tattoos.

T.J. was in his bed, in his boxer shorts, propped against the wall beneath his Confederate naval flag.

"How long have you had your tattoo, T.J.?" Bob asked, dropping his navigation text to his lap.

T.J. dropped his gaze to his bare chest as he placed his hand reverently over the red and blue USMC, in large, Gothic script.

"The day I graduated from boot camp. Some of me mates and I went to a tattoo parlor in San Diego to get them. It's over me heart, you notice. Do you like it?"

"Yeah," Bob said.

"How about you, Bill. Do you like me tattoo?"

"On you, sure. I don't think I want one, though," Billy said.

"I thought I might get a little one, someday," Bob said. "You know, small enough to be hidden under my wristwatch."

"What would you get?" Billy asked Bob.

"I don't know. Certainly not one of those tigers, clawing my arm. Maybe a little anchor, like Popeye's."

"I'll bet you've seen a lot of them, haven't you, T.J.?" Billy asked.

"Right. And a lot of them like this," he said, patting his chest again.

"Although I saw one bloke with big hinges on his elbows and knees."

"Man, I'll bet that hurt," Billy said.

"Probably. Me dad had bluebirds around his neck. I always meant to ask him if he was drunk when he got them, but I never did."

"Were you drunk when you got yours?" Billy asked.

"I don't know. I was so drunk I don't remember."

They laughed.

"And I saw one chap with a big screw on each cheek of his arse."

"A screw?" Bob asked.

"Right. Ship's screws. Propellers, you know."

"Oh."

"And get this: one chap at basic had decorated his Willie with a pair of snake's eyes, right on the foreskin."

Billy grimaced.

"Damn!" Bob exclaimed.

"Oh, it gets worse. Another bloke had decorated his with a red stripe, you know, like a barber's pole."

"On his pecker?" Bob asked for clarification.

T.J. nodded.

"Man! That's self-mutilation," Billy said.

"No worse than those chaps who have their foreskins surgically removed," T.J. said.

"You think so?" Bob asked.

"What else? God put them there. Why have 'em cut off? Who the bloody hell's going to look at his Willie, anyway, except the bloke himself, or his girlfriend? That's why they're called private parts, isn't it?"

"Still, a lot of guys are having it done," Bob said.

"I know," T.J. agreed."One chap told me so many of his mates had it done on a carrier cruise, the mess cook baked a Willie-shaped cake for the crew after the hundredth man was circumcised."

"The men ate a penis-shaped cake?" Billy asked with a look of disgust on his face.

"Blimey, Benson! It was just a bloody cake. Not like it was a real Willie or anything like that," T.J. said.

"Again, I ask you," T.J. continued, "why would any man want to have an operation to make his Willie smaller, I want to know? Most blokes want a bigger one than they've got, so they'll be like our mate, Peter Stiff, out there."

"Let's change the subject," Billy said. "This conversation is getting perverted."

*   *   *

THE FOLLOWING SATURDAY EVENING, Billy and Suzanne boarded the city bus that shuttled between the base and downtown Pensacola. They sat in different sections of the bus to lessen the likelihood they would be seen together.

Christmas decorations were already up in store windows and over the streets, however, the preponderance of palm trees, palmetto, live oaks, and cool, not cold, weather seemed to be incorrect for the season.

Virtually every other store on both sides of the streets appeared to be either a military uniform shop or tattoo parlor.

Throngs of people were milling about on the sidewalks and in the stores, shopping or looking at window decorations.

As the bus rolled past the Florida Theatre on Palafox Street, Billy noticed that the movie *Arizona Stagecoach* was playing, featuring two of his childhood favorites, Crash Corrigan and his young sidekick, Dusty King. He smiled to himself, thinking how, only a few years ago, he would have chosen that movie over a mushy romance like *Casablanca*, which they were going to see that evening.

They got off near the Saenger Theatre, where *Casablanca* was being shown.

Billy bought tickets at the box office outside the theatre and they walked up the long tiled and mirrored foyer that led to the lobby. A uniformed female usher met them and guided them down one of the aisles of the ornate theatre. She shone her flashlight on two empty seats for them.

A *March of Time* newsreel quickly covered the weekly news on both war fronts and news from the home front. The long, bloody battle between U.S. Marines and the Japanese for Henderson Field in Guadalcanal was finally winding down and the Russians had launched a counter-offensive against the Nazis at Stalingrad. The Andrews Sisters entertained wounded GI's in the ward of a Los Angeles Army hospital and more women's baseball teams were forming up as men were sent to fight.

Casablanca was good choice, Billy realized, not only for its patriotic theme, but also for the romantic story line. He recognized many of his favorite actors and with a little imagination, could see Suzanne as Ingrid Bergman's character, Ilsa.

Billy held Suzanne's hand throughout the movie, except toward the end, when she had to use both her hands to blot her eyes with a handkerchief and quietly blow her nose.

A light drizzle was falling when they came out of the movie. Billy waited outside until the bus arrived. He turned to her and raised his hand to get her attention. Again, they boarded the bus individually and sat apart.

Suzanne's car was parked near enough the bus stop that they didn't get very wet as they made a dash for the bus for the ride back to the base, where Suzanne had left her car near the front gate.

"I need to get in early tonight. I'm covering for Miss Harkins tomorrow morning," she said, as she started the car.

"Okay."

She drove to his quarters and shut off the engine.

"I enjoyed the movie. Thanks for going with me," he said.

"I liked it, too. Thanks for taking me."

He took her hand and looked at it.

He lifted her it to his lips and kissed the back of her fingers.

When he looked up, their eyes met.

She returned his smile.

Maybe she's beginning to trust me.

As he moved his face to hers, she leaned toward him and tilted her face.

He placed his hand gently behind her head.

Billy closed his eyes as he savored the sweetness and warmth and softness of her lips.

He could feel the stirring in his shorts and his strength leaving him.

She ended the kiss by pulling away slightly and turning her head, but she let him keep his cheek next to hers.

His eyes were still closed, as he thought of how he could remain like that for as long as she would let him.

Let the flight training go on without me. Let the war go on without me. Just let me be near Suzanne Walker.

"I need to go," she said softly, moving away from him.

He took a deep breath, inhaling the light floral scent and sat up.

He looked into her eyes and lifted her hand to his lips again. She smiled as he turned her hand over and kissed her fingers.

He leaned over again and gave her a quick kiss on the mouth.

"Thanks again. I'll call you."

"Okay. Goodnight," she said.

"Goodnight."

* * *

BILLY AND SUZANNE had only one more date, on the night before his Christmas leave began. Suzanne drove them to Martine's nightclub for an early supper before attending a Christmas concert in Pensacola. Afterward they drove slowly through the Spanish-inspired downtown business district to take in the activity and effervescent energy the holiday generated.

When they returned to the base, she again permitted him only one kiss, but she surprised him by pressing a small, wrapped gift into his hand as he prepared to leave the car.

He looked at it and felt the blood go to his face.

"Gosh, Suzanne. I didn't get you anything."

"I didn't give you that so I'd get something from you."

"I'm embarrassed."

"Don't be."

"Thanks. I really appreciate this."

"You're welcome."

"Wait. I *do* have something for you."

"Hm?"

He leaned over and gave her another kiss.

"There!" he said. "Merry Christmas!"

She smiled.

"And Merry Christmas to you."

When he walked into his room, he set the small package on his rack, sat sat beside it, staring at it.

Before their date that evening, he had wondered if there would be enough of a relationship to hope for a continuation when he returned from his Christmas break, especially if he were transferred to another base

The gift was a confirmation.

I'll send her a Christmas card from Riverton. And write or call her during final squadron. That should be a long enough period for us to know if we had a possible future together.

He looked at the gift.

Should I open it gift or save it for Christmas?

He didn't have to wonder long.

He untied the bow, carefully removed the paper and lifted the top from the box.

Inside was a pair of oval gold cuff links with the engraved wings of a Navy pilot.

He was overwhelmed. To him, the gift meant that she cared for him, that she shared his dream of his becoming a naval officer and pilot.

Perhaps she was saying she, too, had hopes for our future together.

Maybe I'm getting ahead of myself.

He removed one of the links and inspected it closely.

Hmm. They aren't new. They're used. I wonder what that means.

*   *   *

BILLY'S CLASS WAS GIVEN CHRISTMAS WEEK OFF. He had invited T.J. and Bob to go to Riverton with him, rather than leave them to spend the holiday in Pensacola. They boarded the train in Pensacola early Thursday morning, arriving late that evening in Riverton, two days before Christmas.

After the overwhelming swarming in the back yard, the group moved indoors.

"Blues and animals aren't compatible," he said as his mother handed him a whiskbroom to remove Buddy's hair from his uniform.

The tree was up, decorations were all around the house, colorful lights mixed with branches of pine were festooned over the front door and the fragrant smells of the season filled the house.

T.J. was accepted immediately by Billy's family and friends. That he was a Marine, Billy's friend and roommate, and an Australian made him special. And especially special for Billy's older sister, Alice, but her boyfriend correctly read what was going on and found ways to keep her occupied during T.J.'s visit.

After his first visit to Riverton, Bob had written thank-you notes to Billy's parents and to Uncle John and Aunt Grace. Following the death of Billy's Uncle Kenneth, Grace had her brother write Bob to formally invite him to visit the farm any time he wanted, with or without Billy. Bob had written back, accepting the invitation. During their Christmas leave, he slept in Uncle Kenneth's room, making it less crowded at the Benson's, with Billy and T.J. sharing Billy's room.

Of course, one reason Bob was eager to stay at the farm was that he secretly hoped Molly might be home on leave from the Army. He was already thinking of ways for them to share the spare bedroom in the loft of the barn. Unfortunately for him, her holiday leave would be over New Years'.

The days were barely long enough for Billy to see his civilian friends: Mrs. Watson, the Rileys, and Jim Hayes, as well as high school classmates who were also home on leave.

He was saddened to learn that Mark Walters and John Valentine, members of his senior class, had been killed in combat. Don Rimes was missing in action in Europe. Billy had not been especially close to any of them, but he knew, nevertheless, how their families must hurt.

And he knew there would be others.

His mother thought he looked tired.

His father thought he had matured.

Uncle John was overjoyed with his military bearing.

"You look more like a Marine every time I see you!" he proudly told Billy again the night he and T.J. drove Bob to the farm.

Uncle John and T.J. hit it off at once, comparing notes on California, basic training experiences and Marine lore. He, too, received an enthusiastic invitation to visit and stay at the farm anytime he chose.

Velma, the Benson's family cook, and Billy's mother cooked his favorite foods at every meal. T.J. was unfamiliar with turnip greens seasoned with salt pork, and Brunswick stew. Velma's rich, dark, chocolate pie called for seconds. T.J. had already eaten cornbread in the Navy, but he raved about Velma's, especially when she made it with cracklings.

The days flew by. They used up all his father's gasoline and accepted neighbor Sally Moore's offer of coupons, in their attempt to cover as much territory and visit as many of Billy's friends as they could.

Sally and Billy's great aunt Ollie, Aunt Grace, Uncle John, Bob, and T.J. gathered for Christmas dinner at the Bensons and spent nearly three hours at the table, eating and talking and enjoying each other's company. .

At church on Sunday, the minister, Dr. Allen, asked Billy and T.J. to stand beside him on the dais as Billy introduced T.J. and Dr. Allen welcomed the men home. He placed his hands lightly on their heads and asked a special blessing on them, their brothers-in-arms and a rapid end of the war.

They returned to sit with Billy's family. When the congregation stood to sing the Navy Hymn—*Eternal Father, strong to save, Whose arm hath bound the restless wave*—Billy had to fight back tears.

The continued deterioration of the Allies' attempts to turn the direction of war in the European theatre cast dark clouds over the men's leave-taking the Tuesday following Christmas.

Jim and Edna drove the three to the train station.

Billy's father kept his lips pressed tightly together as he bravely waved to the three as the train pulled out of the station. Edna waited until the train was out of sight and heading south before she broke down into tears.

Billy, Bob and T.J. arrived at the air station late afternoon.

Billy immediately called Suzanne, who was working the three p.m. to midnight shift on the ward.

"Let me come by long enough to say 'Hello!' "

"I'll be going to dinner at eighteen hundred. Meet me outside the ward then," she said.

"I'll be waiting," he promised.

After Billy had gone to chow with his class, he brushed his teeth, brushed his hair, smoothed his tie, and walked about anxiously, looking frequently at his watch, until 1745. He walked briskly to the hospital, pushed through the wooden doors to the stairs and ran up them, two at a time.

He could see her through the small glass windows in the ward's doors. She was at the nurse's station, talking to her ward corpsman.

He smiled when he saw her look at her watch and start for the doors where he was standing.

"Hey!" he greeted her as she walked into the passageway.

She smiled broadly.

"Hey, yourself."

"Is there any place we can kind of duck inside?" he asked.

"Maybe the doctor's office," she said, pointing to a door across the passageway.

"But we can't stay long, you know. It *is* his office."

"Oh, sure," he said, turning the knob and pushing the door open, allowing her to enter before he did.

He closed the door behind them and walked straight to her, wrapped her in his arms and kissed her long and passionately.

"Oh, Suzanne. I missed you so much. I thought about you the entire time," he said.

"I missed you, too. Thanks for the Christmas card."

"You're welcome. Did you have a good Christmas?" he asked.

"Probably not as good as yours."

"Thanks for the cuff links."

"You're welcome. Have you worn them yet?"

"Oh, no. As much as I'd like to. Not until I get my wings."

He kissed her again.

"When can I see you again?"

"This weekend?"

"Friday? Saturday?" he asked.

She smiled.

"How about both?" she asked.

"Great!"

"We need to leave."

"Okay. Just one more, for the road."

He took her in his arms again and was encouraged when he felt her arms around his shoulders.

He looked into her eyes.

"Suzanne Walker, I think I'm falling in love with you."

She put her finger over his lips.

"Don't rush into anything."

"Right."

*   *   *

WHEN THE MEN RETURNED from Christmas break, they received orders for advanced training. Half would be assigned to Barin Field and half to Bronson Field.

Billy would be transferred to the former, an out-lying field, or OLF, in Foley, Alabama. All satellite fields in the Pensacola area were under the command of NAS Whiting Field, in nearby Milton, which meant he would receive his wings in Pensacola.

Orders to Barin produced mixed reactions in Billy: He would be separated from Suzanne, but close enough to see her on weekends. That happy prospect was overshadowed by the reputation of Barin Field, however, known infamously as "Bloody Barin."

Bob had also been assigned to fighters at Barin, while T.J. and Barry received orders to nearby Bronson Field for multi-engine training. They would also receive their wings at Pensacola.

But before intermediate training ended, one assignment remained, however: a solo cross-country flight.

The men walked to their planes, looking rather like schoolboys, with parachutes under one arm and maneuvering boards under the other. Each performed the pre-flight inspections of their Vultees, climbed in, started their engines and took off one after the other, in a mighty cacophonous roar of pure, radial horsepower.

Billy grinned with pleasure as he anticipated what he considered an easy navigation assignment: north to Selma, Alabama, west to Meridian, Mississippi, and southeast over Mobile, Alabama, and back to Pensacola.

The skies were perfect for flying, cloudless and brilliant blue. Visibility was unlimited. The sun and skies reflected off the bodies of water that dotted the landscape, especially the rivers and marshes that made up broad, delta-shaped Mobile Bay.

He unfolded his Airways Chart to give it a quick perusal for prominent landmarks, to confirm their identity and location visually on the ground.

As he traveled north, he observed with idle curiosity the minuscule automobiles creeping along twisting and turning narrow roads below. Train rails made excellent landmarks to confirm his flight.

He marveled at this pilot's life he was fast discovering: flying for hours in a powerful plane through a perfect sky; a instrument-filled control panel before him that he controlled by a myriad of switches, controls, levers and pedals, and whose operation was now as second nature as talking, and, equally as important, knowing a beautiful woman he loved would be waiting when he returned to base.

As the men completed their missions by early afternoon, they met at their hangar and waited at the assignment board for the mandatory post-flight critique. One by one they arrived, eagerly reviewing their flights with members of their wing and discussing plans for the evening.

Finally, all were accounted for except Wrong Way Carrigan.

The men were getting concerned that he was nearly an hour overdue.

The flight operations officer, Mr. Springer, approached the wing.

Attention on deck!

"Stand at ease, men."

The men complied.

"I just got a call from Carrigan. He flew east instead of west and got lost. He landed before he ran out of fuel and we need two volunteers to take him some gas."

The men groaned.

"No wonder he's called 'Wrong Way,'" somebody complained.

"How long will it take, sir?" one of the men asked.

"I have no idea. Not less than three hours, I feel safe in saying."

No hands went up. The men were anxious to put all things intermediate behind them and hit the beach.

"Any volunteers?"

The men avoided the officer's eyes.

"Do I have to volunteer somebody?" Mr. Springer asked.

Still, no one spoke up.

"Okay," Mr. Springer said, pointing to T.J., "I volunteer you and..."

Billy raised his hand.

"I'll go with him, sir."

"Okay, you two. Come with me. The rest of you hang around for your critique."

Billy asked Bob to call Suzanne and tell her he would be delayed.

Mr. Springer led Billy and T.J. to his office.

"Thanks for volunteering, mate," T.J. said as they made their way.

"All for one," Billy reminded him.

"We've got some Stearmans ready for you," Mr. Springer told them after arriving at his office.

Billy and T.J. looked at each other. Even though they were on the Gulf Coast, it was late December and the chill factor from the air rushing through the open cockpits would be brutal.

They had mistakenly assumed they would be flying Vultees.

"The Vultees may not be able to land or take off if Carrigan is on a short field. I only hope he'll be able to get it back into the air," Mr. Springer added.

"Where is he, sir?" Billy asked.

"In a field outside Eclectic, Alabama."

"Where's that, sir?" T.J. asked.

"Damned if I know," Mr. Springer replied. "We're going to have to look it up on a map."

Eclectic was so small it wasn't on any Navy maps.

One of the plane captains from Alabama had a road map he brought into Mr. Springer's office.

"It's here, sir," the sailor said, pointing to a dot on the map. "North of Montgomery and just west of Auburn. It could have been worse," he added.

"How's that?" Mr. Springer asked.

"It might have been Flea Hop."

"That's a town?" Billy asked.

"Right. And that isn't on any maps."

"We'll need to change into some warmer clothes, sir." Billy said.

"You're right there," Mr. Springer agreed. "Have a safe trip."

Billy and T.J. changed into their cold weather clothing issue: long underwear, leather jackets, helmets, gloves, a scarf. They walked to the flight line where cans of gasoline had been placed into the bed of a pickup truck. They carefully transferred and secured the gasoline in the front cockpits of two Yellow Perils. They performed their preflight inspections, climbed into the rear seats of the planes, snugged their helmets tightly over their heads, buckled them under their chins, pulled the goggles down and wrapped the scarves about their faces.

After plane captains wound up their starters, Billy and T.J. taxied to the runway and lifted off.

Billy had the road map he would use to follow roads from the air, to the field where Carrigan was waiting. T.J. flew 10 feet behind, 10 feet below, and 10 feet to the right of Billy's plane.

They located the town and then the field as the sun was getting low in the west. Carrigan was vigorously waving to them from the ground. Several cars and trucks were parked near the airplane and people were standing around as the Stearmans circled for their landings.

Billy and T.J. landed their planes and after a brief, friendly exchange, the three began tanking up the Vultee's wing tanks.

They replaced the empty cans in the N2S's storage compartments and opened the engine compartments to retrieve the cranks they would need to energize their starters.

Neither man could locate a starter crank.

"Okay, Wrong Way. You'll have to fly back and tell somebody to send us a crank," Billy said.

"Okay."

Carrigan looked in his engine compartment for a starter crank, but none was there, either.

"Don't worry," he said. "I can crank this one with the starter."

He climbed into his cockpit and began his start-up procedure. He held down the battery-powered starter that turned a flywheel which would, in turn, start the engine.

The engine wouldn't catch.

"I think it's flooded," Wrong Way called to his friends on the ground.

"It's set on *full rich*?" Billy asked.

"Yes."

"Ignition switch to *both*?" T.J. asked.

"Yes."

"Well, give it another go," T.J. said.

Carrigan held down the starter again, only to hear the motor that turned the flywheel grinding slower and slower until the battery was too low to be of any use.

"Okay, Wrong Way," T.J. said. "Ask one of these gentlemen to take you to a telephone. Call Saufley and tell somebody to send us a crank before it gets dark."

Wrong Way climbed back down from his plane, dropped his parachute onto the wing and left in the truck with one of the locals, followed by the entourage.

"Let's see if we can get a little shuteye while they're gone," T.J. suggested.

They climbed into the Vultee, closed the cockpits and promptly fell asleep. They were awakened by the sounds of the cars returning.

They looked out to see the same three cars bumping across the field.

"This must be the only game in town," Billy commented.

"Mr. Lipscomb and one of the mechs are going to bring us a crank from Saufley," Carrigan said. "Since it's probably going to be too dark to land, he said they'll make two low passes and drop it on the second pass."

He pointed to the farmer who drove him back.

"Mr. Jackson and his friends will make a triangle with their cars and shine their lights so Mr. Lipscomb will know where to drop the crank."

The three locals positioned their cars and the six men stood around, waiting for the plane to arrive.

Just as the sun was setting, they heard the sound of a Stearman approaching from the southwest.

The men jumped into their cars, started them up and switched on their headlights.

The Stearman dropped low and passed overhead slowly, turned and to everybody's surprise, landed.

The pilot, Mr. Lipscomb, jumped from the plane, leaving the engine running, followed by the mech. Mr. Lipscomb was swearing like the proverbial sailor, as the two approached the gathering. Bevis, the mech, was trying to defend himself.

"Bevis dropped the f***ing crank on the first pass," Mr. Lipscomb said, gesturing with his thumb at the luckless mech. "He was supposed to wait until the second pass," he said, still fuming, his fists planted firmly on each hip.

"Did any of you see it drop?"

Nobody had.

"Did you hear it hit the ground?"

"The car motors were running and your plane was too noisy for us to hear, sir," Billy said.

"Okay, scatter out. Let's see if we can find it," Mr. Lipscomb said.

The men scoured the area, but were unable to locate the crank.

"Well," Mr. Lipscomb said, glaring at Bevis, "the only thing to do now, is for me to get back to Saufley. Bevis, you stay here. I'll need to make a short takeoff and your weight will interfere.

"If one of these gentlemen will be so kind as to take you three to a hotel or rooming house, you guys stay over and somebody will be back at 0800 tomorrow and drop you a whole, f***ing sea bag full of cranks. Okay?"

"Aye, sir," Wrong Way said.

"Bevis, I want you to stay here, right here, in this pasture, with the planes tonight. Make sure nobody damages them and if a herd of cows decides to stroll over for a midnight snack, run them off. Can you do that?"

"Aye, sir."

Mr. Lipscomb returned to his plane, kicking the dirt with the heel of his shoe and swearing with every step he made.

When Mr. Lipscomb was out of earshot, Bevis made one more effort to defend himself.

"I dropped the crank on his command."

Carrigan turned to Bevis. "Don't worry about it. I brought some snacks along. They're in the cockpit. Help yourself."

Bevis smiled for the first time since he arrived.

"Thanks."

Mr. Lipscomb gunned his plane and lifted off into the rapidly darkening sky.

Billy, T.J., and Wrong Way climbed into Mr. Jackson's car and the procession headed for Eclectic.

The three cadets had only four dollars and some pocket change among them, but Mrs. Thomas, a tall, gregarious woman who operated the only rooming house in the small town, as well as serving as the town's telephone operator, said she trusted the men and let them owe her for a night's lodging. Billy called Suzanne to apologize for canceling their date and then joined his friends in the dining room as their hostess began serving them an ample and much-appreciated home-cooked fried chicken dinner with mashed potatoes, home-canned green beans, hot biscuits, and gravy.

When the three men were shown to their room, there were only two beds in it: one double four-poster and a small trundle bed that pulled out from under the larger bed. Billy and T.J. agreed initially to sleep in the four-poster bed together and Carrigan was given the trundle bed.

"On second thought," Billy said to T.J., recalling that his Marine friend always slept in the nude, "you're not sleeping in your birthday suit, are you?"

"Sorry, mate. I could sleep in shorts in a pinch, but not these long johns," T.J. replied.

"Okay, Wrong Way," Billy said, motioning toward the double bed. "You sleep with Nature Boy."

"Why me?" he protested.

"Because you got us into this predicament."

Carrigan watched as T.J.—185 solid pounds of hairy, muscular Marine—peeled off his long underwear and climbed naked into the bed.

T.J. pulled the sheets to his waist and patted the unoccupied side of the bed.

"Come, on, mate," he said to Wrong Way, a wicked smile on his face.

"Uh. I'll think I'll sleep in that chair," Carrigan said, pointing to a wing chair in the corner of the room.

*　　*　　*

"MATES," T.J. ANNOUNCED to Bob and Billy, "Since the Navy, in its infinite wisdom, made us return from leave in the bloody middle of the week between holidays, I've got a little surprise for you."

Billy and Bob waited for him to continue.

"I thought I'd have a little New Years' luau for you and some of the other blokes in our wing and, of course, a few damsels."

"What's a luau?" Billy asked.

"Spoken like a poor, misguided mainlander," T.J. replied.

"A luau is a great feast we hold on the islands, always outside, often on a beautiful beach. The guest of honor is a pig, roasted whole, and lots of other delicious treats, like baked fish, poi—one finger or two, depending on how thick it is—sweet potatoes, pineapple, bananas, papayas, mangoes, coconuts, macadamia nuts, and mai tais.

"Oh, yes. And ukulele music, although me mum used to say if you ate sweet potatoes with pineapples, you could make your own Hawaiian music."

"What's poi?" Bob inquired.

"Taro root that's been pounded into a paste. It's really nasty stuff. People eat it only because it's a tradition."

"What's a mai tai?" Billy asked.

"A mixed drink served over ice. Rum and lime juice and a few other tasty ingredients. I'm going to make me own Aussie version of it, however. Light and dark rum, vodka and citrus fruit juices. Quite delicious—and bloody lethal, I might add."

"Where do you plan to find a whole pig to roast?" Bob asked.

"I've got that all taken care of. You just find some girls who like to hula-hula and be at the Marine barracks' chow hall at eight o'clock New Year's Eve. Grass skirts for the girls is optional.

"And I'll need a little monetary backing. Five dollars a couple. Okay?"

Okay.

When Billy and Suzanne and the other guests arrived, the chow hall had been transformed into a Marine grunt's version of a Hawaiian beach. Gunny Gillespie and the Marines who performed most of the guard duty on the base, had constructed palm trees from heavy, cardboard linoleum rollers and real, albeit contraband, palm fronds, hacked from a grove behind Fort Barancas. A huge yellow cardboard moon had been nailed to the bulkhead behind the palm trees. Nets borrowed from local fishermen were hung about, adding atmosphere and the unmistakable faint aroma of dead fish. A sand "beach" had been poured onto a large drop cloth.

On the central table on a fishnet tablecloth was displayed the culinary guest of honor: a pig carved from commercial, restaurant-sized logs of Spam. The Spam had been decorated with chunks of sweet potatoes, sliced pineapples and bright red cherries, all of which had been baked in a brown sugar, clove, rum, and raisin sauce.

An aromatic shrimp dish made with pineapple chunks and their juice, soy sauce, ginger, and garlic, stood steaming and ready in a large rectangular pan over a Sterno burner next to a large bowl of cooked white rice.

Bananas and cracked coconuts lay decoratively about the table.

An enormous steel cook pot with handles held the beverage *du jour*: the juice of pineapples, lemons, limes, and oranges, fortified with vodka and the two kinds of rum as promised, chilled by a large block of ice.

Colorful crepe paper leis hung on either side of the entry.

A phonograph played scratchy 78 rpm records of Hawaiian music.

T.J. was barefoot, his trousers rolled up to his calves, sported a hat made from palm fronds, with the ends sticking out all around, and one of his colorful tropical shirts.

"Leis for the lasses first, lads. You can have any leftovers," T.J. instructed as the guests arrived, mostly men from their wing and nurses from the hospital, along with a few female civilians.

"What's with the fishing poles?" Barry asked, pointing to the pair of vertical bamboo poles with one horizontal one attached.

"We're going to have a limbo contest," T.J. announced proudly.

"I didn't know the limbo is Hawaiian," Barry commented.

"It isn't. Neither is the ukulele, but that doesn't mean we can't enjoy them, does it?

"But before we get started, let me read you a little poem from the *Bayou Tale Spinner*, the base paper over at NAS New Orleans.

He cleared his throat noisily.

The moon was yellow, he read, pointing to the artificial moon behind him,

The lane was bright,

As she turned to me on that Autumn night.

Ah!

Every movement, every glance

Said to me she craved romance.

I stammered and stuttered while time fled by.

The moon was yellow…

And so was I.

Everybody laughed appreciatively.

"All right, mates. We Marines have done all we can do for you squids to set the mood. Whether you want to be yellow or not is up to you."

The men made lecherous passes at their girl friends.

"Okay," T.J. invited, strumming on his ukulele, "let's get everybody loosened up. Come on up and try a bit of me Aussie Mai Tai punch.

"Come on, ladies. Don't be shy."

As the alcohol in the punch began dislodging inhibitions from members of the gathering, some of the women set their punch cups aside and performed their versions of the hula-hula, cheered on by the gathering.

After some of the couples tried to dance to the Hawaiian music. T.J. signaled for one of the Marine privates to put on some faster music. He started off with Woody Herman's *G.I. Jive*, on a black, 10-inch disc, which filled the floor instantly with energetic jitterbuggers.

When it came time to eat, T.J. informed the crowd that fingers would have to do the work of forks and knives. Feeding each other quickly became a merry variation on the theme of spontaneity, encouraged by the quantities of liquor consumed.

The rum and vodka had its effect on Billy, too, who thought everything was hilarious, especially when T.J. won the limbo contest.

After passing underneath the horizontal fishing pole, T.J. stood and shook his joined hands over either side of his head the way a victorious prizefighter does. He presumed everyone was shouting and screaming approval because the pole was barely three feet from the deck when he passed under it.

"It's not what you think, T.J." Billy called, wiping tears from his eyes as everyone looked on and listened.

"Oh?" T.J. asked, innocently. "What do you mean, mate?"

"You split your pants at the crotch when you went under the pole," Billy said.

"Oh," T.J. commented, looking down to see the evidence for himself as his friends continued looking and laughing.

"And you're not wearing any skivvies."

"Oh! Right!" he said calmly. "It did seem a bit drafty."

Shortly after 2300, Billy suggested to Suzanne that they sit on the steps outside the chow hall and talk, despite the cold January air blowing from the bay.

"Let's get in the car. It's getting too cold out here," he suggested after only a few minutes.

He suddenly seemed different to her. She looked at him suspiciously for an instant before climbing into the rear seat of her car.

Her look was well deserved, for Billy, emboldened by the liquor, had determined to have his way with her that night. His kisses were hard and forceful. The inside surfaces of the car's windows car became completely covered with steam.

His hands pressed against her soft body as he forced her flat on the seat and his free hand groped her breasts and slid down her thigh and moved under her skirt.

His mouth was pressed so tightly over her mouth she was unable to speak. She pressed her hands against his shoulders in an effort to move him off her.

He used his strength to subdue her, but in an act of desperation, she twisted her head, pulled free and shouted at him, "Stop, Bill! Stop!"

He was deaf to her command.

He was oblivious to her hands pushing desperately against him.

He did feel—and hear—her hand as it angrily slapped him across his face.

He looked into her eyes in the dim light and saw fierce, burning fury and resolve.

He pulled himself off her and fell back onto the seat. He was breathing heavily.

She sat up and straightened her clothes.

They sat in silence.

He was too embarrassed to speak.

She was too angry.

Presently she spoke tersely between pressed lips.

"I need to explain something to you before you walk back to your quarters."

Billy looked into her face.

"I was raised right, I want you to know that," she said, jabbing at the air with her hand to emphasize her words.

"I know what a lot of people assume about single women in the military. But a lot of us aren't here because men are everywhere and easy to get."

She paused before continuing.

"Before I came into the Navy, I dated a doctor for a long time. I loved him and wanted to marry him. After we were engaged, he began to put pressure on me to go to bed with him. I wouldn't do it. But he kept it up. Every time we were together, he said if I really loved him, I would sleep with him."

She stopped again.

"So I did."

Billy swallowed.

She was less angry now and feeling more in command of the situation.

"The next day he called me every name he could think of. He said only one kind of a woman sleeps with a man before she marries him."

Billy's head lurched back with surprise.

"He hurt me more than anyone ever had. Not physically, but emotionally. And you, Bill Benson, you are the first man I've dated since Steve. Believe me, I know about young men who are away from women and all that. But listen to me, Bill Benson, if you think I'm going to make the same mistake twice, you've been going out with the wrong girl."

Billy's brain swirled dizzily. He, too, had been "raised right" and on this night he had tossed away all he had been taught at home and at church. All he had learned and believed spun inside his head and collided with his carnal craving.

He had had only one burning thought when he left the party that night: to seduce Suzanne. He knew that would have been wrong, but he hadn't cared. In his youthful lust and emboldened by false courage from the alcohol, he displaced all propriety with licentious desire.

He had wanted to take her virginity and her to take his.

But now the realization that he was the virgin and not she, at once wiped out the scenario he had anticipated: that two virgins in love with each other would be deflowered simultaneously; that they would, by mutual and romantic consent, be equal partners in the amorous act.

And now that she had informed him she was not a virgin, he was chauvinistically judging Suzanne, as her seducer had done.

He and his Uncle John had had this conversation long ago, one night at the farm, when Billy had indicated that he understood it was unfair for the man to expect the woman to remain unsullied, while the man chased and seduced anything he could catch.

He sat silent.

She waited for him to speak.

He cleared his throat.

"I-ah, I need to think. Uh…" and he blew air from his lungs.

He pulled the door handle. He stepped outside and closed the door. He stood motionless, his hands against the roof of the car.

She got out on the other side of the car and closed the door.

"I'll call you," he said quietly, turned and began walking to his quarters.

Except for the man on watch, the barracks were empty when Billy arrived.

Before leaving the head, he looked at his cheek, still bearing the red imprint of her hand.

He left the light off in his room as he removed his clothes, draping them over the desk chair.

He stood at the window.

His brain continued to whirl with what had transpired and Suzanne's disclosure. He tried to force himself to begin making sense of the emotional quagmire in which he found himself.

I was wrong.

I acted indecently, ungentlemanly.

I violated her trust, something I would have never done to one of my friends in Riverton and definitely not to one of my mates.

He was ashamed and angry with himself.

He felt he could never forgive what he had done and couldn't expect her to, either.

He climbed into his bunk and lay on top of the sheets, starring at the ceiling, listening to the steam clanging and echoing in the radiators throughout the building.

Outside, he heard whistles and sirens blowing and the rapid cracking of fireworks ushering in 1944.

What a rotten way to end the year.

* * *

AFTER SUNDAY BRUNCH the next day, Billy was in his rack, reviewing the SNJ manual, in anticipation of final squadron.

T.J. entered the room with a small volume under his arm.

"Hello, Bill, me boy!" he called out cheerily

Billy mustered a smile and responded, "Hey, T.J. How are you?"

"Wonderful!"

"Did you enjoy the party?"

"Yes, I did. Thanks. You did a good job. Sorry I didn't stick around to help you clean up."

"Me Marine mates did it. A trade for all the leftover food and drink. I had to borrow a pair of trousers."

T.J. removed his uniform and hung it carefully in the closet. He went to his bureau drawer and removed a pair of shorts. He pulled them on, snapped the waist and walked to his bed. He shifted his pillow to the foot of the bed, fell onto his rack and stretched luxuriantly. He opened the book he had brought and began to read to himself.

A half-hour passed.

"Bill?" T.J. asked.

"Yeah?"

"Listen to this."

T.J. tossed his pillow to the head of his bed and leaned against it as he read aloud:

Shakespeare, Sonnet One Hundred Sixteen.

Let me not to the marriage of true minds
Admit impediments. Love is not love
Which alters when it alteration finds,
Or bends with the remover to remove:
O no, it is an ever-fixed mark,
That looks on tempests, and is never shaken;
It is the star to every wandering bark,
Whose worth's unknown, although his height be taken.
Love's not Time's fool, though rosy lips and cheeks
Within his bending sickle's compass come;
Love alters not with his brief hours and weeks,
But bears it out even to the edge of doom.
If this be error, and upon me prov'd,
I never writ, nor no woman ever lov'd.

Billy had dropped the manual he had been reading, as T.J.'s rich Australian accent lyrically stroked the Elizabethan sonnet.

Americans shouldn't attempt to read Shakespeare aloud, Billy decided.

When T.J. finished the reading, Billy sat up and looked down across the room at his friend.

"I changed 'man' to 'woman' in that next-to-last line," T.J. explained. I thought it sounded better."

"Read it again," Billy said.

T.J. complied with the request, reading the passage a bit more slowly and with more feeling.

"Love is not love which alters when it alteration finds…" Billy recited. "And what was the next line?"

"Or bends with the remover to remove. O no: it is an ever-fixed mark, That looks on tempests and is never shaken."

"Why did you read that to me?" Billy asked.

"I thought it was appropriate."

"Appropriate for what?"

"The way things are."

"The way things are?" Billy asked. "Have you talked to anybody?"

"Well, now, let me see. Oh, yes. To the mess cook at chow this morning. He nearly splattered SOS on me shirt. And of course to the librarian when I checked out this book just now."

"To Suzanne?"

"Suzanne? No. Should I have?"

"What a fool I am! What a moron!"

He tossed the manual aside, jumped to the deck, bent over T.J., and kissed him on the cheek.

"T.J., I love you!"

"Well, thanks, mate. I'm fond of you, too, but isn't this rather sudden?"

Billy smiled, threw on his uniform, dashed out the door, and double-timed it to the nurses' quarters.

He rushed into the lobby and stopped one of the nurses he knew.

"Kay, would you see if Suzanne is in her room?"

"Sure. Just a minute."

Billy paced back and forth as he waited.

The nurse returned.

"She took Bev's shift this morning. She's on the ward until eighteen hundred."

"Thanks," Billy called, as he dashed out the front door, letting the screen door slam behind him.

He walked rapidly to the hospital, slowing down and saluting smartly whenever officers' cars passed.

Inside the front lobby of the hospital, he asked the duty corpsman at the information desk, "Which ward is Miss Walker on today?"

The medic looked at the lighted board on the bulkhead behind him.

"Ward F. Up the ladder here to the second deck."

Billy dashed up the stairs, down the passageway and pushed through the ward's double swinging doors like a provoked cowpoke itching for a saloon fight. He walked briskly down the polished aisle between the neatly arranged beds covered with blue and white striped cotton spreads. The pharmacist's mate and patients looked up as he strode past them, straight to the nurse's station where Suzanne was seated, working on patients' charts.

He took her totally by surprise. She looked up just as he reached her desk, a look of determination on his face. She had no time to respond.

He went behind the desk, took her by the arms and pulled her to her feet.

"Suzanne Walker, I am the biggest fool on the face of the Earth, but I'm smart enough to know that I love you and that I want you to marry me," he announced.

The patients on both ends of the ward stopped talking and sat up in their beds or stood beside them for a better view of the duo at the nurses' station in the center of the long room.

"Bill," she began.

"Don't say, 'Bill.' Say 'yes.' "

The patients leaned closer.

"I'm not sure I even want to talk to you."

"You will if you love me."

"Bill, we've known each other for just a few weeks."

"Long enough."

"Bill."

"Don't say 'Bill.' Say 'yes.' "

"Bill."

"I know my name. Tell me you'll marry me. Say, 'yes.'"

She broke into a smile.

"Yes, Bill. Yes, I'll marry you."

"And will you forgive me for making a bleedin' arse of meself last night?

"Yes, Bill. I forgive you. And I love you, too."

The men on the ward broke into shouts, whistles and applause.

Billy pulled Suzanne into his arms and kissed her fiercely, knocking off her nurses' cap in the process, as their audience continued its noisy, enthusiastic endorsement.

SNJ's—"The Texan"—on ramp at Barin Field, Foley , Alabama
(Source: Curtiss Silvernail)

CHAPTER FOUR
ADVANCED TRAINING
BARIN FIELD, FOLEY, ALABAMA

W ITH 65 FLIGHT HOURS in primary and 75 in intermediate
training behind them, all Billy and other members of the
"final squadron" needed for graduation were another 75 hours in
the air, approximately the same number of hours of ground school,
plus a similar number of hours devoted to military and physical
training, to complete the requirements for the V-5 program

Three months.

Twelve weeks.

Just twelve more weeks.

The survivors of the gaggle of raw troops that had entered the V-
5 flight program some 10 months earlier in Athens, Georgia, had
steadily evolved into uniformly physically fit, superbly trained, and
highly-motivated naval pilots, soon to be sent out to the fleet to
apply what they had learned and experienced toward bringing the
world war to an end.

And in only 12 weeks, all on one monumental day in his young
life, 3 March 1944, Billy would graduate from flight training,
receive his commission as a Naval officer, pin on the coveted Navy
wings of gold, and marry Suzanne.

While never doubting his eventual success in the program, Billy
nevertheless had not permitted himself to become overconfident
with his progress in the program or the prospects for what lay
beyond commissioning. He couldn't become lax, for cadets were
still being cut from the program for technical as well as academic
failures, including the maddening Morse code tests, plus, with the
deadly, notorious reputation of Barin Field looming ahead of him,
there remained the very real possibility that he could be injured for
life or killed.

On the Navy bus taking the cadets to their advanced training, the
mood was upbeat and energetic. Preflight, primary and intermediate training had been the same for all: learning to fly basic trainers.

This final leg of preparation, however, was what the men on this bus had long been anticipating, some since childhood: fighter training, with its challenging aerial dog fights, gunnery training, and bombing practice.

All had seen, at least once, the 1927 Academy Award-winning silent film, "Wings," not for the love interest between two World War I pilots and the "It" girl, Clara Bow, but for the vicarious thrill of the incredible and exciting dog fighting sequences.

T.J. had once confided to Billy how, as an adolescent, he replayed images of the movie's dogfights to keep his hands off himself in his bed at night.

"In that scene," he had excitedly and dramatically recounted, "where the German pilot in his Fokker D-Seven, with those evil-looking, squared-off goggles and black leather helmet, that pencil-thin mustache and demonic grin, in a forty-five degree dive angle, his twin Spandow machine guns blazing away as he chased down the doomed Allied pilot...To me, that was the only thing more powerful than the sex drive."

At Barin Field, the men could at last fulfill their aggressive dreams of being fighter pilots.

Now, the men thought, we'll separate the falcons from the finches.

A fighter pilot rockets unimpeded, breakneck through the clouds at speeds up to 300 miles an hour, five miles above the earth, while those on the ground rattle along at a snail's pace of only 35 miles an hour.

On land, the fighter pilot runs when others walk.

He walks when others drive or hitch rides.

He stands when others sit.

He sits when others lie down.

His body is always taut, charged.

The fighter pilot is intelligent, curious, energetic, adroit, confident, demanding, driven, aggressive, prone to recklessness, often raucous and quite frequently the exhibitor of a rather perverted sense of humor and finally, if he is not totally arrogant, he certainly borders on it.

Billy knew he didn't quite fit the mold and and that made him work even harder.

The next important 12 weeks would determine if he was, indeed, cut out for the inherent danger and prestigious title of fighter pilot. The outcome would, of course, indicate the direction the rest of his military and personal life would take.

He was mentally, physically and emotionally prepared for final squadron. He was, as T.J. frequently enthusiastically expressed-- motivated.

The bus drove west along the natural beaches of the Florida pan-handle, across the narrow bridge that led to Alabama's pristine, undeveloped beaches, dotted by occasional cinder block vacation cottages and one locally-owned hotel, to Gulf Shores. It turned north on Highway 59, a typical two-lane, sparsely traveled country road that led northward through Baldwin County—known for its fertile potato and strawberry fields, pecan, peach, and satsuma orchards—to Foley, Alabama, a small, country crossroads town. The bus turned east on Highway 98 and slowly passed between the married enlisted and officers' quarters on either side of the road until it turned onto a narrow road that led south a few yards to 950-acre Barin Field, opened only two years earlier in 1942, and named for Lt. Louis T. Barin, Naval Aviator No 56, who was killed in a plane crash.

Between 1942, when flight training began, and 1944, 6000 cadets were trained at Barin but 40 of them were killed, giving it the record for the highest mortality figure of any one naval flight-training site. Consequently, the outlying field became infamously known in the fleet as "Bloody Barin."

Did its namesake curse the field named for him? Billy won-dered.

After the aviation cadet nephew of famed news correspondent Drew Pearson revealed the dubious record to his uncle, Pearson publicized the revelation in his nationally syndicated Scripps-Howard newspaper column.

Some blamed the high fatalities, however, on British Royal Air Force cadets, who unlike the Americans, had not grown up working on Model A's. The Brits, it was joked, knew only two positions on their throttles: wide open and closed completely.

After the bus passed through the main gate, the cadets moved to the row of windows on the right side. They could see the two fields ahead: East and West. Each had four asphalt runways, the longest one of which was 4000 feet and separated by four hangars, before which now stood row upon neat row of hundreds of gleaming SNJs, lined up precisely across the ramps, facing the hangars.

A cluster of easily forgotten buildings behind the hangars to the north, provided housing, medical, and administrative support for the cadets and the sizeable staff that was needed to maintain the 400 SNJ fighter trainers— "Texans," or "J Birds"—a handful of OS2Us (the Vought Kingfisher, the Navy's most popular floatplane) and N2S Stearmans, the familiar Yellow Perils.

The driver stopped the bus beside the extraordinarily tall flag-pole that rose in front of the wood frame administration building, oddly topped by a partial second story smack in its center.

"Take your orders inside and begin your check-in procedure," the driver said mechanically, as he swung open the double-hinged door and pointed.

After leaving their records with the duty yeoman, the men marched to the Cadet Barracks, a sprawling, two-storied frame structure rising from a pine tree setting. The rooms were consider-ably more inviting than those in Splinterville: newer, cleaner, with six men to a room, sharing three double-deck beds and a lavatory. The standard open heads were located at the ends of the buildings.

The base was quite small, especially when compared to Memphis or Pensacola. Everything north of the airfields was arranged more or less in a square around the baseball field: their quarters, the crews' quarters, the Aviation Cadets' Recreation Center, known as the Ac Rec—complete with billiard tables and bowling lanes, chow hall, gymnasium and library, which doubled on Sundays as a chapel—officers' club, bachelor officers' quarters, hospital, hobby shop, swimming pool and exchange. The airfields, nearly a quarter of a mile away from their barracks would be reached by marching in formation, still their exclusive means of transportation on base.

The popular saying among the men, "If you go to Barin, you can't leave," referred to the isolation of the base. One passenger train passed through Foley daily. Since cadets were not permitted to drive cars, free military bus service to Pensacola and other Navy fields was available.

Telephone calls to Pensacola, only 34 miles to the southeast, but across the state line, were considered long distance and expensive for the cadets.

For those who wanted to try their hand at farming as a weekend distraction, local farmers around Foley welcomed sailors who wanted to help in picking fruit or harvesting potatoes, the biggest crop in the agrarian community.

In Foley and in communities all across America, the United Service Organization—the USO—provided weekend entertainment for all military personnel. The traveling entertainers put on shows as well as dances at the bases, attended by busloads of single women in each area that were welcome and refreshing weekend diversions.

The girls of the nearby and unique Single Tax Colony of Fairhope—a charming, scenic, artist's retreat on Mobile Bay's eastern shore—who came to the dances, teased the young cadets with shorts they rolled up to reveal more flesh. The men who preferred better odds, however, traveled over the bay to Mobile.

The proximity and easy access by train and bus to Mobile on the weekends provided opportunities for the men who longed for the special kinds of comfort provided by the hundreds of young women who had come from far and wide to replace men at the large, bustling shipyards.

The women quickly discovered they could serve their country in more ways than just constructing ships.

Since the majority of the women tended to be independent, free-spirited, adventurous and "available" for bar dates and other, more intimate adventures, many of the libido-charged cadets, with an ample supply of cash and cache of Navy-issue condoms in their wallets, filled the coaches and regularly took advantage of the prospects for meeting and possibly bedding, one or more of the accessible riveters, welders and grinders in the port city.

As they excitedly prepared for weekend liberties on Friday afternoons, the hopeful cadets were wont to strike up the chant, "No soap in Fair-hope! Big deal in Mo-bile!"

Other than those brief weekend diversions, the men were trapped in an isolated outlying field with nothing to do but study, fly and stay occupied the best way they could.

Fortunately, the men could entertain each other. So many of them had been together from the beginning of their training, they were now close—as close as any fraternity or even blood brothers.

Bob Hawthorne and Billy were assigned to the same room, along with Peter Stiff, Chris Singleton, Nick Overstreet, and Tom Lumpkin.

Billy had known Peter in intermediate training and had wondered about his name at their first meeting, as possibly everybody else did. Since the military recorded each man by his last name first, it was necessary to resist the natural urge to permit one's eyes to drift southward to determine if Stiff, Peter, proved to be a name or a graphic erotic display.

Who would give a son a name so fraught with sexual innuendo? Billy had wondered.

On the contrary, Peter showed no discomfort with his name. In fact, he left no question that it was a proud manifestation of his personae, since he bore as an audacious emblem the actual, visceral appendage, a literal, corporeal namesake.

Peter had always thrown off his clothes as soon as he arrived at the open bay berthing spaces in Splinterville and enjoyed parading about, bull-bold nude, to and from the head and, it seemed, especially in the mornings, when his appendage, a veritable genital gerund—a noun used as a verb—was fully realized as both a proud moniker and a physical state.

Too, Peter made no secret of his passionate attraction to women. He lusted after them openly, pinned up voluptuous Vargas nudes inside his locker door and, like an enthusiastic mechanic with a unique power tool, he wasted no time in finding ways to display and demonstrate his special talent whenever he was with females. He claimed to be a modern day Don Juan, seducing women right and left.

His reputation was confirmed by the perfumed letters that arrived daily, in which women begged him, he said, for his manly ministrations. He even claimed he was seduced by one of the Barin Field nurses—on a sofa in the lab—when he went to sick call one evening to have a splinter removed from his hand.

Consequently, Peter Stiff was on the bus nearly every weekend, bound for Mobile.

Adding to another level of his sexual resume, was his refusal to use condoms.

I'm a bareback rider. Always have been, always will be.

He boasted of having impregnated two women already, both of whom he had refused to marry.

Ironically, he was engaged to marry Miss Amy Scott, the daughter of the rector of St. Paul's Episcopal Church in Spring Hill, an exclusive community just west of Mobile, where the well heeled could escape the heat, mosquitoes and war-time commotion found in town. A talented piano student, the studious, attractive and virtuous Miss Scott, of course, knew nothing of the sexual exploits of her fiancée.

In all honesty, Billy would have to admit Peter was probably not much different from the other men in his overt, casual nudity or sexual activity, just that he possessed a larger package.

The studying and training demands fortunately took precedence over sexual "bull sessions" which Billy did not particularly enjoy. He could always find other things to do to prevent being drawn in to such.

Additionally, Billy was relieved Peter did not lie about their room naked.

The new men who joined them at Barin were welcomed into their company, quickly becoming assimilated into the wing.

Two transfers—identical twin Marines, Gary and Barry Lucas— were assigned a room across from Billy's. Only their nametags made it possible to distinguish one from the other. They may have had a speech or stuttering problem, for Billy noticed when the one who was speaking, paused, perhaps to prevent repeating a sound, the other immediately picked up the conversation. When the second one abruptly paused, the other picked it up again. They were so expert in their methodology, it was a nearly seamless conversation.

The pair seemed to have two identical, albeit independent bodies but shared the same mind. Their cheery dispositions, sparkling wit and indissoluble loyalty to each other very quickly made them favorites of all the men.

As had been the routine at primary and intermediate training, physical conditioning remained a fixed segment of the cadet's daily schedule: calisthenics, sports and military drill.

When their formal introduction to the base and instruction began, Billy was impressed with the large number of mechs on board—over 130. But he wondered if the cadets should be comforted to know that 25 full-time firefighters, seven crash trucks, one crash crane truck and four ambulances were standing by at all times.

And the plane they would fly was the legendary SNJ Texan.

A real plane, at last!! the men expressed to one another. Not a trainer, *per se*, as had been the endearing little Yellow Peril or the cumbersome and deafening Vultee Vibrator. The SNJ Texan, the third and final plane the men would pilot, was actually used in combat as a fighter or bomber.

*   *   *

THE ARMY AIR CORPS authorized the Texan in 1937, to be used as a combat-effective trainer or combat plane. The Army referred to the plane as either the Texan or the AT-6.

Its manufacturer, North American Aviation, had once been an aviation division of the General Motors Corporation, which had emerged independently from the parent company in 1935, and relocated in Inglewood, California.

The original plane, known as the NA-16, was designed principally by chief designer R.H. Rice and James Kindelberger as a low-wing, full cantilever airplane. It featured an all-metal wing, steel-tube fuselage, removable fabric-covered side panels and single-leg, fixed landing gear.

In 1938, the British government ordered a version of the NA-16A to be known as the Harvard. Its wingtips were more rounded, the rudder more squared off and powered by a constant-speed propeller.

Improvements and changes continued, including a controllable-pitch propeller and retractable landing gear. A high-pressure oxygen system permitted pilots to attain an altitude of 26,000 feet. A relief tube for distended bladders extended flights considerably.

When World War II broke out, virtually every Allied country with a military—33, in fact—ordered the AT-6/SNJ. Ironically, even Italy and Germany—members of the Axis Powers—procured a number of the planes for their air forces before hostilities broke out. The versatile plane could be rigged as a fighter, with guns mounted in the wings, or as a bomber or even for use in aerial photography.

Difficult to taxi but easy to fly, with proper maintenance the Texan was practically indestructible. It proved to be the nearly perfect combat plane and quickly became the most widely-used trainer of the war.

Unfortunately, the SNJ turned out to be as noisy as the Vultee. Pilots stuffed their ears with cotton pulled from bulkhead-mounted dispensers in their ready rooms and pressed their headphones against their ears to help block the noise of the powerful nine-cylinder, air-cooled, 550-horsepower Pratt and Whitney R1340-AN-1 radial engine.

The auditory inconvenience mattered little to the cadets, however, for the Texan was the plane that would take them from bucolic Barin Field in rural south Alabama to the adventurous combat zones of the Pacific.

*   *   *

AS HAD BEEN THE CASE with the previous two trainers, hours of ground school familiarized the cadets with the SNJ's technical specifications, its cockpits and instrument panel.

And, as he always did, Bob Hawthorne counted the controls in the front cockpit.

"Look at this!" he exclaimed to his roommates, all of whom had been quietly engrossed in their own lessons. "Sixty-one gages and power plant controls, and that doesn't include the electrical control panel. And look!" he said, pointing enthusiastically to the control stick. "A gun selector for cowl or wing guns. Here's the gun trigger switch on the top of the joystick!"

He pointed with his fingers and broke into a staccato *Ba-a-a-a-a-a-a-a!* to simulate gunfire.

"And look at this! A bomb-release switch! Man! I can hardly wait to take this baby up!"

Billy smiled at his roommate's enthusiasm, crawled from his rack, stretched, excused himself and walked to the pay telephone in the lobby to call Suzanne and invite her to drive up for a dance Saturday night.

"It'll be so late, I wouldn't want to have to drive back afterward," she said. "Do you think you could find out if I could stay in the nurses' quarters?" she asked.

"I'll see what I can do," he promised.

The only officers he knew were his ground school instructors.

Maybe Mr. Chambers would help me. He seems easy to get along with.

The next morning as his class was heading outside for muster, Billy caught up with Mr. Chambers, on his way to the instructors' ready room, to pose Suzanne's request

"Why doesn't she just plan on staying with my wife and me?" Mr. Chambers asked.

"You can stay, too, if you'd like. You two could share the extra bedroom."

Billy smiled.

"We're not that, uh, intimate, sir," Billy explained.

"No matter. Just tell her to plan to stay over with us. My wife's going to be one of the chaperones and she'd be happy to have another gal to go to the dance with."

Billy thanked Mr. Chambers and called Suzanne again.

"I don't know, Bill, that just seems kind of strange, you know?"

"Well, I don't know anybody else to ask. Maybe you could call the hospital or something."

"Okay. I'll get there around seventeen hundred. Will we be able to eat somewhere?"

"You know I'm still unwashed enlisted trash," he reminded her. "You could eat at the O Club or in the hospital mess. Or, there's a gedunk where both of us could go."

"That'll be all right. We'll eat a hamburger and some greasy French fries at the gedunk," she agreed. "I'll bring along a bottle of antacid tablets."

"Okay. I'll meet you in front of the admin building. It's where the only flagpole is on base. You can't miss it; it's about four stories high."

When Suzanne drove up Saturday afternoon, T.J. was in the front seat with her and Barry and two women were in the back seat of the car.

"Miss Casey! Miss Riley! T.J.! Barry! Welcome to Bloody Barin," Billy said as he opened the doors.

"Good to see you, mate!" T.J. said, pumping his hand. "Barry and I wanted to check out your digs, to compare them with our luxurious accommodations over at Bronson."

The dance was held at the gymnasium. Music would be provided by the base band, known as the Barin Bombers, made up of base crewmembers and led by a chief petty officer.

After Billy introduced his friends to Mr. Chambers and his wife and explained that Suzanne would be returning to Pensacola after the dance and wouldn't stay overnight with them, Mrs. Chambers quickly said, "Well, I expect the grand march with you, Mr. Benson. And then, you, Mr. Macintosh."

"Candy" Chambers held on to Billy as the men made one large circle and the other women formed another for the grand march. As the band played and the circles began rotating, whoever landed together were partners for at least the first dance.

Billy and Candy danced together, not only the first dance but the second and third as well. Billy was the least bit annoyed that Suzanne was in the clutches of Peter Stiff. He hoped she had told Peter whose guest she was.

T.J. and Barry were enjoying themselves on the dance floor with two girls from Fairhope who had worn short, pleated skirts that offered brief glimpses of petticoats and even panties and lots of leg as they energetically danced the jitterbug.

Billy waved desperately to T.J. for relief. Candy Chambers was a jitterbug fanatic and Billy was sweating profusely.

Mr. Chambers eventually rescued Billy and danced with his wife, making it possible for Billy to break in on Suzanne and Peter.

Candy Chambers left her husband immediately and broke in on T.J. and his dance partner.

"I thought I'd never get away from her," Billy said with some frustration in his voice. "Could you see what she was doing to me while we were dancing?"

Suzanne shook her head.

"She kept grabbing me arse," if you'll pardon my Australian French.

"Are you serious?" Suzanne asked.

"And they had wanted you and me to spend the night with them," he added, privately wondering what she would have thought about the arrangement. "I think you were right when you suspected something strange was going on with them."

He was tempted to share a conversation he and his Uncle John had had about couples he knew of in California who enjoyed swapping sex partners.

Suzanne didn't respond to his previous comment. She was focused on Candy Chapman and T.J, who were now slow dancing.

"Look!" Suzanne said, nodding toward T.J. and his partner.

T.J. had a curious look of befuddlement on his face. The side of Candy Chapman's face was pressed contentedly against his chest and both her hands were firmly gripping his buttocks.

"I think your flight instructor should spend less time in the air and more time at home with his wife," Suzanne said.

*   *   *

THE FLIGHT SYLLABUS each man received outlined the amount of time and order of training to be followed in final squadron: aircraft familiarization, formation flying, acrobatics, cross-country, rocketry, bombing and strafing. Except for the latter three areas, the curriculum was a review and refinement of training they had learned in primary and intermediate schools.

"Now, let me review some definite 'no-no's' for you," Lt. Chambers began in his ground school aircraft familiarization lecture.

"The landing gear. This is the first plane in which you've had to raise or lower the wheels. The Navy wanted to wait until you've had enough experience under your belts before you got this added challenge. As soon as you're sufficiently airborne, clear of the ground, push the hydraulic power control forward.

"Never, never, never push the handle forward while you're on the ground. There isn't a safety mechanism to prevent the gear from retracting. But I saw it happen when I was in final squadron. Some Dilbert activated the handle while he was sitting on the mat and the plane just slowly sank to the deck, like it was a big balloon and somebody was letting the air out of it.

"On the other hand, if you're about to land and the landing gear isn't locked in the down position, a warning horn will sound when the throttle is slowed for landing.

"And I want you cowboys to keep your itchy thumbs off the bomb release switch. Ditto for your fingers on the gun trigger switches."

Billy sneaked a glance at Bob, who winked at him.

"Now, follow along with me on that handout I gave you.

"No outside loops. Got that?

"Repeat after me: No outside loops, ever."

No outside loops, ever.

"One hotshot I know tried it once. Lucky for him North American built a plane strong enough for such abuse. He made it back safely but without any dihedral left.

"What's the dihedral, Mr. Hawthorne?"

Bob stood beside his desk and snapped to attention.

"The upward slope of the wing, sir."

"Very good, Mr. Hawthorne. Be seated.

"Okay, no inverted flight in excess of ten seconds. You might find yourself without power and falling like a stone, nose first, straight to the ground.

"Repeat after me: No snap rolls in excess of one hundred and ninety knots per hour."

No slow rolls in excess of one hundred and ninety knots.

"No solo flights from the rear cockpit."

No solo flights from the rear cockpit.

"Don't dive at speeds over two hundred and forty knots."

Don't dive at speeds over two hundred and forty knots.

"If you do," he added with a smile, "You might try to pull up and find you've left your wings behind."

"Finally, men, we cannot emphasize safety enough.

"I know all of you are anxious to get out into the fleet and bag a few Zeros but if you don't follow exactly the correct procedures for piloting the Texan, you'll be sent home in a box.

"Go slow.

"Go cautious.

"Go home alive."

*   *   *

BILLY'S FLIGHT INSTRUCTOR was a Marine captain, Bob Mosley, who had served in the Pacific before being trained as a flight instructor. He looked to be in his late thirties, but Billy found out from one of the plane captains, "Skippy" Marks, that Mosley was barely 28 years old.

"Combat does that to 'em," Skippy had told Billy. "We've got a chief here who was in the Aleutians for a year. He looks like he's fifty but he's only in his mid-thirties.

"When you see him it the shower, it's really weird. He's got the face of an old guy but the body of a young man."

Capt. Mosley met Billy at the assignment board. He returned Billy's salute and shook his hand.

"Let's sign the yellow sheet and then check out the plane, Mr. Benson."

On the flight line, Billy met his plane captain, "Zoomie" Willis and laid his parachute on the elevator to begin his preflight inspection.

"Always check your propeller carefully, Mr. Benson," Capt. Mosley said "On one of my pre-flight checks, I found a chunk missing from the backside of it. Enough that it probably would have unbalanced the prop and either slung it off in the air or while we were on the ground, killing who knows how many."

Billy completed the inspection and climbed into the front cockpit.

He stuffed cotton in his ears and pulled his helmet snugly over his head, fastened it under his chin and plugged the jack for the headset into his helmet.

The Texans were equipped with two-way communications: each cockpit had a microphone and helmet earphones.

After Zoomie had climbed onto the wings to assist both men with their shoulder harnesses, Capt. Mosley spoke to Billy.

"Go ahead and adjust your rudder pedals and seat level."

"Aye, sir."

"Is the ignition switch off?"

"Aye, sir."

"Set your parking brakes."

"Aye, sir."

"Make sure all armament switches are off."

"Aye, sir."

"Landing gear control handle in the *down* position."

"Aye, sir."

"Unlock the surface control lock."

"Aye, sir."

"Set your altimeter to the correct barometric pressure. Do you know what it should be for Barin Field?"

"Seventy-four feet, sir."

"Correct. Never forget to do that, Mr. Benson. It could save your life some day."

"Aye, sir."

"Place the battery-disconnect switch in the *on* position."

"Aye, sir."

Billy completed the remainder of his check off before pressing the foot-operated starter pedal to activate the inertia motor.

When the engine started, he signaled to Zoomie to pull the wheel chocks. Billy turned the plane into the wind, set the brakes and waited for the oil pressure to build. When it reached 70 pounds per square inch, he opened the throttle to rev the engine up to 1000 rpms.

He rotated the fuel selector to check the reserve, left and right fuel systems, electrical controls, wing flaps—both hand operated and hydraulic—and other flying controls for free movement, made further propeller adjustments, set the elevator and rudder trim tabs, the mags and released the parking brakes.

"Ready for takeoff, sir," he said to Capt. Mosley, over the intercom.

"Very well, Mr. Benson."

Billy taxied out toward the take-off area, making his zigzag way with the other planes and halted for a clear view of approaching planes. He make a final check of his generator line, confirmed that the fuel mixture control was set to *full rich*, and the fuel selector on *reserve*. He made one more check of his fuel pressure, prop control and carburetor air control. He confirmed that his wing flaps were up and the gyro instruments uncaged.

He completed the check and when permission to proceed to the runway was granted, he paused and concentrated on the lights in the tower.

When the green light flashed, he pushed the throttle forward, taking care to keep the tail wheel on the tarmac to prevent any possible torquing action of the plane, produced by the spinning propeller. As he approached takeoff speed, he slowly raised the tail, pulled back on the stick and rose into the air.

As soon as they were clear of the ground, Capt. Mosley came back onto the inter-com.

"You can push your hydraulic power control lever forward now, Mr. Benson," he said.

"Aye, sir," Billy responded with a nod of his head.

"And retract the landing gear."

"Aye, sir."

Billy took the landing gear handle in his left hand and pulled it up and back. He was unable to hear the wheels pull into their wells under the fuselage but he suddenly felt vulnerable, the way he imagined a legless man in bed might feel.

His reflection was short lived.

"Ease back on your throttle, to thirty-two and a half inches of mercury."

"Aye, sir."

"Your propeller control should be about twenty-two hundred rpms."

"Aye, sir."

"Have you been checking out possible emergency landing sites?"

"Aye, sir."

"Climb at one hundred fifteen miles per hour, IAS.

"You know that term, IAS, don't you?"

Billy lifted his microphone to respond.

"Aye, sir. Indicated air speed."

Mosley nodded his head. "I don't mean to insult your intelligence, Mr. Benson, but since my life is in your hands, I prefer to leave nothing to chance."

Billy smiled and nodded.

"Aye, sir."

"Swing westward and climb to five thousand feet. We need to check out our air space."

"Aye, sir."

As the plane banked to the right and continued its steady, roaring ascent, Billy watched in awe and fascination as the landscape beneath the plane became a literal patchwork quilt of fields, pastures and farmsteads.

The sun was behind him, permitting a glorious, unlimited view to the west.

The brilliant, blue Gulf of Mexico came into view to his south.

Immense cloud formations in the brilliant blue sky sailed ahead of him like frothy, weightless, floating islands of cotton.

He shivered from the sight that so few could ever experience.

A silver ship, sailing serenely in the upper seas of heaven.

Once he had attained 5000 feet, Capt. Mosley came back on the intercom.

"Would you show me your outside loop roll, Mr. Benson?" he asked.

"Negative, sir. Those are not permitted."

"Very good, Mr. Benson. How about inverted flight?"

"Not to exceed ten seconds, sir."

"Right, again. Let's see what you can do."

Billy complied and performed the inverted flight maneuver.

"Very good. How are your slow rolls?"

"Good, sir."

"Okay, show me one."

"Aye, sir."

Billy visually cleared the area, pushed the throttle forward to accelerate the plane's speed to 140 knots, sighted the horizon to confirm that the nose of the plane was level with it and in one fluid motion, pushed the control stick to the left as he pressed the right rudder, taking care to keep the nose up, since there was no lift in the wings during the seconds they were vertical during the roll.

"Very good, Mr. Benson.

"What are the limits on a snap roll?"

"Not in excess of one hundred thirty knots per hour, IAS, sir."

"Correct. Show me one."

"Aye, sir."

"How about another?"

"Aye, sir."

"Can you do an eight-point slow roll?"

"Aye, sir, but it needs work."

"Try it anyway."

"Aye, sir."

The eight-point roll required precise control to stop the wings at eight measured points in the roll. The level of difficulty is increased in maintaining altitude, since the vertical position of the wings compromises the amount of lift available.

"You're right. It needs work," Captain Mosley confirmed after Billy's demonstration.

"Aye, sir."

"Let's see another inverted flight."

"Aye, sir."

"Barrel roll?"

"Aye, sir."

For nearly an hour, Billy demonstrated the maneuvers he had learned in primary and intermediate training, all to Capt. Mosley's satisfaction.

"Alles gut, Mr. Benson. You're a good pilot. You must have had Marine instructors."

Billy smiled.

"Thank you, sir."

"Okay, let's take her home. Since the east and west fields are so close together, we'll have to be extra watchful when we enter Barin's air space."

"Aye, sir."

The euphoria of a successful introductory flight was shattered by the intrusion of approximately 100 other SNJs returning to base at the same time.

Following Captain Mosley's instructions, Billy flew north, fell in at the end of the single column of planes ahead of him, 500 feet over Highway 59 leading to Foley. He made a right turn and headed east to the duty runway, which was always determined by wind direction.

His eyes darted up and down and all around as he entered Barin's air space. He had no desire to be another bloody statistic.

"Landing gear down."

"Aye, sir."

"Flaps down."

"Aye, sir."

"Mixture *rich*."

"Aye, sir."

"Prop pitch *low*."

"Aye, sir."

Billy felt perspiration soaking through his clothes as he kept his eyes on his surroundings and instrument panel as he corrected his air speed.

Suddenly, he missed the simpler days of flying the Yellow Peril.

*   *   *

IT WAS JUST A BROKEN PENCIL POINT, a barely visible piece of black graphite lying on the deck in the room that Billy shared with his five roommates. The men had stood confidently at attention that Friday morning, their arms stiffly at their sides and chins pulled into their chests as the inspection party entered the open room and spotted the offending discrepancy right away.

Despite its small size, it was enough to ground all six of the men, meaning they would be required to attend Extra Military Instruction, or EMI, Saturday, and remain confined to base all weekend.

Not only would he not see Suzanne, he and his fellow delinquents would be at the discretion of the officer of the day for punishment.

On Saturday morning, the men reported to the yeoman at the administrative office with the other cadets who had accrued penalties that week. Wrong Way was already there. He was such a regular at the Saturday morning sessions, he had taken on the duties of a staff member.

The men drew pieces, dummy M-1 rifles, at the armory and for four hours performed close order drills, marching to specific commands with the rifles.

They were dismissed at 1200 for chow, to return for two more hours of close order drill, followed by instructions to report to the chief of the day at the hangars, at 1600, for two final hours of punitive EMI.

The 20 or so men marched in formation to the open door of Hangar One where Chief Duffy was leaning against the door opening, drinking a cup of coffee from a thick, white mug. He was wearing khaki shirt and pants, black tie and a leather flight jacket. His chief's hat was placed on his head at a salty angle.

He was gazing intently at the tree line far beyond the ramp and didn't even look at the cadets when they halted on the ramp and broke formation.

"I'll bet you fellas have noticed how clean our ramp always is, haven't you?"

The men waited for the chief to continue.

"But I bet you never gave a thought how we keep it that way, did you?"

The men looked at the acres of asphalt where the rows of Texans were parked.

"Prop wash keeps the ramp cleaned off, but the shit gets blown out there in the wire grass," he said, motioning with his mug.

"Guess what you're going to do for the next couple hours."

The men looked again at the expanse before them

The chief motioned once more with his mug as he spoke.

"Get one of those cardboard boxes over there in the corner and form a line along the front of these hangars and start moving forward, picking up all the loose shit. Don't stop until you get to that line of trees out there.

"Watch out for fire ants, though. They've been known to bring a full-grown bull to his knees."

"Pick up paper, cigarette butts, litter, anything and everything on the ramp and paper and any other shit out there in the grass. When you reach the trees, turn around and come back and pick up what you missed on the first pass. I want those boxes full when you get back."

The men each silently picked up boxes that had BRIG RAT in bold, hand-lettered letters on each side and took positions along the front of the four hangars and began the slow task of policing the area.

At around 1700, as the sun was about to set and the men were slowly making their way back to the hangar, one of the men in Billy's wing, Rick Shawley, known as "Rickshaw," was walking toward them. He had a local girl on one arm and his Navy blanket under the other.

"Hey, guys!" he called cheerily.

The girl smiled shyly.

"We're going out there to watch the night ops."

The men laughed and nodded knowingly.

Night ops. Sure! We know what kind of night ops you're talking about.

The men continued to work their way slowly back to the hangar, scanning the ground for any litter they had missed on the first sweep.

Chief Duffy was still leaning against the hangar door, nursing another mug of Navy coffee.

The sun had set and the lights had been turned on inside all the hangars and on the ramps in front where the SNJ's were lined up.

"Okay, let me see what you've got in those boxes."

The men paraded in front of the chief, holding their boxes for his inspection.

"Okay. Dump'em in that shit can over there. Stack'em back up where you found'em and go on to chow."

As the men were emptying their boxes into the large metal trash-can just outside the hangar door, they heard panic-stricken shouting from the darkened field beyond the ramps.

They could barely see two white figures in the lingering twilight, shouting hysterically and running madly toward the hangars.

It was Rickshaw and his girlfriend, both stark naked, screaming, jumping and wildly hitting at themselves with their hands, frantically running as if their lives were at stake.

The chief shook his head and grunted. "Fire ants," he said, as Rick and his girl disappeared inside the door of the sick bay.

"Dumb shits."

*   *   *

THE CADETS POLISHED THEIR FORMATION, night, cross country and acrobatic flying, day after day in the Texans, in preparation for one of the highly anticipated elements of fighter pilots: combat flight training.

Brief ground school lectures and "chalk talks" explained and demonstrated the objectives of aerial combat.

"Remember, men, that surprise is your greatest advantage," gunnery officer Lt. Hardy told the cadets.

"Deflection shooting is a U.S. trait. Neither the Japs nor the Krauts use that technique and I don't know why they don't. Of course, it's to our advantage that they don't, because the side of your enemy's plane is a target too big to miss.

"They like to shoot head on or from the rear, but those are only fractions of the size of the fuselage.

"In deflection shooting, you come at the enemy from his side and you start firing before he knows what hit'im. You're sure to get the pilot or the engine. If you're good, you'll get both.

"When your enemy is in sight, remember, the man with the greatest altitude has the advantage.

"If he sees you, however, he'll position for the top spot.

"Move fast. Strafe his side and get under him as soon as possible, out of his line of fire. Come back around and fill your windshield with his plane. Blow him away from underneath.

"What's going to happen, though, when he sees you, is that both of you will start making a lot of passes over or under each other. We call that scissoring."

Mr. Hardy demonstrated with his hands as he continued.

"Back and forth, back and forth. And all the while, you've got to keep your altitude.

"Watch the horizon. Watch the ground. Watch him.

"Don't let'im take the high road.

"Never let'im out of your sight. Never. You'll have to turn your head back and forth and around and around like an owl to follow his plane. By now you should have developed your hundred and eighty-five degree vision. You have to know where he is at every moment, because, the very second you get sloppy or lazy is the second he'll take the advantage.

"Get sloppy and you're a goner.

"Get lazy and you can just kiss your sweet, white ass goodbye."

*   *   *

THE WING SUITED UP and checked out the SNJs to practice the first exercise in dog fighting.

Billy and Bob Hawthorne were teamed up. They were instructed to climb to 5000 feet and fly to the north end of Baldwin County to safe air space to explore, experiment and refine the crucial art of air dominance.

They began slowly, getting the feel of passing each other, turning their heads, looking over their shoulders to follow each other. As they gained confidence, they sped up their passes, turns and reversals.

The head-twisting exercise reminded Billy of the little toy black and white Scottish terriers, outfitted with magnets of opposing polarity he used to amuse himself with. There was no way one could sneak up on the other: as one approached the other's electromagnetic field from any direction, the other would spin quickly to face his aggressor.

Whenever one of the two friends assumed the strategic higher altitude, the other would quickly do the same.

After nearly an hour of non-stop scissoring, their necks were sore and tired from the constant rotating, keeping each other in eye contact. Consequently, they became less and less vigilant and eventually lost sight of each other in the clouds.

Billy circled widely to search for Bob, who had, unknown to Billy, elected to perform the same maneuver but from the opposite direction.

Suddenly, there was a break in the clouds and there they were: two planes on a deadly collision course, closing in on each other at 180 knots per hour.

Bob was banking sharply, clockwise, his plane still in a vertical position, speeding toward Billy's plane, which was in a horizontal position.

Without thinking, Billy instantly and reflexively executed a snap roll to his right, holding the vertical position as the momentum forced him away from Bob's lethal path.

The bottom of Bob's plane filled Billy's cockpit canopy, seemingly in slow motion, passing directly and only feet underneath his right wing. Billy saw one large, fat, black rubber wheel, tucked tightly in the plane's wheel well, zoom past him, as well as a sudden, brief flash of daylight around the aileron in the trailing edge of Bob's right wing.

When the planes had safely passed each other, the two men slowed down, looped back, leveled off, and met up, wing-tip to wing-tip. Billy shuddered visibly for Bob's benefit, looked over to his friend and dramatically wiped his brow. Bob nodded enthusiastically and blew air from his lungs.

Billy gave the hand signal to head back for the base.

Bob nodded, patted his head, pointed to himself and took the lead.

It was then that Billy became aware of the wet warmth spreading in his shorts and darkening his flight suit.

He couldn't expect it to dry before he joined his wing for the debriefing that followed all maneuvers.

That mattered little to him. He was alive. That was what counted.

A little embarrassment and gentle ribbing won't be a burden, he convinced himself, especially when considering the terminal toll the afternoon encounter might have taken.

*   *   *

Returning from a night operation in what had begun as a three-plane formation, Billy and Bob Hawthorne landed and waited just inside Hangar Two for their instructor, Mr. Coleman, to arrive and critique their performance.

"Mr. Stiff seems to be missing," he said upon entering the hangar. "All of you secure for tonight and we'll talk about this when all of us are here."

Billy and Bob saluted and returned to their quarters.

At 1000—ten hundred—mandatory time for lights out, Billy and his roommates had showered, turned out the light in their room, slipped between the sheets of their racks and promptly fallen asleep.

Billy was awakened just past midnight by "Snuffy" Smith, the barracks watch.

"Bill? Wake up," Snuffy called, shaking Billy's shoulder.

Billy rolled over and opened his eyes.

"Hey, Snuffy," he said huskily. "What's up?"

"I just got a call from the flight line. Peter's crashed his plane."

Billy slid up and braced himself against the bulkhead behind his rack.

"What happened?"

"We don't know yet. Just that he crashed his plane in Mobile. That's the second time that's happened."

"You mean for Peter?" Billy asked.

"No. For a Barin cadet being killed in Mobile. Another one was buzzing his girlfriend last year and hit one of the towers on the big cathedral downtown and crashed."

"Was he killed?"

"Oh, sure."

"And there's no word if Peter is alive or not?"

"Not yet."

"Is there anything any of us should be doing?" Billy asked.

"No, but if I hear anything else, I'll let you know."

"Okay. Thanks," Billy said, as Snuffy left, closing the door behind him.

Billy got out of his rack and walked unsteadily across the darkened room to the window. He stood there, looking out over the tall, shadowy, pine trees that surrounded the barracks.

His mind tried to focus on the event. He wondered if he should pray for Peter. He didn't know what to pray, since he didn't know if Peter even had actually crashed and if he had, was he living or dead.

Bob stirred.

"What's up, Bill?" he asked sleepily.

"Snuffy just came in to say that Peter crashed his plane," he answered.

Bob propped himself up with his elbow.

"Is he dead?"

"Dunno. Snuffy said he'd let us know if he hears anything."

After breakfast the next morning, Mr. Coleman met with the wing and announced that Peter had been killed when he hit a church steeple in Mobile.

"That's all we know right now," he said. "We'll keep you informed."

The rest of the story came in piecemeal over the next few days:

Peter had left the formation over Mobile, without permission, where he planned to buzz the house of his girlfriend, Amy Scott, before he returned to Barin Field.

Amy's father, Doctor of Divinity Charley Scott, was in the basement office of his uncompleted church, St. Paul's, across Old Shell Road from the parsonage, where she was practicing Chopin's thunderous *Revolutionary Etude* on the piano.

Wartime shortages had curtailed construction of anything not vital to the war effort and the church could not be finished until the war ended. The steel framework, however, had been erected and the exterior brickwork completed. The interior of the church was a cavernous, empty space. The roof had been shingled, but the tall, slender steeple was as yet only the towering, steel framework of a great needle pointing to heaven, built sturdy enough to support a 2½ ton carillon. Dr. Scott wanted it to be the tallest steeple on the Gulf Coast.

Peter had made one pass, two passes, three passes, each time at a lower altitude.

On the third pass, he failed to see the dark, pointed, metal skeleton protruding from the roof of St. Paul's church against the gigantic, live oak trees that grew in profusion in the area.

The steel propeller of the plane made unforgiving, grinding contact with the steel steeple, producing a shower of sparks. The wounded projectile continued on in a plunging nosedive over a narrow ravine to the adjoining campus of Spring Hill College, where it partially buried itself in the side lawn of the library.

A startled Dr. Scott ran from his study at the loud, shattering clamor that had interrupted his sermon preparation for Sunday.

An astronomy class of second-year Spring Hill College Jesuit novices in long, black cassocks and Roman collars were in front of the library studying the surface of Mars through a telescope when they heard the plane hit the steeple. They watched in stunned horror as it crashed on the opposite side of the library.

The young men picked up their long skirts and dashed to the plane. One of them jumped onto a wing and reached through the broken Plexiglas canopy, unlocked it, pushed it back and unfastened the harness holding the motionless young pilot in his seat.

"Hurry, Aaron. Before the plane catches fire," one of the students called out.

The young man released Peter's harness and pulled him from the plane. The other students reached their hands under the cadet's limp body to hastily carry him from harm's way.

When they were a safe distance from the plane, the men gently lowered Peter to the ground. Aaron pulled off the pilot's helmet and felt his neck for a pulse.

"Is he alive?" one of the students asked.

Aaron looked blankly at his friend for an instant and then shook his head slowly.

The young men knelt in a circle around Peter, crossed themselves and bowed their heads in prayer.

Miss Amy Scott continued practicing her concert piece, totally unaware of the demise of her fiancé.

* * *

THEIR SCHEDULES AND THE DISTANCE between them prevented Billy and Suzanne from spending much time with each other while Billy was in advanced training. Their courtship was restricted by several factors, which more or less dictated that Saturdays were the most expeditious times for them to be together: he was still enlisted, after all; and they had to be careful where they were seen together; gas rationing kept them close to their bases; and finally, his limited salary. They might drive to town and mingle with the crowds on the sidewalks or department stores or wander through public parks or sit in a quiet corner of the lounge at the nurses' quarters, since her friends knew of their engagement and understood the wartime situation they were in. When it was time for her to go on the wards or for him to leave, she would drop him off at the Marine Corps barracks where T.J. had arranged for him to stay overnight whenever he was in Pensacola.

When they both had the opportunity to attend a beach party at Gulf Shores, they eagerly made plans to go.

She drove over from Pensacola with some of her nurse friends and he hitched a ride in Alphonso Larkins' rusting, 12-cylinder Lincoln, driven by his girlfriend from nearby Point Clear, an exclusive enclave of summer homes owned by blue-blooded Mobilians.

The car was a legend at Barin Field. The paint was peeling, the headliner in shreds and Alphons, as he was called, had placed plywood over the holes in the rusted floor. That it had been driven all the way from Memphis, Tennessee—by whom, Alphons would not say—was a feat in itself. Once when he boasted of the gas mileage the car got, he was quickly reminded that happened because the relic was pushed or towed much of the time.

By the time Billy and his friends arrived that Saturday afternoon, Suzanne, T.J. and Barry were already there, along with a sizeable gathering from the Navy Nurse Corps and the cadet flight program. A fire had been built, tubs filled with iced beer and soft drinks, a volleyball net was in place and music from car radios filled the air.

The women wore civilian one-piece swimsuits but the men wore Navy issue dark, form-fitting, knit brief suits with white belts.

At dusk, as the group jostled for positions around the fire to roast hot dogs on long sticks, one of the planes from Barin passed overhead, heading south over the Gulf. It was flying low enough for the party to read the numbers on the tail.

Less than a half hour the same plane returned, bound for Barin Field.

Approximately an hour later, when the couples at the party had had their fill of hot dogs and burnt marshmallows, they settled down in pairs on blankets for what T.J. called "beach maneuvers."

The same plane passed over them, heading once more for the Gulf of Mexico.

It was only minutes before the beach party was rocked by the sound of an explosion just south of where they lay. Everybody sat up suddenly and looked southward to see a red fireball rising far out in the dark waters of the Gulf.

"What the hell was that?" Alphons asked, jumping onto the hood of his car for a better view.

"Beats me," Bob Hawthorne answered, pointing. "It looks like that plane dropped a bomb on a ship or something."

Monday, back at the base, the word circulated that Chief Duffy and Zoomie Willis had rigged a bomb underneath the wing of an SNJ and dropped it onto a Nazi sub.

"I don't know who started that scuttlebutt," the chief said when anyone asked him about the rumor

Zoomie, likewise, was mum on the matter.

Throughout the war, there had been rumors on every U.S. coast that Nazi submarines had been spotted. In the Gulf of Mexico, from Galveston to New Orleans to Miami, reports were made concerning the presence of a German sub, operating in full view on the surface, possibly running its engines to recharge the batteries.

It had been confirmed earlier that one Nazi submarine ran aground near Fort Morgan, a Confederate fort on the south-easternmost point of Mobile Bay, not far from Foley, and the bewildered crew was captured by alarmed Baldwin County farmers, armed with pitchforks and axes, not unlike in scenes in the old Frankenstein movies.

Some of the techs in the hangar had begun the rumor about the bombing of the Nazi submarine. They had surmised that the chief, who was a NA—a naval aviation pilot who had earned his gold wings—and the plane captain had perpetrated the deed. The rumor was based on the frequent clandestine sessions at the chief's workbench, late into the night. Too, it was well known that Chief Duffy had been trying to design a method of suspending a bomb from underneath the wing of a Texan trainer.

Evidently, he had succeeded.

Confirmation of the attack would have to wait until 1953, however, when records of the Nazi high command were released: a Nazi submarine had, indeed, disappeared while on patrol in the Gulf of Mexico on the night the two obscure enlisted men from Barin Field delivered a knock out punch to one of *der Fuehrer's* U-boats with a jerry-rigged, homemade bomb.

*   *   *

"WE'LL FLY TO COTTON BAYOU," Mr. Hardy said, "where you'll see four white crosses arranged in a two-hundred foot circle, with a fifth one in the center. Aim for the center cross."

The men were preparing to go on their first bombing exercises.

"Today we'll start easy, making a couple of practice runs, utilizing glide bombing. Approach the target area slowly, at about a thirty-five or forty degree angle, using your bombsights. Make a couple practice runs, pull up and go around again. When you've gotten the hang of it, we'll go on to actually dropping practice bombs."

He pointed to a circular device attached to the underside of a Texan.

"There are six practice bombs in this cluster here. Arm it before you begin your run and press the button on top of your stick to release one bomb at a time.

"There's a shotgun shell inside, activated by a plunger when it impacts the ground. You'll see a puff of smoke when it goes off. I'll be in a chase plane, circling you and, of course, scoring you. I'll be talking to you on your radios so make sure you maintain radio contact.

"Remember everything we told you about angle of attack and pulling G's. Fly at the specified air speed for each part of your bombing circuit. Go slow. We don't want you to turn yourselves inside out or rip the wings off the planes.

"Be sure to stay in order so I can score you correctly. Understood?"

The men nodded.

Aye, sir.

"Okay, men, go to your planes and meet me at Cotton Bayou."

Aye, sir.

The men saluted and hurried to the field.

They flew in a 'V' formation to Cotton Bayou, a swampy tract of land just north of the Gulf of Mexico, assuming an echelon, or "step-down" formation, as they approached the bombing site. They circled overhead at 3000 feet to check out the target area below.

Billy observed that three of the crosses were under water but still visible.

Each of the men made practice glide bomb runs before returning to the formation for the real run.

Billy was third in line for his run and watched carefully from a large overhead circle the men had created as members of the wing dropped their first bomb, all listening to Mr. Hardy's comments from his chase plane.

When it was his time, Billy announced over his radio he was going in.

He peeled off and began his descent. He dropped his nose and dove headlong at the prescribed 45 degrees. He leaned forward to aim through the optical bombsight mounted on top of his instrument panel. He focused on the center cross and watched intently as it grew larger and larger. At 500 feet, he released the bomb, silently counted *One second* before pulling up, feeling the weight of four times the force of gravity—"Gs" —pressing against his body as he climbed back to join his wing.

He missed the center cross but hit inside the circle.

It'll get better, he promised himself.

The next day, flying at 7000 feet, Billy led his formation back to Cotton Bayou in a 'V' formation, like a flock of geese, which was the most aerodynamically expeditious manner of travel. As they approached their area of operation, Billy raised his right arm through his open canopy as a signal to the men on his left that they were about to assume the echelon formation. He shook his ailerons—causing the plane to rapidly and briefly flutter horizontally—to execute. The two planes to his left were to slip underneath him, one at a time, beginning with the outboard plane and then under the other planes on the right side and join up at the end of the formation.

The "10-foot rule" was strictly adhered to in formation flying: each man stayed 10 feet beneath, behind and away from the other planes. When a plane slipped below the others to form a 'V' or return to the echelon formation, the plane in motion was to drop an additional 10 feet for safety and, when in position, resume the original 10-foot clearance.

Preacher was in the first plane to begin the maneuver. He dropped 10 feet, passed under Ted Miller, beneath Bill, then below Bob Hawthorne—the wingman—and beneath Snuffy Smith, and took his place to Snuffy's right before bringing his plane up 10 feet again.

Ted Miller then began his lateral move, but was blinded and so distracted by the sun that he failed to drop the required 10 feet. He passed unseen by the men in the formation, underneath Billy's plane and then Bob's.

Mr. Hardy, in his chase plane, saw the violation and immediately went on his radio, ordering Ted to drop the extra 10 feet.

Ted, confused in his inability to see the other planes, was passing beneath Snuffy when, for reasons no one would ever understand, he accelerated his plane, moved ahead of the formation and climbed rapidly. The propeller of Snuffy's plane slashed like a lumber mill saw through Miller's cockpit, killing him instantly. Snuffy's prop was severely damaged when it made contact with the steel framework of the plane, sending him and his plane plunging toward the ground.

Snuffy successfully bailed out as the two wounded planes continued their Earthward plunge, crashing less than 20 feet from each other.

Mr. Hardy spoke to the wing over the radio.

"Mr. Benson, take your wing back to Barin. I'll call in an ambulance and crash crew. Wait for me at Hangar One."

"Aye, sir."

None of the men spoke when they left their planes and walked silently to their muster area. They looked at one another but did not speak. Preacher hugged them all individually.

They stood or hunkered beside the hangar door or walked from Hangar One to Hangar Four and back again. The smokers lit up and puffed nervously.

Billy replayed his time spent with Miller over the months they had been in the flight program. Only that morning, in the head, Ted had asked Billy to lend him some toothpaste. Billy recalled that Ted had kept pictures of his girlfriend and his dog taped inside his locker door in primary, intermediate and advanced training.

It came so fast.

It happened and then it was over.

He was here and now he's gone.

Billy knew by the time the men returned to their quarters, all traces of Miller, Theodore, would be removed.

Mr. Hardy arrived. The men walked to meet him.

"First of all, Mr. Smith is okay. He'll spend the night at medical.

"But, Mr. Miller…Well, let me tell you, gentlemen, these things happen. This is training for combat. That's what we do here. It may happen again. And it will, for sure, happen every day somewhere in the fleet. I'd like to say you'll get used to it but you never will.

"You can't forget it. You'll remember this day for as long as you live.

"But it can't stop the training. It can't stop the war."

He paused, shook his head and continued.

"I'll need to get a written report from each of you. Tell us what you saw. It may help determine the cause of the crash. Let's go do that now and then you can go to chow. Try to get some sleep tonight and get your heads straight.

"We'll try it all again tomorrow."

*   *   *

"OKAY, MEN," GUNNERY OFFICER HARDY was reminding

the wing of six cadets, shortly after they had completed the requisite bombing runs, air-to-ground straffing practice—at crosses and other stable targets—and progressed to air-to-air tactics, in which the men would fire at a target pulled behind a plane. "I hope today you do a better job than you did yesterday. I've never seen such a piss-poor firing exercise since I've been teaching final squadron.

"And don't forget that you must stay in the order you've been assigned.

"Yesterday, every one of you got out of position at the beginning of the run and drifted so far ahead of the tow plane, I didn't know if it was a firing practice or a cross country."

The men stood silently as they were upbraided again for the failed exercise that resulted in down arrows for the entire wing.

"I'll be in my chase plane again, watching you.

"Maintain your echelon formation and go after the target—in order! Remember, if you get out of order, I might score you incorrectly. I repeat: Stay in formation. Go in the order you were assigned. Understood?"

Aye, aye, sir!

"Today, we'll be doing the high side runs. You'll climb one thousand feet above the target and dive at a forty-five degree angle.

"We'll try the flat side and low side runs after we get this one down pat.

"Let's head on out for the Gulf. When we get there, Mr. Carrigan will be pulling the target and will fly north and south. Go in, one at a time. Okay? In order!"

The men responded, *Aye, aye, sir!*

All, that is, but Carrigan.

"Dismissed."

Carrigan, standing at the rear of the other cadets, mumbled, "Why do I get all the shitty details?"

"Because you flew the wrong way on your cross country, Wrong Way," Pat O'Hara answered, patting him playfully on the back.

"Because you ran out of gas over Eclectic, Alabama," Preacher added.

"Because you didn't have a crank in your plane," Billy reminded him.

"And, most important," Bob Hawthorne concluded, emphasizing his words with his index finger, "because you wouldn't sleep with T.J."

The men erupted in raucous laughter.

"But we love you, Wrong Way, even if it seems the Navy doesn't," Preacher said, dropping his arm around his short friend's shoulders and giving him a gentle squeeze.

The ordnance crew had loaded each man's plane with 100 M-2, .30 caliber rounds, with seven to 10 tracers. Tracers were used in the first few years of strafing and actual WWII combat but were discontinued when it was discovered the enemy could trace the fiery projectiles back to the attackers during nighttime operations. Too, for a time, a tracer signaled the end of the cartridge belt. Enemy pilots quickly learned that signal and eagerly looked forward to attacking a defenseless plane.

For training purposes, each man's bullets had been coated a different color with non-permanent paint, to determine how many hits each would make in the fabric tow.

That afternoon, five flights of six planes each, followed by instructors in chase planes, took off and headed south to conduct their strafing run practice.

Billy again led the 'V' formation to the rendezvous point. As they flew over the shoreline, he signaled for the men to form up in the echelon position.

Billy felt himself tense up as the two planes to his left passed under his plane and the others in formation to assume their positions to the right. He took a deep breath of relief and blew it out when the maneuver was completed.

As the men continued south at 5000 feet, Billy frequently glanced over his right shoulder to observe the smart-looking line of gleaming SNJ's, holding steady in the step-down echelon. Each time he looked, a rush of electrically-charged neurons traversed his body. He smiled with satisfaction and returned the smiles, nods and waves from Bob Hawthorne, his wingman, as the men caught each other's eyes.

Wrong Way—and the other cadets assigned to pull targets for their flights—had taxied to the runway after the other men had taken off and paused. There, coiled lines were attached to target sleeves 100 feet long and three feet in diameter, secured to the bellies of their planes. The tow planes took off one at a time and banked slowly to prevent the lines from getting tangled in their planes' empennages as well as the tall pine trees that surrounded the field.

Wrong Way climbed to 5,000 feet as he flew to the Gulf of Mexico, where the members of his group were now circling and waiting a mile from the shoreline. He continued south, set his speed at 120 knots an hour and flew straight and level to the formation.

Their instructor in the chase plane ordered Billy to begin the exercise.

The formation ceased its circling and flew alongside Carrigan in an echelon formation.

Billy turned on his gun sight, charged his fuselage—or cowl—gun by pulling back on the charge handle on the instrument panel to the right of the gun sight, and switched the selector and safety switches to *fire*.

He announced on his radio to all the planes in his formation that he was commencing his run.

He peeled off to his left, carefully maintaining his 6000-foot altitude. As he crossed the imaginary line of attack, he nosed over into a steep dive.

He was now going in the opposite direction of the tow plane to intercept the southbound sleeve.

As his diving speed increased, he felt the controls of the plane becoming increasingly stiff. He looked through the gun sight and aimed 20 to 30 mils—or degrees— ahead of the target, to compensate for the deflection angle and speed of the sleeve.

Beginning at the front of the target, the approximate size of an enemy plane's fuselage, he squeezed the trigger on the control stick to send a burst of rounds along the length of the sleeve, before he rolled back underneath the sleeve to complete the strafing.

It was important that he didn't cut his speed as he made the pass. Even though that presented no problem for most of the men, it was difficult for many to continue firing as they came from the rear and underneath the target, fearing one of their live rounds might strike the tow plane and possibly the pilot.

Unfortunately, Billy had been momentarily distracted by the *pop-pop-popping* of his machine gun, long enough to lose his deflection lead and none of his bullets hit the target.

Damn!

He flew back up to the tail end of the echelon formation as the next plane made its diving run.

Billy reviewed his mistakes and mentally performed the exercise again as he waited for his second attempt. He made two more runs, each more successful than the first but Mr. Hardy interrupted the exercise from his chase plane

"All right men," he announced on his radio, "your formation is losing altitude and you're making runs that are too flat.

"Remember, these are supposed to be high side runs. You should start one thousand feet above the sleeve. Always check your altimeter before you start your run."

"Let's get back upstairs and try it again."

The formation climbed to 5000 feet for two more runs.

The entire exercise had lasted less than an hour, ending when each of the five planes had made four passes and shot up their hundred rounds.

As the sun sank lower and the first part of the exercise was concluded, Wrong Way reached the southern limit of his allotted track and turned back.

Everybody else is having all the fun, he had told himself, *diving, shooting, pulling G's.*

Because of the boredom and with some degree of resentment of his tedious assignment, he made a hard turn that exceeded the plane's normal banking limits. The result was that the tow line became firmly wedged in his left elevator, locking the critical control surface in place.

Billy radioed Wrong Way as soon as he saw the snagged tow line.

Carrigan's plane, consequently, could turn only and each turn was tighter than the last. Nearly immediately, the plane became completely inverted and out of control.

Carrigan tried to clear the line with his manual controls but to no avail. With a stuck elevator, the plane could go in only one direction—straight down.

"Bail out! Bail out!" Billy called into his radio as Wrong Way's plane continued its downward plunge.

Billy watched helplessly, circling overhead, as Carrigan's plane sped toward the choppy waters of the Gulf. The distance and dim light prevented his knowing if his friend had bailed out or not.

He saw an explosive geyser of water shoot up as the plane and the target disappeared beneath the churning foam.

Then, from the corner of his eye, he saw a momentary flick of white, not much bigger than the whitecaps covering the surface of the water.

"Parachute!" he said aloud.

As confidently and instinctively as a raptor after its prey, Billy dropped his plane into a vertical dive while maintaining visual contact with the point on the water where he had seen the white flick.

Leveling off above the water, he spotted the parachute spread out in the water but no Carrigan.

He continued to circle the area and soon saw Wrong Way, fighting his way from underneath the wet, clinging folds of the parachute.

Billy relayed his sighting to the chase pilot and continued circling Carrigan until he saw his friend safely on his raft. Carrigan smiled and waved at Billy.

Billy waved back, relieved that Wrong Way was safe.

Lt. Hardy, circling above, called Billy on his radio, ordering him back to the base before night set in.

"I'll stay with him, Mr. Benson. I've called in a Catalina flying boat from Bronson Field. It should be here in about an hour."

Billy returned to base and joined up in the hangar with other members of his wing, to await their debriefing with Mr. Hardy and, hopefully, news of Wrong Way's rescue.

When Mr. Hardy returned, the men stood as he approached them.

"The PBY is on the way," he announced. "I was about to run out of fuel and couldn't wait. Mr. Carrigan has flares, though, and the

Catalina can taxi right up to him. They'll take him to the hospital at NAS Pensacola for a checkup. He probably won't be back here until tomorrow morning.

"I don't have any complaints about your performance today. It was a hell of a lot better than yesterday's."

He stopped and smiled. "But, then, it couldn't have been any worse, could it? Unfortunately, since the target went down with Mr. Carrigan's plane and we can't score your runs, we'll have to scrap this exercise and try it again later."

After evening chow, Preacher stopped by Billy's room where Billy and Bob were discussing Wrong Way's crash.

"Am I disturbing you guys?" Preacher asked after he tapped on the door and opened it slightly.

"No, not at all," Bob said. "Come on in. Have a seat."

Preacher sat on Peter's empty rack.

"We were just talking about Wrong Way," Billy said.

"Following on the heels of Peter's crash and then Ted Miller, you know, it kinda changes the way we have to look at things, doesn't it?" Preacher asked.

"Yeah," Bob agreed.

"I'm glad Wrong Way is okay. He could've been killed, too," Billy said.

The men nodded agreement and sat quietly.

"Do you ever think about dying?" Bob asked Preacher.

"Sure. I guess all of us do."

"Do you think Ted and Peter did?" Bob asked.

"I didn't know Ted very well. And you guys knew Peter better than I did."

"I don't think he thought about dying," Billy said. "I think he was one of those who thought he'd live forever."

"He lived that way," Bob suggested. "But I guess I do, too."

The men sat silently again.

"What do you think happens to us? I mean, after we die," Billy asked.

"I don't know. I do know we're not like Rover and dead all over, the way some people believe," Preacher said.

"Our souls go somewhere," he said, "to wait for the Judgment."

"You believe in heaven and hell?" Bob asked.

"Sure. Don't you?" Preacher replied.

Bob laughed softly.

"I'm afraid so."

"When you say 'afraid,' do you mean you're afraid there'll be a hell? Or a heaven?" Preacher asked.

Bob laughed again.

"Hell! I hope there's a heaven but afraid there's a hell. That's about all I heard in church when I was growing up at the orphanage.

"How about you, Bill?" Bob asked.

"Oh, sure. I was raised on belief in heaven and hell. And like Bob, a lot of it was about hell."

"Yeah, I think we hear way too much about hell," Preacher said, "and not enough about God's Grace."

"My Aunt Grace was well named," Billy volunteered. "If it hadn't been for her, I'd have been scared out of my wits by those fire-breathing preachers I heard at that little country church she and my uncle took me to.

"She'd hold my hand during those sermons and the hotter the preacher got, the tighter she'd hold my hand. A lot of times, when things really got hot, she'd put her arm around me and hold me tight and whisper in my ear, 'This is the way Jesus wants to hold you. This is how the Grace of Jesus holds you so you'll never fall away from Him.'

"Of course, when I was real little, I wasn't sure just what 'Grace' meant. Did it mean my aunt? Or the love of God?

"Eventually, I just came to accept them both as more or less the same. She's a good woman and she believes as long as we're committed to Jesus, we're locked so tight in His Grace, He'll never let us go."

"I believe that, too," Preacher said.

"It takes a lot of faith, doesn't it?" Billy asked.

"Considering what's at stake, can you think of any reason not to believe it?" Preacher asked.

Bob looked at the deck.

"I've been so bad all my life," he said. "I've gotten so stinking, fall-down drunk so many times and screwed so many girls, I just don't see how God could love me and Jesus could save me."

"He does and He will, brother. Jesus' death on the cross wasn't wasted," Preacher said, his hand firmly on Bob's shoulder. "Believe it."

Wrong Way arrived back at Barin Field early in the afternoon the next day.

"Tell us what happened," Pat O'Hara requested as Wrong Way's friends gathered around him after their day of gunnery practice.

"Yeah," Billy said, "like why did you wait so long to open your 'chute?"

Wrong Way laughed.

"After I jumped out of the plane, I remembered to grab my nuts and pull them up tight with my hands, but I clean forgot that I was supposed to pull the ripcord. Of course I did but, just in time."

He held up one finger and shook it for emphasis.

"It took one swing before I hit the drink."

"That was close," someone said.

"Too close," Wrong Way agreed.

"What did they say at the hospital?" another man asked.

"That I was fine. They kept me overnight to be sure everything is okay."

"Now what?" Rickshaw asked.

"Safety flight check," Wrong Way answered.

"When?" Pat O'Hara asked.

"Tomorrow morning."

The door to Wrong Way's room stood open when the men returned from bombing practice the next day. Wrong Way sat on his rack, his head in his hands.

"What's the verdict, Wrong Way?" Preacher asked.

The men gathered behind him, to hear Wrong Way's response.

He looked up from his rack and threw up his hands before standing and walking to the doorway.

"It looks like I'm out of the program, guys," he said.

"What happened?" Pat O'Hara asked.

Wrong Way extended his arms.

"My arms were too short to recover from a spin."

"What do you mean?" Billy asked.

"I went up with Captain Mosley and when we got to five thousand feet, he told me to put the plane into a spin. I slammed the rudder in okay but my arm was too short to snap the stick hard enough to come out of the spin."

He hesitated and dropped his head.

"Captain Mosley had to do it for me."

"But, haven't you done that already?" Gary Lucas asked.

"Well, sure but I had always had another cushion. I didn't have one today, though."

"Why didn't you ask for another cushion so you could be closer to the controls?" Billy asked.

"I don't know. I guess I forgot to."

"Why don't you ask them if you can do it with another cushion?" Billy asked again.

"Aw, it's too late for that. They're pretty pissed that I lost one of their planes because of my own actions. And I've racked up more demerits than anyone in the history of the program. You know how many times I've screwed up. Frankly, I wasn't that great a pilot, guys. I think they're just tired of me."

"What happens now?" Barry Lucas asked.

"I'm heading for the fleet. To boot camp."

"Where?" Gary asked.

"Bainbridge, Maryland."

"Never heard of it." Preacher asked.

"Me either. I thought they'd send me to Great Lakes."

"When do you leave?" Preacher asked.

"As soon as I can get my bags packed. Man, I hate showing up in khakis. Everybody's going to know I flunked out of flight school."

"You won't be alone," Rickshaw said."You've seen how many have already been dropped. It's no disgrace. We're the *crème de la crème*. Remember?"

"Sure," Wrong Way said, "the cream that went sour."

"Bow your heads, everybody," Preacher announced.

The men did as Preacher instructed.

Preacher placed his hand firmly on Wrong Way's head.

"Father, we approach Thy throne of Grace to ask Thy continued blessings on us all and, especially on our good friend, Wrong Way Carrigan.

"We have grown to love Wrong Way, Father, as we know You do and we ask that You go with him to his new assignment, strengthen him and give him the resolve to do his duty proudly and bring honor and glory to Thee and to our country.

"Father, continue to bless our country and our president and strengthen us in our righteous battle against evil men.

"We ask these things in the name of Thy Son Jesus. Amen."

Amen.

"By the way, Wrong Way," Preacher said. "I think you were misnamed. I think we should call you 'Right Way.'"

"Thanks, Preacher."

Each of the assembled men shook Wrong Way's hand. Some embraced him. The twins remained and helped him carry his gear to the front of the quarters.

Billy and his roommates watched from their window as Wrong Way walked to the admin building.

"He was so close to finishing," Bob said. "It must really hurt."

"It's still not too late for any of us," Nick Overstreet reminded them.

*   *   *

THE MEN WERE MARCHED to the Ac Rec building for studio photographs to be included in the hard-bound yearbook, the *Flight Jacket*, which would include cadets from airfields in Pensacola and Jacksonville.

Each man slipped into a white choker jacket with ensign's shoulder boards and took his turn before the camera. The coat was split up the back, "Like they put on stiffs at the funeral home," Bob said.

And then a group picture was made in cadet uniforms, in front of the Ac Rec building.

When only two days of advanced training were left, the mood in the Cadet Barracks suddenly became chaotic, even wacky.

No one in the showers was safe from stinging smacks on any unsuspecting body part with well-aimed, snapping wet towels or sudden dousings with swab buckets filled with cold water. Uniforms reeked of cheap perfume, attributable to unknown interlopers who sneaked into rooms armed with small, blue, tasseled bottles of "Evening in Paris." Heavy sleepers woke up with their palms filled with dollops of shaving cream, 25-cent pieces and thank-you notes. Bottles of Listerine mouthwash were mysteriously filled with vegetable oil.

The Lucas twins stripped naked, penciled moustaches onto their upper lips, donned their issue boondockers, homemade Zorro masks, black capes and bandanas and one large golden earring apiece. They ran loudly and wildly up and down the passageways, springing noisily, spider-like into rooms, brandishing combat knives, identifying themselves as the Mad, Masked Marine Bombers and announcing the formation of the Barin Field Flying Circus, with tryouts after the final flight training exercise the next day.

Once inside their cockpits the following afternoon, the Marine twins donned their Zorro masks, bandanas and capes over their helmets and flying suits and, as promised at the end of formation flying, clasped their knives between their teeth and left the formation to give an acrobatic, follow-the-leader demonstration. Only Pat O'Hara was fool-hardy enough to follow and replicate the antics of the wild, uninhibited pair: flat-hatting across a potato field that forced the field hands—men and women—to throw themselves desperately face down into the plowed earth; a low pass across the parking lot of a livestock auction barn that panicked the animals inside, as well as clipped aerials from the cars lined up outside; a vertical, barrel roll high into the clouds and a terrifying Kamikaze dive underneath a stand of ancient oaks near Cotton Bayou.

The twins had been eyeing the oaks since they had arrived at Barin, secretly plotting the assault. They lined up, leveled off mere yards from the ground, passed beneath the spreading limbs of the trees and between the trunks, out the other side, followed by another long, graceful, spiraling barrel roll into the sky.

Barry took the lead, followed closely by Gary, while Pat thoughtfully and prudently hesitated, circling overhead to see if the

Texans emerged safely from the tunnel beneath the leafy canopy of live oaks.

When the twins swooped upward dramatically from the other side and climbed steeply into the air, Pat continued to circle, still unsure of his skills.

The twins joined him and signaled to him to fall in behind them as they made another pass underneath the trees.

Pat, not one to allow Marines to have the upper hand over a Navy pilot, swallowed, pressed his lips tightly together, put his plane into a dive and headed in directly behind the twins' single file. He centered his plane between the trees ahead but the prop wash from the Lucas' planes produced enough turbulence that Pat feared he was losing control of his Texan. The plane dropped enough for the propeller to chew up the topsoil before the Irishman jerked up the nose, which now caused the prop to act as a rip saw on the low-hanging oak limbs as he emerged.

He could tell right away as he began climbing, that his propeller had been damaged and left aerodynamically defective.

"I'm not going to be able to make it back to Barin," he told the twins over his radio as he leveled off over the trees.

"Keep heading south," Gary said.

"Canal Field is dead ahead," Barry added.

Pat dropped his landing gear and looked ahead for the small field, used primarily for touch and go's.

"There it is," Gary said, from his position 1000 feet up.

"Okay," Pat said, as the south-north landing field appeared.

Pat landed without incident and taxied to a stop. The twins landed behind him and climbed from their planes.

Pat shut off his engine, scrambled from his cockpit and walked to the front of his plane to inspect the damage to his propeller.

"Well, it isn't as bad as I thought," Pat said. "Bad enough but not terrible."

"We'll fly back to Barin," Barry said.

"You stay here," Gary added.

The twins returned to their planes to report the incident and summon help.

"What are we going to tell them?" Barry asked his brother as they walked toward the hangar.

"Engine trouble?" Gary suggested.

"Let's talk to Chief Duffy first. I think he likes us enough that we can just tell him the truth. Maybe he'll help us."

The men walked into the hangar where the chief was supervising the overhaul of a Texan engine. He smiled and waved as soon as he saw the two heading his way, their parachutes under their arms, their Zorro gear tucked inside their flight suits.

"Well, now, if it isn't Frick and Frack!" he said, wiping his hands on a shop rag.

"Hi, Chief," Gary said.

"Hi, Chief.

"Can we talk to you, Chief?" Barry asked.

"Sure. Come on over to my workbench," he said, leading the two across the hangar.

He poured a cup of his infamous, thick, mid-watch coffee from a squat, aluminum percolator, kept warm over a single-eye electric hot plate.

"Okay, what can I do for you Gy-rines?"

"Well, Chief," Barry began.

"We've got a little problem," Gary added, "and we thought you might help us out."

"Sure, guys, anything for you two. Just name it."

The twins looked at each other.

"You see, Chief, Gary and I kind of formed a flying circus today, you know, to kind of celebrate the end of training, and O'Hara kind of decided to join us."

The chief looked outside the hangar.

"Where's O'Hara now?" he asked.

"Well, he kind of..." Gary began.

"He kind of hurt one of my Texans?" the chief asked.

"Well, maybe just a little," Barry said.

Chief Duffy put his mug on the workbench and crossed his arms as he waited for their explanation.

"O'Hara's prop kind of got chewed up, Chief," Gary said.

"But it's probably our fault."

"Where is he?"

"He's at Canal Field," Gary said.

"Is he okay?"

The twins nodded.

Yes, Chief.

"How did it happen?"

"He tried to fly underneath some trees down at Cotton Bayou," Gary said, "and his prop hit the ground first and then the limbs of the trees."

Chief Duffy looked unsmiling at the young Marines.

They gave him a shy, imploring look.

The chief shook his head but said nothing.

The twins looked at each other and shifted uncomfortably.

The chief put his fists threateningly on his hips.

"You know that all three of you shitbirds could be dropped from the program for this, don't you?"

Yes, Chief, the twins said together.

"And you wouldn't get your commissions, would you?"

No, Chief.

"You two would go to Parris Island."

We've already been, Chief.

"Okay. But you'd be just another couple of jarhead grunts. Enlisted, like me."

Yes, Chief.

"You wouldn't like that, would you?"

The twins looked at each other again.

No, Chief.

"So, you came to good ole Chief Duffy because you hoped he wouldn't give you a ration of shit, and maybe wouldn't report you, didn't you?"

Yes, Chief.

"And you've told me the truth?"

Yes, Chief.

The chief looked at them sternly before his face broke into a broad grin.

He placed his hands on their shoulders and gave them friendly shakes.

"I swear. If it was anybody else but you two, I'd throw the book at 'im. But you guys?"

"Okay, fly me down there. If it's just the prop and not the engine, well, it'll be our secret."

"Admiral Radford's already here for tomorrow's inspection and I sure as hell don't want him to know you might have damaged one of his planes."

"Thank you, Chief," Gary said, extending his hand.

"Thanks, Chief," Barry added, also shaking the chief's hand.

Chief Duffy climbed into the cockpit with Gary and the three flew the short distance to Canal Field, constructed alongside the Intercoastal Waterway.

The twins followed the chief to O'Hara's plane and waited quietly as he inspected the damage to the propeller.

"Stand back," the chief said, as he climbed into the cockpit and started up the engine.

He listened carefully and observed the plane's vibrations as he revved up the engine and then let it idle.

He switched it off and climbed out.

"I think the engine is going to be all right. We'll have to replace the prop. You guys are lucky.

"I'll send my men out here to pick the plane up. If you don't hear from me before Admiral Radford inspects you tomorrow morning, you're safe.

"Okay, get back in your planes and let's head back to Barin. Come on, O'Hara."

Thanks, Chief.

*   *   *

An all-hands inspection was ordered for the last day at Barin Field.

Dress blues were the uniform of the day and the men had spent the previous evening removing lint with adhesive tape rolled the wrong way around their fingers, spit-shining shoes and polishing the patent leather visors on their hats.

This would be their last inspection as enlisted men and spirits were high.

Admiral A.W. Radford, Director of Aviation Training, Bureau of Aeronautics, would lead the inspection party.

The men were marched onto the ramp in front of the hangars and lined up in wings. The colors were presented and Admiral Radford began his inspection, followed by base skipper Commander Weatherford and other administrative members of the command. A chief carrying a clipboard was prepared to write down gigs or commendations.

Radford stood in front of the man at the far right side of the first rank and side stepped his way down the line of cadets.

Billy could see him approaching, from the corner of his eye.

When he stood directly in front of Billy, the two men were eyeball to eyeball. Billy looked beyond the admiral as the officer's eyes swept over Billy's cover, his uniform and his highly polished shoes.

He reached out and smoothed one of Billy's lapels.

"Give this man a four-o," he said to the chief.

"Aye, Admiral."

"You look fine, son," he said. "You make me proud."

"Thank you, sir."

"How have you liked the V-5 program?"

"Fine, sir."

"Let me shake your hand, Mr. Benson."

Billy extended his hand.

"Good luck, son."

"Thank you, sir."

*   *   *

WHEN THE INSPECTION ENDED, the men marched back to their quarters, erupting in shouts of victory as soon as they were dismissed to change back into their khakis. They grabbed their bags and loaded onto the waiting bus. The jubilation continued on the return to NAS Pensacola.

The men held on to their blues carefully, for the dance that night at the Mustin Beach Club. It would not be at all like T.J.'s uninhibited luau: the cadets would have to be on their best behavior since senior base officers and their wives, instructors and their wives would attend.

That was the last time the men would wear the cadet uniform, for the next morning they would don their blue officer's uniform with single gold braid on their sleeves and an embroidered gold star above each. Navy wings had been embroidered onto the left breasts of the uniforms as an expedient measure to spare the officers in charge the time-consuming task of pinning on so many of them.

Billy had bought a shirt with French cuffs at the base uniform shop to wear the links Suzanne had given him.

The next morning, the men marched in formation to the area designated as "Under the Oaks," in Officers' Country, surrounded by the massive, moss-festooned trees. The romantic setting seemed at odds with the purpose of the gathering: a celebration of young warriors who would leave that place of peace and loveliness to destroy their enemies in the air, on the seas, on the ground.

The men assembled in smartly lined up companies and were ordered by the student battalion leader to stand at parade rest.

As laudable exemplars of Uncle Sam's "pretty soldiers," T.J., the Lucas twins and the other Marines in the company were resplendent in their choker blue uniforms with red piping and bright brass buttons on the sleeves, bold, red stripes down the outboard sides of their trousers, highly polished brass belt buckles, gleaming white hats with the officers' large embroidered cloverleaf designs on the tops, white gloves and shoes so brightly shined, each swore he could shave in them. The Marines wore the actual gold-plated aviator's wings on their tunics, rather than the embroidered type, beneath which their marksman medals hung proudly.

Suzanne, wearing her dress blues, and the other guests sat in folding chairs to the sides of the formation.

At precisely 1000—10 hundred—hours, the student battalion leader advanced from the rear of the assemblage to face the graduating class. He bellowed out at the top of his voice, "Comp-nee! Ah-tenn-HUT!"

The men came to sharp attention, feet together, eyes straight ahead, shoulders back and spines ramrod straight, as the senior officers of the base and Admiral Radford walked from the sides of the formation and faced the cadets, standing before metal wardroom chairs that had been fitted with white sailcloth covers.

Parade the colors!

The military personnel saluted. Guests stood and placed their right hands over their hearts as the color guard moved briskly from the rear of the formation.

The flag of United States, with its 48 embroidered stars, the Navy flag, with the fouled anchor on a white diamond on a field of blue and the colorful Marine Corps flag, with the eagle, anchor and globe on a field of red, along with the chaplain's flag, were brought forward by gloved cadets and placed in holders behind the row of officers' chairs.

Hand salute!

The color guard saluted the national ensign and stood at attention on each side of the flag display.

Company! Two!

The men dropped their hands smartly to their sides.

Uncover, two!

The men removed their hats as the chaplain walked to the wooden lectern.

"Let us pray.

"Almighty God,

"We are gathered before You this beautiful day to commission these fine young men who will pilot the planes that we pray will help end the hostilities that plague our planet.

"We ask, O Father, that You bless this service, these men who are being honored today, their families and loved ones and that You will go with each one of the men as they leave this historic place today to join the fight.

"Bless them, O Lord. Care for them. Watch over them. Keep them from danger. For those, our Heavenly Father, who will be called upon to sacrifice their lives for our country, we pray sincerely and fervently that You will welcome them into Your heavenly kingdom and grant unto them Grace and Mercy and eternal rest.

"We ask that You bless our president, Father and our country and our allies.

"We ask all these blessings in the name of Your Son, the Prince of Peace, Jesus Christ.

Amen"

The chaplain returned to his place before his covered chair.

Comp-nee! Cover, two!

The men replaced their hats

Color guard! Post!

The color guard retreated to the rear of formation.

Another officer walked to the lectern as the others sat.

"Would our guests please be seated?

"Stand at parade rest, men."

Parade rest!

As one man, the cadets placed their hands behind their backs and shifted their left feet 12 inches.

"Admiral Radford, honored guests, welcome.

"I am Captain Henry Marsh, commandant of naval flight training here in Pensacola.

"Before I make my remarks, I invite Admiral Radford to make whatever comments he wishes."

"Admiral, sir?"

Admiral Radford stepped before the assembly.

"Thank you, Hank.

"Since I met with the cadets yesterday, I want to briefly address the parents and families of the cadets.

"I want to sincerely thank you for doing such a wonderful job rearing your sons. I am sure you are proud of them. I am. All of us are. They are the best of the best. To have been accepted for the V-5 program was an honor in itself but to have completed it successfully is even more exceptional.

"I have every confidence they will continue to make us all proud.

"Thank you, again."

Captain Marsh returned to the podium.

"Thank you, Admiral Radford.

"I am particularly pleased to stand before all of you today, Friday, 3 March 1944, especially you cadets, the day of your commissioning and graduation. I am certain this is a day you will never forget.

"You have worked hard, you have achieved much and you and your families, too, have every right to be pleased with your great accomplishment.

"I congratulate you. I applaud you. I am proud of you. When you go out into the fleet, don't forget Pensacola and the things you have learned here. Represent us well. Represent the Navy and Marine Corps well.

"Your country needs you. You have been trained to be the finest pilots in the world. Whether you fly bombers, fighters, transports or train other cadets to fly, or perhaps even find yourself, like me, behind a desk, each of you has a place in the war that has already taken untold numbers of lives. Whatever your assignment, give it your best. Do your duty and do it well, knowing that that you will play a major role in ending the most destructive war since recorded time."

He paused and then smiled.

"I know you're anxious to get this over with, so without further ado, as I call your name, my boss, Admiral Harris Murray, Chief of Naval Air Training, will present you with your commissions."

He turned to the row of officers behind him.

"Admiral Murray, sir."

The two saluted and Admiral Murray walked to the table beside the lectern.

As each man's name was called, he snapped to attention, walked to the table, took his diploma, saluted, shook the admiral's hand and returned to the formation.

Billy looked at the paper he had received:

Know all men by these presents that
James William Benson Jr.
has completed the prescribed course of training and
having met successfully the requirements of the
course is designated a
NAVAL AVIATOR

B.J. and the Marines were presented their pairs of single gold bars in small, rectangular black boxes.

When all certificates had been given out, the color guard retrieved the flags, the ceremony was declared concluded and the men threw their covers into the air with shouts of victory, causing a blinding avalanche of falling hats.

Billy retrieved his cover and ran immediately to give Suzanne a kiss and an embrace. T.J. appeared and asked Suzanne to pin his bars on the shoulders of his uniform.

Barry Dorsey's parents and grandparents had arrived at the graduation in a chauffeur-driven Cadillac. A second car, a Ford convertible, was close behind.

"Come on and meet my family," Barry invited his friends.

"His father is a member of Congress," Billy told Suzanne as they, Bob, and T.J. followed Barry to the two cars where a well-dressed and amiable group of people was waiting at the edge of the grassy area.

After introducing his immediate family, Barry placed his arm around the quiet man who had driven the convertible.

"And this is Bobby Jones," he said proudly. "Taught me all I know about golf."

Jones shook hands all around. When he spoke to T.J., he reminded the group of the special Marine bodyguards who had protected him from his fans at his second U.S. Amateur in Philadelphia.

Later, Suzanne, who was not a golf fan, would remark to Billy on the argyle socks Jones had been wearing.

"Hah!" Billy would respond. "If you were Bobby Jones, you could wear your argyle *drawers* in public and get away with it."

"Follow us to the O Club," Barry invited his family.

T.J., Bob, Barry climbed into the back seat of Suzanne's Buick as Billy happily slid behind the wheel—after nearly a year—to drive to the Officer's Club where a buffet lunch had been set up for the graduates and their guests.

The five friends and Barry's family and Bobby Jones took a table in a large room across the back, where glassed-in brick arches looked out over the bay. There they excitedly rehashed the events leading up to the morning's ceremony as they ate.

"And what time are we supposed to be at the chapel for the wedding?" Bob asked.

"Sixteen hundred hours," Suzanne declared.

"Spoken like a true bosun's mate," T.J. declared.

"And be sober and be dressed," she told them.

"Aye, aye, ma'am," Barry replied.

"And I made sure T.J. wore some skivvies," Bob volunteered.

"Will there be another limbo contest?" Suzanne asked.

"You can never tell about T.J.," Bob said.

"Thanks, T.J.," Suzanne said. "That's probably a sacrifice for you."

"Anything for you, love," he replied.

"And back here for the reception afterward," she reminded them, indicating the Officer's Club.

"Maybe we should have just set up our racks down here," Barry suggested. "The dance last night, this buffet, reception this afternoon and another dance tonight."

"And to the personnel office at ten hundred hours tomorrow for our orders," Billy reminded them.

"Hey!" Bob said, as he remembered the old folk tale, "Isn't it supposed to be bad luck for the groom to see the bride on the day of the wedding, before the wedding?"

"No," Suzanne replied quickly.

"I didn't think so," Bob replied, regretting that he had reminded them of possible bad luck.

*   *   *

BARRY AND BOB AND TWO OF SUZANNE'S NURSE friends, all in dress blues, stood on either side of Billy before the altar in the base chapel, facing the congregation.

Billy was pleased that several nurses and nearly his entire company had filed into the chapel to witness their marriage. Since the men had not received their orders, it was a pleasant way for them to pass the time and, too, the promise of more free food and drinks afterward were friendly lures. Billy smiled broadly as several of his friends waved cheerfully and greeted him from their pews.

The organist began the traditional wedding march. The doors in the back of the sanctuary opened and Suzanne entered on the arm of T.J. She carried a bouquet of white flowers, her face fairly glowing. She was still wearing her dress blue uniform, the female officers' hat worn toward the back of her head, similar to the men's but without a visor.

Billy smiled proudly and watched every careful step she made down the aisle.

After they exchanged rings, and the chaplain pronounced them "man and wife," the men from his class stood, cheered, whistled and repeated the toss of their hats into the air.

While Billy and Suzanne waited in the lobby, the dozen or so men who had purchased sabers lined up in a double column in front of the chapel to make an arch with their swords.

T.J., Barry, and Bob had paid one of the base photographers to take pictures of the wedding and the reception.

"But not the honeymoon," Billy had insisted.

"That would be the most interesting part," T.J. had commented salaciously.

T.J. drove the five back to the Officer's Club for the reception and when the men from his company arrived, T.J., Bob and Barry each bought the assembly a round of drinks, which continued after Billy and Suzanne slipped away for the drive to a small beach house east of Pensacola, that one of the doctors had lent them for their honeymoon.

They stopped at a restaurant for their evening meal before continuing on to their cottage. They passed up dessert. Billy wickedly looked directly into Suzanne's eyes while telling the waitress they would have it later.

Suzanne lowered her head and smiled at his boldness.

After he paid the check, he pointed to a wall-mounted pay telephone.

"I think I should call my folks. Come on. I'll introduce you."

"Mom?"

"Billy. How are you, son?"

"Fine, Mom."

"Well, how did things go today?"

"Oh, it was a good day. We had the commissioning outside under the trees and then we went to the chapel. It was all really nice."

"I wish we could have been there."

"So do I, Mom."

"Did you receive our card?" she asked.

"No, ma'am. Don't worry. It'll catch up with me eventually.

"Is Dad there?"

"Oh, sure. He's right here."

"Hi, Son."

"Hey, Dad."

"Sorry we couldn't be there on your big day. We were thinking about you."

"I'm sorry, too. I'll get some pictures to you."

"We'd like that."

"Suzanne is here with me."

"Put her on."

"Mr. Benson?"

"Jim."

"Jim."

"Suzanne, we're really happy for you and Billy. We know you must be somebody special and we're anxious to meet you."

"Thanks, Jim. I'm anxious to meet all of you, too."

"I know this call is costing you a lot of money. Here's Edna."

"Suzanne?"

"Hi."

"I guess Jim said everything I would say."

"Even though we don't know you yet, all of us love you because Billy loves you."

"Thank you."

"Please come see us as soon as you can."

"Okay. We will. Thanks.

"Here's Bill."

"Mom, thanks for everything you and Dad have done for me. I appreciate you more every day. I love you both. And everybody else there. Please tell them for me."

"I will, son. We love you, too."

Billy hung up the phone and looked at Suzanne.

"They seem like really good people," she said.

"They are. I'm anxious for you to meet them."

She put her arms around his neck.

"I love you, Bill Benson."

"I love you, Susanne Benson."

Later that night, Billy was sequestered in the bedroom of the cottage as Suzanne changed her clothes in the small bathroom across the hall. He snapped out the ceiling light, leaving only a low wattage, shaded lamp on the dressing table to softly illuminate the room.

He removed his uniform and draped it over a chair, laid his underwear in the chair and wrapped a short, native Polynesian skirt with red and white designs, around his waist and tucked in the waistband to secure it. He sat in the bed, resting his back against the pillows piled against the headboard. He crossed his ankles, dropped his hands onto his chest and moved his thumbs against each other as he passed the time, anxiously anticipating her arrival.

Billy looked up when he heard her turn the doorknob and slowly open the door.

She stood in the doorway momentarily, a soft illumination from the hall framing her dramatically.

Her hair hung softly over her shoulders. A lacy, white negligee covered a long, sheer nightgown that reached to her bare feet.

Billy leaned forward in the bed.

"Oh, Suzanne. You are so beautiful," he said in awe of her nuptial splendor.

Suzanne walked shyly to the center of the room.

He eased from the bed and walked toward her slowly, not taking his eyes off her, his mouth slightly slack.

She saw his loincloth, threw her hand to her mouth and bent over with laughter.

"Heavenly days! What is that?" she asked, pointing.

"Oh," he said, looking at his loincloth. "It's a lava-lava. T.J. let me borrow it. It's from Somoa or Fiji or someplace in the Pacific. Don't you like it?"

"Are you sure it's not a flag?"

Billy looked down again.

"No, that's just the effect you have on me. It has a mind of its own."

She laughed again. "It's a good thing Casey or Riley aren't here."

"What do Casey and Riley have to do with it?" a frown crossing his face.

"When that happens to the guys on the wards, they give them a good thump."

"Come on, Suzanne, this is supposed to be romantic!"

"I'm sorry," she said, trying not to laugh.

He reached out to her face.

She laughed again.

"Suzanne!"

"I'm sorry, Billy. It's just that silly skirt you're wearing."

He reached for his waist and pulled the fabric free, letting the lava-lava fall to the floor.

"How's that?" he asked.

"Much better," she said and looking again, exclaimed enthusiastically, "Much better!"

"Suzanne!"

"Okay. I'm sorry. I'm okay now."

He was mesmerized by her beauty. He stepped to her, lifted her hair with his fingers and let it fall back softly to her shoulders. He ran his hands across her shoulders and gently pushed her negligee free.

"You are so beautiful," he said again, moving to her, kissing her shoulders delicately.

He released the gown's thin, pink bows on each of her shoulders, letting the gown slip smoothly and silently down her body.

He gasped quietly.

His hands gently touched the underside of her breasts.

"Oh, Suzanne! I've never seen anything so gorgeous. You are the most stunning woman in the world."

She put her arms around his neck and kissed him passionately.

"And you are the most beautiful man I have ever seen," she said. "I thought that the first time I saw you."

"Just a minute," he said, as he closed the bedroom door and snapped off the boudoir lamp.

Moonlight from outside the cottage filtered in through the wooden Venetian blinds.

He swooped her up into his arms and started toward the bed when, from outside the window, came the unmistakable sound of a ukulele. Seven chords were struck and then the sound of three drunken male voices:

A-lo-ha o-ee,
A-lo-ha o-ee...

Billy put Suzanne down and lifted a slat of the blinds.

He laughed aloud.

"Oh, no! Look at this!" he said to Suzanne.

She looked though the small opening and shrieked with laughter.

Outside their window, in the light of a full moon, Barry and Bob stood on either side of T.J., who was wearing his native hat made of palm fronds, and playing the ukulele. Bob was waving a bottle of rum in his free hand as he and Barry attempted to balance themselves by holding onto T.J.'s shoulders

All three were wearing Hawaiian shirts that came to just below their waists.

That was all.

No trousers, no underwear, no shoes, no socks.

Just three drunks in Hawaiian shirts.

"Hmm," Billy said. "Their first day as officers and they're out of uniform already. And T.J. promised Bob he'd wear skivvies."

"Did you know about this, Bill Benson?" Suzanne asked threateningly.

Billy laughed and shook his head. "No, I promise you. I didn't."

Suzanne looked out the window again and laughed.

"Well, this is certainly going to a night to remember," she said.

Billy pulled her gently from the window, swept her up into his arms again and held her over the bed.

"You bet it is, lady. Captain Billy is going to see to that. And it begins right now."

Stearmans on the NAS New Orleans flight line.

CHAPTER FIVE

FLIGHT INSTRUCTORS' SCHOOL
NEW ORLEANS, LOUISIANA

B ILLY FUMBLED FOR THE CHAIN connected to the light over the lavatory in the small bathroom of the beach cottage. He pulled it and placed his hands firmly on the edges of the pedestal lavatory for support as he leaned into the bathroom mirror to examine his face.

This too, too sullied flesh, he thought.

Puffy, dark bags hung under his red-veined eyes. He had to blink several times to clear his vision. His mouth was dry. He looked like…what was it Velma liked to say? *Like death warmed over*? He thought he might have felt even worse than that.

Maybe I could call in sick. Pick up my orders Monday.

He knew he had no choice, however: he had to report for his orders at 1000 hours that morning.

He shaved carefully, taking care not to nick himself with his unsteady hand. He showered in the narrow metal stall in the corner of the room, brushed his teeth, and returned to the bedroom to quietly put on his dress blues. He tip-toed out of the little house and drove Suzanne's Buick to the base personnel office.

He knew the ribbing and crude honeymoon remarks he would receive from his classmates.

Maybe it wouldn't be so bad.

The way I feel, I really don't care.

He stopped at the main gate, rolled down his window and, from force of habit, pulled his identification card from his shirt pocket and held it up. The young Marine corporal took a quick look at the base sticker on the car's front bumper, leaned over to compare the ID card picture with the face in the flesh. Billy hoped he resembled the photograph. The sentry quickly stiffened to attention and executed a smart salute—so military, in fact, that his perfectly flattened hand vibrated when it touched the visor of his hat. Billy saluted and started to drive away but stopped quickly.

"Yes, sir?" the sentry asked, leaning down.

Billy pulled his wallet from his hip pocket and removed a one-dollar bill.

"You're the first to salute me," he said, handing the guard the bill.

The Marine took the money and snapped to attention and presented another perfect salute. "Congratulations, sir! Thank you, sir!"

Billy returned the salute and drove off.

As he parked the car, he saw members of his class across the street from the oyster-shell covered parking lot, standing around on the lawn outside the personnel office. They were neither in formation nor in the festive mood he had anticipated.

As he walked toward them, he realized they looked worse than he did. Patrick O'Hara was approaching, Billy thought, to speak, but rushed past to his real target, a large trashcan near the sidewalk and vomited violently into it.

The men squinted against the painful morning light as they looked at Billy. Some lifted their hands in a half-spirited acknowledgement. Some mumbled an indecipherable greeting.

They were wobbly on their feet and their faces were green-tinged. All of them were hung over from their extended celebration party at the Officers' Club the night before.

He saw T.J. in the middle of the group. He was bent over, gripping his knees firmly. He righted himself and waved weakly when he saw, through bloodshot eyes, Billy making his way toward him.

"Ohhhhhh, Blimey, Bill. I am so f***in' sick, I want to die."

"I think you already have."

"Oh, please, don't shout."

Billy laughed quietly.

"How did things go last night?" T.J. asked.

"Fine."

T.J. dropped his hand clumsily onto Billy's shoulder and gave it a shake.

"I'm glad to hear it. You're a good man, Bill Benson. You deserve the best and Suzanne is the perfect girl for you. You deserve each other."

"Thanks, T.J."

"I think I should have stayed outside your window last night instead of going back to the O Club," he confessed.

"I don't know. You already looked a little looped then."

"I guess I was. It's all a blur."

"Any word from our orders, yet?" Billy asked.

"No. The chief was just out to tell us they're about ready for us."

"Where's Bob?"

"He and Barry are in the head, puking up their insides."

"Must have been a good party."

"Right, from the looks of all our mates here. But I doubt if anybody remembers."

The door to the personnel office opened and Lieutenant Sheeley, the personnel officer, and his assistant, Chief Birdwell, stepped out onto the covered porch.

"You guys look like hell!" the chief said, looking at the undulating, insalubrious group before him.

"Where's your flight leader?" the officer asked.

"Here, sir," Barry said, as he came through the door the officer had just exited. Bob was behind him.

"And this one looks even worse," the chief said, gesturing with his thumb at Barry.

And he did. His face was totally devoid of color. His coat was unbuttoned, his tie and collar were loose. He carried his cover.

The chief called out to the ragged assembly: "Don't any of you guys attempt to salute today if you're eating an ice cream cone!"

"Get your men in formation, Mr. Dorsey," Mr. Sheeley said.

Barry put on his hat, buttoned his coat and straightened his tie.

"Aye, aye, sir," he said, giving a semi-salute.

He did an about face and called to the men, "Final squadron, ah-tenn-hut!"

The men attempted a formation.

Barry did a quick head count and turned to face the personnel officer.

"All men present or accounted for, sir," Barry said, again making an effort to salute.

"Very well, Mr. Dorsey. Thank you.

"Stand at ease, men" he said mercifully.

The men complied.

"Men, your orders were delayed until this morning because we have sincerely been trying to give you what you requested. It took a little more time than we anticipated but I want you to know we didn't take the easy way out to assign you just anywhere.

"A lot of you are going to be pleased with your orders. Some of you won't be. I'm sorry we couldn't give all of you what you requested but it just didn't work out that way.

"If you don't like what you got, you can always put in a request for change of orders. Meanwhile, take what you're assigned and wait until you get to your next duty station before giving the personnel office a hard time. Okay?

"Now, Mr. Dorsey, after you dismiss your men, Chief Birdwell will call the names and when you hear your name, come on up and I'll give you the envelope."

"Aye, aye, sir."

Barry did a wobbly about face.

"Well, guys, it's been good. I hope we see each other here and there. Smooth sailing, clear skies, and all that. A-tenn-hut!"

He added, "Fall out!" as he saluted them.

The men saluted, broke ranks and moved closer to the chief and the officer. As they heard their names, they sounded off and reached for their envelopes.

Billy's name was one of the first to be called. He took the envelope and walked away from the group to open it. He removed the paper inside, unfolded it and read silently. He shook his head slowly in quiet protest: he had been assigned to flight instructors' school in New Orleans and upon completion of training was to be attached permanently to NAS Memphis as a primary flight instructor.

He read the orders again to be sure he hadn't misread them the first time.

T.J., Bob and Barry walked over with their opened envelopes.

"Not so good?" Bob asked, seeing the expression of disappointment on Billy's face.

"The Naval College for Primary Flight Instructors in New Orleans," he read, holding it up for them to see. "I have to report

Monday after next. And then I go back to Memphis to teach V-5 cadets. It looks like I'm in some sort of a SNAFU loop. Not exactly what I was hoping for. Back to the Yellow Perils. How about you guys?"

"Multi-engines for Barry and me," T.J. said.

"And fighters for me," Bob added.

"Well, I'm glad for you," Billy said.

"Reapply for fighters," T.J. said.

"I will. Don't doubt that I won't."

The four stood awkwardly together.

"I hope you have a good visit with my folks in Riverton," Billy said to Bob and T.J.

"We will. You won't mind if we sleep in your room, will you?" T.J. asked.

"No, but Buddy may. Mom says he's been sleeping on my bed."

"That'll be okay. I've slept with some dogs in my lifetime," Bob said.

"Four-legged ones?" Barry asked.

"Them, too," Bob answered with as much a smile as he could muster.

"And Uncle John and Aunt Grace want us to spend one or two nights with them," Bob added.

"Give them my regards," Billy said. "I'll write everybody before I leave for New Orleans."

"Oh, when you get to your new duty stations," he added, "send your addresses to my folks. They'll get them to me."

They agreed.

"Speaking of bed," Billy began.

"And just who was speaking of bed, mate?" T.J. teased.

"You were. You're going to be sleeping in my bed."

"Ah! Right-o."

"As I was about to say, 'Speaking of bed,' I think I'll get back to the little woman. Maybe we can think of something to do together to cheer me up."

T.J. nodded his head and smiled. He then held out his hand, palm down.

"All for one…"

The others stacked their hands on his.

"And one for all," they repeated together.

They looked at each other, not knowing what to say, and not wanting to remove their hands.

"Thanks, guys," Billy said. "Keep in touch."

"Right," the other three said.

They removed their hands from the stack, looked at each other again, nodded, turned slowly and walked away.

* * *

SUZANNE WAS DRESSED AND WAITING for him when he returned to the cottage.

She greeted him at the door with a kiss.

"You don't have to tell me anything about your orders. You must be a terrible poker player."

He laughed quietly.

"Written all over my face, eh?"

"Down to your toes."

He handed her the envelope and went into the bedroom to remove his coat and tie and then to the little kitchen to pour a cup of coffee.

"Do you want me to bring you some more coffee?" he asked.

"No, thanks. I still have some."

He sat beside her on the rattan settee and took a sip of coffee.

She refolded the paper and slipped it back into the envelope.

"Okay," she said. "Let's have it."

He placed his coffee cup on the table in front of the settee, stretched his legs under it and locked his hands behind his head.

"I guess you'd better get in a request for transfer to the hospital at NAS Memphis."

"That's it?"

"A green ensign doesn't have much weight in this man's Navy. You told me that enough times. I'll play along for now but I'll see if I can get orders to fighter school later."

She turned to face him.

"Bill, if these orders mean you and I can stay together and you won't have to go into combat, I think—I think they're perfect."

"I know that. And I know I should be grateful that I got them. But, selfish man that I am, I didn't join the Navy to teach a bunch of teen-agers to fly."

"I know."

She snuggled against him. He dropped his arm around her shoulder. They sat quietly, one not wanting to gloat and the other not wanting to be bitter.

"Do we have anything to eat?" he said presently. "My wife didn't make me any breakfast this morning and I'm about to starve."

She pulled away from him and sat up.

"Drink your coffee while I rustle us up something."

"And then," he said, "after I eat, I'm going back into the bedroom, take off my clothes, climb into bed and take a nice, long nap. Every time I fell asleep last night, my wife woke me up. There was something I had that she wanted. And that went on all night. Oh, it was cruel. And all I wanted to do was sleep."

"Really?" she asked. "And have you considered that she might not let you sleep this morning, either?"

"As a matter of fact," he said, "I'd be mighty disappointed if she didn't."

* * *

BILLY AND SUZANNE left their beach cottage two days later, on Sunday afternoon and loaded the trunk of her car with their luggage. They drove into Pensacola, to Mrs. McCauhey's Tea Room, at the corner of Strong and Spring Streets, where they would spend the week before Billy left for New Orleans the following Sunday.

Billy rang the bell at the front door and a black man in a dark suit greeted them and showed them to a small formal living room where they waited on a couch for their hostess. The man took their bags and left the room.

Through the double doors they faced they could see the dining room, where a long table was being set for dinner.

Billy stood when Mrs. McCauhey entered the room and introduced himself.

"And this is my wife, Suzanne. She's a naval officer, too. A nurse at NAS."

Suzanne stood and shook the hand Mrs. McCaughey extended.

271

"Nice to meet you. Welcome to my boarding house.

"We have a lot of officers, junior and senior, staying here and I have tried to make my dining room as close to a wardroom as I could. I'm sure you understood my reason for the written recommendation from Mr. Sheeley," their hostess said.

"Yes, ma'am," Billy said.

"I'm going to give you a room occupied by our most famous naval hero," Mrs. McCaughey said, leading them up the stairs near the main front entrance, to a room on the second floor.

"This was Admiral Halsey's room when he was commanding officer of the main air station back in the thirties."

She opened the door to the high-ceilinged room and led them inside. A framed, autographed photograph of Admiral "Bull" Halsey hung on the wall.

"He was only a captain when he stayed here," she explained.

"It's a nice room," Suzanne said.

"Yes, it's our best one. Big windows. A little sitting area over there. You've even got your own bathroom," she said, pointing to a partially opened door.

Suzanne and Billy looked into the bathroom that held a large lavatory on a pedestal, a toilet with a pull handle to the flush tank above it and a commodious bathtub supported by heavy, cast-iron, claw-foot legs.

"Good. Thanks," Billy said.

"We had another famous person who stayed here during the First World War," Mrs. McCaughey said. "I don't know if you'd know her or not."

Billy and Suzanne looked at her expectantly.

"Have you heard of Mrs. Wallis Simpson?" she asked.

Billy shook his head.

"Oh," Suzanne said, "isn't she the woman the king of England gave up his throne for?"

"The very one. But when she stayed here, she was Mrs. Earl Winfield. She was married to a Navy lieutenant. A pilot, like you, Mr. Benson. Nice chap. Everybody called him 'Win.'"

"Who was Simpson?" Suzanne asked. "Her second husband?"

"Yes. After the war, Win began to drink heavily and they separated and finally divorced. A lot of men returning from the war had problems with peace after fighting for so long, you know," Mrs. McCauhey said.

"So she was divorced twice," Suzanne said. "It sounds like a soap opera, doesn't it? Heavenly days! No wonder everybody in England was so upset over the affair."

"She's a duchess now. Living in France," their hostess added.

"Well, back to the real world. The hours the meals are served are posted behind the door. I prefer for everybody to be seated when we serve. I like for everything to be done correctly.

"We've developed quite a reputation for serving good food. Of course, war-time rationing has hurt us a bit, but the local fishermen and the farmers over in Baldwin County keep us supplied with seafood and fresh vegetables and my cook knows how to serve chicken at least a hundred ways," Mrs. McCaughey said with a laugh.

"Yes, ma'am, we've heard about your meals. We're looking forward to them," Billy said.

"It's French-style roasted chicken tonight."

"Okay, young people, I'll leave you alone. Enjoy your stay. If you need anything, just let me know."

"Thank you. We will," Billy assured her.

He shut the door and reviewed the meal schedule in a picture frame that was screwed to the back of the wooden door. He pulled off his coat and hung it over the back of a chair and walked across the room to Suzanne, who was looking out the windows onto Spring Street. He put his arms around her, pulled her gently against his chest, and rested his chin on top of her head.

"Your hair smells good."

She smiled and gripped his hands, pressed across her chest.

"It's about two hours before they serve supper," he said, "and I'd like to get cleaned up before I eat. Did you see that big tub in our bathroom? Think of how much water we could save if we took a bath together. I'll bet Mrs. McCaughy would really be pleased."

*   *   *

BILLY DROVE SUZANNE to the nurses' quarters the next morning and let her off. She would change into her uniform in her room and walk over to the hospital to work her shift on the ward.

Billy then drove to the base library to write letters on the Red Cross stationary available free at the hospital and the library, to his parents, his Uncle John and Aunt Grace, and other Riverton friends, to bring them up to date on his graduation, wedding and orders to flight instructors' school.

He joined Suzanne for lunch at the officers' mess at the hospital and afterward he drove to Chevalier Field to get more flight time in an SNJ.

He and Suzanne returned to the boarding house after she got off from ward duty and had gone by her room at the nurses' quarters to change into a civilian dress. Following a meal of chicken pot pie and apple tart with whipped cream for dessert, they sat in the living room for an hour or so, becoming acquainted with some of the other guests, nearly all of whom were military, married to military, or related to military, before going up to bed.

The week passed too quickly.

They enjoyed the time they spent together but the upcoming day of his departure loomed as ominous and inescapable as a storm cloud, growing larger and darker as each day passed.

They drove east on Cervantes Street toward the train station early Sunday morning, speaking very little as they drove. Only church bells and the whining gears of the Buick broke the silence.

He parked at the station, shut off the engine and turned to face her.

"Our first separation," he said.

"But think about this," she said quietly, lowering her hand to cover his, pressed against the seat between them. "You'll just be a few miles away in New Orleans and for only six weeks, not thousands of miles away, somewhere in the Pacific, who knows where and for how long."

He smiled.

"And you're not going to let me forget it, are you?" he asked.

"I'm going to do all I can to keep you close to me for as long as I can.

"How wide the bed with none beside thee," she recited.

"True," he agreed. "But you know, Barry tells me there are a lot of women in New Orleans."

"One is all you need, kiddo, and you've got her. For life."

He lifted her hand and kissed the tips of her fingers.

"You betchum, Red Ryder."

"I'll call you as soon as I find out when you can come over. And I'll see if I can fly one of their planes over here. But I'd really like for us to see the French Quarter together. And maybe spend a night at the Roosevelt Hotel."

"Okay."

"You're not going to cry, are you?" he asked.

"Not while you're still here."

"I miss you already."

"Remember that when you start requesting combat duty."

He smiled again.

"Okay."

He looked at his watch.

"I'd better go. Time waits for no man and very few women."

He removed his hat, pulled her close and kissed her passionately.

He looked into her face and saw tears welling up in her eyes.

"You said you wouldn't do that until I left."

She wiped her eyes with her fingers.

"I lied."

He opened the door and walked to the trunk for his bag as she slid under the steering wheel. He returned to her window, leaned inside it and kissed her again.

"I'll call you."

*   *   *

NAS NEW ORLEANS had been constructed in 1940 on the southern shores of Lake Ponchartrain, lifted literally from a swamp on 182 marshy acres the City of New Orleans had donated to the military. By 1942, a hangar, two barracks, airplane assembly and repair shops, storage for 50,000 gallons of fuel, a ground school and an auditorium had been erected.

It was used first as an Elimination Base, or E-Base, for V-5 cadet candidates and later as a primary training base. A total of 179 V-5 cadets were trained there until the end of 1943, when the chief mission of the station changed again. The Navy ordered a merger of its other two primary flight instructor schools at Dallas and Atlanta into one, at New Orleans.

Three asphalt and concrete runways—the longest only 3300 feet—accommodated the 230 Stearman N2Ss and the Naval Aircraft Factory's N3N Canaries that were assigned for flight training.

The N3N trainers were very similar to the "Yellow Perils" in dimensions and power, but fitted with a Wright 235-horsepower R-760-2-Whirlwind 7 radial engine, as opposed to the Stearman's Continental 220-horsepower R-670-5 piston radial.

Quite small by Navy standards, with its back to the lake, the base had berthing, messing and administrative facilities for only 72 full-time officers and 1179 permanent enlisted personnel. An additional 62 civilians provided administrative support.

The instructors' flight school had been organized under the oversight of prominent Pensacola-based aerial educator, Lieutenant Commander Hugh B. Jenkins, who was now the station's executive officer.

By war's end, 1700 flight instructors would be trained; the hearty little Yellow Perils would be aloft for a total of 139,000 hours, logging 11,000,000 air miles, with only three fatalities.

*   *   *

Upon arriving in New Orleans, Billy took a taxi northward from the train station to the base. One of two sailor sentries at the main gate checked his identification and orders and waved his cab through. He entered the personnel office and began his check-in process.

His first inquiry was if he would be permitted to fly to Pensacola on weekends.

"Yes, sir," the yeoman assured him. "Just request an R-O-N—that's a 'Remain Overnight' chit—and as long as you're flying to a military base, you're okay."

"Could I take my wife up sometime?" Billy asked. "She's a Navy nurse at Pensacola."

"That's an affirmative, sir. Active duty personnel are welcome to go along with you as long as it doesn't interfere with your training time. When you fill out your flight plan, just include her name as your passenger. And once a year, you can even take someone who isn't service related."

Billy felt better. Flying to Pensacola in a Stearman would be quicker, easier and much cheaper than having Suzanne come by train to New Orleans.

He completed the check-in and asked directions to the Bachelor Officers' Quarters, or B-O-Q, or simply the Q, a white, squared-off, two-story structure, with a single-story lounge and recreation extension, giving the building a T-shape. He quietly welcomed the news he wouldn't have to share his space.

The neatly-made bed was covered with a spread that matched the draperies: no more drawing linen or having to make his own bed each morning.

A small lavatory was mounted to the bulkhead in one corner, but he would have to share one of two "all hands" heads with the other officers assigned to his deck.

Much better than what we had back in flight training, he thought.

No more walking naked to the showers, though, he thought, as was the cadets' practice in flight training. *I guess I'll have to buy a robe.*

Even in the least-expected place—the head—would he discover yet another example of RHIP, or "Rank Has Its Privileges," in the quality of the toilet paper. In the heads of the cadet flight training schools, as in all enlisted heads of the fleet and as was the case in many civilian homes, the toilet paper was made from wood pulp of such poor quality that splinters embedded in the paper were not uncommon because of inadequate processing. In the officers' heads, however, the toilet paper was of a superior quality: smooth, soft and splinter-free.

He walked down to the cheerful, spacious lounge, furnished with several multi-colored sofas arranged in groupings around coffee tables constructed of light-colored wood. Across the room, a group of male officers and two WAVES sat on two of the facing sofas, engaged in animated conversation.

The click and quiet rolling of billiard balls across a felt-covered slate top and the muffled sounds of balls dropping into the table's pockets could be heard in the adjoining recreation room. Through another door, in a smaller room with smaller scale furniture and natural-wood Venetian blinds between draperies bearing a geometric design, he saw men in armchairs, reading, relaxing and listening to what was identified during a station break later, as WWL, New Orleans.

He recognized Scott Wood, who had been in his final squadron class in Pensacola, sitting in one of the groupings near the entrance. He was with two other ensigns, approximately his age, poring over a war map in the *Times-Picayune*, depicting a battle in the European theatre, with arrows showing movement and labels identifying the nations' armies. He greeted Scott and shook hands with him and was introduced to the two other instructor candidates, George Freeman and Kevin Snyder. After becoming acquainted, they agreed to meet later to eat dinner in the officer's club

Billy showered and put on a fresh shirt. He noted that he had finally grown enough hair to hold a part if he brushed it firmly while it was wet. His face was still tanned from hours in the Florida sunshine and the regular exercise in Pensacola had helped him maintain his muscle tone.

Back in his room, he stepped away from the full-length mirror attached to the back of the door for an overall look, seeing only Bill Benson in a blue uniform. Satisfied he was presentable, he took his cover, snapped out the overhead light and walked back down the stairs to the lounge to meet his friends.

Hand-carved steamship round of beef was featured on Sunday nights at the O Club. Near the center of the carpeted, wood-paneled room, was a long table covered with white table cloths, starched and ironed, holding individual silver-plated chaffers filled with vegetables and breads, kept hot by cans of blue-flamed Sterno. At one end of the table stood neat stacks of large, heavy, white plates, each decorated with a pair of widely-spaced blue circles around the outside edge and, at the top, a matching blue anchor between the bands, the same as used in wardrooms in the fleet. A smiling Negro staff member in starched white coat and trousers removed a plate as each guest arrived at the table. The food selected was carefully tipped—not splashed—into the plates with large, long-handled serving spoons.

A heroic-sized leg of beef was presented upright under heat lamps. A burly, friendly chef in a tall, white toque, and wielding an enormous carving knife and fork, sliced the roasted meat—progressing from a dark brown crust on the outside, to lighter brown, to pink, to bright red nearer the bone—into thick, juicy, generous portions.

Billy and his three companions carried their plates to a cloth-covered table, carefully set with bread plates, each with a perfect, square pat of butter to one side, starched and ironed white napkins, polished silverware with a small anchor stamped near the end of each piece, short-stemmed glasses and, carefully placed in the center of the table—near the silver-plated sugar bowl with a hinged top and a spoon projecting from a small opening, and salt and pepper shakers—a real carnation in a crystal bud vase.

The four junior officers exchanged sea stories and speculated on the five-week-long instructor's school as they enjoyed their meal.

During a momentary lull in their conversation, Billy looked about the room, occupied by fellow officers: ensigns, lieutenants, commanders and a four-striper or two. Navy aviator's wings—gold pins, not embroidered—were worn proudly on the left sides of their double-breasted, dark blue uniforms. All the senior officers displayed rows of colorful ribbons under the gold wings. At three other white-cloth-covered tables sat Navy families, chatting amicably. Polite Negro waiters in white coats stopped regularly at the tables, quietly offering water, coffee or tea to the diners.

Billy turned his attention to the embroidered gold wings on the coats of his tablemates, to the single, half-inch bands of gold braid that encircled the cuffs of their sleeves and the embroidered gold star above each band. He held his sleeves out slightly and, as for the first time, studied his own gold braid and five-pointed star. He suddenly realized he would no longer be subjugated to having to wear a "slick arm" uniform—a term given to the sleeves of senior enlisted chief petty officers' coats without the hash marks that marked four years of service—or, in his case, the naked sleeves (and blank shoulder boards) that branded him merely a cadet.

Everything had moved so fast since graduation, he hadn't paused long enough to assess his present status and

suddenly,

the revelation came to him,

in a flash,

as an epiphany:

Hold on! He thought. *I'm no longer just some unidentifiable person in between enlisted and commissioned, neither fish nor fowl, nor good red herring, wearing a blue uniform.*

Oh, no! I am now, in every sense of the word, a full-fledged Navy officer and I have my gold stripes to prove it!

More than that, my gold wings mean I'm a Navy pilot!

And, here I am, at a Naval Air Station's Officers' Club, talking leisurely with my friends, eating good food off real plates, not rushing to gobble it up like a pig from a metal tray in a noisy, crowded chow hall. And I'm drinking water with ice cubes in it, from a stemmed glass instead of from a heavy porcelain mug, poured from a beat-up metal pitcher.

These are the fruits I've earned after nearly a year of flight training.

The recruiter told the truth. I worked hard and the Navy delivered.

He put down his knife and fork, leaned back in his chair, patted his Navy wings lightly as if to confirm their presence and confidently folded his arms. His tablemates observed his sudden shift in position, demeanor and the uncharacteristic smug look on his face. They stopped eating momentarily and waited for him to speak.

"You know, guys," he announced cheerfully, gesturing and nodding at their surroundings, "this is all right. I think I could get used to living like this."

*   *   *

THE NEXT MORNING, Billy and other ensigns approached the Instructor School Building, whose exterior was identical to the enlisted barracks: two stories tall, a peaked roof, asbestos-shingled siding, a wooden ladder which ran from the ground to a small deck beneath a second deck window and continued to the roof.

"Why do you think the escape ladder goes all the way up to the roof?" Scott Wood asked, pointing to the end of the building. "Does somebody think you can escape a fire by climbing onto the roof?"

The men looked at the architectural phenomenon but had no answer.

They joined other ensigns in a classroom, all wearing khakis with dark ties, gold wings pinned to their shirts and gold bars on their collars. They filled white glass mugs with coffee from a metal percolator at a coffee mess near the door as they introduced themselves to each other.

When a lieutenant with a manila folder under his arm came through the door, one of the men called, "Attention on deck!"

The men placed their mugs on the desks nearest them and came to attention.

"At ease, men," the officer said. "Take a seat and let's get started."

"Good morning," he said cheerfully. "Welcome to the swamp we call NAS New Orleans.

"I'm Lieutenant Greg Morrison and I'm your indoc instructor."

He opened the manila folder.

"Raise your hand when I call your name."

He had called only the first few names when another officer entered the room

Attention on deck!

"Carry on, men," the officer said. The men returned to their desks.

"Men, this is Lieutenant Commander Jenkins, our XO," Mr. Morrison said. "I'm sure he has some pearls of wisdom to share with us.

"Commander?"

"Men, I want to welcome you to New Orleans. I came here directly from Pensacola to get this place on line a couple of years ago. I hope you have the same pleasant memories of Pensacola that I did.

"My office is just down the passageway and I want you to drop by any time you like. Maybe we can swap a few sea stories about Pensacola. I don't have a receptionist outside my door to screen you, so just pop in. I'm always interested in your comments.

"Contrary to Mr. Morrison's optimism, I don't have any real pearls of wisdom for you. I just wanted to come by to welcome you to New Orleans and wish all of you good luck while you're here with us."

He gestured with his index finger.

"Oh, wait. Maybe I do have something for you. Later this week we'll have a crew flying in from California to start making the first of seventeen scheduled films for the flight-training program. Robert Taylor, the actor, who is a j.g., by the way, and became a flight instructor here, will be back to narrate the films. They've asked me to be the technical advisor. We're going to try to stay out of your way, though, so your training won't be compromised by Hollywood.

"Now, if you happen to spot Taylor on the base, treat him just like any other officer. I think you heard while you were in Pensacola, that Ted Williams and Errol Flynn were trained there, too. Celluloid celebrities are everywhere: Jimmy Stewart and Clark Gable are two more but they're in the Army Air Corps.

"On the other hand, if you happen see Taylor's wife, Barbara Stanwyck, no wolf whistles, please. She might get the idea that all those stories about sailors really are true.

"And if your girl friend or wife asks you to take her to a restaurant called L'Enfant's, down on Canal Boulevard, because she heard Taylor and Stanwyck eat lunch there, don't go. That's just a rumor the owner started to get more people into his restaurant."

He gave the class a big smile and lifted his hand in farewell as he started from the room.

"Good luck, men."

The indoctrination instructor called, "Attention on deck!" and then an "At ease" when Commander Jenkins left..

"All this standing and sitting is a bit like going to church, isn't it?" Mr. Morrison asked rhetorically. He completed the roll call and began his indoctrination lecture. Another "Attention on deck!" was called for two more officers who walked into the room together: a full commander and a lieutenant.

"Men," Mr. Morrison announced after the men had been reseated, "these two gentlemen are your commanding officer, Commander Paul Gillespie and Lieutenant Lewis Davis, our school's superintendent.

"Skipper?"

"Good morning, men."

Good morning, sir.

"I want Mr. Davis to have his say first. Lew?"

"Thank you, Skipper.

"Men, I've reviewed the orders of every man at this school. We take only the best. *You* are the best. I'll be following your progress and wish you the best of luck while you're here.

"I'll be dropping by your various venues and my door is always open. Come see me any time you have a complaint or a compliment. We want this to be the best flight instructors' school in the world. Okay?

"Again, welcome to N'awlins and the Navy's graduate school of flying." He flashed a broad smile.

"Skipper?"

"Thank you, Lew.

"Men, not many of you volunteered for our program here and I want you to know I appreciate the frustrations some of you may have about being assigned to flight instructors' school. I know where each of you would rather be.

"I left the States during the Big War to learn to fly in France. I came back to the States and joined the Navy as an enlisted man. Like you, I just *had* to be a naval pilot. I think you can relate to that. So I set my sights on the stars, literally, and here I am with my wings of gold but I'm flying a desk and not a plane.

"Quite frankly, I still love to fly and if I had my druthers, I'd be in the thickest part of any battle I could get. The Navy says otherwise. So, here I am, pushing pencils at a school in the middle of a Louisiana swamp.

"Get my drift?

"Nobody in this room was drafted. We all joined up of our own volition. We all took the same oath to obey the lawful orders of our superior officers.

"We take what we're dished out whether we like it or not. We do our best and bring credit to ourselves and the Navy and our country. You may never see actual combat, but you're here to give your best so hundreds upon hundreds of others may engage the enemy and beat him.

"Let me fill you in on why each one of you is here. You are here because your instructors in primary, intermediate and advanced told us you were their best students. That's the truth. Each one of you was hand picked to become flight instructors. You're the best of the best.

"And one-third of our IUTs—that's what you are, by the way, Instructors Under Training—one-third are combat pilots, men returned from combat duty in the Pacific. They'll share their expertise with you and with the students they'll teach in primary training.

"Men, let me tell you something else. You won't believe it until it happens to you. You take a youngster who knows nothing about flying and, in just eight lessons, you watch him take off on his first solo. That is a thrill! Why, I've seen hard-boiled instructors get up and leave a poker game on some trumped-up excuse, just to slip out to the landing strip to watch one of his students come in for a landing.

"For that matter, I've done the same thing myself. You say to yourself: 'I taught that young man to fly.' What a great feeling that is!

"I'm being honest with you again when I say, I believe primary is the most interesting stage of flight training, because it covers all phases of flying, from straight and level to acrobatics.

"I believe that. I really do.

"And seated before me here are true, unsung heroes."

He paused and pointed to the men seated before him.

"I believe, in this room, are the unsung heroes who would prefer the glory and honors of battle but realize that, in teaching, they are doing more than their share to bring victory in this world war.

"Don't grumble, men. Don't complain about your orders. Don't let anything compromise your training, your safety or the instructors who'll be teaching you to teach or the safety of the students you'll teach after you leave here. I don't want to hear about any bad attitudes.

"Finish the school. Report to your new duty station and cheerfully carry out your responsibilities. If you're so inclined, request orders to fighters or multi-engine or bombers or whatever it is your heart tells you to do.

"But while you are carrying out your duties as flight instructor students or as flight instructors, do so professionally. As naval officers. Above that, as naval aviators.

"Understood?"

Aye, aye, sir.

"Good.

"Now hear this: I didn't say, 'Don't try to get orders out of the program later, did I?'"

No, sir.

"Carry out the lawful orders of your superior officers.

"Mr. Morrison."

Attention on deck!

The two officers left and Mr. Morrison resumed his lecture.

"Let's see. Where was I?" he asked himself.

"Ah, yes. Some good news. Something we think will improve instruction: You'll be pleased to know we're in the process of replacing the Gosports with honest-to-goodness, two-way electronic communication in the Stearmans."

The class of 20 young ensigns and Marine second lieutenants smiled and nodded in approval.

After the welcomes and introduction to the program, the men were issued the instructors' handbooks that formed the basis for the five weeks of ground school and instruction began.

Billy called Suzanne that night from a phone booth in the Q.

"Oh, Suzanne! I miss you so much. I'll be so glad when we have a house of our own and we won't have to live like gypsies," he said.

"Me, too."

"I just called the Roosevelt Hotel and told them we were newly-weds and in the Navy and that you'll be coming over this weekend and guess what? They're reserving a room for us."

"Bill, that's swell, but honey, we can't afford anything like that."

"Oh, no, here's the best part: It's free! It's their wedding gift to us. Everybody loves the military down here."

"Heavenly days, Bill! That's wonderful! I can hardly wait."

"You can hardly wait? Listen, I'm counting the seconds. I'm as randy as a billy goat. Bill the billy goat! Ha! That's a good one, isn't it?"

She laughed appreciatively and then told him, "I'm taking PMs this week so I can leave Friday morning. The train should be there at around seven o'clock.

"Oh, I've mailed off a request for a duty swap with the nurses in Memphis. From what I've heard, half the girls in up there want to get down here to snare a Navy pilot husband, the way I did."

"Heavenly days, McGee!" he laughed. "Do you mean I didn't have to drop my pants to get your attention?"

*   *   *

THE NAVY HAD DEVELOPED a well-organized program for teaching pilots to teach, beginning with its syllabus that was carefully followed to the letter by the instructors.

Classroom lectures employed slide presentations, for example, to demonstrate how to fill out the many types of flight records. Movies that had been shown in primary training were shown again but with emphasis on the reversed teacher-cadet role perspective. Blackboards, as well as small, indoor, desk-sized or room-sized landing fields outdoors, and hand-held trainer models permitted the instructors to review the correct techniques for computing wind direction, wind speed and where and when to cut the throttle for landing. Invariably, however, the favored method for demonstrating flight maneuvers was the use of one or both hands.

Until the gosports were replaced, which was still ongoing when the war ended, the IUTs were given communication classes. The student donned his gosport mouthpiece and read a prepared script through the plastic tube into a transmitter and speaker that let him and his instructor listen to how clearly he enunciated his words.

The most demanding ground school application of speaking clearly placed an "instructor" five feet from a "student." The two men were connected by the flexible tube that carried instructions to the student's earpieces and separated by a pair of ordinary household washing machines. As the water-filled washers ran, the instructor practiced speaking to the student. The ultimate test of course was performed while actually flying in the noisy, open cockpit of a Stearman N2S.

*   *   *

BILLY WAS WAITING FOR SUZANNE when she stepped down from one of the passenger cars of the famed Crescent City, traveling from Pensacola to New Orleans and on to San Francisco.

She wore a dark suit with broad, padded shoulders and a light, two-tone, cylindrical hat, tapering at the top, and dark gloves. The miniature gold aviator's wings he had given her were pinned onto the left lapel of her jacket.

He took the suitcase from her, placed it on the platform floor and swept her into his arms to kiss her.

"You are so beautiful!" he said. "You make me so proud."

"You took the words out of my mouth," she said.

"Let's get a taxi and get on over to the hotel. I can give you a better welcome there."

He lifted their cases, took her by the hand and led her out onto the street where a line of taxis was waiting.

"The Roosevelt Hotel. The shortest route you know," he told the driver, climbing into the back of the cab.

The driver looked at his passengers through his rearview mirror. "Aye, aye, admiral," he said and pulled into the traffic.

They walked up the short flight of stairs to the grand marble hall leading to the lobby, taking in the opulence as they made their way to the desk.

A smiling, attractive couple passed by them going the opposite direction.

Billy and Suzanne looked at each other, stopped and then turned to look at the naval officer and the woman wearing a slinky evening dress.

"Heavenly days!" she said. "That was Robert Taylor and Barbara Stanwyck!"

"They're staying here while he's making flight training films at the flight instructors' school," Billy explained.

"That was exciting, wasn't it?" she asked.

The bellhop opened the door to their room, stepped aside and gestured for them to enter. They waited politely as he brought their bags in, set them on the pair of racks at the foot of the bed, adjusted the shades and pointed to the special offerings displayed on the dresser.

"Complimentary champagne, brandy, cigars, ice bucket. Here's a coupon for two free cocktails in the Sazerac Bar. Try the Sazerac cocktail."

Billy pulled a quarter from his pocket and handed it to the bellhop. "Thank you. We appreciate it."

"Thank you, sir! Oh, here's the 'Do Not Disturb' sign."

"Yes, that'll come in handy," Billy said, taking the sign.

"Enjoy your stay at the Roosevelt."

The bellhop left, Billy hung the sign on the doorknob outside the door, closed it, swept her into his arms again, and kissed her fervently.

"I can't wait any longer, Suzanne. I'm about to explode. You don't mind if we eat late, do you?"

"I don't care if we eat at all."

But they did eat, stopping first at the Sazerac Bar for their first experience with a Sazerac, touted as the first cocktail in history.

"How do you like it?" Billy asked after he had taken a sip of the spicy drink.

Suzanne fanned her face with her hand.

"It's hot. Do they put hot sauce in it?"

"I don't know. But I like it."

They walked down Bourbon Street, to Galatoire's Restaurant, where they stood in line on the sidewalk outside.

"I always think of my father whenever I have to stand in a line," she said, observing the jovial people in the line in front of them.

"How's that?"

"He would grumble that doctors shouldn't have to stand in line, 'like a bunch of peasants.'"

"But everybody stands in line at Galatoire's," Billy said. "Even heads of state."

They were soon shown into the spacious, mirrored, high-ceilinged, main dining room and seated against the wall at a table for two.

Their waiter, an older white man dressed in a black suit with a long white apron hanging from his waist nearly to the floor, poured ice water from the side of a silver pitcher, into the empty glasses at their places and took their orders.

They ate their first raw oysters, from the cold, salty Gulf of Mexico, served with lemon wedges and a zesty blend of catsup and horseradish. Cups of thick, dark, mahogany-colored seafood gumbo preceded crawfish etouffe, spicy eggplant and shrimp casse-role and little loaves of crusty French bread—"baguettes"—that the waiter placed directly on the pristine white tablecloth. They washed down the Creole offerings with glasses of crisp, cold, dry white wine. For dessert, they shared a serving of bread pudding with whiskey sauce, followed by Creole coffee *au lait*, served in demi-tasse cups.

Billy moved away from the table and brushed crumbs from his lap with his oversized napkin, onto the tiled floor of small, white hexagons.

"Man! That was good! I must have really worked up more of an appetite back there in the hotel room than I realized," he said.

"Me, too."

"One of the things I've noticed since I've been at the air station here, is the great chow. We've had fried oysters, fried shrimp, gumbo and jambalaya, but I think the best one of all is red beans and rice."

She made a face. "Red beans and rice? It sounds awful."

"It sounded bad to me, too, until I tasted it. I promise you, Suzanne, I could hurt myself eating it. But you know how I love beans.

"Well, now what?" he asked, leaning toward her, lowering his volume, "I mean, before we do *that* again."

She laughed.

"Let's just walk around a bit. Maybe take a buggy ride," she suggested.

"Okay. Let's see if we can walk off some of this food before we take the buggy ride."

The narrow streets of the French Quarter were filled with carefree sailors and civilian men with laughing women on their arms.

Dissonant sounds of jazz spilled from the clubs and bars along Bourbon Street, joyfully colliding in the center of the streets where merry revelers strolled or staggered.

Delicious smells of piquant Cajun and Creole foods drifted through the cool, night air from the restaurants, tantalizing all who breathed the complex aromas.

As they passed through the ancient streets, pushed through the happy throngs, it was hard for Billy to believe the rest of the world was at war.

Let them come to New Orleans, he thought. *Let them come eat the good food here; let them listen to the music; let them live the good life. They'll discover there are better things to do in life than kill each other.*

They walked hand in hand to Jackson Square where a column of mule-drawn carriages was lined up along the curb. They took a peaceful, leisurely ride through the bustling streets and afterward walked back to their hotel.

A 2330 (11:30 p.m.) curfew for military personnel was in effect, except for Saturday nights, forcing them to cut their evening short.

"Would you like to go up to the Blue Room and dance or just have a drink and listen to the orchestra?" he asked as they waited for an elevator.

"Don't they broadcast that orchestra on the radio?" she asked.

"Yes."

"Is there a radio in our room?"

"Probably."

"Maybe we can listen to the orchestra on the radio while we..."

"...do something else? Great idea," he said enthusiastically.

They returned to their room. As he locked the door behind them, he said, "There's no need to turn on the light, is there? Let me get out of this uniform and brush my teeth and then we'll listen to the radio."

*   *   *

BILLY'S TRAINING to be an instructor moved in a much different direction from his cadet training.

The total of 50 hours of flight time they would accrue while in New Orleans was devoted to reversing roles, since Billy was the instructor in the front seat, "instructing" another IUT in the back seat.

Much time was spent in emphasizing safety and anticipating possible mistakes that could be fatal. A staff back-seat instructor would set up situations for Billy to overcome and quickly trim the plane, as had been the case in the three phases of V-5 cadet training.

Very frequently, however, the instructor students would go up with each other more or less informally, simply to log airtime, perfect maneuvers and share helpful information with each other.

Even though they often flew over the city of New Orleans, most of their time was spent over Lake Ponchatrain and air space west of NAS New Orleans, although the young instructors enjoyed flying out over the Gulf in hopes of spotting enemy submarines.

Billy enjoyed, too, picking out the landmarks in the Crescent City: St. Louis Cathedral in Jackson Square, the trolley lines on Canal and out St. Charles to Carrolton, to the racetracks, and he nearly always made a pass over the large Falstaff Beer billboard, especially at night, with its large, round, lighted clock at the corner of Chantilly and Elysian Fields, to compare the time with his wristwatch.

For entertainment, base movies were shown in the auditorium where USO Camp shows, the Camel Caravan and the Curtiss Candy's "Baby Ruth Quiz Show" were also featured. Dances, jitterbug contests (music provided at the latter two events by Negro members of the base's station band, directed by a white chief petty officer), blood drives and war bond sales relieved the tedium of military life.

Billy passed up a performance by a musician known only by his last name: Rubinoff, who billed himself as "The world's greatest violinist."

"He came to our school to play once," Billy told his friends. "If he's the world's greatest violinist, why is he playing small-town high schools and military bases?"

Billy attended one USO show because it featured Bobby "Uke" Henshaw who played the ukulele. Billy liked T.J.'s playing better. He did enjoy watching Helen Wall, however, who performed an acrobatic novelty act she concluded by balancing, while blindfolded, on a slender revolving pedestal.

He took advantage of only one base movie, *Buffalo Bill*, with Maureen O'Sullivan and Joel McCrea, because of his appreciation of westerns.

A large amusement park, Lincoln Beach, was separated from the air base by only a road. Admission to the park was free—to whites only—and the men enjoyed taking their dates there, especially to ride the Zephyr, a large, wooden roller coaster.

Once a week, men, and sometimes WAVES, from the base produced a popular one-hour variety show called "The Skyway to Victory," broadcast over clear channel radio station WWL from its downtown New Orleans studios.

*   *   *

THE SECOND WEEKEND at instructors' training school, Billy took advantage of the RON availability and flew a Yellow Peril to Pensacola.

"It's like arriving in a Model-T," he confessed to Suzanne, referring to the Stearman, when she picked him up at Chevalier Field. "But I'd come in a cattle car—the Navy's version or a real one—to be with you."

He and Suzanne returned to Mrs. McCaughey's Tea Room, where they were greeted like old friends.

Suzanne made one more trip to New Orleans. This time they stayed at an inn on St. Charles Avenue on the trolley line. They took a streetcar to Canal Street and walked to Antoine's for dinner: Oysters Rockefeller and oysters on brochette for him, shrimp

Creole for her. For dessert they ate crème brulet and enjoyed the veritable light show at their table, in the production of café Diablo.

"I've been told that eating oysters is supposed to improve a man's, uh, shall we say, performance in bed," Billy said to her as they walked back to Canal Street to catch a streetcar back to their inn. "I've eaten so many since I've been here, I was wondering if you tell any improvement?"

"I don't think that's possible," Suzanne replied happily, squeezing his upper arm with both her hands. "I can't imagine how it could be any better."

Billy proudly agreed with her but didn't say so.

*   *   *

THE INSTRUCTOR-STUDENTS, as the men were also called, were introduced by the "Gunair" instructor to a new technology called "Synthetic Training and Gunnery" in a building behind the Link Trainer building. The student sat in a cockpit mockup built into the forward section of a wingless fuselage and in front of a large movie screen. As targets were projected onto the screen, the pilot "fired" at the target, moving the horizon realistically with his controls.

"Try not to get too aggressive when you're chasing the enemy blip on the screen," Billy's Gunair instructor told him.

"This is designed just to give you a feel for leading the target. I have an overpower lever that lets me stay ahead of you, no matter how hard you try to pull a lead on me."

It was difficult for Billy to remain humble after he "flamed" the target blip.

Additional target practice took place on the skeet range located at the Menefee Outlying Range, to enhance the Navy's philosophy of "deflection gunnery."

*   *   *

ATHLETICS WERE STILL EMPHASIZED at NAS New Orleans. A baseball team competed with small colleges in the area and teams from other military bases. Touch football, volleyball, swimming and workouts in the gym allowed the men to stay in shape and aided in reducing tension.

A popular device Billy had enjoyed as a cadet was the Aerowheel, a six-foot-high, drum-shaped, tubular steel structure that men could exercise inside to improve equilibrium and muscle tone. A pair of loops held the men's feet in place as they grasped the top handles and set the wheel rolling fore or aft. It could also be tilted over and spun around downward and then upright again.

Archery and pitching horseshoes were less exhausting recreations many men enjoyed.

All the instructor-students were offered the opportunity to earn an optional Instrument Card in their off time. After 15 hours of Link trainer time, the men flew under hoods—"Blackout Howards"—in the back seats of planes, in which 18 to 20 different prescribed patterns could be "flown."

Training in following radio beams was also offered. The final check for the Instrument Card was a four-and-a-half-hour cross-country flight, solely by instruments: to Mobile, Alabama, to Jackson, Mississippi, to Baton Rouge, Louisiana, and back to NAS New Orleans, accompanied by a check instructor in the forward cockpit. Each candidate made an instrument "letdown" upon his return to New Orleans, in which he dropped to a point he had calculated to be the center of the field.

Most of the instructor-students, Billy included, chose not to attempt the time-consuming honor, although the Instrument Card was highly prized among those who earned it.

*　　*　　*

MOST EVENINGS, Billy joined the instructor-students who gathered in the BOQ lounge after dinner. Some evenings they amused themselves with cribbage, a card game popular with the enlisted men, played with pegs placed into a small pegboard, to mark points.

Billy, Scott, George and Kevin were in the billiard room one evening as George was teaching them to play "cake," a form of snooker where numbers written on small, folded pieces of paper and drawn at random, determined the order of play.

As they played, the conversation turned to the subject of Women Accepted for Emergency Service, or WAVES.

"They're all over the base, doing just about everything the men do," Kevin was saying. "Packing parachutes, running the Link Trainers. They're even serving as airplane mechs."

"Have you seen that storekeeper WAVE, the one who was a Rockette?" Scott asked, enthusiastically.

"Vera Richter!" George responded. "Da-um! What a luscious cupcake! I'd like to see her doing some high kicks."

"I've even seen a couple of WAVES in flight suits and carrying 'chutes under their arms out there on the flight line," Kevin added.

"Are they pilots?" Scott asked.

"I don't know," he answered. "Maybe they ferry planes. Frankly, I don't know what they are or what they do."

"Ha!" George said, with an evil laugh. "I know what they do and I know how much they like to do it. They're just like all the other women in the Navy." He waved his index finger knowingly as he added, "And, there is only one thing those sweet, little Cupie Dolls want."

Billy looked up unsmiling from the paper he had taken from the ball case and was unfolding.

"And what would that be?" he asked flatly.

"That big sausage you've got swinging between your legs, Billy boy," George added with another dirty laugh.

Billy crushed the piece of paper as his hands squeezed into fists.

He felt his face turn red and his scalp prickle.

He slammed the balled scrap of paper onto the billiard table and hurriedly left the room, hearing only the first part of Scott's angry response: "George, you dumb sonuvabitch. You don't know shit from Shinola, do you?"

Billy, in his white rage, didn't remember climbing the stairs or entering his room.

He found himself standing beside his bed, smashing his fist into his hand, not knowing how to vent his anger.

He couldn't recall the last time he had been this heated about anything. But, just now, he had wanted to punch George in the face. As soon as he heard the demeaning remark, Billy's mind flashed a captain's mast scenario: He was on report for having struck a fellow officer.

He was frustrated in his fury.

He was too old to cry.

He couldn't hit, yell or throw furniture.

He was now what John Paul Jones first identified a "gentleman and an officer."

He didn't know what to do.

He began walking in a circle to cool off as he mentally replayed the scene in the billiard room.

He knew the perceived notions people held about women in the military. And he had heard enough stories from his buddies about sexual liaisons to know that many of the tales were likely true. Even Suzanne had teased about trapping him. And he had joked lightly about the same thing with her, too.

He was confused. Maybe he wasn't angry because he felt his wife had been insulted but because he suspected there was truth to what George had said about the real reason women were in the military.

His brooding was interrupted by a quiet knocking at his door.

"Bill, it's George. I need to talk to you."

Billy looked at the door. He wanted to ignore the knock. He was a slave to conscience, however, and knew he would have to let George in.

He took a deep breath, walked to the door, hesitated before turning the knob and then silently pulled the door open.

"Will you let me come in?"

Billy said nothing as he stood aside for George to enter.

"Bill," George began, while standing in the center of the room, his palms presented upward and then placed against his heart as his hands struggled to say what his words could not, "I am truly sorry for what I said. I promise you, from the bottom of my heart. I wouldn't have made that crack if I had known you were married to a Navy nurse."

Billy only stared coldly at George, making no comment or effort to accept his apology.

"Bill, I swear to you, I would never, never say anything to insult you or your wife. I'm so ashamed. I didn't know. I shouldn't have said it. I'm truly sorry and really want you to forgive me."

Billy looked at his friend who was clearly in distress.

Even in his anger, Billy knew it was wrong to let George suffer. He nodded and said through tight lips, "Thank you, George."

George extended his hand.

Billy looked at it. He didn't want to shake it. That would mean he forgave George and he couldn't be angry with him any more.

"Please, Bill."

Why do I have to do this? Why can't he just leave and let me get over it at my own pace?

He looked at the hand again and reluctantly extended his own.

George took his hand eagerly in both his.

"Thank you, Bill. I want you to know I am sincere in this: of all the guys I've met since I entered the flight program," he said, "I've never met anybody I respect more than I respect you. Nobody."

Billy stiffened slightly at the revelation.

"Scott has told all of us how much your wing thought of you and I understand why. I-I…"

"Thank you, George. I believe you. I'll get over it. I don't want you to feel bad about this."

They were startled at the sound of loud pounding on the door followed by solid banging at the bottom of it.

"Hey, Benson! It's Scott. I know you're in there. Come out with your hands in the air!"

Billy had to smile.

Scott evidently hung around T.J. too much. He's acting just like him.

Billy opened the door. He was half-expecting to see Scott wearing a colorful shirt and straw hat. Instead he was carrying a bottle of Cutty Sark. Kevin was behind him, holding four short glasses.

"Can we come in?"

"Sure."

"It's a good thing you let me in, Benson. I would have kicked the damned hatch off its hinges if you hadn't," Scott said.

"Shouldn't you be in a fighter squadron in the Pacific somewhere, blowing Japs to smithereens instead of flying those harmless little Yellow Perils around New Orleans?" Billy asked as he closed the door.

"Sure. Rub it in, you sonuvabitch."

"Sorry. I couldn't resist," Billy said.

"We thought this might be appropriate," Scott said, holding up the bottle of liquor.

Billy smiled. "Thanks."

"Is everything okay in here?" Kevin asked.

The two men looked at each other, smiled and nodded their heads.

"The comic relief helped," Billy said.

"I'm glad," Scott said as he removed the cork cap and poured a generous amount of the pale amber whisky into the glasses and handed one to each of his friends.

"Bill, I know how close you and T.J., Barry and Bob were back in Pensacola. Maybe it's time for you to establish a New Orleans branch of the Four Musketeers."

He held out his glass. The other three did the same.

"One for all…," he said.

"… and all for one," they recited together, clinking their glasses and drinking.

*   *   *

BILLY LAY IN HIS BED later that night, propped up on his pillow, his hands locked behind his head. Perhaps because of the drama that had just played out or the warming, philosophical-inducing effects of the Scotch, his drifting mind pondered the mysteries and complexities of life, love, family and friendship.

Men in the Navy:

Friends.

Pals.

Buddies.

Shipmates.

He was pleased to learn his friends respected him. Unassuming man that he was, his humility would have never permitted him to contemplate such an honor. Hearing it pronounced by another, however, gave him a modicum of satisfaction. Pride, perhaps.

Not too much.

Just a little.

Just enough.

And the topic that began it all that evening:

Women in the Navy.

The sex thing.

He had often heard men joke that they had joined the Navy to "ride the WAVES" and he had heard how the women in offices of all branches of the military couldn't type very well but were only "huntin' peckers."

Maybe women did *enter the service to find sex partners.*

The men took advantage of the situation. Why shouldn't the women?

He couldn't say because he was no an expert on matters related to sex.

His sexual experiences were confined only to Suzanne. Even though he was frequently a captive audience as his friends singled him out to discuss their intimacies with women, he didn't encourage the topic nor did he draw any conclusions from their true confessions of conquest—or their braggadocio.

Before he was married, he had no tales to tell, from lack of experience. He never entered the bragging contests boys and men invent about their sexual conquests or potency. Nothing changed after he married, since he felt his private life was just that—his and private.

He had always naively perceived women as being God's gentle little creatures, innocent in all things related to sex, who only responded to men's aggressive carnal cravings, rather than assertively pursuing their own gratification as his friends claimed, which had caused the conflicts in his values earlier that evening.

He knew there were girls like Nookie Sanderson and Jerri Alexander, the "easy" girls back in high school, the school whores but he truly believed women like that were in the smallest of minorities.

Marriage had changed some of his preconceived notions about the nature of women in love, however.

He was pleasantly surprised—delighted, even elated—to discover that Suzanne proved to be an eager, active contributor to their lovemaking. She was not the limp, lifeless, rag doll devoid of passion that he had heard Europeans claimed that American women were.

Not only was his wife a vigorous, reciprocal partner but on several occasions he had been gratefully and blissfully awakened from a deep sleep when he felt the exquisite, shivering sensations brought on by his wife's warm, exploring hand and fingernails— dragged sensuously backward over his bare skin—moving slowly and maddeningly back and forth across and down, down, down his chest and abdomen, to the sensitive inside surfaces of his thighs and then delicately fondling the independently and sensuously tightening and relaxing ovoids in what she called his velvet pouch of mystery, before her roving hand finally arrived at the swollen, rigid, pulsating object of her desire—throbbing simultaneously with the same energetic intensity of his strong, young, passionate heart— that she firmly grasped, causing him to shudder with rapture, taking his breath away.

He found himself being aroused as he mentally replayed the leisurely voyages of discovery each of them frequently enjoyed— taking turns at unhurried exploration, using their hands, their fingers and fingertips, followed by lips, teeth and tongues—tasting, feeling, sampling every plane, every hillock, every valley, every warm centimeter of each other's perfect body.

He smiled as he recalled the first afternoon at Mrs. McCaughey's Tea Room. They had undressed each other little by little in the late afternoon light. Still standing in the center of the room, they covered each other's body with kisses and sensual nibbles.

"I think we'd better stop this and take a bath before something happens we didn't plan," he had suggested.

She smiled.

"Okay. I'll lead the way. This will make a good handle," she said, gripping his engorged phallus.

He quickly bent over, pulling his pelvis away from her as he removed her hand.

"Oh, no, lady. I wouldn't do that if I were you. That weapon is loaded and cocked. It has a hair trigger and no safety."

"It goes off that easy?"

He gave a quick laugh.

"Hah! Every night I returned to my room from a date with you, I had to wash out my shorts and take a shower."

"Loaded and cocked, eh?" she asked.

"Ready on the left. Ready on the right. Ready on the firing line," he recited.

"You've been in the Navy too long, Benson. Now you're making love like a ordnance officer," she said.

His premarital orgasms had been limited to nocturnal emissions and an occasional experiment with masturbation. Both forms of sexual release shamed him deeply. He was embarrassed for Velma, their maid, who washed his underwear and sheets. He said nothing of course, nor would she but the increasingly regular occurrences as he progressed well into healthy puberty caused him to wonder if she might have, somehow, thought less of him for the voluntary, natural, biological, nocturnal phenomenon.

Billy's boyhood chum Lee Roy Cunningham, who made no secret of "lending Mother Nature a hand," said he always used a sock so he could wash it out the next morning and his mother wouldn't know.

Now that Billy was married, however, he was afforded frequent opportunities to engage all his fantasies with the woman he loved, letting her do the same to him and more importantly for him—without guilt. Everything they did together or to each other seemed totally natural and innocent to him.

He had never dreamed a woman's body could be so soft and smooth and beautiful and sensual. He had memorized each mole, each freckle, each curve and depression of her body, as she had his.

He recollected and now appreciated Bob's post-bath testimonial of how Molly's hands could create sensations on his own body he could not achieve himself nor even dream of.

And Billy understood how men—and women—could become addicted to the maddening power of sexual gratification.

Ironically, his sheltered life had created such idealized and romanticized prepubescent precepts when he began to understand more about procreation, that he believed the people he loved and who had created him, namely his parents, would not engage in such sweating, rutting, bestial behavior as sexual intercourse.

Billy recalled the embarrassment and frustration he had felt when Lee Roy first explained the facts of life to him. He absolutely refused to believe his parents would ever do THAT to produce him. But on a family vacation to Gulf Shores, he had discovered the foil pouches of condoms in his father's suitcase. He realized then that Lee Roy was right; his parents *did* have intimate lives.

Billy wondered now if they had ever shared or still shared the experimentations and passions their son had with his wife.

He hoped they had.

Billy reflected again on George's declaration earlier that night that he, Billy, was held in such high regard, not just by George but by the cadets in flight training and now, evidently, at flight instructors' school. He knew he liked the men but had no idea they thought so highly of him.

Billy contemplated that and the ensuing thoughts came in a jumble, wanting to be sorted out.

Tonight, when George apologized to him. Billy thought George might cry.

Billy wanted to cry, too, but didn't because men don't cry.

When he felt so moved, he always recalled Friar Laurence's charge to Romeo: "Thy tears are womanish."

George's eyes had been wet, whether tears fell or not. And Billy felt George wanted to hug him. Billy would have tolerated it. But men don't do that, certainly not naval officers.

He had seen men, happy with a day's flying, however, walking off the flight line together, their arms solidly around each other's shoulders. Or men at the O Club bar, standing face to face, their arms firmly holding on to each other's shoulders.

The touching we do. The masculine embraces. That's almost hugging. But that was public. Public displays of friendship or, perhaps, even affection, are they okay? Uncle John and I hug. Not just side-to-side-arm-across-the-shoulder but a tight, body-to-body embrace.

I love Uncle John and I can say it. It isn't sexual, but I love him. I love him more than any other man I know.

What would people say if they knew that?

302

But my own immediate family. I've never hugged my dad. Only the women, including Velma, a colored woman.

He determined to hug his father when he went home.

Would he permit it?

Billy felt confident he would.

But back to Velma.

She's lived in the house longer than I have. And Robert came to live with us when he was still a baby.

But why do she and Robert have to eat in the kitchen by themselves? Any time any of us individual members of the family are there, we eat at the table in the kitchen with them. Why can't they eat in the dining room with the rest of us?

He knew the unwritten rule: *It isn't done in the South. Whites and coloreds don't mix. They don't eat together.* His own Uncle Kenneth felt so strongly about the rule that he had brought his Klan friends to stand in the street outside the house to protest Velma's presence in the Benson house.

In Memphis, black actors were cut out of Hollywood films.

Less radical people would probably agree that whites and coloreds shouldn't socialize.

He knew many people who believed that, but he felt what people thought didn't necessarily make something wrong, especially if he thought it is right.

His mother had reminded him often of how he had slept with Velma, as an infant, when she and his father were away overnight.

A lot of people would say that was wrong.

He resolved he would talk to his parents about doing what they knew was the right thing, regardless of what people might think or say.

Velma's a part of our family. She should be treated like family. Robert, too, of course.

Billy smiled as he thought about Robert, who had been raised by Velma since infancy, after his mother was killed.

The first time they went fishing with Billy's father, the two boys ducked into a canebrake to change into swimming trunks. Billy was surprised to see that Robert was black all over. He had somehow assumed Robert's penis would be white, like his.

He wondered now if Robert had considered the same thing about Billy.

It's funny what we believe when we're young.

In Billy's case, Lee Roy had passed on many of the beliefs, sexual or not, correct or otherwise, that Billy had accepted in his innocent youth:

A man's shoe size indicates the size of his penis
Asian women have horizontal vaginas.
A horsehair left in a bucket of water will turn into a snake.
Handling toads causes warts.
Burying a potato or dishrag will cure warts.

He stretched and smiled as he thought about Suzanne and what she was doing. He rolled onto his side, pulled the covers over his shoulders, closed his eyes and fell asleep.

*   *   *

"THAT'S RIGHT, MOM," Billy was saying from the pay telephone booth at the Q. "I'll complete training Thursday. Suzanne is picking me up but we'll have to stay overnight some place along the way. We should be there sometime late Friday morning."

"How long will you be able to stay?" she asked.

"Until Sunday. I have to report for duty Monday morning."

"I'm sorry you can't stay longer, but as close as Memphis is, you can come down after you get settled, can't you?"

"Sure, Mom."

"We're so anxious to meet Suzanne."

"She's anxious to meet you, too."

"We're going to push the beds in your room together and try to make everything as comfortable as we can. Will that be all right?"

"Of course, Mom."

"Okay, son. We're really excited. Drive safely."

"We will. See you Friday."

Billy knew his family and friends would accept and love Suzanne. But this was an entirely new set of situations for him and for them. After all, he had never had a serious relationship with any Riverton girls. And he fell in love with a Navy nurse the first time he saw her. What would they think of his impulsive choice and hasty behavior, marrying a girl they had never seen and knew noth-

ing about? Did they secretly harbor feelings of recklessness or irre-
sponsibility on his part, despite their explicit assurances? Did they,
as George had charged, wonder if military women were immoral,
promiscuous?

And Suzanne had her own fears and reservations, too, despite
Billy's assurances. Her family had never been close and she was
unsure about and unaccustomed to the overt shows of love Billy
had assured her his family would demonstrate.

*   *   *

BILLY'S CLASS ASSEMBLED in formation on the flight line for
his mid-April graduation from flight instructors' school. An inspection by Skipper Gillespie and BuAer Chief, Admiral Ramsey, was
followed by addresses from Louisiana dignitaries.

Suzanne stood alongside the formation, in a Navy blue and
white polka-dot dress that emphasized her figure, a broad-brimmed
hat she told him was a cartwheel and high heels that showed off her
shapely calves. Billy was so proud of her, he kept cutting his eyes
in her direction to watch the breezes play with her dress.

Commander Gillespie introduced "the honorable James Davis,
Governor of the great state of Louisiana."

Billy smiled as the governor approached the microphone to
make comments. Because of Uncle John's fondness of country and
western songs, Billy knew that "Jimmy" Davis had written one of
the nation's all-time hits, *You Are My Sunshine.*

Billy wondered if the governor might break into song before the
assembly.

A.J. Higgins Sr., owner of New Orleans-based Higgins
Industries that manufactured the famous Higgins Boats—the landing craft used by every branch of the service, except the Air Corps
and Coast Guard—was the main speaker for the program. The men
didn't throw their hats into the air after they received their rolled-
up certificates. Instead, they were dismissed to assemble under an
open-sided tent where punch and cookies were served and the graduates could introduce their wives and girlfriends.

Billy shook hands with members of the New Orleans' branch of
the Four Musketeers, chatted awhile, took Suzanne's elbow and
escorted her to the Buick. They drove to the Q, where he changed

from whites to aviator greens and she to slacks before they struck out northward.

*   *   *

AS BILLY AND SUZANNE drove into the back yard and parked behind his father's car, the back door opened and his family tumbled down the stairs like fruit from an overturned basket.

"Just roll with the punches," he said, patting her hand before he exited his door that had been opened by his sister Susie.

They were all over Billy.

Billy hugged his father tightly and was touched when his father returned his hug with even more energy. And Billy, emboldened by his father's response, planted a gentle kiss on his cheek.

Jim looked at his son, wiped his eyes and walked to Suzanne's side of the car to open the door for her.

"Welcome to the family, Suzanne."

She climbed out and returned his warm, welcoming embrace.

The rest of the family followed, as Billy introduced each by name. Sally Clark Moore had heard the commotion from her house across the alley and joined them.

His mother cried.

His father cried.

The rest of his family cried, except for Robert, who was grinning broadly, stoically trying not to cry, and Buddy, who was tearing around and around the gathering of kith and kin, barking hysterically.

"Come on inside," his mother said. "Jim, you and Robert bring in their bags.

"Sally, come on in and eat with us."

The group moved to the living room *en masse*, still so tightly clumped together, they resembled a Nordic nomadic clan.

A short time later, Billy's mother excused herself and went to her bedroom. She returned with a large box wrapped in white paper and tied with an extravagant white ribbon.

"Suzanne and Billy, we wanted to get you something as a wedding present but weren't quite sure what you needed. There are so many shortages because of the war, we didn't have a lot of options.

Anyway, take this for now. When the war is over and you're settled in your own house, we'll try again."

She placed the box on the coffee table in front of the guests of honor.

"It's from all of us," his mother explained. "Velma, Ollie, Robert...all of us."

"Thank you, everybody," Billy said.

"You open it," he told Suzanne.

She carefully untied the bow and removed the paper without tearing it, exposing a large box with *Keenum's Department Store, Since 1899*, written in large, blue letters, diagonally across the top.

She pulled the lid straight up and placed it on the floor. She folded back the tissue paper, revealing a heavy, white bedspread.

"It's the Martha Washington pattern," his mother explained.

"It's beautiful!" Suzanne exclaimed, stroking the bedspread. "Thank you so much."

She stood and gave Edna a hug.

"Thank you again, everybody," Billy said. "It's nice."

"Suzanne and I have some things for you, too, in my bag."

He excused himself and went into the dining room where his suitcase had been left, returning with his hands full of gifts.

After he handed out all but one present, he knelt on one knee beside his mother and held up a box. He removed the top and lifted out a pin.

"Mom, this is a special pin like the wings Navy pilots wear, except it's a little smaller. Only mothers and wives can wear them."

"Like this," Suzanne said, proudly patting hers, which she was wearing at the top of her blouse.

Billy freed the pin on the back of the wings and carefully slipped it through the left side of his mother's dress.

Edna's hand went to the shining gold wings.

"Thank you, Billy. We are all so proud of you."

She placed her hands at the back of his neck and pulled him over to kiss his cheek, as everybody gathered around her to admire the pin.

"I have something for you, too," Aunt Ollie said.

Everybody looked at her.

"Robert, would you look on my bed? There's a small box there."

Robert dashed to the back of the house and retrieved the box.

"I haven't worn this in years," Aunt Ollie said. "My arthritis has swollen my joints so."

"This is for your bride," she said, handing Billy the box..

Billy passed the white cardboard box to Suzanne. Inside, she found a dark-blue, velvet-covered box with a mother-of-pearl button on the front. She lifted out the blue box and carefully pushed the button, causing the domed lid to pop open.

Suzanne's eyes lighted up.

"Bill! Look at this!" she said enthusiastically.

She held up a silver ring with two large Tiffany-mounted diamonds set at angles to each other.

"Oh, thank you, Aunt Ollie!" she said.

"Wow!" Billy exclaimed.

"Try it on!" Alice called.

Suzanne removed her white gold wedding band and handed it and the velvet box to Billy.

"You put it on," she said.

"You have to kneel!" Robert said, causing the family to applaud and echo Robert's demand.

Billy immediately went to one knee and reached for Suzanne's hand.

"Suzanne Walker Benson, will you please accept this extravagantly beautiful ring from my beautiful and thoughtful Aunt Ollie, with all the love my family and I can offer you."

"Yes, I will, James William Benson Jr."

He slipped the ring on her finger. She leaned forward and kissed the top of his head.

She held out her hand for everybody to see.

All the women were crying.

"And to seal it," he said, "here is the fifteen dollar wedding band I bought you."

He slipped the ring back onto Suzanne's finger.

She went over to Ollie to hug her and thank her again.

Billy stood and faced his Aunt Ollie with mock anger.

"And, tell us, please, Aunt Ollie, why you waited until you met Suzanne before you sent Robert for the ring?"

"If I didn't like her, I'd keep it. I might get married again, you know."

He knelt and hugged his great aunt and kissed her on the cheek.

"If you do, I'll buy you a fifteen dollar wedding band."

A short time later, Billy's mother suggested that everybody get washed up for the evening meal.

Billy grabbed their bags and escorted Suzanne up to his old room, followed closely by Buddy. He paused outside the door and set their bags on the floor.

"Watch the ceiling when I open the door."

He stood out of the way so she could see as he flung the door open wide. The airplanes hanging from the ceiling stirred to life.

"I always like to see how they swing back and forth like that when I open the door. It's like they recognize me and are welcoming me home."

She squeezed his arm.

"I'm sure they are," she said. "The way everybody else did."

He dropped the bags onto the beds that had been pushed together.

"So, this is the real Bill Benson," she said, studying the pictures and books and model airplanes in the room.

"Yep. The pre-Navy Bill Benson, anyway. Maybe I should say, 'the pre-Navy Billy Benson.'"

"Yes. I noticed that. Will they know who I'm talking about when I refer to you as 'Bill'?"

"Oh, sure. I'm the only Bill or Billy here."

She closed the door and walked back to him.

Tears were welling in her eyes.

"You are such a wonderful man," she said. "I love you so much. I love your family."

"My family loves you, too."

She put her arms around his neck, pressed against him and kissed him lovingly.

"Thank you for being such a wonderful human being, good friend, excellent lover and sweet, caring husband," she said.

He removed her hands from his neck.

"I think if this goes any farther, I may not be able to go downstairs for a week."

She stepped back from him, looked at his pants and laughed.

"Oh, Bill. You just can't hide the truth, can you? It doesn't matter if I look at your face or your pants, I can always tell what you're thinking."

"The curse of being a man in love," he confessed.

"Well, if it doesn't go down in time, let me know and I'll give it a good thump," she said, demonstrating with her middle finger, arched against the back tip of her thumb.

"Oh, no you don't," he said laughing. "You leave that to Nurse Riley and those other abusive ward nurses. It stays sore enough already, just doing what a dutiful husband has to do."

"Has to do?"

"Okay. Likes to do."

"Only likes to do?"

"All right. How about this? Couldn't live without?"

"That's better. Now let's get ready for dinner."

"Here it's called supper."

"Supper."

"It's too bad we won't be able to come back up here for dessert," he added.

*   *   *

THE DINING ROOM TABLE had been laid out with a white linen tablecloth, the best china and silverware. An extra leaf had been added to provide more seating.

"Billy, you and Suzanne sit over here," his mother said, pointing to the chairs on his father's right.

"Sally, you sit on the other side of Jim."

"Susie and Alice, there."

"And I'll sit here, at the other end of the table."

As members of his family took their places at the table, Billy remained standing.

"How about if we bring in chairs for Velma and Robert?" he asked the group.

Velma, who was in the process of placing a basket of hot rolls on the table, looked up disapprovingly at Billy.

"Don't you start giving orders as soon as you get home, Admiral Billy Benson," she said with conviction. "Robert and I will eat in the kitchen, the way we always have."

Billy looked at his father.

"Dad?"

His father jumped up from his chair and disappeared into the kitchen. He emerged with two chairs that he placed on either side of the table.

"Grab a couple more plates, Velma," he said.

"Mister Jim?" she asked.

"Robert?" Jim called.

Robert came to the dining room door.

"Yes, sir?"

"You and Velma will be eating in here from now on."

Robert smiled.

"Yes, sir!"

Billy sat beside his father and grasped his wrist lightly

"Thanks, Dad."

"No, thank you, son. We should have done this a long time ago."

*　　*　　*

"LET'S LET BILLY DRIVE and Jim and I'll sit in the back," Edna said at the back door of her house the next day.

They were driving to Mrs. Watson's house for lunch.

Billy pointed out to Suzanne Riverton High, the family's church and other highlights as they drove to the quiet street lined with grand old Victorian houses.

Mrs. Watson opened the door to welcome the Bensons.

"Billy! How fit you look! Give me a big hug. And this must be Suzanne! You give me one, too. Come on in, everybody."

They followed her into her formal living room.

"Please, make yourselves at home. I'll bring Marcus in to meet you all."

Billy looked around the room. It was the same but looked brighter. He realized the windows had been washed and the draperies had been cleaned and pulled back, letting in the natural light from outside.

"Everything looks very nice, Mrs. Watson."

"Marcus has painted and cleaned and made this old house shine," she said.

"Has Billy told you he used to deliver my groceries and drive me to my study club?" Mrs. Watson asked Suzanne.

"Yes, ma'am. And I really want to see that car. What kind is it?"

"A LaSalle," Billy said.

Marcus Aurelius Brown appeared in the doorway of the living room.

"Everybody, this is Marcus, Mrs. Watson announced. "He has cooked the most scrumptious meal for us."

Marcus lifted his hand and nodded politely.

Hello, Marcus.

"This is Billy, Marcus."

"Hi, Marcus."

Marcus took Billy's hand and shook it but didn't say anything.

"And this is my wife, Suzanne."

Marcus nodded at her.

"And these are my parents, Marcus," Billy said.

Marcus nodded at Edna, shook hands with Jim, waved and left the room.

"Miz Watson took Marcus in after his brother moved to Detroit," Billy said.

"Billy, I'm so glad how all this worked out."

"So am I, Mrs. Watson. I'm glad you have somebody with you now."

"And be sure to show Suzanne the car before you go. Maybe you'd even like to take her for a ride in it," Mrs. Watson said.

"Thanks. Maybe we will."

Robert returned with a plate of appetizers atop a tray of short glasses. He carried a pitcher in his other hand.

"Marcus has made us a few little appetizers before we go in to eat. And this is a pitcher of fruit juice."

Robert left the tray and returned to the kitchen.

Suzanne pointed to the music box in front of the marble fire-place.

"Is that the bumblebee music box?" she asked Billy.

"Would you like to hear it?" Mrs. Watson asked.

"Oh, yes," Suzanne said. Everybody walked to the wooden box as Mrs. Watson wound it and pressed the start key.

They watched in fascination as the bronze bees vibrated the bells with their tails.

Afterward they all returned to the hand-carved, velvet-covered furniture, as Mrs. Watson held court from her Belter chair.

Marcus reappeared in the doorway.

"Are you ready for us, Marcus?"

He nodded.

"Pull me up, Billy."

He took her hand and gently helped her to her feet.

"Marcus, come over here and take me to the dining room.

"Everybody else, follow me."

"I think you've made some changes in here, too, Mrs. Watson," Billy said as he entered the spacious dining room.

"Oh, Marcus keeps the entire house as spotless as Buckingham Palace," she said, as Marcus held her chair for her.

"He's even cleaned the crystal chandeliers. He is a real treasure."

Mrs. Watson was right about the food. Marcus had prepared an excellent lunch of *coq au vin*, with fresh mushrooms and pearl onions.

Everybody raved about their lunch as they consumed it eagerly.

For dessert, they had fruit sorbet and little Swedish cookies.

After Marcus had cleared away the table, Mrs. Watson spoke to Billy.

"Go to my bedroom and bring me that long package on the bed."

He excused himself and disappeared from the room, returning nearly immediately with a large cylindrical object wrapped in brown paper.

"Billy, as we grow older we wind up with more things than we can use.

"Suzanne, I want you and Billy to have this. It's been in my family for over fifty years and I'd like for you to pass it on when you've had it fifty years."

Billy unwrapped the package and rolled an oriental rug onto the floor.

Suzanne walked over to look at it more closely.

"It's a genuine oriental, although it was made in India. The pattern is called Shariz and it's all hand-made. I think the size is something like five feet by eight feet."

"Oh, it's beautiful!" Suzanne said.

"Thank you, Mrs. Watson. It is really nice," Billy added.

He bent over her and kissed her cheek.

"Thank you," he said again.

"You're welcome. Think of me every time you tromp across it."

He laughed. "We will."

*   *   *

"THIS IS THE OTHER HALF of my civilian life," Billy said as he turned the Buick into the driveway at his Uncle John and Aunt Grace's country home.

"It's beautiful. I could live in a place like this."

"So could I. And Bob Hawthorne. And T.J.

"I'm next in line for it, but I'm sure Uncle John and Aunt Grace will stay here until they die. And, from the way they're all talking, Bob will probably move in with them after he gets out of the Navy."

He stopped the car in front of the garage, got out and opened Suzanne's door.

Uncle John called to them from the barn loft.

"Hello, down there!"

"Uncle John! Come on down and meet Suzanne!"

"On my way!"

Uncle John's shirt was wet with perspiration. He removed his work gloves as he strode toward them.

He extended his hand to Billy. Billy took it but pulled his uncle to him and embraced him.

"I'm soaked, nephew. I'd hate to mess up that Navy uniform."

"A little sweat won't hurt it."

John studied the uniform closely.

"It looks like a Marine uniform, doesn't it? Are you *sure* you're in the Navy?"

"Oh, yeah. Our aviation greens do look a lot like the Marines' uniform.

"Uncle John, this is Suzanne."

"Hi, Suzanne."

He offered his hand. She took it and shook it firmly and pressed her cheek against his.

"It's good to meet you at last. Bob and T.J. were right. You are every bit as beautiful as everybody said."

She smiled shyly.

"Thanks."

"Check out these diamonds Aunt Ollie gave her."

John held Suzanne's hand and admired the ring.

"Oh, boy! They're knock-outs, all right.

"Well," he said. "Come on in to the kitchen. Grace went over to old Miz Harris's place to help her work on a quilt. She should be back before dark."

As they walked to the house, Rattler ambled up to the back door of the kitchen. Billy rubbed his head and the old dog returned to his nest in the grass.

The three entered the kitchen and sat at the table.

"Can I get you anything?" he offered.

"Oh, no! We ate a big meal at Mrs. Watson's house. Thanks, anyway."

"Thanks for the letter," John said. "I'm sorry you didn't get a fighter squadron."

"So am I. I'll reapply after I get to Memphis, if Suzanne lets me."

"From what T.J. said," his uncle remarked, "you're too good a pilot for your own good. He said you were sent to instructors' school because of your high scores in flying."

"Looks that way. If I had it to do over again, I think I'd crack up a couple of planes."

"Oh, by the way," John said, pointing to a wrapped gift on the Hoosier cabinet. "That's a wedding gift from your Aunt Grace and me but she wants to give it to you, herself. It's a coffee maker."

Billy laughed.

"You do have electricity up in Memphis, don't you?" John asked.

Billy nodded. "Oh, yes, and running water, too."

They passed the next half hour catching up on all the news, permitting John and Suzanne become better acquainted.

After showing Suzanne through the house and pointing across the road to the creek, Billy excused himself and pulled his uncle aside.

"Uncle John, uh, Suzanne and I slept in my bed last night. It's over mom and dad's room, you know, and we, uh, we didn't want to make any noise, you know, so we couldn't, uh, you know, have sex. And when we get to Memphis, we'll have to stay in segregated officers' quarters until we can find a place to live. It might be a couple of weeks before we can, uh, you know."

"So, you married one of those screamers, eh?"

"Well, I have to admit I do my share, too."

"And you want me to get lost so you can use my bed to catch up?"

"Oh, no. The room up in the barn loft will be fine."

"Those are just single beds up there."

"Sure, I know that. But there's only one of us on the bed at a time, if you know what I mean. We kind of, uh, stack up, you know. A single bed is fine."

John put his arm around Billy's shoulder and pulled him close. "Nephew, you just take that pretty lady up there and stay as long as you like."

"Thanks, Uncle John."

"But there's one thing I'd like to ask."

"What's that?"

"Please, don't ya'll make so much noise that you scare the livestock. I don't want those chickens laying doorknobs or the cows giving sour milk."

"You've got it."

Instructor and student wait as mech winds up inertia starter in the Stearman N2S-3.

CHAPTER SIX

FLIGHT SCHOOL

NAS MEMPHIS

EVEN BEFORE BILLY AND SUZANNE passed through the northern outskirts of Memphis that Sunday afternoon in mid-April 1944, NAS Memphis made its presence known in the distance before them, as the small, slow-moving yellow specks in the clear April sky materialized as Stearman N2S trainers.

Suzanne occupied herself during the drive up the narrow, two-lane county road by following the planes as they crossed and criss-crossed each other in the ether, weaving a haphazard, trackless pattern.

Billy sighed as he rolled down the window of the car and stopped at the main gate where he and Suzanne handed their orders to the Marine sentry. The unremitting and ubiquitous drone of the little yellow planes filled the car. The Marine returned their orders, stood aside and saluted them smartly as they drove onto the base.

"Well, this is one place I hoped I'd never see again," Billy said, rolling up his window.

Suzanne looked at the drab, monolithic structures on both sides of the long, straight asphalt streets and along the acres of asphalt grinders as they drove slowly toward the hospital.

"I see now why there were so many nurses who were anxious to swap with me," she said. "This place looks like something you might see on the moon. Aren't there any trees?"

"They're probably considered hazards to aviation," Billy said off-handedly.

"It really wouldn't be so bad for us if there were married quarters on base. At least we could enjoy our bedspread and rug together," he commented.

"Is it always this noisy?" she asked.

"I'm afraid so."

"It didn't seem this loud at Pensacola," she said.

"I think the earth absorbed it down there," he said. "Up here, everything is asphalt. It just reflects it and probably amplifies it."

He reached the hospital, parked the car and walked inside with Suzanne, stopping at the information desk for check-in instructions for her.

"I'll log you in, Ma'am," the corpsman said, reaching for her orders.

He wrote her arrival time beside her name and handed back the envelope.

"You'll need to give your orders to the OOD tomorrow morning. His office is just around the corner.

"The chief nurse is here today. She'll need a copy, too. Her office is right down that passageway there," he said, pointing.

Lieutenant Commander Elizabeth Pavlick stood, shook hands with Billy and Suzanne invited them to sit in the chairs that faced her immaculate, flight deck-sized desk.

Suzanne had never known of a case in Pensacola where the chief of nursing was working in her office on a Sunday afternoon

Miss Pavlick's brilliantly white uniform was so stiffly starched it appeared to be made of a white, malleable sheet of metal. As they spoke, she sat with her unmoving hands clasped tightly on the highly polished wooden desk. Her rigid cuffs held gold Navy officers' insignia cufflinks.

Her skin was milk white and it was obvious she had darkened her hair. A neat circle of rouge on each cheek gave her a strong resemblance to Elizabeth, the Virgin Queen.

As they chatted, Suzanne perceived Miss Pavlick as a perfectionist who would tolerate nothing less than excellence from her nursing staff. After a short visit, Suzanne left a copy of her orders and walked back to the car with Billy.

"She seems like a tough old bird, doesn't she?" Suzanne commented.

"T.J. calls the old, salty ones, 'sea bags.' But that's probably how she got to be a lieutenant commander and chief of nursing. Don't let that happen to you."

"We need to find her a husband like you," Suzanne said suggestively. "That would put a smile on her face."

"Hmmm. Do you mean I'd tickle her to death? How am I supposed to take that?"

"As a profound compliment."

Billy drove to the nurses' quarters and carried her bags inside.

"I'll call you after I get checked in," he said. "Let's go to the O Club for dinner. Maybe we'll be able to get a feel for what we're facing."

"Okay."

He squeezed her arm. "I'd love to devour you right now but I guess we have roles to play, don't we?"

She smiled. "I'm afraid so."

"Talk to you in an hour or so."

"Okay. I love you."

"I love you, too."

*   *   *

"YOU'RE LOOKING FOR A PLACE for yourself and your wife to stay?" Brad Kendrick, Billy's new squadron commander, asked the next morning in his office after Billy had checked in with the OOD and met the commanding officer.

"Out here near the base, if possible," Billy specified. "I think the drive in from Memphis would be too long."

"There's precious little housing out this way, for sure. This is almost…no, it *is* rural. There's no question. But I'll check it out.

"Meanwhile, pick up a copy of the *Commercial Appeal*…yesterday's if you can. Sunday is the big day for ads."

"Okay. Thanks, Commander."

"Call me Brad."

"Brad."

"Meanwhile, come on back to the ready room. Let's see who's here."

Billy was pleased to learn that Jim Harris, his principal flight instructor when he was a cadet, was still attached. Jack Loper (The 'Mad Looper') was still on board and as taciturn on a personal level as he was on the instructor-student level.

Billy also was introduced to others he had not known as a student.

"And you're going to see some more new faces out on the flight line," Brad told him. "We've got a full complement of WAVES in our program now, doing everything the men do except fly or teach flight."

"I'm sure the air crews appreciate that," Billy said.

"And not just them," Jim Harris volunteered. "We've seen a couple of little romances blossoming between the cadets and their mechs."

"I guess everything changes," Billy commented.

"Especially the changes," Brad said as they left the ready room

Billy met Suzanne for lunch at the hospital wardroom every noon. They compared notes on locating housing but without luck.

"It's getting discouraging, isn't it?" he asked. "I'm beginning to think our renting something in Memphis might be the only way we can be together."

"No. Let's take our time," she said. "I'm sure something will show up sooner or later."

And it did. If only a temporary respite but from an unlikely source.

During her morning rounds, Commander Pavlick, her head erect, shoulders pulled back and her spine as straight as a ship's mast, walked up to the nursing station on the pediatric ward where Suzanne had been assigned.

Suzanne looked up and stood as she heard Miss Pavlick's over-starched uniform, which was rustling loudly and solidly with each step,

"Have you and your husband found a residence yet, Suzanne?" Miss Pavlick asked.

Suzanne was surprised on two counts: that the chief of nursing showed interest in her personal life and that she called her by her first name.

"No, ma'am. We've been looking in the paper and making telephone calls but no luck yet. We're going to drive around this weekend to see if any signs are up anywhere."

Miss Pavlick reached into her waist pocket, pressed a key into Suzanne's palm and then folded Suzanne's fingers tightly over it.

"This is a key to the VIP suite on the SOQ," she said quietly. "Until you find quarters, if we don't have any patients there over the weekends, you and your husband can stay in it Saturdays and Sundays. I'm the only person who can unlock that door or authorize its use, so you shouldn't be disturbed." She tapped Suzanne's wrist gently with her index finger. "But not during the week. Okay? Saturday afternoons and nights and Sundays only, if it is not occupied by a senior officer. Understood?"

Suzanne smiled. "Aye, aye, ma'am. Understood. Thank you, Miss Pavlick."

"You're welcome. And if I hear of any vacancies off base, I'll let you know."

* * *

BILLY SETTLED INTO HIS ROUTINE as a flight instructor. He was assigned to two squadrons with two wings each, divided into morning and afternoon sessions. He would teach four students a day, one and a half hours each session, one squadron at a time, 10 days on and two days off. When he returned from the short, two-day break, he would take cadets in the alternate squadron.

Neither he nor Suzanne welcomed his schedule. If it had not been for their meals together at the hospital wardroom and occasional evening meals at the Officers' Club and the opportunity to rendezvous in the Sick Officers' Quarters suite, he told his wife he felt the two of them should consider loading a Stearman with their rug, bedspread and coffee maker and fly down to Havana to wait out the war.

When a letter arrived from Bob Hawthorne later during Billy's third week in Memphis, Billy was in just the right frame of mind to be interested in his friend's proposal:

Brother Bill!

I'm out here on the West Coast, having a wonderful time!

We'll be getting our flying assignments within the next few days but thought you'd like to know there are several billets open for fighter pilots, flying Avengers. Even though they prefer carrier-trained pilots, that isn't essential. They can teach you.

Beat the rush! Apply today!

My best to you and to Suzanne.

Been to the Peabody yet to check out the ducks? Quack! Quack!
Have you heard from T.J. and Barry? Let me have their address-
es when you get them.
A card today from Molly. She's still in D.C.
Bob

Billy reread the letter and stood at a window of the ready room, looking absently at the rows of Yellow Perils on the flight line. He looked at the letter again: *Beat the rush! Apply today*! He pressed his lips tightly together, folded the single slip of paper and slipped it into his hip pocket.

He proceeded down the passageway to the personnel office, where he requested an application for a transfer. He filled it out and left it with the yeoman.

*   *   *

BILLY WAS SURPRISED how young the cadets—his students— seemed. He was only 22, but the two or three year differential between him and the cadets' average ages seemed more like a decade.

The students looked at him as if he were not just older, but old. They called him "Sir," as if he were a senior officer and treated him as if he were, in every way, senior to them.

In his present unhappy frame of mind, Billy *felt* old.

On his first day as instructor when he had trooped his little band of fledglings out to the flight line to give them their introductions to the Stearman, he suddenly felt as if he were in a time warp. It had been less than a year since he was standing where they were, receiving the same talk he was about to deliver:

"Okay men. Here it is. Your passage to naval aviation," he began.

"This is the Stearman Kaydet trainer. . . "

*   *   *

SUZANNE WAS FAIRLY BEAMING when Billy joined her for lunch in the officers' mess at the hospital during their fourth week at Memphis.

"Bill, Karen Larkin told me there's a garage apartment for rent just about a mile and a half from the main gate.

324

"Do you think we could drive over there after work today?"

"You bet! Right now, I'd settle just for a garage, if it meant we could have some privacy together.

"This is my son's room," Louis McKenzie said to Billy and Suzanne as he led them up the wooden stairs built onto the outside wall of the neat frame garage behind the McKenzie's home.

"He's in the Army in Europe and won't be back until the war is over. I thought it would be unpatriotic not to offer it to somebody in the military. And I'll put the rent money into the bank for him, so's he can have a little nest-egg started when he gets out."

"What's his name?" Suzanne asked as they paused under the small porch roof while McKenzie unlocked the wooden door with a large glass window in its top half.

"Sonny."

He pushed the door open and stepped aside as Billy and Suzanne walked in.

"There's a light switch beside the door," McKenzie said.

The single room had a ceiling that followed the roofline, with rows of windows on each side and at the end. A large brass bed, similar to Uncle John's, stood against the back wall. A small bed-side table with a shaded lamp was located on the right side of the bed. A chest of drawers was against the center of the wall to the left. A small wooden table with two matching chairs was located to their immediate right. They were standing in front of a counter into which a combination sink, stove and refrigerator had been built. A bathtub on legs, toilet and lavatory were in plain view in the opposite corner.

"He lived up here alone and didn't have to hide anything he did from anybody," Mr. McKenzie said, pointing to the open bathroom.

"If you're shy, you might not be comfortable with this arrangement."

"I love to look at my wife," Billy said.

Suzanne smiled at her husband. "I'd put a screen in front of the commode, just the same."

"It's got electric heat," McKenzie said. "TVA makes that afford-able. Sonny installed that exhaust fan up there and that ceiling fan. He said with all these big trees around, the fans do a good job keep-

Flights of Angels

ing it cool. Nice hardwood floors, easy to keep clean. Sonny thought it's a right comfortable little apartment."

"What do you think, Suzanne?"

"I like it."

"How much is the rent, Mr. McKenzie?"

"I don't want to take advantage of you. How does twenty dollars a month sound?"

"Just about what we could afford," Billy said.

"Do we have to sign any contracts? I mean, in case I get orders or something, would we still have to pay?"

Billy ignored the look Suzanne gave him.

"No, sir. I know how the military is. I fought in World War One. No. Whenever you have to leave, just let me know and then pay up, pack up and we'll look for somebody else."

"We'll take it."

"Good," McKenzie said. "My wife and I were hoping we'd find a young couple who'd enjoy it and take good care of it."

"We will," Suzanne assured him.

"When can we move in?" Billy asked.

"Right now."

"We'll need to buy some sheets and pots and pans and things," Suzanne said. "All we have is a bedspread and rug."

"I think Sonny left some stuff for the bed in that closet over there," Mr. McKenzie said, pointing to a closet between the galley and bathroom area. "And everything for the kitchen is in these cabinets. Even dishes and knives and forks and things like that."

Billy opened the door. Linens had been neatly folded and stored on the shelves.

Suzanne looked at the cabinets over and beside the sink.

"Honey, I think everything we need is here," Billy said.

"Do you think Sonny will mind if we use everything?" Suzanne asked.

"I think he'd be proud if you did," Mr. McKenzie said.

"We can use the laundry on base," Billy said.

"How about if we move in tomorrow afternoon?" he asked.

"Fine. Here's your key."

*   *   *

BILLY AND SUZANNE returned the next afternoon after work, brought in most of their clothes and held field day on the little apartment. They made the bed with Sonny's sheets, carefully placed the spread Billy's mother had given them over the sheets and unrolled the rug from Mrs. Watson at the foot of the bed.

She turned on the lamp beside the bed and the pin-up lamp over the dining table.

Billy stood with his arm around Suzanne as they looked proudly at the room.

"It looks quite homey, doesn't it?" she said. "Maybe a couple of plants would help."

"Before it gets dark," he suggested, "let's get the rest of our things, pick up some groceries on base and get back to see how Sonny's sheets hold up."

He gave her a couple of tight squeezes for emphasis. "Hm?"

She gave his buttock a pat.

"Is that a 'Yes'?"

"Yes."

When they climbed the stairs later, Billy unlocked the door and instructed Suzanne to remain on the little porch while he took the groceries and boxes of personal effects inside.

He came back for her and swept her into his arms.

"Do you realize this is the first time we've had anything we could call our own?"

She locked her arms around his neck, squeezed him and kissed his cheek.

"Okay, wife, here we go. Across the threshold of our own little bungalow."

*   *   *

WHEN BILLY BEGAN TEACHING primary flight, he promised himself he would not be the type instructor who confused students—who were already befuddled enough—with anger or sarcasm. For several weeks, he was successful in adhering to the professionalism he had been encouraged to apply while he was at instructors' flight training school in New Orleans.

The first time calm and reason failed repeatedly, however, he resorted to subtle cynicism:

A cadet was making practice landings in an out-lying field, but kept pulling the nose of the plane up to the extent the plane's speed dropped and the craft was difficult to control.

"Why don't you just pull the nose up and spin us in," Billy finally said in exasperation after several unsuccessful attempts.

The stick immediately came back into Billy's hand as the plane's nose went up and the speed slowed dramatically.

The cadet had taken Billy at his word.

Billy grabbed the stick and pushed it and the throttle forward, just as the wheels of the plane hit the ground between a ditch and a fence. The plane bounced over the fence and onto a field before he could safely get the plane airborne again.

He never again used sarcasm as a teaching method.

He was later assigned to teach a British cadet how to recover from spins.

As they climbed to 3000 feet, Billy instructed the student to tighten his seat belt before beginning the exercise.

Billy put the plane into a spin and then, as they were approaching the safest low altitude for recovery, he told the student to pull the plane out of the spin.

There was no response.

Billy looked in his mirror but saw no student.

He pulled the plane out mere yards from the ground. It was then he saw the student, in his parachute, floating toward the ground

Instead of tightening his belt, the cadet had unfastened it. Billy wondered how his instructions got lost in the translation from American English to British English.

Billy flew to the field and borrowed a car to return for the student.

From then on, he personally checked his students' seat belts before leaving the ground.

* * *

"SUZANNE?" BILLY SAID TWO DAYS LATER as he stood shaving at the lavatory, a towel around his waist. She was scooping coffee from a flat, round Maxwell House can into the basket of the percolator Uncle John and Aunt Grace had given them, "Why don't I check out a Stearman this weekend, request an RON and we fly down to Riverton or maybe even down to Rio?"

"Oh, Bill, you know I don't like to fly."

"It'll be fun. The weather is going to be perfect. Warmer than usual. Riverton is always pretty in May. We'll just follow the river down and land at the river bottom. We'll take our time, you know. It'll be a good weekend."

"Only if you promise not to scare me."

"Hey! Have a little faith in my piloting skills. Why do you think the Navy selected me to teach flight?"

"I don't care. Flying still scares me."

He removed the towel from around his waist, wiped the shaving cream from his face as he walked to her and gave her a quick kiss on her lips.

"I promise not to scare you."

"Get some clothes on. You know how you get when you start kissing me."

*   *   *

"BILL, YOU DIDN'T TELL ME about the parachute!" Suzanne said, her voice clearly tense with apprehension.

"Navy regs, honey. Don't give it a second thought. I'll stay so close to the ground you can just step right out of the plane if we have trouble."

"Remember that you promised not to scare me."

"I remember. Come on, let's get you buckled in."

"You mean I'm going to be tied down with that?" she said, pointing to the webbing that formed the seatbelt.

"Navy regs, Honey. Don't…"

"I know. Don't give it a second thought."

She pulled her helmet over her head and buckled it under her chin as he secured her in the rear seat.

He took his place in the forward cockpit and strapped himself in as Rex Porter, his plane captain, stood by the inertia energizer.

"Okay, Rex, wind 'er up."

The engine cranked up on the first try. As Billy let it warm up, he leaned back and turned his head to call to Suzanne.

"You won't be able to talk to me. There's a note pad on the side-wall if you need to tell me anything. Just tap me on the shoulder and hand it up. Okay?"

"If you don't scare me, I won't have to write anything," she shouted.

"Okay. Pull your goggles down and just enjoy the ride."

They taxied to the end of the runway and waited until the light in the tower turned green. He pushed the throttle forward and raced down the runway. He pulled back on the stick for a smooth takeoff and a slow, arching climb westward toward Memphis and the Mississippi River.

She held on to the sides of the cockpit and sat stiffly, trying not to look at the ground below.

After circling Memphis, he banked gently to the southeast, leveled off at 1500 feet and flew to the Cherokee River. He centered the plane on the flat, shiny ribbon of dark water, lined on both sides with vast stretches of greenery, flying first over the Charles Town Dam.

Down below, he could see small boats where tiny fishermen were trying to pull catfish from the river's deep, murky bottom.

Billy waved at the men who waved back enthusiastically.

Suzanne found the courage to look cautiously over the side of the cockpit.

Ahead, a long procession of barges filled with black mountains of coal, pushed by a single diesel boat called a tow, was headed east, creating graceful, elongated, parabolic ripples, liquid silver bands, curving uniformly across the bow of the lead barge and extending back along both sides of the connected vessels.

She slowly relaxed enough to enjoy the scenery on either side of the placid river.

Ahead lay Jefferson Dam, appearing first as a gray line across the river just east of Riverton. Billy steered the plane south of the river, over the sheer cliffs that formed the limits of Jackson's Bluff, Riverton's sister city, connected by a narrow, two-lane bridge with a single, shared set of train and trolley tracks across its upper structure. He pointed to his left where the river bottom landing field was located, where he had been taught to fly. He then turned gently northward, waving at his family standing at the hangar. They waved back and watched him disappear over the trees.

He continued northward toward town, lowering his altitude a bit as he flew over the center of the Riverton business district, above the farmer's market. As he approached the row of crude buildings where the farmers were selling their produce, he slowed the plane and gently rocked it before making a lazy circle overhead. Several people looked up. Some waved. He waved back, hoping one of the men in overalls was Uncle John.

He increased his speed and altitude, turned south again and headed for the landing field. It appeared suddenly as they cleared the cypress trees that ran along the field's northern boundary. His family began waving again. He dropped and slowed, looking at the windsock to determine wind direction.

Bill and Suzanne both waved again to his family, standing beside the Hudson and Uncle Kenneth's pickup truck. Suzanne felt braver as the flight was about to end and even mustered a bright smile.

He reduced his power further, began his descent, circled the field, located his landing site, reduced his power again for landing.

Members of his family held their hands over their eyes to cut the glare of the bright morning sun as he brought the plane in as gracefully as a seagull.

He taxied to the hangar and shut off the engine.

As soon as he released his seat belt and began helping Suzanne from her cockpit, his family rushed to the plane

He helped her out onto the wing. Billy's father reached for her hand and steadied her as she jumped to the ground.

"I thought Billy had brought Amelia Earhart with him," Jim Benson said jokingly.

"I certainly feel like her in this get-up," Suzanne responded, removing the helmet and shaking her hair free.

After a full round of welcome hugs, Billy shared a condensed version of his Stearman N2S orientation lecture with his parents, sisters, Velma and Robert.

"Listen, folks," Billy said, as he removed a suitcase from the plane's storage compartment behind the rear cockpit, "Suzanne and

I are going to make a couple of calls in Uncle Kenneth's truck before we go to the house. We should be there by mid-afternoon. Okay?"

His father had driven Uncle Kenneth's truck to the landing field as Billy had requested.

"You're not going to change first?" his mother asked.

Billy pointed to the hangar office.

"I know where Jim hides the key to the office. We'll change in there."

"Where will you eat?" his mother asked.

"Suzanne made some sandwiches."

"Okay," his mother said. "Hurry on to the house. Aunt Ollie is anxious to see ya'll."

"Okay, Mom."

He kissed his mother's cheek again and waved as his family climbed into the Hudson and drove away.

"What's all this about?" Suzanne asked, as they were changing clothes inside the office.

"Uncle John and Aunt Grace will be at the curb market until about four. I thought maybe we'd go to the creek and get cleaned up and go back up to the loft in the barn."

She placed her hands on her hips.

"Is this why we flew down here, Bill Benson? Just to skinny dip in Uncle John's creek and make whoopee in the barn?" she demanded.

"Partially."

She smiled at him."Why didn't I think of it?"

*   *   *

"NO, I DON'T WANT YOU TO DO A THING," Billy told her upon their arrival at the creek and she had begun removing her blouse.

"Let me do that."

"Are you sure nobody will see us?" she asked, looking about.

"Only a bird or two and maybe a few curious pilots passing overhead."

"You would never do a thing like that, would you?"

He smiled. "Ask me in fifty years."

He turned her around gently. He carefully and slowly unbuttoned her blouse. He laid the blouse on the smooth gravel creek bed and knelt before her. He then removed her shoes and short, white cotton socks, undid the side button of her slacks and gently unzipped them as she placed her hand on his head to steady herself.

He stood again and removed her brassiere, adding it to the clothing on the ground. As he stood behind her, he reached around her and held her breasts lightly as he kissed her on the side of her neck.

He had bought her several matching bras and panties, like the ones she was wearing that day, in a lingerie shop in the French Quarter. Instead of loosely covering her entire pelvic area up to the navel, as was the conventional style, which he found unattractive and sexually unappealing, the new panties were handmade from finely woven cotton by Ursuline nuns in New Orleans. Not only were the panties well fitting, conforming perfectly to her anatomy and trimmed with exquisite white lace and tiny pink bows on each leg opening, they extended only halfway to her waist, which Billy found overtly sensual. Nearly transparent, they seemed pink against her skin, darker in her pubic area.

He knelt before her again and reached for the lacy edges of the leg openings of her panties. His mouth dropped slightly as his eyes drank in the beauty of her body. With the tips of his thumbs and fingers, he gently, very gently, slipped her underwear down her thighs, her knees, her calves, to her ankles. He removed them as she lifted her small, bare feet.

Still on his knees, he placed his hands on each side of her hips and marveled at her magnificence.

"Oh, Suzanne! I think you get more beautiful every time I see you."

She closed her eyes as he leaned forward, slid his hands to her buttocks and pressed his face against her. As he inhaled deeply her delicious, luscious heat and slowly, gently tasted her sweet nectar of Venus, he heard her groan and felt her knees weaken. He stood, pulled her body to his and began kissing her hungrily: first her lips, her neck, her breasts.

Even as he was covering her body with kisses, she reached for his shirt and began undressing him, dropping his clothes beside hers.

When she dropped his pants and saw the barometric bulge of his boxers, she said, "I thought we were going to bathe first and go to the loft later."

He smiled.

"Let's save the loft for another visit, when it's too cold to come down here."

*   *   *

A LETTER FROM T.J. was in Billy's mailbox at the ready room Monday morning when he reported to work.

Bill, old boy,

Barry and I have been assigned flying a PB4Y Privateer, the Navy's version of the B-24 Liberator. It has a single tail and a few other improvements, but basically the same craft the Army Air Corps is flying over the Himalayas.

And what are we doing, you ask?

Taking bloody photographs, mate!

That's how we're using all that flight training! I can't tell you exactly where we're taking these snapshots, of course, but here's a hint: we fly in the area I told you me mum and I moved after me dad died.

All kidding aside, we're learning a lot and are getting some good flight experiences. Sure beats flying over all those potato fields in lower Alabama.

Anyway, you've got me address now. Write!

Me best to Suzanne.

Barry says "Hello."

Your mate,

T.J.

And Billy did write. Even though he attempted to be upbeat and chipper about the boring routine of having to teach cadets to fly, it would not have been difficult for T.J. to read between the lines: Billy hated his duty assignment.

*   *   *

TWO WEEKS AFTER BILLY mailed the letter, his life changed suddenly.

"What happened to you today, Suzanne?" Billy asked as he walked from the car to meet her behind the hospital after work. "Why didn't you meet me for lunch?"

"Let me tell you when we get home," was all she would say.

As hard as he tried to get her to explain her sudden absence, she doggedly changed the subject each time, preferring to bring him up to date on the prognosis of a newborn diagnosed with encephalitis or the career Marine father who nearly fainted as the pediatrician, Dr. Strauss, had to draw blood from the femoral artery of the Marine's son in a last-ditch effort to get a blood sample.

She talks a lot about this Dr. Strauss.

At the apartment, she instructed him to sit and wait and watch her change from her uniform to slacks, sneakers and a cotton shirt.

When she completed the transition to comfortable wear, she sat in the chair opposite him at the small dining table.

He waited anxiously.

She lowered her hand to his and studied his face.

"Bill Benson," she began, "I believe you are one of the finest men in the world."

He looked into her eyes and swallowed hard.

Uh oh! Only one of the finest? Has she fallen in love with someone else? Someone finer? This Dr. Strauss?

"The minute I saw you in that treatment room in Pensacola, I knew you were special."

What is it? Why doesn't she tell me why she missed lunch?

"I loved my father and mother. There's no doubt about that. But I guess I only liked my brothers and sister."

He felt his hands begin to tremble.

Oh, no! Now, she loves somebody else. Dr. Strauss. And just likes me.

"But Bill, until you came along, I didn't think I could just totally love anyone the way I fell in love with you."

Fell? As in past tense?

He pressed his fingers against his eyes, breathed deeply and shook his head in disbelief.

She leaned forward, a worried look on her face and stroked his head.

"Bill, what is it? What's wrong?" she asked.

He straightened up and faced her.

"What is it, Bill?" she asked again.

"You've fallen in love with someone else," he said, with finality, looking into her eyes.

She knelt at his side, threw her arms around his waist and held him closely.

"Oh, no, Bill! I could never love anyone else the way I love you. Never!"

He looked up, his eyes moist with tears.

"Oh, Bill, no. No! There isn't anybody else. There never will be."

He leaned over her, pressed his cheek against her head and encircled her shoulders with his arms.

"Suzanne, I don't think I could go on living without you. I've never loved anybody the way I love you."

"And that goes for me, too, Bill and there isn't anybody else. There never could be."

"Please, Suzanne! Tell me what all this is about. I don't think I can take any more suspense."

She stood and pulled him up from his chair.

She wrapped her arms around his waist and pulled him tightly to her body as she pressed her face against his chest.

"Bill Benson?"

"Yes?"

She lifted her head, smiled at him and placed her hands around his neck.

"You're going to be a father."

He held her at arms length and looked into her eyes, which were misty and anxiously waiting for his response.

He pulled her close to his body and hugged her tightly.

"Oh, Suzanne, I am so happy."

He released her quickly.

"I didn't squeeze you too hard, did I?" he asked.

"Oh, no. You could never squeeze me too hard."

"Well, come on and sit down," he said, helping her to the chair beside the table. "I guess we need to start making some plans for the immediate future."

"Would you like some coffee or a Coke?" he asked before he sat down.

She shook her head. "No. I'm fine, thank you."

He sat across from her and took her hands in his.

"Do you know when it's due?" he asked.

"Early December."

"I'd like to think it happened in Uncle John's barn loft," he said thoughtfully. "Is there any way to tell?"

"Why don't we say it happened in the loft?"

"Well, I'm not so sure we should actually *say* where it happened. That was just a figure of speech."

"I know," she said, smiling and stroking his hair gently with her hands.

"The Navy will take care of all our medical bills," he continued. "That's one worry we won't have."

"Oh, wait," he said as he remembered Navy policy about pregnancies. "You'll have to resign from the Nurse Corps, won't you?"

"I'm afraid so."

"How do you feel about that?"

"I'm going to have a lot of time on my hands."

He looked around their small one-room apartment.

"We'll have to find a bigger place, and on the ground floor," he said. "I don't want you climbing a lot of stairs."

She pulled one of her hands free and patted the back of his hand.

"I'll put out the word," he said. "As many personnel transferring out as we do, surely something will come up pretty soon.

"Will we still be able to…you know, have sex?" he asked.

"Oh, sure."

"Good. I think you know I really like that."

"I do, too," she smiled.

He leaned over the table and gave her a light kiss on her mouth.

"And you don't have any regrets over having to resign from the Navy?"

"If you mean, 'Would I prefer to be in the Navy or be the mother of your child? the answer is simple: I can't think of anything that could make me happier, than having your child; that is, as long as I still have you, too."

He smiled and leaned across the table to kiss her again.

"Thank you, Suzanne Benson. You have me. Don't worry about that. You'll always have me. Oh, I do love you so."

She smiled back. "And I love you, too, Bill Benson."

"We won't have as much money coming in," he said after a moment, "but when you're released from the Navy, I'll apply for a dependent's allotment. That should help a little. And when the baby is born, we can get a little more."

"Maybe I can work as a civilian nurse in Memphis," she suggested.

"As long as you think it won't interfere with your...the baby.

"I was never allowed to use the words 'pregnancy' or 'pregnant,'" he confessed. "The stigma remains."

"I know. It was the same at my house. We had to say things like, 'She's going to have a baby,' or 'She's expecting.'"

"Me, too," he agreed. "'Pregnant' was supposed to be vulgar."

"You know? I'll think I'll call my folks tomorrow and say something really diplomatic, like, 'Hey, Mom and Dad! Guess what! Suzanne is pregnant and I knocked her up in Uncle John's barn!'"

"Is this a rebellious side of you I've never seen?" she teased.

He laughed. "No. Just having a little fun."

"I know everybody there will really be happy that you're...what? That you're with child?"

"That sounds like the Virgin Mary, doesn't it?"

He smiled and nodded agreement.

"Your parents will be good grandparents," she said.

"Are you going to call any of your family?" he asked.

"No, I'll just drop them a note. I doubt if they care very much one way or the other."

"Well, when do you have to tell Miss Pavlick?"

"I suppose tomorrow. She's been straight with me and I don't want to keep anything from her."

*   *   *

"SINCE WE'RE SHORT-HANDED, SUZANNE," Lieutenant Commander Pavlick told Suzanne the next day in the office of the Chief of Nursing, "let me assign you to the OR for a couple of months so you can wear scrubs. Nobody will be able to tell that you're pregnant. When you can't hide it anymore, you can resign from the Navy and we'll see if you can't get on as a civilian nurse for a month or two more."

"Miss Pavlick," Suzanne began, "I really appreciate your support. Thanks."

"You're welcome, Suzanne. And call me 'Mary' in social settings or when we're alone. Okay?" She stood and extended her hand.

"Okay, Mary," Suzanne said. "Thanks again."

*   *   *

IT WAS TO HAVE BEEN just a routine flight: Billy and Jack Snow were to fly to New Orleans to pick up a Stearman that had developed engine trouble on a cross-country flight. The plane was repaired and Jack would fly it back.

Jack had attended flight instructors' school in New Orleans also, and both men were looking forward to a return visit to the Crescent City.

They filed their flight plan and left on an early spring morning.

The flight was uneventful, although tracing the Mississippi River all the way south was exciting for Billy. Being able to communicate over the new intercoms made the journey more enjoyable as they talked and pointed out features to each other.

They dropped low enough over sternwheelers to get a good look at the large, lumbering, graceful, anachronisms. The passengers waved to them and they waved back, wagging their wings in salute.

Lake Pontchatrain came into view east of the river as they approached the complex of waterways that comprised the Mississippi Delta. Billy guided the plane toward the lake and approached the air station where he and his companion had been taught to teach flight.

Billy circled the field until he was signaled that he was clear to land on Runway Three. He landed the plane and taxied to a parking space as directed by one of the ground crew.

"Let's check in with the chief flight officer and see about a room at the Q and then maybe visit the Quarter," Jack suggested.

"Good plan," Billy agreed.

"Would you like to go to Tujague's Restaurant for some good Creole chow?" Jack asked later after they stepped from the base shuttle bus.

"Two Jacks?" Billy asked. "Two guys named Jack own it? You, maybe?"

"No. It's French."

"Oh. Sure, let's go," Billy said as he followed his friend down the crowded Bourbon Street sidewalk leading to the eastern end of the Quarter and the French Market.

They walked farther down the loud, colorful street as he and Suzanne had done. Barkers stood on the sidewalks in front of clubs, advertising the girls, drinks and fun to be enjoyed inside. As the two men passed by the doors of the various establishments, the barkers swung open the louvered saloon doors to graphically display the sights and sounds to be enjoyed within.

"They have to screen the girls from cars passing by," Jack said, explaining the swinging doors. "Especially from police patrol cars and the vice squad."

They turned south down Dumaine Street and west onto Decatur Street until they came to the elegant corner entrance of the French restaurant underneath a wrought-iron sunburst.

"M'sieur Snow," the *maitre d'hotel* greeted them as they entered. "How good it is to see you again."

"Merci, Jean-Pierre. It's good to be back," he responded.

"Only two in your party?"

"Yes."

"Are you not expecting some mademoiselles?"

"No, not tonight, Jean-Pierre," he answered with a laugh.

"Right this way, please."

The exciting and tantalizing aroma of exotic seasonings and jovial, high-spirited conversation greeted the pair.

Jean-Pierre led them to a table near the center of the room, handed each an oversized menu and signaled for a Negro man to fill their water glasses.

"Enjoy your meal, gentlemen."

"Thank you, Jean-Pierre."

"The specialties here are shrimp remoulade and beef brisket with Creole sauce," Jack said.

"I've never had either."

"The shrimp is an appetizer," Jack explained. "Really good. The brisket comes with a horseradish sauce. It's better than good. I think you should try both of them. Billy took Jack's suggestion and wolfed down the exquisite food as if he were starved. He hardly had room for the bread pudding with whiskey sauce but he ate most of it anyway.

"Jack, that was four-o! Outstanding!" Billy said, wiping his mouth with the large napkin.

"Glad you enjoyed it. I've never been disappointed here," Jack said, pushing slightly away from the table and sipping his Creole coffee.

"Since you seem to know the Quarter so well, what else is on the agenda?" Billy asked.

"How about a visit with an old friend?" Jack asked.

"Fine."

They finished their demitasse cups of coffee, paid their bills and emerged from the restaurant onto the street again.

Jack gestured. "It's up this way. On Dauphine Street."

They walked up the crowded sidewalk, back through the French Market, past the open Café Du Monde, filled with buoyant natives and visitors, enjoying steaming cups of chicory-laced *café au lait*, the color of a Creole, and eating beignets covered with powdered sugar, then past Jackson Square with St. Louis Cathedral as a backdrop, the Jackson Brewery to their left on the banks of the Mississippi, to Toulouse Street and finally to Dauphine Street where they walked west toward Canal Street.

Billy noticed an increasing number of colorfully dressed denizens, unusually friendly and familiar, speaking to Jack and to him as they passed on the narrow sidewalks. Heavily made up women in scanty costumes stood seductively in doorways, giving the male passers-by the once-over and invitations to step inside.

One woman was demonstrating her skills with a yo-yo. She flung it from her doorway in front of Billy and Jack as they passed her.

Jack paused to speak to her.

"Can you rock the cradle?" he asked.

"Yes, but I'd rather go around the world," she replied.

"I rather suspected that you might," he said with a knowing smile as they moved on up the street.

Bill wasn't sure what had just transpired but he didn't comment.

Another pedestrian that Billy noticed approaching them was a tall, willowy woman, unusually beautiful, attractively coifed and exquisitely made up. She walked up to Billy and stood in front of him, blocking his passage.

Jack stopped to observe Billy's response.

The woman smiled and put out her hand to gently touch Billy's cheek.

Billy looked at her with mixed feelings: interest and vanity.

"Hi there, tall, blond, and gorgeous."

She had a man's voice.

Billy was openly taken aback.

"Damn!"

Jack laughed loudly.

"Come on, Bill," he said, as he patted him on the back and began walking again. "Always check out the Adam's apples on these night creatures. Many an unsuspecting sailor has gotten one of them to a hotel room and when he reached under her skirt, realized he had picked up a man."

Billy, humiliated, didn't speak but eyed the passing foot traffic with a new awareness.

"Here we are," Jack said, pointing to a plain, narrow, two-storied building ahead on the left side of Dauphine Street, where the sound of a piano spilled from the open window, framed by solid wood shutters, on the other side of the doorway.

"Norma Wallace's place," he said.

"She has forty acres in St. Tammany Parish at Shady Pond Farm that's a lot more impressive than this," Jack added.

The only identification was over the door: 410.

"What is it?" Billy asked.

"I told you. Norma Wallace's place."

"Who's Norma Wallace?"

"Let's go inside and see."

Jack led the way up the short flight of stairs and, without knocking, opened one of the pair of glass-paned, wooden doors.

They crossed a small, undecorated foyer and stepped into a dimly lighted double parlor, divided by doors that had been shoved into their wall pockets.

Before their eyes adjusted to the lights, they heard *Anchors, Aweigh!* strike up on the piano.

Women screamed, "Look! It's Big Jack!" and ran to greet Billy's guide.

Billy saw that they were all wearing minimal lingerie under thin, multihued wrappers, open down the center, exposing breasts of different sizes and shapes.

"Jack!" a woman with a husky voice called out.

"Norma!" he responded.

An attractive and well-coifed woman, dressed in a smart business suit and carrying a cigarette between the knuckles of one hand, walked assertively toward them.

Billy thought of Bette Davis as she strode in their direction.

She embraced Jack.

"It's good to see you again," she said in a voice more Manhattan than New Orleans.

"Norma, this is a good friend, Bill Benson. We flew down from Memphis this afternoon."

She extended her hand. Billy shook it warily.

"Hello," he said pleasantly.

"Hello, yourself, handsome. Would you like to meet some of my girls?"

Before Billy could respond, two of the girls who had their arms around Jack, jumped to either side of Billy, kissed him on the neck, squeezed his hands gently and one rubbed his chest under his tie.

"Uh, no. I just came by with Jack."

"You don't want to stay and let us make you feel really good?" one of the girls said, now gently squeezing his crotch.

Billy tried to be congenial.

"No, really. I'm married and think I should get back to the base."

"Okay, but you don't know what you're missing," she said, continuing to massage him.

"Thanks, anyway," Billy said, backing away and lifting his hand in farewell. "See you back at the base, Jack."

Back on the sidewalk, Billy walked quickly to Canal Street to wait for a taxi or a cattle car back to the base, whichever one came along first.

Each step of the way from Norma Wallace's Place, Billy felt the weight of his regrettable decision to walk up the steps to what he should have known was a bordello.

Am I so naïve and such a fool I didn't know what I was walking into? he asked himself angrily.

He smelled his hands. The aroma of perfume lingered.

And the girl playing with me was getting me hard, he accused himself angrily.

Dammit, Benson! What kind of a fickle husband are you?

What kind of a man are you?

He flagged down a taxi.

Two sailors were in the back seat. Both were so drunk they were already sleeping: the one beside the door was slumped with his arms locked across his chest, his head on his buddy's shoulder.

In his room at the Q, Billy pulled off his coat and sniffed it. It smelled faintly of perfume.

I can have it cleaned at the base laundry when I get back to Memphis.

He removed his tie and smelled it.

And the tie.

He went to the mirror over his lavatory to check for lipstick.

Damn! How could I have been so gullible?

He pulled off his shirt and reached for his toothbrush.

He wet it and rubbed it across a bar of soap and began to scrub the red stain from his collar.

I'll drop this by the cleaner, too.

Satisfied the incriminating stains were gone, he removed his shoes and socks, trousers and underwear hurriedly, pulled a bathrobe from his bag, lifted the towel from the foot of his bed and went to the head where he showered longer than usual.

Back in his room, he put out the light and walked to the window. He stared absently at the airfield.

"Oh, God," he said. "I still feel dirty. I'm so ashamed. I've been unfaithful to Suzanne and to You. Oh, Father, I am so ashamed. I am so sorry."

He sat on his bed and dropped his head into his hands.

Billy had made mistakes as a boy, of course. He would be sent to his room to wait for one of his parents, usually his father, to explain to him why what he had done was wrong.

A feeling of redemption always followed after he apologized and promised not to repeat the error.

But this is different.

I'm grown now. I should have known better. I can't tell Suzanne but she can read me like a book. She'll know something is wrong: "Oh, Bill, I can always tell what you're thinking. I can just look at your face or your pants."

He threw his robe onto the chair beside his desk and climbed into bed for a night of fitful sleep.

The next morning, Billy arose, showered, packed up his clothes, pulled on his flight suit and set out for the hangar where he had parked his plane. He still felt the weight of his previous evening's indiscretion heavily and he lacked the enthusiasm for returning to Memphis he should have. He went back to the ready room where Jim Harris and other instructors were drinking coffee from thick, white mugs with their names written on them in black letters.

"Good morning, Bill," Harris called to him, rising to shake his hand. "I'm sorry I missed you yesterday. How was your flight down?"

Billy forced good cheer and greeted the instructors he knew and was introduced to the others. He poured himself a cup of coffee and took a McKenzie's Bakery pastry from a large, flat box.

Jack Snow appeared and walked stiffly to the coffee mess.

It was obvious he had not slept much, if at all.

"Bill, you should have made me leave when you did," he said, easing into a chair and sliding down to the back of his neck.

"Ohhhhhhh," he moaned. "Do you think you could tow my plane like a glider and I could ride back in your plane?"

"Wish I could, Jack."

"Are you ready to head north?" Jack asked.

"As ready as I'll ever be. I'll check the weather conditions and meet you outside. Okay?"

Jack nodded.

"We've got some cloud cover moving in from the central states," the flight officer said. "Looks like something might shape up in northern Mississippi."

"Any airfields up there we could use if the need arises?"

"Oh, sure," the officer said, pulling a map out of a folder on his bookshelves.

"Up here in Columbus," he said, pointing. "That's Army. Another one over here near Oxford. One near New Albany. They're civilian. May not be anybody there. Just don't take any chances with the weather."

"Right," Billy said. "Thanks."

He walked to his plane, performed his pre-flight inspection and retrieved his parachute from the wing as Jack came walking slowly to the plane.

"What's the weather going to be like?" he asked.

"A little cloud cover the first and second legs. Probable clouds and rain in north Mississippi. There are fields in Columbus, Oxford, and New Albany if we need to set'em down for the duration."

"Okay, buddy," Jack said, clapping Billy on his back. "Lead the way. I'll try to keep up. I hope it *does* rain. It'll help keep me awake."

Billy climbed into his plane, set his controls, waited for the plane captain to energize his starter and taxied to the runway to await permission to take off.

Billy felt so heavy from guilt, he was mildly surprised his plane got off the ground. Once he was airborne, the cloudy weather mirrored his mood.

They reached 2000 feet and leveled off. Light gray clouds dusted the sky, increasing as the planes continued north. In his rearview mirror, he could see Jack occasionally through the clouds.

As they passed over Yazoo City, the clouds grew ominously darker.

Billy slowed and beat on the side of his plane for Jack to come alongside him. When his friend was off Billy's port side, Billy pointed to the clouds, waved his hatchet-hand in front of his face, toward Memphis and then pointed to the ground.

Jack opened his hands and shrugged to indicate he had no preference.

Billy gestured toward Memphis.

Jack nodded and fell behind again as they flew on northward.

By the time they reached Oxford, their exposure to the sporadic rain showers reduced their visibility and the rapidly deteriorating weather called for another conference.

When Jack pulled alongside again, Billy pointed to the ground.

Jack nodded and fell behind again.

They dropped closer to the ground, looking for the Oxford airfield.

The rain was being whipped by steady, 30-knot winds, blowing in sheets across their lines of sight.

Billy had lost contact with Jack by the time he spotted the field and dropped low enough to begin his glide path for a landing.

He was about 20 feet off the ground when, suddenly, without any warning, he collided head-on with Jack's plane. The planes dropped nose-first into a crashing heap, onto the rain-whipped field, landing face-to-face.

His harness held him in place, but a spar broken by the collision caught him in his forehead.

He switched off the mags and the gas supply, fumbled with his safety belt latch and threw off the shoulder harness. He climbed carefully from the nearly vertical plane, stepping down the wing struts to the ground. He removed his parachute and proceeded to Jack's plane, also positioned at a steep angle, barely 10 feet away.

Jack was unmoving and his head was bent forward. Billy climbed up the struts and called out, "Jack! Jack!"

He could see blood on his friend's cheek. Jack had obviously been hit by flying debris also.

Billy shook Jack's shoulder.

"Jack! Jack!"

Jack raised his head and opened his eyes. He blinked a few times, put his hand to his face, looked at the blood on his glove, and then at Billy.

"Hey, Bill!" he said cheerfully. "Funny running into you out here."

"Can you climb out?"

"Yeah."

Jack released his belt buckle as Billy worked on the shoulder harness.

"Give me your hand. Don't let me fall."

Billy steadied Jack as he climbed down from the wreckage of his plane and then helped him out of his parachute.

"Can you walk?" Billy asked.

"Yeah, but where are we going?"

"There's some sort of a building over there," Billy said, pointing. "Let's see if anybody is there."

The two walked through the rain to the small, covered porch on the front of the little shed.

Billy tried the doorknob. The door was locked. He jumped to the ground and looked through the window. The building was empty.

A car with a county agent's license tag was parked beside the building.

"Stay here," Billy said.

He went to the car and tried the driver's side door. It was unlocked.

He opened the door in hopes the keys might have been left in the ignition.

Jack walked up behind him. "Find the keys?"

"Not yet."

"Know how to hot wire it?" Jack asked.

"If I have to," Billy said, lifting the rubber floor mat.

"We're in luck. Here are the keys. Climb in. We're about to steal the county agent's car."

They left the field and followed a narrow country road to a service station.

"Stay here," Billy said. "I'm going to call the base to report the crash and request instructions. I'll see if we can get a ride back. Meanwhile, we need to see if there's a hospital nearby so we can get you checked out."

Billy called Brad Kendrick and gave him his report. He also asked his skipper to call Suzanne and tell her, not that he had crashed his plane, but he was just held up by bad weather.

By the time the two men had cleared up the theft of the car with the county agent and were checked out at a small clinic in Oxford, a member of the National Guard introduced himself and told the two that he had been dispatched to drive them back to Memphis.

Jack was sent immediately to the base hospital upon his return to Kendrick's office at the Millington air station.

"I called Suzanne like you asked me," Brad said, "But you're going to have a hard time explaining that bandage on your head."

That's not the only thing I'm going to have a hard time explaining, Billy thought.

He went to the telephone to call Suzanne at the little house they had moved into after they left the garage apartment.

"Hi, honey," he said, trying to be casual. "I'm back. Can you pick me up at the ready room?"

"I'm on my way," she said.

Billy was relieved that he and Brad could spend the time making out their reports on the collision.

When Suzanne entered Brad's office, her smile immediately left her face when she saw her husband still in his wet, stained flight suit, a bandage on his forehead and the look of a condemned man in his eyes.

"Oh, Honey!" she said, rushing to him, throwing her arms around his wet clothes, "What happened to you?"

He tried to make light of the incident.

"Oh, Jack and I tried to use the same air space landing during a storm down in Mississippi."

"Are you all right?" she asked, standing back to survey him.

"Oh, sure. I've got a hard head. Unfortunately, the planes weren't so lucky."

"Is he in trouble?" she asked Brad.

"Just a ton of paper work," he replied.

She embraced Billy again and held him tightly.

"Oh, honey! I'm so glad you're okay."

"Thanks. So am I."

"Can he leave now?" Suzanne asked her husband's commanding officer.

"Sure. But he has to be back tomorrow morning."

"Thanks, Brad. See you later," she said.

They walked to the car and Billy opened the driver's door and held it for her.

"Do you mind driving, honey?" he asked.

"Of course not."

He closed her door and walked to the passenger's seat.

Their conversation on the way home was forced. Billy tried to be upbeat and reviewed the accident with humor but was not entirely convinced he was succeeding.

Inside their small living room, she put her arms around him and laid her head on his chest.

"Oh, Bill, I am so glad you're all right. I'd die if anything happened to you."

He put his arms around her and pressed the side of his head on hers but he didn't speak.

"Are you hungry?" she asked."I didn't cook anything. When Brad called, I thought you might not be back until tomorrow morning. Will a sandwich and some soup be okay?"

"Sure. And while you do that, I want to get out of these wet clothes and take a shower."

As he undressed, he remembered the suitcase he had left in the plane.

Maybe someone will steal it. Maybe it'll get lost.

He showered and put on a dry flight suit.

"I left my bathrobe in the plane," he explained as he sat at the small table in the tiny kitchen.

They ate, but again, he had to force himself to keep up the conversation.

As he helped her clean the kitchen afterward, she stopped and looked at him.

"Okay, Bill, what is it?"

He wouldn't look at her.

"Look at me," she said.

He turned and looked at her.

She looked into his eyes and then at his crotch.

"Okay, I know what it isn't. Now, tell me what it *is*."

"Let's sit down," he said.

He walked to the chair at the table and sat.

She pulled the other chair up to him, sat in it and held his hands.

He shook his head and pressed his lips together.

"Suzanne," he began, and then fell silent.

"Is it about the crash?" she asked.

He shook his head.

"Is it about Jack?"

He made a gesture that it might be.

"Did you have a fight or something?"

Again, he shook his head.

"No. He, uh, asked me if I'd like to visit one of his friends in the French Quarter."

She waited for him to continue.

"As it turned out, his friend was a madam."

He stopped and looked at her. She waited for him to continue.

"He took me to a…to a…whorehouse."

Again he paused.

"Well?" she asked.

"Well? I went to a whorehouse, Suzanne!"

"Did you sleep with one of the girls?"

He gave her a stern look.

"No! You know I wouldn't do anything like that, Suzanne!"

"Well, what's bothering you?"

"I let two of the girls kiss me. Well, I didn't let them, actually. They just sort of pounced on me and before I knew it, they kissed me. On the neck."

"So?"

"And one of them grabbed my crotch."

"Okay."

"I got hard."

"Well, of course you did. They're professionals. That's how they stay in business."

"You mean, you're not mad at me?"

"Bill, have you already forgotten that sonnet T.J. found, that you wrote out for me?" she asked, gripping his hand in hers.

"Love is not love," she began as a reminder to him, "Which alters when it alteration finds, Or bends with the remover to remove."

He relaxed, looked into her eyes and joined her on the next three lines:

O, no; it is an ever-fixed mark,

That looks on tempests, and is never shaken;

It is the star to every wandering bark...

"Oh, Bill, honey," she said, "I would trust you anywhere. I know who you are and *what* you are. I would never get mad at you for anything like that."

"Do you mean I've worried myself sick about all this for nothing?

"I even thought I had the accident because God was punishing me."

She squeezed his hand with both of hers.

"Oh, no, honey. God wouldn't punish you for that. You're a good man and you have a good heart. He wouldn't cause you to crash your plane."

He leaned over to her, wrapped his arms around her and dropped his head onto her shoulder.

"Oh, Suzanne! I don't deserve you. You're just too good for me."

"My poor, sweet, innocent Bill. He doesn't know how much he is loved. And trusted."

She pulled away from him.

"Look at me."

He looked into her eyes.

"Nothing you could ever do would make me love you less or especially, not at all. Nothing. And I believe God feels the same way about you that I do."

He pulled her to her feet and looked intently into her face.

"Thank you, Suzanne, for being the incredible woman that you are. I love you so much, I can't express it with words."

He wrapped his arms around her tightly and kissed her long and deep.

She pushed away from him slightly after the kiss.

"Uh, oh," she said.

"What?"

"I know what you're thinking."

*   *   *

ONE MORNING IN EARLY JUNE 1944, Brad Kendrick sent his yeoman to the ready room to put up an announcement on the bulletin board for the instructors to assemble at 1600 hours for an important meeting.

Formal assemblies were rare and the pilots stood at attention when an unsmiling Kendrick entered the room.

"Okay, men, at ease," he said. "I want cut right to the chase and give you a heads up on the newest wrinkle in our flight program."

The men looked at each other. Change was a constant in the military.

"I think you all need to know about the latest from Admiral Radford. Let me read you two paragraphs from this directive you're going to be hearing a lot about in the next few days:

"When war broke out, a great many naval aviators had to man the new carriers and to fill aviation shore billets. Rapidly, however, we are reaching the point where only replacement pilots need to be trained.

"The number of pilots lost in combat has been much smaller than originally expected. Thanks to the excellent training of Navy pilots, and to the superior planes which they fly, combat and other losses have been small and it is not necessary to provide replacements on the scale which had been planned."

"Before I go on," Brad added, "let me echo the admiral's congratulations to you for having done a superb job taking these young men and shaping them up as you have.

"A job well done.

"Now, back to this letter," he said, holding it up for them to see.

"A copy will be going out to all preflight cadets in just a few days, on 17 June. And what this means is that we have been ordered to cut our enrollments by half."

The men looked at each other again.

Half? Someone asked.

"Half," Brad repeated. "As in fifty per cent.

"Admiral Radford judiciously calls this 'deselection.' You can call it anything you want but it still means we have to kick out half our cadets.

"I think you know the men will not be quite so kind in what they call this.

"Unfortunately, gentlemen, this puts the burden of being bad-ass bastards on all of you. You are, therefore, mandated to use any reason, any excuse necessary to drop our numbers by fifty percent, commencing 18 June."

*   *   *

BETWEEN 1935 AND 1940, some 1800 naval flight cadets had been trained to fly. In 1941, the number increased to 7000, and in 1944, the year of "The Great Purge," the program's peak year, the enrollment increased to over 21,000.

By war's end, a total of 54,000 reservists—83 percent of the total pilot strength— transitioned from civilian life to pre-flight and to the fleet in the V-5 program. And suddenly, without warning, half of the cadets were to be unceremoniously cut and transferred to other naval programs, primarily enlisted, instead of the commissioned ranks they had anticipated and been promised.

Brad Kendrick was right in his prediction of the dissatisfaction with the directive: considerable ire was raised and many cadets filed lawsuits.

The next months were not easy ones for conscientious instructors like Billy, who had been trained to be positive and helpful and to devote long hours to producing superior pilots.

A negative pall fell over the V-5 program. *Any* discrepancy in military, physical, ground school, or flight training was terminal. Any flaw, any miscalculation, any mistake, regardless of its size, would result in immediate expulsion from the coveted program.

One down arrow was terminal. There would be no second chance.

The "It isn't fair!" lament of the disqualified cadets fell on deaf ears.

*   *   *

DESPITE THE TURMOIL in pre-flight training, Billy and Suzanne's lives continued. She tearfully resigned her commission, they attended a farewell party by the hospital staff but only days later, she returned as a Civil Service nurse.

They began attending the base's Livermore Chapel services regularly on Sunday mornings and shared potluck suppers on Sunday nights. He volunteered as an assistant Boy Scout leader for the troop that met at the chapel each Monday evening and helped coach the youth basketball team as he had the time.

Billy had listened with wonder to the miraculous sound of the fetal heartbeat during her second month of pregnancy. He gently stroked and inspected her abdomen daily, watching in enthrallment as it grew in response to the budding life inside her. When her obstetrician announced the presence of two heartbeats, Billy was overwhelmed with fascination and listened every night for the separate heartbeats.

Will they be boys? *Would they be like the Lucas twins*? he wondered. *Completing each other's conversations*?

He called his parents to announce the news of the second heartbeat.

He wrote Bob Hawthorne, T.J., and Barry, crowing like a proud rooster at the news. In his blustering pride over his impending fatherhood, he felt emboldened enough to grouse to his former roommates about having to teach incompetent cadets to fly, crab about night flying, recount occasional near-accidents, and carp about how difficult his job now was, having to give his students down arrows for the least mistake.

When they moved from the garage apartment to a small, four-room apartment, virtually everything in their new house was borrowed from the Navy warehouse on the base, except for their own double bed and a sleeper-sofa in the living room.

"Each time the National Anthem is played on the radio," Billy enjoyed saying, "everything in the house snaps to attention."

Suzanne stopped working altogether six months into her pregnancy and set about readying the diminutive spare bedroom as a nursery.

Her nurse friends and the flight instructors donated two rocking chairs. Brad Kendrick's wife, Irene, lent them a bathinette, with storage for pins, swabs, powder, clothes and other bathing supplies, and a cover that allowed it to double as a changing table. She also let them borrow a baby bed and a white wicker bassinette, plus a sizeable collection of infant clothing her children had used.

Billy's sisters, Alice and Susie, mailed them some inexpensive framed pictures of babies, puppies and kittens to hang on the walls.

Baby showers were given by her nurse friends, wives of flight instructors and women from the chapel.

As Suzanne's December delivery time approached, Billy grew more and more anxious but not to the point of sharing her bouts with morning sickness or false labor pains. He eagerly waited on her, helped her up from her chair, held the car door for her and offered to run errands for her. He had arranged with Irene Kendrick and Chaplain Weber and his wife to be available to drive her to the hospital in the event he was flying when the contractions began and one of the others was not available to drive her.

He was gratified he was at home with her on the evening of December 8, 1944, when she calmly announced, "Bill, I think it's time."

He grabbed the bag she had packed weeks before, helped her to the car and began the drive to the base hospital.

"I'd prefer to be in an open plane in a thunder storm, than having to drive you to the hospital right now," he announced as he cautiously and nervously made his way to the base.

He checked her in and went to the waiting room to pace and tried to read worn-out magazines as the hands on the wall clock slowly continued their rotation. Shortly after one o'clock the next morning, a nurse in a delivery room scrub suit pushed through one of the heavy doors to inform him he was the father of twin boys. A half hour later, he was taken to the large plate-glass window of the nursery where two green-gowned, masked nurses held the bundled babies up for him to see.

He went to Suzanne's room and kissed her.

"Hi, honey. Are you okay?" he asked, holding her hand.

She smiled. "A little sore but I'm fine. How are you?"

"Relieved."

"Have you seen the boys yet?"

"Yes. I couldn't tell much about them. The nurses had them all wrapped up. Have you seen them?"

"Just for a few minutes. They'll bring them back at feeding time."

He stayed with her until the nurse suggested he leave and let Suzanne rest.

Billy drove out the gate with a big smile on his face. The sentry cocked his head as Billy stopped to be waved through.

"I'm a father!" Billy announced.

"Congratulations, sir," the sentry said, saluting.

He called his parents when he arrived home to give them the news and to confirm the arrival time of the train that would bring them to Memphis.

He awoke Brad to tell him about the twins and to request the day off.

"Glad to do it, Bill," his commanding officer said.

"What are you naming them?"

"Gosh!" Billy said. "I don't know. I'll have to talk to Suzanne about that."

He climbed into bed and placed his hands behind his head.

He was too excited to sleep.

Boys. Two of them. Twin boys.

How often does that happen?

Boys.

Thank you, Father, for giving to our care two fine, healthy boys.

He returned to Suzanne's room the next morning as she finished feeding the twins.

A nurse took them away and Billy sat beside Suzanne's bed, holding her hand.

"Brad asked me what we were naming the boys. I told him I didn't know.

"Have you thought of names for them?" he asked.

"Sure," she said with a smile. "I don't know of a prospective mother who doesn't.

"I think it wouldn't be fair to name only one of them the third. What do you think?" she asked.

"I agree."

"Maybe we could name one of them after your side of the family and one after mine," she suggested.

"Okay. Ladies first."

"How about John as a first name, for my father and your Uncle John, too, and Walker, my maiden name?"

"Fine," he replied. "And James as a first name, for my dad, and Grant for a second name."

"Who's the Grant for?"

"Nobody. I just like the sound. Solid, like granite, don't you think?"

"Solid. Whatever you want, honey."

"Will we be able to tell which is which?" he asked.

"Of course."

"How?"

She laughed. "A mother knows."

"Well, how does she know? They look identical. Do they smell different or something?"

"Mothers just know."

They heard a soft rapping at the door.

Billy walked to the door and opened it. A doctor wearing a long, white, cotton coat over green scrubs was waiting.

"Mister Benson?"

"Yes."

"I'm Doctor Morales."

"Oh, sure," Billy said, offering his hand. "You're Suzanne's doctor. Come on in. Thanks for doing such a good job."

"You're welcome but I feel your wife did all the work."

"See, Bill? I told you."

"How do you feel, Mrs. Benson?" the doctor asked, in a heavy Cuban accent, as he walked to the side of her bed.

"I don't feel like doing any foot races but I guess I'm all right."

"They're fine, healthy boys."

"Thank you," Billy said.

Doctor Morales turned to Billy.

"I wanted to ask you if you're planning to circumcise your boys."

"When do you do it?" Billy asked.

"Normally the third day," the doctor replied. "To give them time to recover from the shock of being born."

"What do you think, honey?" Billy asked his wife.

"I'll leave that decision to you."

"Would you explain the procedure, Doctor Morales?" Billy asked.

"We strap them to a board—one at a time, of course—and remove their foreskins with a scalpel."

"Do you use anesthesia?" Billy asked.

"Not usually. It causes the foreskin to swell and interferes with the surgery."

"Does it hurt?"

"Of course it hurts. It's very sensitive tissue and filled with nerves."

"Does it bleed?"

"Yes."

"Are there ever accidents? I mean, when the scalpel slips or something, you know, and you cut off the penis?"

"Very rarely. I've never had that misfortune."

"Very rarely. Hmmm."

Billy looked at Suzanne.

"T.J. thinks Americans are obsessed with foreskins."

She smiled to think the topic would have come up.

"What do you think, Doctor Morales?" Billy asked.

"I agree with your friend."

"Is there any good reason to circumcise them?" Billy asked.

"Are you Jews?"

"With a name like Benson?" he laughed. "No."

"Then I know of no reason."

"Well, let's let them make that decision when they're older," Billy said. "I think they should be the ones to say."

"Is that all right with you, honey?"

She nodded.

"Let's leave them as they are," Billy said.

"Good," Dr. Morales said and then added, "One of my colleagues in Cuba says removing the foreskin is like removing the eyelids."

"Thank you, Doctor."

"Thank you. And let me know if I can do anything for you," the doctor said.

He shook Billy's hand and left.

Billy's parents arrived the next afternoon and remained a week, until Suzanne was fully recovered and could handle both boys by herself.

"Thanks again for the diaper service," Billy told his parents at the railroad station.

"Thank you for two beautiful grandchildren," his mother said. "They look just the way you did."

"And we really want you to try to visit us Christmas," his father said. "Everybody is eager to see the boys."

"We'll try," he said.

He hugged and kissed his mother, shook hands with his father and hugged him, too.

"Thanks for coming up. We really appreciate it."

"Wouldn't have missed it. We're ready to come back whenever you need us," his father said.

Billy waved at them as they boarded the train. He returned to his car and drove back to his small house.

Suzanne had finished feeding the twins and was leaving their room when Billy entered the living room.

"Got them off okay?" she asked.

He nodded.

"They really want us to come down for Christmas," he said.

"I know. We have every reason not to go," she said, quietly closing the bedroom door and walking to the kitchen.

"The twins will barely be three weeks old, and those stairs up to your room are going to get a good workout."

"What are you saying?" he asked.

"I think it would mean a lot to them if we made the effort."

He walked behind her and tied the strings to her apron.

"I think so, too."

*   *   *

CHRISTMAS EVE IN THE BENSON'S HOME was festive and filled with the collection of family and extended family: Velma and Robert and Sally Clark.

The mantle of the fireplace had been hung with 13 stockings, one for each member of the Benson extended family, one for Sally and another for Buddy. Lights decorated a cedar tree from Uncle John's farm and candles placed around the room and on the piano provided the only illumination in the living room that evening. Alice was seated at the upright piano, playing Christmas carols as the family stood around the piano or sat about the room, enthusiastically joining in on the songs.

The twins were asleep in their father's room in the single baby bed the Bensons had kept stored in their basement.

Edna and Velma excused themselves from the songfest to set up the dining table with glass plates filled with candies, cake and cookies. They carefully filled a large clear-glass punchbowl with the eggnog Sally Moore had brought over in a gallon jug.

Sally had made extra, without alcohol, for Susie and Robert.

When the family gathered in the dining room and everyone's punch cup was filled, Jim announced that he wanted to make a toast.

He lifted his cup as the others did the same.

"May this be the last wartime Christmas we'll have to celebrate. May Billy soon be a civilian, with Suzanne and my grandsons in a home of their own. May all our military friends soon be with their families and may God bless America."

Billy didn't drink his eggnog with the rest.

"What if I don't want all of those things to happen, Dad?" he asked.

"I don't know. Did I miss something, son?" his father answered.

"What if I want to stay in the Navy?"

"Oh, well," his father said cheerfully, "if you want to stay in, that's fine."

"What do you say, Suzanne?" Edna asked.

"If he makes j.g. soon and we can get out of that tiny apartment, a Navy career would be okay with me."

"Okay. I'll amend my toast, "Jim said. "To Captain Billy, his lovely bride, our fine twin boys and a Navy career: Calm seas and fair weather."

"I'll drink to that!" Billy said and emptied his cup in one gulp.

*   *   *

SUZANNE LAY WITH HER HEAD ON BILLY'S ARM, in the twin beds that had been pushed together, the mattresses laid crossways. The twins were sleeping soundly side by side in the crib beside the door. Buddy was curled up on a rug near Billy, between the bed and the windows.

"This was always the longest night of the year for me when I was young," Billy said quietly.

"For me, too," she said.

He pointed to the open transom over his door.

"Can you smell the turkey?"

She sniffed the air.

"Yes. It smells good," she said.

"That's always been part of Christmas. Mom starts the turkey before she goes to bed and slow cooks it all night.

"And I could hear the mantle clock striking every hour. I'd go downstairs at least a half dozen times before morning to see if Santa Claus had come. A couple of times I had to duck behind the stair rail so Mom wouldn't see me on her way in or out of the kitchen to baste the turkey."

"What else was special for you when you were young?" she asked.

"Oh," he said, pointing to the airplanes hanging from the ceiling, "making model planes, listening to radio programs up here Sunday afternoons or downstairs with the family after supper during the week before coming back up here to do my homework.

"What radio programs did you like?"

He laughed quietly.

"Anything western. Gene Autry's Melody Ranch. Red Ryder. Oh, and Jack Armstrong, even though it wasn't a western."

"Jack Armstrong, Jack Armstrong, Jack Armstrong. The A-l-l-l American Boy!" he recited dramatically.

"And, at night, Jack Benny, Edgar Bergen, Jimmy Durante, and of course, Fibber McGee and Molly."

"Heavenly days! Imagine that!" Suzanne said.

"I never got tired of hearing him open that closet door."

"Oh, no, McGee!" Suzanne mimicked. "Not that door!"

"T'ain't funny, McGee," Billy added.

"What else did you like to do?" she asked.

"Helping Uncle John work on his car or Uncle Kenneth's truck or the tractor."

"You and your Uncle John are really close, aren't you?"

"You bet. Closer, I guess, in a personal way, than with anybody in my own family. I could tell him anything or ask him anything. He always treated me as an equal and never laughed at my questions.

"When I stayed out there, mostly in the summers, I always slept with him. When I was very young, I used to go to sleep just the way you are, with my head in the crook of his arm.

"Next to Mom and Dad, I love him more than anybody else in the family."

"Excuse me?" she asked, turning her face to him.

"What?"

"Where does your own wife fit in? And your twins?"

He laughed quietly and pressed the side of her face to his with his arm.

He relaxed his arm and dropped his hand to clasp both of hers, which were resting across her chest.

"Oh, Suzanne, our love transcends theirs totally. I love them and they love me but it's an altogether different kind of kind of love. I guess I'd have to call theirs more of an emotional love, with a bit of spirituality.

"But ours? Emotional, physical, spiritual, sensual, erotic. You name it.

"I think the twins are a proof of that.

"Our love is so different, it's impossible for me to put into words, which is why I can show you how much I love you when we make love.

"I think…I think we are totally, totally connected, body and soul, heart and mind and on every other level we could think of, all the time. When we make love, though, I think we are more than just physically united. I guess that would be part of the spiritual aspect. I want to hold you so tightly that I can, somehow, just merge my entire body and soul inside your body, inside your soul. I want us to literally be one.

"I think we really are one, Suzanne. I feel I am part of you and you are a part of me, then and now and forever.

"I thank God so often for you and for the way He brought us together and made us fit each other so perfectly. And I don't mean just making love. Doing everyday stuff together. Helping you wash dishes, helping you care for the twins. Talking with you at supper. It is so easy for me to talk to you. Big thing, little things, anything.

"And for the passion and intense feelings, the ability to pour out our love—and I'm not talking about just the orgasms, which are wonderful—but the ability to express our love in such a way that our entire bodies can celebrate the sensuality and the spirituality.

"I love you, Suzanne Walker Benson, with a love that is more than love."

He lifted her hands with each of his four affirmations:

"I love you, I adore you, I admire you, I worship you."

He waited for her to reply.

She didn't speak.

"How'd I do?" he asked, giving her hands a gentle squeeze.

"Did I squirm out of it all right?"

She turned over and lay across his chest and kissed him on the mouth.

He smiled.

"Oh, Benson, you old seadog, you!" he teased, wrapping his arms around her and squeezing her gently. "She fell for it again, hook, line and sinker."

"Don't forget the worm," she said, slipping her hand into his shorts.

"Don't start something we'll have to finish."

She withdrew her hand.

"Hold it! Just a minute there, lady! Worm?" he asked, with mock resentment.

"Since when did my boa constrictor become a worm?"

"Maybe you used the wrong analogy," she answered. "To constrict means to get smaller. Maybe you should have used another one. Something like 'puff adder.'"

The living room clock struck twelve, ending the erotic, reptilian references.

They silently counted the chimes.

"It's Christmas," he said. "Merry Christmas, darling," he said, looking up at her.

She smiled and kissed him lightly.

"Our first Christmas together," she said. "Merry Christmas. And many, many more."

"And all with you," he said.

He paused.

"Speaking of Christmas," he began cautiously. "There's something I've wanted to ask you."

"Sure. We have no secrets from each other," she assured him.

"Well, I wonder if you'd let me ask you about the cuff links you gave me last Christmas."

"Sure."

"Well, I have sort of wondered why…hmm…let's see, how do I phrase this?"

"Why did I give you second-hand cuff links?" she said for him.

"Exactly. Yes. Thanks. You know that I appreciate them and enjoy wearing them. I just wanted to know."

She hesitated a few seconds before speaking.

"One of my first patients as a Navy nurse in Pensacola was a young Marine pilot who had crashed his plane and was seriously injured. Both his legs and one arm were broken. His legs were in traction and he had an airplane splint on his arm. He was receiving IV's, his face was nearly completely bandaged so I had no idea what he looked like. I could see just his eyes and mouth. He was dependent on us for everything."

She paused.

"I was new to the Navy and admit I got sort of a crush on him right away.

"He teased me about not being married and all that and he called me his sweetheart, you know. I played along with him and then the second day he told me he wanted me to have his cuff links in case anything happened to him. They were about all he had with him. In the pocket of his flight suit with his change.

"Anyway, I thanked him but told him not to think about that.

"But he lapsed into a coma just three days after he was admitted. I'd go in on my off hours and sit with him. I talked to him and read to him and held his hand. I was with him when he died because I didn't want him to be alone. I hope he knew I was there with him."

She paused.

"I was sure his family would come and claim his body and personal effects, so I had no intention of keeping the cuff links.

She paused again.

Billy knew she was weeping and put his arm around her tighter.

"Nobody came, Bill. Nobody called. Evidently, nobody cared. He was just all alone. It was so sad.

"He was buried in the National Cemetery there in Pensacola and just the chaplain, a Marine color guard, our XO, the chief of nursing and the people who took care of him on SOQ were at the graveside service.

"Anyway, I kept the cuff links."

They were momentarily alone with their thoughts.

"Thank you, honey, for the cuff links.

"What was his name?"

"Adam McAllister."

"Adam McAllister," he repeated. "Great name."

"Do you remember where his grave is?"

"Yes."

"Let's go there sometime and put some flowers on it."

"I'd like that."

"Thanks, honey."

She turned and lay with her back to him. He snuggled up behind her, placed his arm over her side and pulled her tighter to him.

He kissed her on her cheek.

"I love you, Suzanne."

She patted his arm.

"I love you, Bill."

They closed their eyes and drifted into a deep, peaceful sleep.

Sleeping like a pair of spoons was, by then, as natural as sleeping alone in a single bed before they were married, even though Billy thought they slept like a pair of Stearman inertia cranks, since that was more anatomically correct. She disagreed: *Spoons are more romantic than airplane cranks*.

*   *   *

IN THE PREVIOUS MONTHS, as Suzanne's delivery time had approached, her pregnancy had temporarily curtailed their intimate relations. Billy respected her physical and emotional condition and abstained from all sexual or sensual overtures, devoting himself, rather, to seeing to her comfort.

A little over a week after her delivery, since they could not engage in sexual intercourse at that time, she, who knew so well her husband's predilection for the corporeal pleasures of the marriage bed, was the one who initiated the sex play.

He was content to stand beside the bed and let her undress him slowly and then guide him to the bed where he would lie, moaning, gasping and crying out with ecstasy as she covered his shuddering body with provocative kisses and wandering, erotic, manipulative hands.

He let her take total control of his body and, with closed eyes and shuddering, undulating body, he relished the sensual, slow building and powerful, sustained, breath-taking climaxes she brought him to, after which he found all his strength drained. As he lay as exhausted and unmoving as a beached whale, she used a warm, damp washcloth to clean him.

She would then slip under the bedcovers beside him, turn onto her side and pull his arms securely around her as they slept like two perfectly-matched spoons—or Stearman cranks—until the twins called the one whose time it was to tend to them.

* * *

BILLY WAS AN ENTHUSIASTIC PARTNER in parenting. He looked forward to bathing the twins, drying them off, dusting them with Johnson and Johnson powder, rubbing them with fragrant oil and changing their diapers and even smiling as he did so.

"They think they've given you something," she had told him. "If you make faces and negative sounds or comments when you change them, they'll think you're rejecting their gift."

"Maybe I could check out a gas mask," he had suggested.

"That would really score points with them, wouldn't it?"

He delighted in nibbling their tiny fingers and toes, making baby talk and over the next weeks as they began to recognize him and register their spontaneous pleasure with flailing arms, kicking legs and exultant, elated faces that lighted up like cherubs, he responded to their enthusiasm with more kisses and more happy talk.

"I'll have to get in all these kisses while they're young," he told Suzanne. "The day will come that they won't let me and I'll have to wait until they're asleep."

He happily sat with her as she nursed them, holding one as she fed the other. They would rock together as they offered them water or diluted juice in sterilized Pyrex bottles fitted with Even-Flo nipples, boiled in a pot of water on the stove.

They often rocked the twins together, just for the pleasure of holding them, each in one of the chairs, cradling their tiny blue bundles, he repeatedly kissing the one he held and frequently joining together in song.

Billy liked an old hymn he had learned from his Aunt Grace and made popular by the Chuck Wagon Gang: *Angels, Rock Me to Sleep.*

When they arrived at the chorus, she sang the lead while he added the bass response:

Angels, rock me to sleep
(Angels, rock me to sleep)
In the cradle of love.
(In the cradle of love.)
Bear me over the sea.
(Bear me over the sea,)
To the haven above.
(To the haven above,)
When the shadows shall call
(When the shadows shall call.)
And the Savior shall call.
(And the Savior shall call.)
Angels, rock me to sleep
(Angels, rock me to sleep)
In the cradle of love.
(In the cradle of love.)

*   *   *

There had never been a disagreement between Billy and Suzanne since their marriage. There had been no friction by either's family or representatives of the Navy, bills, job assignments nor friends or neighbors.

Billy knew he was blessed and lived a life totally unlike so many others in their tortured world.

In his private as well as spoken prayers, he thanked God repeatedly for leading him to Suzanne, for making his life so special, so happy and so secure.

Except for the New Orleans indiscretion, Billy felt he had succeeded as a thoughtful and considerate husband. Additionally, with the arrival of the twins, he had willingly and cheerfully assumed the role of a devoted father.

His world, therefore, outside his avocation as a Navy flight instructor, lay inside the walls of the little house where his three greatest treasures awaited his arrival at the end of each working day.

After supper, when he did not have the duty, after the dishes were washed and the kitchen tidied up and before they listened to a radio program or he read the newspaper as she mended clothes or worked on a knitting project, they would walk quietly into the twins' room. There they would stand together, his arm around her shoulder, her hand around his waist, and look with pride at the twins as they lay sleeping in the single bed.

"They are so beautiful, Suzanne. I could stand here for hours just looking at them.

"And, you," he said, turning to her, "I just don't think I could have found a better wife in the world."

Tears welled up in his eyes.

"Suzanne, I'm the luckiest man in the world.

"Thank you so much for marrying me and giving me these perfect boys and for making my life complete."

She slipped her other hand around his waist and laid her head on his chest.

He rested his head on the top of hers and dropped his arms lightly around her shoulders.

"It works both ways, man of my life."

The Himalaya Mountains (Photo credit: U.S. Air Force)

CHAPTER SEVEN
SECRET MISSION

B ILLY ENTERED the flight instructors' ready room office Friday morning at 0645, greeted Scooter Scarbrough, the yeoman who was already at work at his large, gray metal desk beside the door and walked over to the coffee mess, on a table against the bulkhead under the window. He took a thick, white mug with the initials J.L., in large, black, block letters, and inspected the black interior of thick layers of dried coffee. Joe Larkin had sworn not to wash his cup until the war ended

Billy replaced the cup onto the green medical department towel and took another, filled it, and turned to walk to the instructors' ready room.

Brad Kendrick called to him.

Billy paused and looked into the squadron leader's office.

"Mornin', Brad."

"Come on in. I have something that may interest you."

Billy walked through the open office door. Kendrick pointed to one of the two heavy wooden chairs in front of his desk.

"I've got some good news and some bad news for you."

Billy uncrossed his legs and pushed himself upright.

"What do you mean? Did I get some orders?"

Kendrick pointed to a small stack of "flimsies," duplicate letters written on onionskin paper.

"Sort of."

"What do you mean 'sort of'?"

"Well, just like I said: 'Sort of,' " he said, holding up the papers.

"Are those for me?" Billy asked.

"Just hold your horses, Bill. I don't want you to get too excited. You *do* have orders, but only for temporary, and I emphasize the word, temporary duty."

"I don't care, Brad. I need a break. I'll take anything. Let me see."

Kendrick handed one of the copies to Billy as he set his coffee mug next to a shiny metal replica of a Pan-Am Clipper on Kendrick's desk.

Billy rapidly scanned the page, reading the key phrases aloud: "Special orders...Washington...," and then he sat up. "Fourteen days! Leaving Monday!"

Kendrick spread his hands, "Like I said, 'Good news and bad news.'"

Billy looked up, over the papers.

"Do you know anything else about this?" he asked.

"Just what you see there," Kendrick answered. "But I *do* have some sealed orders for you."

He nodded toward his safe. "I'll give those to you when you leave."

"So, you don't have any idea what all this is all about?"

Kendrick shook his head.

Billy handed the papers back.

"Well, I guess I should be grateful for small favors. I just wish I knew what's cooking."

"You can refuse them," Kendrick said. "I can kill those orders with one phone call. Since so many instructors have been transferred out, your being gone just two weeks is going to hurt us."

Billy stood and took his mug by the thick handle. "Oh, no, you don't! I'm not about to turn down any chance in this man's war to see something besides Tennessee cornfields from the air."

Brad smiled.

"I don't blame you. I'd do the same thing if given half a chance.

"Have Scooter call operations and see about getting you a hop to D.C."

"Right! Thanks!"

"Are you going to be able to keep your mind on flight training today?"

"Oh, sure. That won't be a problem. Anyway, thanks again!" Billy said, as he threw up his hand, turned and left the office.

He stopped by Scooter's desk to ask him to call about flights to National Airport but he resisted the temptation to call Suzanne. He doubted she would share his enthusiasm for the mysterious mission.

*   *   *

AFTER CLEARING THE SMALL WOODEN KITCHEN TABLE in the tiny kitchen where they ate all their meals, Billy stood beside Suzanne at the white porcelain kitchen sink. He was drying the supper dishes as she washed them and placed them into a metal pan filled with hot rinse water.

"I have an announcement to make," he said, trying to be casual.

"Am I going to like it?" she asked.

"Probably not."

She stopped washing the dish she held and looked at him.

"I got some orders today," he said.

She bit her lip.

"Now, don't get excited. It's only for two weeks."

She took a sudden breath, dropped the dish into the sink and turned away from him.

He placed the glass he had been drying on the sink top, threw the towel over his shoulder and put his arms around her.

She began to cry.

"Oh, honey! Don't do that!" he said, turning her gently toward him.

She buried her face in his chest as he hugged her tightly.

"It's just for two weeks. And you know how much I need to get away from the school."

"It's bad enough that I worry about you every morning you leave," she said tearfully. "I just couldn't stand it if you got sent off to the Pacific or someplace where the fighting is so bad."

"I know, but this is probably my last chance to do anything. The Germans are about whipped and the war's going to end and my entire service time will have been spent flying around in open cockpits in Tennessee. That'll be some story to tell my grandkids, won't it?"

"At least you'll be alive to tell them," she said, pulling away from him and drying her eyes with the hem of her apron.

"Where are you going, anyway?" she asked as she picked up the plate from the soapy water and began washing it.

He laughed. "I haven't the slightest idea. All I know is that Brad called me into his office this morning and showed me the flimsies. He has some sealed orders for me to pick up when I leave Monday. I have a hop from here to National Airport in D.C."

She paused in her washing again.

"Monday?"

He nodded.

She bit her lip again and shook her head.

"Honey, if this is going to be this hard on you, I can tell Brad to kill the orders."

She handed him the plate she had washed.

He took it, dipped it into the rinse water and began to wipe it dry.

"No," she said, softening. "I guess I owe you that much. Even though you haven't said anything to me about it, I've known how much you'd like to get away from flight training.

"I know it's boring to you, Bill, but like I've told you, from my point of view, it's perfect. You come home nearly every night, just like a civilian. You get to spend time with the boys.

"I read all those war casualty reports and I thank God every day that you're right here at home with your family and not over there, somewhere, getting shot at. I just couldn't stand it if...if..."

He laid the plate aside and took her into his arms again.

"Oh, Suzanne, honey. Please, don't ever worry about me. Believe me, I never take chances. Never. Even with those knuckle-headed cadets I try to teach to fly. I'm always ready for any surprises. I want to grow old with you as much as you do with me."

"I know that. But I still worry. I want you to be happy. And I know you won't be until you see what the rest of the Navy is about."

"I don't have any idea what these orders are for, but I promise you, Suzanne Benson, I'm coming back."

*   *   *

BILLY EASED OUT OF BED early Monday morning, took a shower and put on the aviation greens that Suzanne had laid out for him the night before. He tiptoed into the twins' room and looked down at them. In the light of their dim nightlight, they looked like the angels his mother called them. Wisps of curly, blond hair glowed like halos. They slept on their backs in perfect serenity, their arms thrown back on each side of their heads, their chests gently rising and falling. He lowered the side of their crib quietly, knelt on one knee and kissed them on their cheeks, lightly touched their faces, raised the side and left the room.

Suzanne was awake when he returned to their bedroom.

He knelt beside her and took her hand.

"Write me," she said in a hoarse whisper.

"I will. But I suspect I'll be back before the letters will."

"I don't care. I want to know you were thinking about me."

"Every minute."

"This is the first time we've been separated, except for New Orleans."

"I know."

He looked into her eyes.

"I love you," he said.

She smiled.

"I love you, too."

He kissed her and squeezed her hand.

"Don't worry about me. I'll feel guilty if you do."

"I can't promise that but do enjoy yourself, anyway."

He smiled.

"Oh, how I love you!" he said.

He lifted her enough to slip his arms around her and hold her as he kissed her again.

"I've gotta go. Brad is probably outside now."

"I know."

He threw her a kiss from the door of the bedroom and left quietly.

Brad was waiting in his car.

Billy tossed his bag into the back seat and quickly opened the door on the passenger's side.

Before he climbed in, he saw Suzanne standing inside the front door, looking through the glass panes.

He smiled and waved energetically. She raised her hand timidly. He got into the car and Brad drove to the base flight operations office where Brad handed Billy a large brown envelope sealed with a strip of tape.

"Don't open these until you receive authorization. You'll get that when you arrive at National."

"Right."

"Also, Suzanne wants you to look in your inside coat pocket when you're airborne. Not before."

Billy smiled. "Okay."

"Have a good time. Think of us down here, risking our lives with these yahoos while you're off on your big adventure."

"Right. Thanks for picking me up."

"Glad to do it."

Billy retrieved his bag from the back seat, shook Brad's hand and entered the flight operations office.

*   *   *

He boarded a Naval Air Transport Service, or NATS, Douglas R4D Skytrain troop and supply plane with large wooden crates stowed down the center of the interior. A narrow fabric bench ran down against each bulkhead for personnel to perch or sit uncomfortably. He nodded at the two men sitting on one side and sat across from them. He opened his case and slipped the brown manila envelope into it.

When he was airborne, he reached into his breast pocket and pulled out a small, nearly square, light-blue envelope. He held it to his nose and inhaled the light rose scent. He broke the seal on the point of the flap and removed a matching blue sheet of paper, folded in half. He unfolded the page to read what she had written in her perfect Palmer-method cursive script:

The Lord watch between me and thee when we are absent one from another.

Tears sprang immediately from his eyes.

He began to address his selfish motives for agreeing to take a 14-day leave of absence. Suzanne had never indicated she wanted to get away from her duties as wife, mother, and housekeeper.

Since she was busy with the twins all day every day, he hoped that she would not miss him too much for just two weeks. He'd buy them all something special to make up for his absence. Maybe a bottle of expensive perfume for Suzanne.

He smiled as he recalled their lovemaking over the weekend. It was as if each of them wanted to desperately and totally consume the other's entire sexual capacity. Both seemed to be attempting to store up enough exploding nerve ends and synapses to last until their next encounter.

Now he found he was already anticipating his return, anxious to be engaged in the exhilarating, arousing, sensual pleasures of the matrimonial bed.

He smiled and kissed the sentiment she had written, refolded the sheet, slipped it back into the envelope and returned it to his inside coat pocket.

Their amorous hours, fortunately, had left him sleep deprived. He shifted to a semblance of comfort and closed his eyes. The loud droning of the engines contributed to his drowsiness and lulled him into a sleep that lasted until the plane made its approach to National Airport.

*   *   *

WHEN THE PLANE LANDED and taxied to the side of the field, stopping with a jerk, Billy stood and stretched. As he was straightening his tie and coat, one of the crewmembers spoke to him.

"Are you Mr. Benson?"

"Yes."

"I have been instructed to tell you that you can open your orders now."

"Thanks."

Billy pulled his green suitcase onto the narrow bench, opened it and lifted out the manila envelope Brad had given him.

He tore open the sealed end and pulled out a smaller envelope stamped with the words TOP SECRET in large, bold type.

Inside that one was yet another, smaller envelope with EYES ONLY, stamped across it in red ink.

Inside it was still another envelope, this one with the typed message: *Super-Duper Secret Shit* and, under that, *Jack Armstrong Secret Junior Commando decoder ring may be necessary.*

"Super-Duper? Secret decoder ring? What is this?" Billy mumbled to himself.

He pulled a folded letter from the envelope and read it.

Ensign Benson,

Proceed from the plane as if nothing is amiss. Descend the stairs and wait on the tarmac for your contact.

The Phantom

"The Phantom? Now, wait a minute!" he said aloud.

He closed the hard-sided suitcase, lifted it by the handles and exited through the door in the side of the plane. He walked down the metal stairs that had been rolled against the plane and stopped at the bottom. He lowered the case and placed his hat on his head. It was then that he heard a ukulele plunking out five familiar chords, followed by the sound of two men singing, "Aloha oeeeee, aloha, oeeeeee."

He turned to face the music coming from underneath the plane, behind the stairs.

"T.J.! Barry!" he called, as his friends came toward him, smiling broadly.

"I should have suspected you two!"

They shook hands enthusiastically.

"And you were behind this all along?" Billy asked.

"Right-o!" T.J. replied. "We got bloody tired of hearing all those bloody, sad stories about how bloody mistreated you are and how you bloody wanted to see the rest of the bloody war, so Barry pulled a few strings and, *voila*! Here you are!"

They began walking toward the large hangar located a few yards from where the plane had landed.

"Is this your first trip to National?" Barry asked Billy.

"Right."

"A lot of this was under water just a few years ago," Barry explained. "Mudflats, they were called but filled in with tons of sand and gravel."

"Your tax dollars at work," T.J. volunteered.

Barry continued: "It started out as two airports in the twenties and thirties: Hoover Field, which was the first one here, and Washington Airport. But both were really hazardous to flying.

High-tension power lines over there, a tall smokestack there and Military Road right down the middle of the only runway. Guards had to flag down automobile traffic during landings and takeoffs.

"In 1938, though, President Roosevelt said, 'Enough is enough!' and got the ball rolling to unite the two. He dedicated it in 1941.

"Nobody still knows if it's in Virginia or in the District of Columbia. They'll probably still be trying to work that out twenty-five years from now."

"Well, thanks for the history lesson, Barry," Billy said. "But I'd really like for one of you to tell me why I'm here."

"We can't tell you yet. We have to play a game," T.J. said. "We can tell you what's happening only as things occur."

"What is this?" Billy asked.

"It really is a secret mission, Bill," Barry said seriously. "And we have to protect you in the event you let something slip."

"Slip? Who to? This place doesn't exactly look like Times Square," he said, observing the scarcity of personnel on the base.

"You might spill the beans in your sleep," T.J. laughed. "You do talk in your sleep, you know."

"The enemy is everywhere," Barry reminded him dramatically.

"A slip of the lips can sink a ship. Shhh!" T.J. said, his right thumb to his lips.

The trio arrived at the hangar and entered a corner office where a Marine corporal sat behind a desk.

"Lieutenant Macintosh, Mr. Dorsey. Good afternoon," he greeted T.J. and Barry.

"Good afternon, Corporal Hart. This is Mr. Benson. He's part of our contingent."

"Yes, sir," the corporal responded to Billy. "Could I see your orders, Mr. Benson?"

"I have them," T.J. replied, removing an envelope from his breast pocket.

The corporal read over the document.

"You have another man listed here."

"Right. Lieutenant, j.g., Collins." T.J. explained. "He'll report tonight or in the morning."

The Marine handed the paper back to T.J. and spoke to Billy again.

"Could I see your I.D. card, sir?"

Billy presented his wallet and opened it to show his identification.

"And your security clearance?" the Marine asked.

"Secret."

The Marine returned the wallet.

"Okay, sirs. You are free to enter the hangar space but leave your suitcase here, please, Mr. Benson."

"Sure," Billy said, dropping his luggage against the office bulkhead.

"Thank you, sir."

"And your guitar, Lieutenant?"

"It's a ukulele." T.J. said, placing the instrument on top of Billy's suitcase.

"Right through here, Bill," T.J. said as he opened a wooden door and held it for his companions.

Inside the cavernous, dimly lit hangar, sat a large, black, four-engine airplane with a double tail. Billy recognized it immediately as a B-24 Liberator bomber, the kind the Army flew over the Himalayas, but this one had a different arrangement of windows along the sides of the fuselage.

A Marine sentry armed with an M-1 rifle hanging from a sling on his back approached them.

"Sirs, could I see your identification cards and orders, please?"

The three complied.

"Thank you," the sentry said, handing back their wallets and orders.

The men walked around the plane, looking it over in awe.

"These Pratt and Whitney engines each produce eighteen hundred horsepower." Barry said.

"Sure out-powers my little Yellow Peril's two-hundred and twenty horses, doesn't it?" Billy said. "And it looks brand new."

"It is," T.J. said, "and only five others like it."

Billy followed them up the narrow, metal stairs that stood against the side of the plane.

"This isn't like any Liberator I've seen," Billy said, looking over the compact, luxurious interior.

"I guess not," Barry said, with a smug smile. "This is the president's airplane."

"President Roosevelt's?" Billy asked incredulously.

"He's the only president I know of," Barry replied.

Billy walked to the Pullman upholstered seats and ran his hand over the back of one of them.

T.J. gestured toward the 16 plush seats. "These convert into double sleeping berths. Curtains for privacy and everything. Just like on the trains."

He pointed to the forward berth. "That first one is ours. They all have upper and lower berths. We'll take turns sleeping. With just five military, initially, we won't have to be doing any hot-racking, the way they have to do on subs."

He moved down the narrow passageway.

"We've got a little galley here, with electric hot plates, running water," he added.

"Carpeting and special noise insulation," T.J. added, gesturing at the overhead. "You can actually hear yourself talk in this one. And heat. Not like the standard issue, where you have to wear fifty pounds of insulated clothes. And it's pressurized."

"And," Barry said, opening the narrow door to a small head, "we have two heads with real sit-down johns! Our Privateer has only relief funnels and a box lined with waxed paper. Of course, without heat, the funnels freeze up so we just try to hold it until we get back."

"Even if the funnels worked," T. J. added, "you'd have to be hung like a bleedin' horse to get your Willie out of all your flight gear and into the funnel. And with heavy gloves, yet."

"Some of the flights are up to sixteen hours long, "Barry said. "In those cases, we just sort of aim and let it freeze. Let the ground crews clean up the mess."

Billy took in the plane's luxurious interior and then asked, "Okay, why are we in the president's airplane?"

"Because we're going for a little ride in the president's airplane," T.J. replied.

"I thought you guys were flying Privateers," Billy said.

"We are," T.J. responded, "Just like this one—well, the military version. Ours has only one tail, not two. And after this mission, it's back to the same old grind. But Barry here—Mr. Big Shot—pulled some strings with his uncle to get us this assignment."

"His Uncle Sam?" Billy asked.

"No, his Uncle Claude."

"Who?"

"Claude Wickard. You know who he is, don't you," T.J. asked.

"I'm sorry but am I supposed to know this Claude Wickard? Oh, wait," Billy said. "I'll bet he's a golfing buddy of Bobby Jones."

"No," Barry said.

"Well, who is he then?" Billy asked.

T.J. laughed and put his hand on Barry's shoulder.

"See, Barry? Your Uncle Claude just doesn't get the same respect and recognition as, say, Harold Ickes or James Forrestal. Why couldn't one of them been your uncle?"

"Who is Claude Wickard?" Billy demanded.

"He's only the Secretary of Agriculture," T.J. said in a quiet voice, as if they might be overheard by an eavesdropper.

Barry bit his lip and shook his head in mock humility.

"But Uncle Claude got us this plane!" he proudly announced. "And he kept T.J. and me together, flying a plane that pilots two grades higher than us usually fly."

"Ain't nepotism grand?" T.J. asked.

"Are we flying your uncle somewhere?" Billy asked.

"We can't say," T.J. said.

"The president?"

"You see?" Barry accused playfully. "That's why we can't tell you anything, Benson. You aren't supposed to know who's going or where he or she might be going."

"She?" Billy asked. "Oh, so, it's Mrs. Roosevelt who is going."

"No, no, no, Benson!" Barry said. "You don't know who's going. And you're not supposed to know. It could be Fala but you still don't know."

"Okay," Billy said, throwing up his hands in pretended disgust. "I give up. Let's just finish the tour and get some chow. I haven't eaten all day except for a sandwich on the plane."

At 0730 the next morning, the three friends were back inside the hangar where two Army officers, First Lieutenants Rick Collins and Don Zimmer, joined them.

Barry introduced the men to Billy, who shook his hand as they exchanged greetings.

"I'll be chief pilot," Barry said. "T.J.'s the co-pilot. Rick is navigator and you're his assistant, Bill. Don is our flight engineer and radio operator. Bill, you'll be the assistant radio operator, too. When our party arrives, Bill, you'll also be host to our guests, chief steward and bottle washer. Okay?"

"Sure."

"Good.

"Now, why don't we get our personal gear stowed and everything ready in the cockpit?" Barry suggested.

"Let me give you a little more in-depth intro to the plane," Barry said after they had secured their baggage. "This is a C-87A, which you've already recognized as a modified B-24 Liberator bomber.

"It has a maximum speed of 220 miles per hour, a cruising speed of 188 miles per hour, a range of 3300 miles, and a service ceiling of 28,000 feet. Oh, and it doesn't have any armament."

"Will we need any?" Billy asked.

"I hope not. Fighter escorts will be assigned later," Barry said.

"Fighter escorts," Billy repeated.

"Fighter escorts," Barry confirmed.

Billy let the remark go without asking for clarification.

"Only six planes like this have been built, as T.J. told you," Barry continued. "The Navy has three and the Army Air Corps has the other three. They're all for VIPs. The president hasn't used this one yet, but Mrs. Roosevelt has, on a trip to South America."

"You'd better explain that, Barry," T.J. said.

"Yes, I guess I had. When one of these customized jobs crashed and burned without any valid reason, the Secret Service wouldn't let the president fly in it until it's modified some more."

"Y'all may remember when an Army version crashed near Millington last April," Billy said. "All ten crewmembers were killed."

"Well, it *is* called the flying coffin but that's because so many have gone down flying the Hump," Rick said.

"And the president let his wife fly to South America in it?" Billy asked.

Barry shrugged his shoulders and held out his palms from bent elbows.

"She's flown in it several times. What can I say?"

"Are you having second thoughts about this?" T.J. asked.

"Are you kidding?" Billy asked. "I wouldn't miss it for the world!"

Barry led Billy to the cockpit. The others followed.

"You can see we've got a pretty extensive layout here. T.J. will sit over there," he said, pointing to the right-hand seat. "I'll be here," he added, indicating the left seat, "and you and Rick will be out here. You can see that the cockpit is big enough for the pilot and co-pilot only. Of course, you can squeeze in any time you want to."

"We have virtually unlimited vision through all these Plexiglas panels: overhead, sides, all around."

"Not like the Stearman, is it?" Billy asked, looking over the impressive instrumentation on three sides of the pilot's seats and overhead.

"We have control wheels instead of joysticks," Barry said. "Just like driving an automobile."

"Is it easy to fly?" Billy asked.

"It's quick to respond to controls," Barry answered. "Almost too quick. That takes some getting used to. It isn't totally unforgiving and it definitely demands our respect. When we're airborne, we'll let you and Rick try your hand at flying it."

"Great! I'd like that," Billy said.

"But when are we supposed to get off?" he asked anxiously.

T.J. laughed. "Right. When are we supposed to get off, chief pilot?"

"When our passengers arrive," Barry said. "That's all I can say. Until then, we follow our orders: Wait patiently."

"Are you allowed to tell me what you have been doing in the Pacific since you left Pensacola?" Billy asked.

"Sure," Barry said. "I think you know T.J. and I have been flying a PB4Y-4P photo studio. We have a total crew of twelve: five to fly the plane and keep it repaired; two camera operators; and five machine gunners. We have four cameras and fly at about twenty-five thousand feet."

"What do you photograph?" Billy asked.

"Enemy air fields. Enemy troop or convoy movements," Barry answered. "Whatever we're told."

"Have you had any combat action yet?" Billy asked.

"A couple of times but at our altitude, not much can touch us," T.J. said.

"So, what do we do now?" Billy asked.

"I brought some cards," Rick said. "Spades, anyone?"

*   *   *

BY 1600, THE MEN HAD PLAYED CARDS, drunk coffee, made head calls, talked, walked around the hangar, eaten box lunches of cold fried chicken, potato salad, celery and carrot sticks and an apple, and had tried to avoid becoming irritated at each other, or the delay in the arrival of their mystery party.

Billy had taken the opportunity to acquaint himself with the galley and the procedure to convert the seats into sleeping berths. The men decided to call it a day. They stood, stretched, went to chow and returned to their quarters for the night.

The following morning, the hangar crew performed its daily maintenance check, including rotating the plane's four large propellers.

At 0730, Billy and his friends returned to the plane and again settled into the upholstered chairs in the passenger's cabin to begin their wait anew.

Less than an hour after their arrival, they heard the sound of two noisy motorcycles rapidly approaching their hangar.

T.J. ran to the cockpit and looked outside through the Plexiglas windows.

"Okay, Marine," he called to the sentry from the open cockpit window, "get those doors open!"

"This is it," he said to Billy, T.J. and Rick, who had rushed to the cockpit to see what was happening.

The men grabbed their covers, scrambled down the ladder at the side of the plane and took positions at the large hangar doors that were being pushed open by the Marine sentry and naval ground crew personnel.

Two black Packard limousines came to a halt behind two uniformed motorcycle-riding capitol police officers, wearing thick, black, leather jackets and tall, black, leather boots.

The drivers of the limousines and the men riding with each of them in the front seats jumped out and opened the back doors of both cars.

Barry walked quickly to the front automobile, saluted and asked, "May I help you, Madame Chiang?"

Small fingers with long, bright red nails took Barry's outstretched hand.

"Thank you, Ensign," she said.

Billy and the others watched as a small woman wearing a long, dark dress with a high collar and long splits at the bottom of each side, stood on the tarmac. She was wearing black high-heeled shoes with large black decorations on the toes, the size and shape of butterflies.

Another woman exited the other side of her car and walked around it.

Two more women left the second car and walked to Madame Chiang as Barry was introducing himself with a salute.

"Madame Chiang, I am Ensign Barry Dorsey, United States Navy, your chief pilot."

"Ensign Dorsey," she replied.

He gestured to the others who saluted her as they were introduced.

"This is Lieutenant T.J. Macintosh, United States Marines, your co-pilot."

Madame Chiang extended her hand. "Lieutenant Macintosh," she said.

"This is Lieutenant, j.g., Rick Dorsey, our navigator."

Madame Chiang extended her hand. "Lieutenant Dorsey," she said.

"And this is Ensign Bill Benson, who will be assistant navigator and radio operator. Mr. Benson will also serve as your host."

"Mr. Benson," she said, extending her hand.

"Pleased to meet you, ma'am," Billy said as he took the fingers of Madame Chiang's outstretched hand lightly in his.

"Are you from the South, Mr. Benson?"

"Yes, ma'am."

"I thought so. I learned to speak English in Georgia. Can you detect my Southern accent?"

"Yes, ma'am," Billy said, returning her smile.

The men who had opened the doors had gone to the trunks of the cars where they were busily removing luggage and placing it onto dollies that the hangar crew had pushed into place.

"Shall we go on board, Madame Chiang?" Barry asked.

"Excuse me a moment, Mr. Dorsey."

Madame Chiang addressed her attendants briefly in Chinese, whereupon they retrieved three small cases from the dollies.

And then to Barry, "Yes, thank you, Mr. Dorsey. I am ready."

Barry led the way to the side of the plane and stood as the women walked up the metal stairway and into the plane.

"Mr. Benson will help you stow your personal effects and show you how to use your seat belts."

*   *   *

AS THE LARGE PLANE was slowly pulled from the hangar by a Caterpillar tractor, Billy, standing behind Barry and T.J.'s seats, asked, "Okay, Barry, T.J., isn't it time you guys let me in on our flight plans?"

"What do you think, co-pilot?"

"Sure. We've made the poor bugger wait long enough."

"Okay, Bill," Barry said. "We're taking Madame Chiang home."

"Home? Do you mean to China?" he asked in disbelief.

"To China," Barry confirmed.

"Wow!" Billy said, a kid again, his eyes bright with anticipation.

"After making refueling stops in the Azores, Morocco, Cairo, Karachi and a lovely little spot in India called Chabua," T.J. added.

"Speaking of Chabua, did you guys bring along some pare-goric?" Barry asked.

"What's that for?" Billy asked.

"You name it," Sam said with a laugh. "For the food. For the water. For the air, I suppose. You show me a GI who doesn't need paregoric in India, and I'll show you a dead GI," Barry said.

After the tractor was disconnected from the plane, Barry and T.J. left the cockpit and walked to the front of the plane. There they removed the covers from the two pitot tubes and performed their walk-around preflight inspection before returning to their seats.

"Rick, you and Bill check out our passengers' seat belts and we'll get set for take off," T.J said. "And then you can come back up and hang around to watch our check off."

Don Zimmer, as flight engineer, turned on the four fuel selector valves, one for each engine, and checked the fuel load totaling 1200 gallons in four systems.

Barry turned his control wheel to each side as T.J. and Don visually checked the movement of the ailerons. As he pushed the wheel back and forth, they checked the elevators and the response of the rudder pedals.

"I'm going out to turn the props," Don said. "Make sure the ignition switches are off, chief pilot."

"Ignition switches off, flight engineer," Barry said.

"And the master ignition switch off," Don said.

"Master ignition switch off," Barry repeated.

Don left the plane.

Billy entered the cockpit again and squatted behind the seats.

"Don is going to pull the props through to clear them of oil and gasoline," Barry said. "This can be a dangerous operation. He'll pull them through two revolutions. We've got all the ignitions switches off but a broken ground wire could cause kick-back and just mess up his day."

After Don completed pulling the propellers through, he stepped back, picked up the fire extinguisher a member of the ground crew provided and walked to engine number one.

The ground crew kicked wheel chocks into place in front of each wheel and moved a safe distance from the propellers.

Barry and T.J. began the involved start-up procedure that entailed turning on the ignition and auxiliary switches, altimeter to the field's barometric pressure and a myriad of other controls, as T.J. read the check list and Barry repeated the commands and set the controls.

"We'll start these babies up one at a time," Barry said, turning on all four ignition switches and the master switch.

"Three, four, two and one. We have to start with number three because it's the only one with a hydraulic pump attached to it."

T.J., who would actually start the engines, looked out of the plane to see that all personnel were clear of the propellers.

"All clear!" he called out his window.

Don answered, "All clear!" as he stood at a safe distance, his fire extinguisher at the ready.

T.J. turned on the fuel booster pumps for priming the engines and then primed the number three engine with one hand and held the starter energizer to ACCEL with his other hand.

One at a time, the four whining engines came to life, coughing and sputtering, spinning the propellers slowly, laboriously at first and then faster and faster.

Don returned to the plane and took his seat behind the cockpit.

T.J. slid his side window closed.

"Secure the hatch, chief steward," Barry called to Billy.

The ground crew wheeled the stairs away from the plane, enabling Billy to close and lock the side door.

He returned to the cockpit as Barry signaled for the wheel chocks to be removed. Barry released the brakes to taxi out to the end of the runway where the brakes were locked again and the throttles were set for a 1000-rpm warm up. The powerful engines turned the large propellers until lights came on on the instrument panel to indicate they had reached their target speed.

"Now we'll exercise the props to check their full range of operation," T.J. said. "I'll bet you didn't know props could be exercised, did you?"

Billy laughed and shook his head.

T.J. slowed the propellers down to low rpm high pitch and then to high rpm low pitch, where they remained for the run-up and take-off.

"Adjust control tabs for takeoff," T.J. read.

Barry set the elevator, aileron and rudder tabs.

"Control tabs set," Barry responded.

"Check the automatic flight control and de-icer for me, again, T.J."

"Right. AFC and de-icer. Check."

"Auto rich mixture set," T.J. continued.

"Auto rich, check."

"Fuel pressure?"

"Off, fifteen pounds pressure."

"Fuel pressure on for run-up and takeoff."

"Fuel pressure on."

"Magnetos?"

"Magnetos. Check."

"And now, my favorite part," Barry said enthusiastically. "The SU-percharger.

T.J. moved the supercharger control forward slowly to ON.

"Supercharger on."

Other controls were checked, the control tower was contacted again and Barry turned his head to announce: "Okay, co-pilot and crew, we're clear for takeoff. Take your seats and fasten your seat belts. It's China, or bust!"

Once in the air and they had reached their cruising altitude of 8000 feet, Barry announced on the plane's intercom that the passengers could move about the plane.

Billy went to his guests.

"Is there anything I could get for you, Madame Chiang?" He asked.

"Yes, thank you, Mr. Benson, would you be so kind to show Kwei Twang your galley? I would like a cup of tea."

"Yes, ma'am," he replied.

Kwei Twang followed him into the small galley.

He showed her the sink and dual hot plates and opened a cabinet over the little counter.

"Here is a kettle," he said. "There are knives and spoons and things in this drawer, here."

"I think I have everything else here, Ensign," Kwei Twang said. "I need only boiling water."

"Okay," he replied. "Fill the kettle with water here and turn this knob on the hot plate. If you can't find something, just let me know."

"Thank you, Mr. Benson," she replied politely.

Billy excused himself and walked to the front of the plane.

"Is all well up here?" he asked.

"Oh, sure. Looks like smooth weather all the way to the Azores," Barry replied.

"How far is it?" he asked.

"You're the assistant navigator," Barry replied. "*You* should know that."

"Of course."

He stepped down to where Rick sat at a small desk with a light over it.

"How far is it to the Azores, chief navigator?" he asked.

"It's twenty-three hundred miles from New York," he said, looking at his map. "Right now, we're eighteen hundred miles to go."

"Do we have a base there?" Billy asked.

"We share Lajas Field with the Brits. We're building a new field on Santa Maria, but it won't be ready for a few months yet. Anyway, it's supposed to be a big secret. Nobody's supposed to know about it."

"Come on up, Bill," Barry called. "You can see what it feels like to fly a real airplane and not one of your little yellow crop dusters down on the farm."

*　　*　　*

"COME HAVE A SEAT OVER HERE, MR. BENSON," Madame Chiang said to Billy, on one of his trips to check on her comfort.

He sat in the seat opposite her.

"Would you like some tea?" she asked, gesturing toward the tray with a teapot and cups, set before them on a table between the seats.

"Yes, thank you."

Madame Chiang poured steaming tea from a white porcelain teapot with a rattan handle, into a small, matching cup, resting on a small, round, jade-green, wooden coaster.

He placed his fingers around the cup but removed them quickly.

"Do you know why our cups have no handles?" she asked.

"No, ma'am."

"If it is too hot to hold, it is too hot to drink," she said with a smile.

"That makes sense," he said, looking at his fingertips.

"How long have you been in the Navy, Mr. Benson?"

"Since nineteen forty-three."

"Is this your usual assignment?"

"No, ma'am. I'm a primary flight instructor in Memphis. This is just a little break for me."

"Where have you been stationed?"

"Memphis, actually, Millington, in west Tennessee, is my first permanent station. I was in Athens, Georgia, for pre-flight, in Pensacola, Florida, and Memphis after that, in flight school. And in New Orleans, for instructors' flight training."

"Did you enjoy Athens?"

"I didn't see much of it, I'm afraid. Pre-flight was only twelve weeks long and pretty intensive."

"I attended school in Demorest, Georgia, when I was only ten. One of my sisters was a student at Wesleyan School for Women in Macon. That's where I learned to speak English."

"You speak it very well."

"Thank you.

"When my husband became Generalissimo, he had the communists to deal with first and then the Japanese. If it were not for the Americans, we would have lost China to the Japanese already.

"The American people have been very kind to my family, my people and to me. We owe all of you a great debt."

"Thank you."

"You probably know that American pilots flying over China wear special silk patches sewn onto on the backs of their flight jackets, identifying them as friends of the Chinese people."

Billy nodded that he knew. He also knew they were called blood chits.

"One pilot who had flown with General Doolittle to bomb Tokyo told me that he had to parachute from his plane over China. When he reached the ground, what seemed to him an entire village rushed out to meet him. He wasn't sure what their intentions were, so he waved his arms and shouted the only Chinese word he knew: 'Mei-kuo, Mei-kuo!' which translates as 'America.'

"In our language, however, it literally means 'beautiful country.'"

"I didn't know that."

"The pilot said the people were so kind to him, he felt as if he were at home, even though that was his first trip to China."

She paused and took a sip of her tea.

"This has little jasmine blossoms in it."

Billy gripped the wooden coaster to lift his cup and inhale the sweet aroma of the fragrant tea.

"It smells good." He tasted it and smiled. "It tastes good, too."

"Are you a Christian, Mr. Benson?" she asked.

Billy was surprised at the question.

"Yes, ma'am," he answered.

"My father was a Bible salesman in China and my mother was, and is, a devout Christian. We are Methodists. When the Generalissimo proposed marriage to me, my mother told him he would have to renounce Buddhism and become a Christian before she would allow our wedding."

"Did he?" Billy asked.

"He told my mother he would need to study Christianity before he could make that decision. She believed him and we were married. He was baptized later, in 1929."

"Well," she said, "tell me about yourself. That is a wedding band you are wearing?"

He looked at his ring. "Yes, ma'am. I married a Navy nurse while I was in Pensacola. She's in Memphis with me now, of course."

"Do you have children?"

"Yes, ma'am. Twin boys. Three months old," he said proudly.

"Congratulations," she said, lifting her cup.

"Thank you."

He lifted his and they took a salutary sip.

"I regret that the Generalissimo and I have no children. They can be a comfort in one's old age."

"And a delight in one's young age, too," Billy said.

"I have a friend in China whose son attended one of your primary flight schools in California," Madame Chiang said. "At Twenty-nine Palms."

"Yes, ma'am," Billy said.

"His entire class was made up of Chinese boys."

"Yes, ma'am."

She smiled.

"It seems two of the Chinese boys demonstrated what might be translated 'saving face.' Do you know that term, Mr. Benson?"

"Yes, ma'am."

"They were driving along on the ground in their planes, headed for each other. Is 'driving' the correct term?" she asked.

"We say 'taxiing'," he said.

"Thank you. They were taxiing on the ground, heading for each other. Since to move out of the way of the other would have been a source of great embarrassment for both the Chinese boys, neither changed his course and they crashed into each other. Both planes were destroyed."

She smiled again.

"Their American instructors could not understand why they collided but 'saving face' is very important for Asian people, especially men," she said.

"I hope it didn't happen too often. That would make for a lot of paper work, wouldn't it?" Billy asked, smiling.

He looked at his watch.

"If you would excuse me, Madame Chiang, I need to get back up to the front. They'll think I'm just a passenger."

"Of course, Mr. Benson. It has been most pleasant talking to you."

He stood to go.

"I've enjoyed talking with you, too, Madame Chiang. And thank you for the tea."

"My pleasure."

When he stepped up to the control deck and stood between the two pilots' seats, T.J. turned and asked, "Well, how are you and the Dragon Lady doing?"

"Fine. I think she likes me."

"*Everybody* likes you, Bill Benson," Barry said.

"Maybe so, but everybody isn't a personal friend of the President of the United States or the wife of a virtual head of state."

"Maybe she'll ask you to take over the Chinese air command," T.J. said.

"Over General Chennault's dead body," Barry said. "If anybody messed with his Flying Tigers, we'd have another world war on our hands."

Barry stretched and yawned noisily.

"I think I'll take a little nap, Bill, me boy," he said. "How about taking over for me?"

"You bet."

The plane continued to the Azores for refueling. The crew and passengers took the occasion to shower, change clothes and enjoy a good meal, as they would do at the next three stopovers. They flew on to Morocco, Cairo, Karachi and then, five days after leaving Washington, the plane touched down on an Army Air Transport Command, or ATC, airstrip in Chabua, India.

A jeep with a large FOLLOW ME sign on the back led the plane to the opening in front of a hangar where two military police, with rifles slung across their backs, were waiting. As soon as the plane stopped, a flight crew emerged from the hangar opening and pushed a wheeled set of metal steps to the side of the plane. One of the MPs immediately climbed the stairs and stood by as the passengers and crew exited. The second MP remained at the foot of the stairs, his rifle at the ready.

The two Army green Ford sedans that had been waiting near the hangar, drove to the foot of the stairs to whisk away Madame Chiang and her party.

"We're supposed to hook up with an Army pilot here who will fly the plane to China," Barry said as they walked to the flight control office.

The men entered the office and stood in front of a long counter. Behind it, airmen sat at desks underneath slow-spinning ceiling fans that seemed to do little more than stir up the hot air.

One man looked up from his desk as the men lined up at the counter.

"Could I help you?" he asked.

Barry spoke for the crew: "We're here with Madame Chiang Kai-shek and are supposed to meet an Army pilot who's flying us into China."

"Just a minute. You'll need to talk to Colonel Hines about that."

The man walked to an office, stuck his head in the door and announced that Madame Chiang's plane had arrived.

The soldier returned. "The colonel will be right with you."

"Captain Patterson is the man who'll fly you to India, gentlemen," the colonel told the men at the counter after Barry had introduced himself. "He flew down to Calcutta for a couple of days. A lot of the guys go down for a little leave time at the Grand Hotel. He should be back tomorrow morning.

"Did the Chinese pick up Madame Chiang?" the colonel asked.

"Yes, sir. They were waiting for us," Barry said.

"Good. We always try to treat her with kid gloves.

"We'll put your plane in the hangar until you leave," the colonel said. "Our guys will do maintenance on it and we'll keep security there around the clock."

"Good. Thanks. So, where do we go for the duration?" Barry asked.

The Army officer looked around the office. "Hey, Brillo," he called.

A private with short, tight, curly hair looked up from his desk. "Yes, sir?"

"We've got some overnight guests. Take 'em over to the pilots' quarters, okay?"

"Yes, sir."

Brillo walked past the men as he removed his cap from his belt and plopped it onto his head. "Right this way, gentlemen."

They grabbed their luggage and followed Brillo out of the office.

An enormous elephant with a native on his neck was lumbering by, just in front of the flight operations office, as they stepped out into the stifling heat of the Indian mid-afternoon.

"Where is he going?" Barry asked.

"Work party," Brillo said. "They use 'em for everything over here. They're really good for loading up those fifty-five gallon barrels of fuel. They hoist 'em right up through the cargo doors like they're made out of balsa wood. You might be surprised but one of those elephants can do the work of twelve natives. Just give 'em some hay, hose 'em down now and then, or take 'em down to the river to play and they'll work all day with nary a complaint.

"You can take a ride on one for a buck."

"No thanks," Barry said.

Brillo pointed the direction they were to go and the men fell in on either side of him as they walked to their quarters.

"What are those camels I saw painted on the noses of the Liberators back at the hangar?" Billy asked.

"Camels. Humps. Get it?" Brillo asked. "One camel for each time the plane flies the Hump."

"Makes sense," Billy said.

"How many Hump flights do these guys have to make?" T.J. asked.

"They operate on a quota of hours, not trips. They need six-hundred and fifty flight hours before they can be rotated back to the States."

Don whistled. "Six-hundred and fifty!"

"That sounds pretty stressful," Barry suggested.

"It is," Brillo agreed.

"But some of these guys are so anxious to get back, they've flown three missions in a twenty-four hour period.

"This entire field was made with gravel the Indians crushed by hand," Brillo said, gesturing toward the tar and gravel-covered landing strip.

The men looked at the expansive field.

"They started out with huge limestone boulders," Brillo continued, "and just kept whacking away at 'em with hammers and hauled the gravel out in straw baskets.

"We have a dozen other fields in India just like this one. And six in China. All of 'em hand made. The field over in Yangtze had a hundred thousand Coolies working on it. When a steamroller wasn't available, they just hooked up two hundred Coolies to a roller.

"We hire native guards to keep their sacred cows off the runways but we have to take care of the snakes ourselves."

"Snakes?" Rick asked, jumping and looking nervously at the ground.

"Yeah, cobras and kraits. The cobras are big enough to see, usually. But the kraits are kinda small. About a foot long. They look just like grass snakes, except for the yellow bands. A pilot killed one under his bunk not long ago."

"Oh, man, I hate snakes!" Rick said. "What do you do if you see one?"

"Shoot 'im. Everybody here packs a sidearm. Especially since, a few months ago, nobody could sleep because of the drums at night over at Gaya. They said it was just like in one of those *Nyoka of the Jungle* pictures. The natives were celebrating a massacre of the British in Calcutta a long time ago. The word went out and all the Americans and Brits were given arms and told to be prepared for anything. But that quieted down eventually.

"We shoot rats, too. One guy died three days after one of 'em bit 'im on his toe. He'd done his hours, too, and was going to be rotated out."

A siren sounded. Brillo looked down the field, seemingly without concern, where a large red cloth ball was being hoisted up a tall pole.

"You guys need to keep an eye on that pole," he said, pointing. "Even though we've destroyed the Jap base over in Myitkyina, Burma, just an hour away by air, we still get visits now and then from planes from some of their other bases. We've got spotters all over who let us know when their planes are headed this way.

"One ball means their planes are airborne. Two balls mean they're twenty minutes away and three mean they're in sight."

"What do we do then?" Billy asked.

"Take cover. Hit one of the trenches. They're all over the base. There's one," he said, pointing to a long, wide excavation in the ground.

"For how long?" Barry asked.

"Until you hear the all clear siren. Sometimes the Japs just like to make us scramble our fighter planes and then they leave. Sometimes they bomb us but our guys always scare 'em off."

"It would just be my luck to jump into a trench with snakes in it," Barry said.

"It's happened," Brillo said casually. "We usually kill one or two a week.

"And it's in the trenches where you can tell the old timers from the new guys. The ones who've been through air raids before grab a chair and a magazine to wait it out. Sometimes we're down there for as long as an hour."

They continued walking to their quarters, keeping their eyes alternately on the pole and the ground, for snakes.

They arrived at a large bamboo structure. They could hear men's voices shouting loudly inside.

"Your basha, gentlemen," Brillo said, leading them up the wooden steps.

Inside the building, metal beds with thin mattresses under mosquito net frames filled the space under a woven bamboo ceiling, supported by a network of exposed wooden beams. Metal trunks were at the feet of most of the beds. Green, cone-shaped metal shades with bare light bulbs hung by long electric cords from the beams.

It reminded Billy of being back at his Boy Scout Camp Cherokee.

The shouting, louder now, came from the other side of the building, from an open porch where a group of men could be seen through a wide opening in the side of the basha, sitting around a low table.

"Everybody plays poker over here. Not much else to do if you're not flying missions," Brillo explained. "Liquor costs seventy-five to a hundred bucks a bottle. And the women have what they call

Chinese syphilis. The natives are immune to it but we aren't. I saw one of our guys over at the clinic who had it. Man! His privates were…Man! It made me sick. We tell all new people the safe thing to do is just keep it in your pants.

"Some guys play in the black market," Brillo continued. "They take Indian rupees to China and exchange them for American dollars. And a carton of cigarettes that costs fifty cents here can get you twenty dollars in China. One pilot I knew was dealing in precious stones and things while he was here. He showed me his footlocker once. It was filled with gold, diamonds, sapphires, emeralds, rubies, jade, a little bit of everything. He said his wife had already bought six houses in Tennessee."

So much for scout camp, Billy thought.

"But shouldn't those guys be scrambling?" T.J. asked, nodding toward the men on the porch.

"No. They're off duty. But we have some planes up now. I heard them taking off right after the siren sounded."

"Oh," T.J. said.

"Okay, gentlemen," Brillo said with a flourish of his hand, "Find an empty rack and start making yourselves at home. I'll get the sheets and pillowcases.

"Believe me. I'm serious about the snakes. Be sure to check for them before you climb in your racks and always shake out your shoes and boots before you put them on. We have scorpions, too. But don't kill the big one. We let him stick around to kill the smaller ones."

He turned to leave but hesitated.

"Oh, one more thing: when you go to the latrine, take a look under the rim of the toilet before you, you know, hang any body parts down there. Spiders have bitten a couple of guys. I guess you know where. This is one place where having big 'nads isn't necessarily a good thing."

Rick grabbed his crotch and grimaced. "Damn! I hate this place already."

"Maybe we should have stayed in the plane," Barry said lightly.

"You'd be cooked in fifteen minutes in this heat, sir," Brillo said. "As a matter of fact, the planes are so hot from the sun during the daytime, all maintenance and repairs have to be done at night."

"And one more thing," Brillo said, "keep your toothpaste and shaving cream secured in your bags. These guys have a pet monkey who likes to come in here when nobody's looking. He gets his kicks out of taking the caps off tubes and squeezing them. Nobody's killed him yet but a few have tried. See those bullet holes in the roof?

"Keeping pets is a good idea, though. Fleas jump onto the pets, not on people. When rich families over here go away for a few days, they'll send servants through the house first when they return so the fleas will jump on *them*."

"Got it," T.J. said.

A siren sounded.

"But what about those Jap planes?" Rick asked.

Brillo walked to the large window at the end of the room.

"That's the all clear. It must have been a false alarm."

"You're awfully calm about all this," Rick said.

"Oh, you get used to it. Earthquakes, typhoons, snakes, native uprisings. All in a day's work," Brillo said, as he left to get their bed linens.

Barry walked to the bamboo porch where the poker game was going on. Some of the men were in their khaki uniforms, wet with perspiration. Some wore only olive drab boxer shorts. Several wore their .45-caliber automatic pistols in shoulder harnesses. Two wore the pilots' trademark hat that had been carefully crushed after their fiftieth mission.

A slight, shirtless, dark-skinned native, the basha's houseboy, wearing thin, baggy shorts and sandals, sat on the bamboo rail of the porch. The basha's monkey sat on the boy's shoulder, seeming to enjoy the poker game.

One of the men looked up from his hand. "We can relax, men. The Navy's landed. You're the guys who flew that customized Liberator over?"

"Right."

The men sitting around an improvised table turned to see the new arrivals.

"Welcome to our little piece of heaven, guys!" one of them said.

"Wanna get in on our game?" another asked.

"Not now," Barry said. "Maybe later."

"We'd love to take some of that Navy pay away from you," one of the men chewing a cigar added.

Brillo returned with their sheets and the men began to make up their beds.

"Pull the mosquito nets all the way around your racks and tuck the edges underneath your mattresses before you turn in," he told them.

"The mess hall's next door. The food's lousy but we eat it anyway. It's about the only thing to do here besides play cards or shoot craps. We show a movie every night but it's usually the same one for a week. Just follow the crowds," he added as he was about to leave.

"You can grab a shower in the latrine but when it rains, most guys strip, grab a bar of soap, run outside and shower there.

"One more thing," he said, pausing. "If you see a leopard walking through, don't shoot it. It's a pet. This one's name's Simba. Most of the bashas have house cats."

"And if you want to ride in to the little village down the road, let me know. I can get you a jeep. The natives speak English and love to take American money. They make a lot of handmade things and sell them dirt-cheap. It's a good place for souvenirs."

Brillo turned to go but stopped and raised his finger to speak.

The men all said with him, "One more thing."

They all laughed.

"Right," Brillo said. "Some trivia for you: India is the place khaki was introduced to the military. The Brits wanted a uniform that wouldn't show dirt, so they used a native cloth. Just thought you'd like to know."

"Thanks, Brillo," Barry called.

"Enjoy your stay, gentlemen" he said, as he left the building.

"How many 'one more things' do you think he thought of?" Barry asked.

"I lost count," Billy said. "But you know what I think? I have the feeling we aren't in Kansas anymore."

*　　*　　*

'PAT' PATTERSON HAD RETURNED by midmorning the next day. Colonel Hines sent Brillo to the pilots' basha to invite the Navy crew to the flight operations office to meet their new pilot.

"Come on into my office," Colonel Hines said when Billy and the crew arrived. He introduced the men to Captain Patterson, still red-eyed from his trip to Calcutta and still wearing his leather flight jacket and crushed hat.

"The weather over the Hump was good last night and it looks good for tonight," he told them after they all shook hands and exchanged pleasantries. "The Japs send in their Zeros whenever we go out during daylight hours, so night flights are best. They have reconnaissance planes up all the time. The safest time," he started to say but rethought his statement. "Hah! There isn't any safe time but the least hazardous time to fly is at night or in bad weather. Since we have the president's plane and Madame Chiang, I opt for nighttime. Do any of you object or do you have any comments on that?"

Barry spoke for the group.

"We're totally at your disposal. You're the expert."

"Okay. Good."

Patterson stood and crossed the room to a map hanging on the colonel's wall. The Navy crew followed.

"This is the CBI theater…China, Burma, India. Here we are." He pointed to Chabua.

"You see how Burma bulges up like this? We'll fly over Ledo, where the Burma Road begins, across Burma and on into China where the Himalayas are. If the clouds permit and the moon is bright enough, we might be able to see the Burma Road. It looks just like a snake from the air.

"Here is Kunming. That's where we're going. It's about five hundred miles away, and if all goes well, it should take us only about five or six hours.

"See this here?" he asked, pointing to a dot inside the Burmese border.

"That's Myitkyina, where the Japs had their air base

"Since we captured Myitkyina, we don't have to worry about Japs from there but you can rest assured they'll come from other bases. Their Zeros shot down fourteen of our transports just last winter. There's a trail of aluminum from here to China and back again. "And," he said, taking a deep breath, "because of their fondness for games, we're forced to fly a higher route to the north and the mountains up there are over fifteen thousand feet high. The ones further north reach twenty thousand feet. Seventeen thousand feet is about the best we can do.

"On one of our usual daily runs, when you factor in the mountains, four tons of cargo, Japs nipping at our tail, freak winds reaching speeds of over two hundred knots, icing, especially with the C-46's—their carburetors are bad about icing up—thunderstorms, unreliable navigation equipment because of the thunderstorms, the Japs' jamming our radio transmissions and turbulence that can flip you over or lift you or drop you three thousand feet a minute, you have some idea of what we have to put up with every time we go up."

"We've lost nearly six hundred men and almost a thousand planes so far.

"A bean counter in Washington or somewhere calculated that we lost three men for every ton of cargo we delivered last year.

"Now, you guys might agree with a lot of people who think Hump pilots are just a loud bunch of snotty, smart-ass, hot-shot pilots but I really believe this is the most stressful job in any man's outfit," he said, rapidly punching his finger on the map.

"As far as I'm concerned, not only do all of these guys have balls, they have *balls*, if you get my drift."

He made a large circle with the fingers and thumbs of both his hands. "Huge balls! And," he added with a laugh, "being a little bit crazy doesn't hurt, either.

"Sorry, guys. Just got a little carried away," he said with a shy grin.

The men laughed politely.

Flights of Angels

"Okay. Let's talk about our flight. We won't be overloaded tonight. That's good. But we won't have any armament. There'll be four fighter planes escorting us, though. Right, colonel?"

Colonel Hines nodded agreement. "P-51s."

* * *

THE P-51 WAS THE MOST ROMANTIC PLANE in the U.S. arsenal. Billy remembered flight school lectures about the legendary craft: The versatile North American Corporation's Mustang P-51 was utilized as an escort fighter, fighter-bomber, dive-bomber, and reconnaissance aircraft. Even with its original Allison V-1710 engine, it was a superlative fighter at low to medium altitudes but its performance dropped off at 12,000 feet. After an experimental Rolls-Royce Merlin engine was installed, high altitude performance and range increased dramatically. The renowned 1590 horsepower, British-made Merlins, supercharged in the States by Packard Motors, became standard equipment.

By adding drop fuel tanks, the nearly 2000-mile range the planes were capable of flying at 445 miles an hour and at altitudes of nearly 40,000 feet, permitted them to escort American bombers to all European or Japanese destinations. Six 50-caliber machine guns and the capacity for 2000 pounds of ordinance made them virtually the Air Corps' flying destroyers. Most experts believed the range, firepower and flexibility of the P-51 contributed vitally to the extensive and successful American bombing raids and ultimate victory over Germany and Japan.

It is little wonder the P-51 Mustang was considered "a fighter pilot's dream" and a source of great relief for the crew of the president's plane.

* * *

"WE'VE TRIED TO KEEP MADAME CHIANG'S trip as quiet as possible," Patterson continued. The Roosevelts are attending a highly publicized reception at the Chinese ambassador's residence in Washington today—tonight, whatever-the-hell time it is there, to throw the Japs off. As far as the Japs know, Madame Chiang's at the party. But if they have any idea she's here, they'll have their entire air force out, looking for us, gunning for us.

"Okay, now. Let's talk about parachutes. If we have to bail out over Burma, we're going to die, either on the way down or when we hit the jungle floor or when we're captured. There are confirmed tribes of headhunters still in the Naga Hills.

"That's one scenario.

"If we have to jump in the Himalayas, we'll freeze before we even hit the ground.

"But in either case, I doubt that any of us would jump if the women refused to jump. So I vote for no 'chutes. What do you say?"

The men looked at each other. The lark suddenly took on a serious turn.

Barry spoke up in a firm voice: "No 'chutes."

The other men nodded their heads.

"Maybe you'd be as lucky as that CBS radio correspondent was," Colonel Hines said.

The men looked at him to finish the anecdote.

"Eric Sevareid. He had to bail out over Naga country. He survived the jump, the landing, as well as the headhunter reception committee. Later, when he made it back to civilization, he complained that he couldn't find any Red Cross girls or bars down there."

The men laughed.

"I think if I landed safely in that place, I'd look for the nearest chapel," Patterson volunteered.

"So would I," Billy said.

"Okay, back to reality," Pat continued. "We'll check out the plane tonight at about twenty hundred hours. We should be able to get in the air by twenty-one hundred hours. I'll go by the weather office for a complete weather check before I meet you at the hangar."

"Which of you will be navigating?" he asked.

"I will," Rick said.

"Okay. How about the radio?"

"That's us," Don said, pointing to himself and Billy.

"You're familiar with the Automatic Directional Finder, the ADF, right?

Rick nodded.

"Two units on board?" Pat asked.

Rick nodded again.

"We have a good homing station here," Patterson continued. "It's especially strong for return trips from China. There's a weak station down in the Hukawng Valley in Burma. The Japs can jam it without too much trouble. We have another at Kunming, China. You'll really have to keep close watch on 'em, though. During thunderstorms, the needle will point toward the electrical disturbance of the storm. It takes a lot of experience to tell if you're getting a radio signal or a storm signal. You already know all this?" he asked.

"Right," Barry said.

"Well, I believe it never hurts to compare ignorances, does it?" Patterson said good-naturedly.

"No," Barry said.

"The Japs have stations on the same frequencies as ours that are powerful enough to make you think their signals are ours. Just let me know if you get confused. I'd rather come back to help you out than lose the plane because we're following the wrong signal. Okay?"

"Okay," Rick agreed.

"Well, that just about wraps up everything from me.

"Anything you want to add, Colonel?" Pat asked.

Colonel Hines smiled. "Yeah. Just be sure you don't run into any cumulo-granite formations when you reach the Himalayas. There's a lot of it up there and it is totally unforgiving."

"We'll try, sir. We'll try," Patterson said.

He pushed his hat back on his head and stretched.

"Well, if you guys will excuse me, I'm going to grab a shower and hit the rack for a while. See you over at the hangar at twenty hundred hours."

* * *

FOR SECURITY REASONS, the lights were kept off inside and outside the hangar where the president's plane was parked.

Madame Chiang and her staff arrived shortly after Billy and the crew walked over from their basha. The headlights of Madame Chiang's cars were masked, with two narrow slits for illumination.

Pat Patterson came briskly up the plane's stairs and walked to the cockpit. He had shaved, showered and was wearing his crushed hat, a leather flight jacket with a Combat Cargo Groups patch and the shield of the CBI theatre: the Nationalist Chinese sun on the top left corner, a white star on the right and vertical red, white and blue stripes underneath. He wore a white silk scarf tied around his neck, with the ends tucked into his jacket.

Billy thought he looked like a poster model for Hump pilots.

"Let's do our pre-flight inspection," he called.

Barry and T.J. followed him down the steps.

*   *   *

"Okay, guys, let's stow our gear and get ready for take off," Barry said, after returning from the walk around.

The plane was towed from the hangar as Patterson took the pilot's left seat. Barry sat in the co-pilot's seat. Billy and T.J. would take one of the seats with Madame Chiang's party during takeoff.

The familiar whirring, whining, coughing of the four engines brought the propellers to life.

The plane taxied to the end of the 6000-foot runway where Pat and Barry went through their pre-takeoff check off list.

When cleared for takeoff, Patterson adjusted the propellers for maximum bite, raced the engines, released the brakes and pushed the throttle forward. The plane proceeded down the crushed stone runway as he and Barry kept their eyes on the manifold pressure gauge as the plane gained speed. When it reached their target manifold pressure, Pat pulled back on the wheel and the plane nosed upward smoothly, banked around to the right and headed for China, followed by four Army Transport Command Mustangs.

A cloud cover prevented their seeing the Burma Road but after the plane had reached its cruising altitude of 17,000 feet, they emerged from the clouds into a night sky, brightly and beautifully lighted by a nearly full moon. Below them was the Burmese Hukawng Valley, three of its boundaries clearly marked by steep, vertical mountains.

The plane droned on reassuringly. Madame Chiang and her travel companions settled into their berths for the overnight flight. Billy and T.J. took turns at the radio and hung over the seats of the pilots to observe their progress through the rounded Plexiglas cockpit.

"Not that I'm superstitious or anything, but everything seems to be going so well, I hate to comment on it," Billy said.

"Same here," Pat said.

As they approached the peaks forming the Himalaya Mountain range, the men were at various windows to observe the rugged mountainous beauty below them, stunning and surreal as a Maxfield Parrish painting in the bright moonlight. Sheer, bare rock cliffs rose sharply to hard, jagged peaks. The valleys were completely covered in snow, leaving no trace of their topography—or the men or airplanes that had gone down.

Once well into the Himalayan environment, the weather began to change dramatically. Cumulus clouds increased, as did precipitation, which presented a potentially dangerous situation.

"We've got a little icing on the wings," Patterson said to Billy, who had returned to the cockpit and was squatting behind the pilots' seats. "We'll have to watch it. When we get over this next ridge, it may get worse."

"How do you check it?" Billy asked.

"Like this," Barry said, pulling a long flashlight from a compartment under the control panel. He aimed it toward the wings and snapped on the light.

Billy could see the frosty coating.

"On one flight back to Chabua," Patterson told them, "we ran out of alcohol and had to drop fast to melt the ice on the wings. We estimated it to be about eighteen inches thick. It was unbelievable."

"Not very aerodynamic, was it?" Billy commented.

"Not at all," he confirmed. "And not a comfortable spot to be in."

"How was your trip to Calcutta?" Billy asked, referring to Patterson's rest and relaxation visit there.

"Hard to say. We go down there to get away from a military environment, so we head straight for the Grand Hotel but just about the only people staying there are British or American officers. It's almost like we're still on base."

"What's the hotel like?" Billy asked.

"Just like the name says: Grand. Veddy, veddy British. Huge dining room with crystal chandeliers, linen tablecloths, napkins, polished silver, crystal. One waiter for each person. Take a sip of water and your glass is refilled immediately."

"Sounds great!" Barry said.

"Beats the Officers' Club," Billy added.

"It might be okay if it weren't for what's outside the hotel."

"What do you mean?" Billy asked.

"The entire drive from Dunn Dunn Airport to the hotel is through some of the most abject poverty anybody could ever see. Sick and starving people on the sidewalks, sick and dying cows on the streets. There's always a crowd at garbage cans when the leftovers are thrown out.

"One of the guys told me about a man who had died on the sidewalk outside his hotel. He told the desk clerk about it but was told it happened all the time and the clerk went on with his work."

Shortly afterward, as Billy was talking to Rick at the navigator's desk, he heard Patterson tell Barry to activate the deicers. Billy squeezed inside the cockpit to watch.

"We need maximum power, Barry," Patterson was saying. "We've got some heavy icing there. Start with the props."

Ice on the propellers can unbalance the blades, creating severe and deadly propeller and fuselage vibrations, while the weight of ice on the wings causes the plane to lose altitude and control.

Isopropyl alcohol was pumped through a nozzle outside the propellers, where it enabled slinger rings to literally hurl ice from the props at high velocity in all directions, including loudly against both sides of the plane's fuselage.

Alcohol pumped into rubber boots in the leading edges of the plane's wings broke up the ice that had formed there, too, as the boots expanded

Madame Chiang and her staff were awakened by the alarming, banging noises and she called out to Billy. He ran to her berth and explained what was happening and assured her they were in no danger. He failed to convince himself completely and wondered if the women really believed him.

Billy rethought his earlier comment about a calm flight. As superstitious as the next person when it came to the belief that commenting on unwanted situations actually brought them on, Billy determined to say nothing further about the progress of their flight, smooth or otherwise.

Less than an hour later, before clearing the highest point of the Hump, Barry looked out his window and saw through the patches in the clouds what looked like a small, unfamiliar airplane reflecting moonlight from its canopy.

"We might have a bandit over here at three o'clock, Pat," he said calmly to Patterson.

Patterson lowered the right wing and looked down. He saw the fighter plane with the dreaded red rising sun, or "meatball" symbols, on its wings and fuselage.

"Oh, shit!" he exclaimed. "It's a Zero! Where the hell are those Mustangs? I don't know if that Jap's seen us or not."

The Mustang escort leader broke radio silence: "This is Gunsmith One. My boys and I are taking our flight out and going down to defend a C-47 transport that's being attacked by those Zeros."

Patterson responded: "Roger your intentions, Gunsmith One. Good luck!"

"Are they deserting us, Mr. Benson?" Madame Chiang asked Billy.

"Oh, no, ma'am. It's better for them to handle those Zeros down there than let them get up here."

The crew members and Madame Chiang's party looked on with rapt fascination as the P-51s tore through the formation of Zeros in the bright moonlight.

As the Zeros scattered, the escort flight leader pulled up into a tight wingover and announced on the radio, "We'll crank it around and make another pass on these guys."

He had barely spoken when one of the Japanese planes began its climb toward the president's plane.

Pat cried out, "Oh, shit! One of 'em's headed this way! Looks like we're on our own," he added as he scanned the horizon to find a protective cloud that could offer them immediate cover.

"We'll head for those clouds over there. Even though it's hard to tell the clouds from the mountains—that cumulo-granite the colonel was talking about—we don't have any other choice. We sure as hell can't outrun 'im."

"It looks like he's losing speed getting up here," Barry said.

"Let's see if I can deal him a few slips and slides," Pat said calmly. At least that'll make it hard for 'im to pick up a lead on us.

"Barry, when I ask for it, crank me a full left rudder trim tab as fast as you can."

Barry's hand immediately grabbed the handle of the trim tab.

The unmistakable red and orange flames from the wings of the Zero stunned the onlookers.

"He's firing at us!" Billy cried.

"Okay, Now! Give me the trim tab, fast!"

Barry spun the handle furiously.

The big plane lurched through the sky, slipping to the left. Billy braced himself as the huge plane skidded like a gangster's getaway car on a wet highway.

Madame Chiang and her compatriots had left their beds, put on their robes, strapped themselves into seats, and were holding onto each other tightly.

Billy and Rick had their faces pressed against windows in an attempt to keep up with the enemy plane. T.J. was hanging over the pilots' seats.

"I think we took some hits on that pass," T.J. called out.

"Yeah," Pat agreed. "I think you're right. I heard some thumps but couldn't tell where they were coming from."

"Look out!" Barry yelled. "He's turning around for another pass!"

"Reverse your trim tab fast!" Pat told Barry.

Barry cranked his rudder trim to its STOP, causing the plane to careen sideways again, changing from a left skid to a right skid as the attacking Zero sped by a second time.

"I'm going into that cloud for cover," Pat said. "He'll shoot us down if we can't hide from 'im."

The big plane disappeared into the temporary safety of the cumulus formation.

They broke out of the cloud and looked again for their assailant.

"There he is!" Barry called, pointing to the enemy craft overhead.

"That crazy sunuvabitch is turning back for another run! Let's see if we can outmaneuver that slanty-eyed f***er for one last time," Pat said with determination. "If he hasn't learned a lesson in dog fighting by now, I've got one more trick up my sleeve. He may be faster but, by damn, I can turn this big boy on a dime."

"You mean we have a shorter turning radius than he does?" Billy asked, hanging over the first pilot's chair.

"Just watch," Pat answered. "He couldn't handle the deflection shots, so now he's going to come in behind us and try to shoot us up our ass.

"Barry, give me full flaps when I call for 'em. When he starts firing, drop your flaps and I'll crank it into a tight turn and he'll shoot right on past us and, with some luck, right into that mountain up ahead."

Pat pulled the throttle back to reduce power and speed as much as he safely could.

"Full flaps! Full flaps!" he called.

As Barry complied with the command, Pat cranked the plane into a sharp left turn and varied his nose position to prevent a complete stall.

Out of the corner of his eye, Pat watched as the Zero angled for a tail shot. As the air speed of the big plane dropped dramatically, the Jap plane whizzed by them and smashed against a jagged mountain peak in a fierce, fiery explosion.

"Banzai, you yellow bastard!" Pat exclaimed.

A cheer went up from the men.

"Now you know why this route is called the 'fireball express'," Pat said cheerfully.

"Good show!" T. J. congratulated the first pilot.

"That was slick!" Billy added.

"Good flying, Pat!" Barry said, squeezing Patterson's arm enthusiastically.

"Don't thank me," he said pointing straight over his head. "Thank Him. Thank you, Jesus! You saved my sorry ass again," he said, looking upward through the Plexiglas.

"Is it okay to say I nearly shit in my pants?" Barry asked.

"If you had, it wouldn't be the first time," Pat said.

"Are all of you guys okay?" Pat asked.

"Man!" Barry said. "Give me the peaceful Pacific any day. I think the stress on this milk run would make an old man out of me fast."

"Same here," T.J. agreed. "Me hat is off to you chaps, Pat. I hope we've seen the last of Jap Zeros. Me nerves are so shot, I don't think I could do it again."

"You're a good pilot," Billy said. "You saved our lives. Thanks."

"All in a day's work. But you're welcome."

"How did you make that sharp turn?" Billy asked.

"This plane is outfitted with what's called a Davis Airfoil, with one of the highest lift efficiencies ever recorded. When you slow the plane down, the foil will let you outturn any fighter in the world and without stalling."

"How are the rest of the Mustangs doing?" Pat asked.

"It looks like they've got the Zeros cleared out," Barry said.

"Good. T.J., how about taking over?" Pat asked. "I need to go to the latrine."

When Billy turned to walk back to check on Madame Chiang, he realized his shirt was soaked with sweat.

Madame Chang was standing in the narrow aisle beside the seats, surrounded by her aides. She was straightening her hair.

"Are you ladies okay?" he asked.

Madame Chiang nodded.

"Yes, I think so. Are all of you all right?" she asked.

"We are now. Ten minutes ago, I wasn't so sure."

"Do you think we are safe?" she asked.

"Yes, ma'am, I do. We're almost in China and not far from Kunming. As a matter of fact, I think it's safe enough to make a pot of coffee," Billy said. "Would you ladies like some?"

"No, thank you. I think I need something stronger," Madame Chiang said with a smile. "Maybe some brandy. Will you join us?"

"I need it," Billy replied. "But no thank you. I'm on duty."

When Patterson returned to his chair, Barry said to him, "The wing flaps aren't responding as sharp as they did before the Jap attack. It feels like something's wrong with the flight control cables for the right wing. I tried to find the problem with the flashlight but couldn't see anything."

Pat moved his wheel.

"Yeah, I think you're right. It feels like it's binding or something. He must have got us there. Well, let's hope we don't have to do any more emergency maneuvers. If we don't stress it too much, it should be okay."

The rest of the flight into Kunming was blissfully uneventful.

When the plane touched down, Billy felt himself relax.

"This has been the longest night of my life," he confessed to T.J.

"Mine, too, mate."

"But I don't regret having had the experience," Billy added cheerfully "I feel the way I did at pre-flight training. I'm motivated!"

The plane followed the FOLLOW ME sign on the back of a jeep and taxied toward a building at the edge of the landing field where a large lighted billboard announced: *Welcome to the City of Eternal Spring.*

"Is that some kind of a joke?" Billy asked, looking over the shoulders of Pat and Barry.

"No, that's really what it's called," Patterson answered.

"It's on the same latitude as Mexico, it's a mile high, like Denver and mild all year round."

"What a lovely place for a war," Barry said.

"Will we have any time for sightseeing?" Billy asked.

"Sightseeing?" Barry asked.

"The great American tourist," T.J. teased.

"Sure. We can probably get somebody to drive you around," Patterson answered.

"Great!" Billy answered. "I need to buy my wife a peace offering."

The plane came to a stop and Pat cut off the engines.

Billy walked quickly to the door. He unlocked it and swung it open as the metal stairs were pushed into place.

The first person up the stairs was a tall Asian man wearing a military uniform.

Madame Chiang went to meet him.

"Hello, darling," she said in English.

The man kissed her cheek.

"This is my husband, Chiang Kai-shek," she said to Billy. "Mr. Benson, darling."

"I'm honored, Generalissimo Chiang," Billy said, shaking his hand.

Madame Chiang then spoke to her husband in Chinese. He smiled broadly, removed his hat and extended his hand to Billy again.

"Thank you for taking such good care of my wife, Mr. Benson," the Generalissimo said in halting English.

"My pleasure, sir."

An Army photographer with a large press camera entered the plane and called, "Would everybody please come to the front of the plane for a group photograph, please? The president's request."

The photographer arranged the passengers and crew with the plane as a backdrop and snapped several pictures, changing flash bulbs between shots.

"Now, one with Mr. Benson," Madame Chiang said to the photographer.

She pulled Billy gently by the arm and positioned him to her right, the Generalissimo to her left. She slipped her hands under the arms of both men, and smiled.

"That will be something to show your grandchildren," the photographer said to Billy. "Give me your address and I'll mail you some copies."

As Madame Chiang's attendants collected her luggage, she spoke to Billy as he started to turn away.

"Oh, Mr. Benson," she said. "I have something for you."

He turned toward her as she was digging in her black purse.

"I want you to give this to your wife," she said, removing her jade ring and placing it into a small, black, velvet-covered box.

"Thank you, Madame Chiang," he said. "It's beautiful."

"I have a note in there, too, but it is for your wife only. Agreed?"

"Yes, ma'am," he said as he took the box from her.

"You may kiss me, right here," she said, touching her cheek.

He bent over and kissed her.

The photographer snapped their picture.

"Thank you again," she said. "I hope you and your wife have a very long, happy life together."

"Thank you, Madame Chiang. You and the Generalissimo, too. And I hope the war is over soon".

"So do we," she said with a smile.

With that, she put her arm in her husband's and left, followed by her attendants and a heavy metal dolly filled with luggage, pushed by a small Asian man.

Billy slipped the box into his coat pocket and joined his friends who were standing under the left wing of the plane.

"Take a look at this, Bill," Pat said. "That Zero got closer than we thought."

He pointed to three holes in the wing.

"Wow!" Billy exclaimed.

"But over here is the worst," Pat said, leading his party to the right wing, where he pointed to a four-inch hole. "Looks like he chewed up our flight control cables pretty bad. I'd say we were lucky to make it here."

"How long will it take to patch it up?" Billy asked.

"I don't know. Maybe a couple of days. We won't know until we can take off some of these wing panels."

"I'm not sure I have a couple of days extra to wait," Billy said. "I'll probably need to get a hop back to the States."

"If you let me have a copy of your orders," Pat suggested, "I'll get one of the guys in operations to find out."

"Sure. Thanks," Billy said, opening his suitcase to retrieve a set of orders.

"Go on to chow and I'll drop these by ops and meet up with you."

The men walked to the chow hall for an early breakfast of fried eggs and coffee, available around the clock for the crews who flew in and out of Kunming.

Patterson talked the photographer into giving the Navy crew a quick tour of Kunming while he and the airfield's maintenance crew began to investigate the damage to the president's plane.

The photographer loaded the men into an old, two-door Chevrolet and drove them through the ancient town, giving a running commentary as he did.

"This place is at least two thousand years old," he told them as he navigated the car through the narrow, crowded streets. "Marco Polo came through here in the late thirteenth century and wrote about the trading and the salt springs. He was really impressed by the fact that husbands didn't mind if their wives fooled around, as long as the women were willing."

"Let's hang around a little bit longer," Barry said with an evil grin.

"Don't forget about that Chinese syphilis," Rick reminded him.

"Right. I forgot."

"Marco Polo said the people here ate their fish and meat raw but dipped it in a garlic sauce."

"That doesn't sound very appetizing, does it?" Billy asked.

"Here's the famous Green Lake. This gate is very old," the photographer continued.

"I'll bet you've photographed that," T.J. commented.

"Many times. It's virtually the symbol of the city."

"This place has really built up since the war began. They've got factories making just about everything they need for the war. And with all those Chinese forced here by the Japs, they've got all the labor they need."

He drove them through the city gate in the wall that surrounded the old town, to the market where they saw lavish displays of fruits and vegetables, seafood, live chickens and plucked fowl hanging by their necks.

"Nothing is wasted here. They'll eat just about anything: squids, sea urchins, anything."

They continued their tour, stopping to walk about or to take photographs of each other standing in front of various venues.

By mid-afternoon, the men were back at the base. They thanked the photographer and walked to the hangar where their plane was being worked on.

"What's the verdict?" Barry asked Patterson, who was on top of the wing with a coverall-clad air force maintenance man.

"We've got to rebuild or replace the flight control lines and pulleys."

"How long will that take?" Billy asked.

"Not less than three days. More like four. But we've got to locate the parts first and then see about getting them flown in."

"Any word for me?" Billy asked.

"Not yet. I know you guys are beat. Let's go to chow, find a place to crash and get a shower. Maybe by the morning we'll know something."

"Good plan," Billy agreed.

None of the men needed any coaxing to get a good night's sleep. They slipped between their sheets and didn't move until reveille the next morning.

After breakfast, Billy walked over to the flight operations office where he spoke to a staff sergeant.

"I'm Mr. Benson. Has anybody gotten any word for my return to the States?"

"Hey, Smitty. Did you get a dispatch for Mr. Benson?"

"Affirmative," the man replied, bringing a typed manifest to the counter. "You're to take the next flight back to the States."

"When's the next plane to India?" Billy asked, looking over the paper.

The staff sergeant looked at a board on the wall. "The next one out is at eleven hundred hours, to Chabua. It has to stop at Myitkina, though, to pick up some wounded. Some of Merrill's Marauders. You've hearda them, ain'tcha?"

Billy nodded.

"There are flights back to the States every day from India as these guys get rotated back," the staff sergeant said. "You won't have any trouble getting there. Grab your gear and be back here by ten hundred. We'll get you on that flight."

He thanked the men and returned to his group, gathered at the president's plane.

"Well, guys, they want me back. I've got a swoop back to India in about two hours." Billy asked.

"A swoop, eh?" T.J. asked with a smile. "We're going to make a Marine out of you yet."

"Anybody else ready to head back that way?" Billy asked.

"No, thanks," Barry said. "We're sticking with this bird."

"I've been ordered to Norfolk after this mission is over," T.J. said. "Maybe we can visit more often."

"You're welcome any time—in Memphis or Riverton," Billy replied.

Billy walked back to his quarters to retrieve his bag and returned to the president's plane.

Barry and T.J. walked their friend to the flight control office.

"We need to get you suited up," the flight control officer said. "Go on back there. Tell O'Neill to fix you up with a flight suit."

Billy walked to the room behind the office and put on the clothing he was issued for the flight in the unheated, unpressurized transport.

He returned to the office where his friends were lounging about waiting for him.

"I feel like the Michelin man," Billy said, his gait slowed and lumbering, his frame enlarged by the fleece-lined leather suit, leather helmet and a parachute slung over his shoulder.

His friends laughed at him.

"Oh, man!" Barry said. "If Madame Chiang could see you now!"

"This will give you an idea of what we have to go through every time we go up," T.J. said.

"I hope you took a piss before you got suited up," Barry added.

"Okay, Mr. Benson," the flight officer said, pointing to a plane a few yards from the office. "Your ride is here."

"Guys," Billy said, "thanks a lot for this little adventure. It's been great being with you again. Without question, it's been the highlight of my short and not-so-fabled naval career."

"Glad you could come along," Barry said.

"Give Suzanne our regards," T.J. said.

The men shook hands and Barry and T.J. stood outside the flight office as their friend waddled across the tarmac to the waiting plane, his parachute hanging from one shoulder, his suitcase in one hand and thick, leather gloves in the other.

Billy stopped before climbing the stairs leading into the rear of the plane. He smiled broadly and gave an energetic wave of his hand.

His friends returned his wave and watched as Billy Benson walked up the stairs and disappeared inside the plane.

Navy Distnguished Service Medal

CHAPTER EIGHT

DEEP REGRET

S UZANNE DIDN'T FEEL WELL. She knew she wasn't ill. She didn't know just what it was. She knew only that some, as yet, undetected demon was skulking just out of her reach, enough to disrupt her peace of mind.

She had gotten up at seven, made coffee, changed the boys and fed them, and was planning on pushing them in their buggy to the small park at the end of the street when the telephone rang.

It was Brad Kendrick.

"Could I come by?" he asked casually.

"Sure," she had answered.

She thought nothing of his call since he often dropped by to see the boys or bring them a toy. But when Suzanne saw his unsmiling wife Irene with him outside the door, her hand went to her chest.

She opened the door cautiously. Her hands were trembling. She knew she was pale. All her blood seemed to have suddenly left her body.

Brad and Irene stood motionless, not confident they were up to their unpleasant task. Irene gripped her purse tightly by the handle with both hands. She looked at Suzanne.

Suzanne knew.

Her hands went to her face and she burst into tears.

Irene handed her husband the purse and stepped into the small room, took Suzanne in her arms, and embraced her tightly.

Brad stood before the open door, trying not to watch the two women.

Irene took Suzanne by the arm and walked her to the sofa.

Brad closed the door, laid the purse on the desk, and pulled the desk chair in front of the sofa and sat in it.

"I knew something was wrong when I got up this morning," Suzanne said. "I didn't know what, but I just knew.

"Am I supposed to ask you or are you supposed to tell me?" she asked.

"I'm supposed to tell you," Brad said, but…"

He walked to the kitchen door and stood with his back to the women. He pulled a handkerchief from his hip pocket, wiped his eyes and blew his nose. He stuffed the handkerchief into his hip pocket, returned to the desk chair, and sat again.

He drew a yellow envelope from his inside coat pocket and handed it to Suzanne.

She held it in her hands and looked at it.

"Have you read it?" she asked Brad.

"I have a copy of it."

"What does it say?"

"What you think it says."

Suzanne tore open the end of the envelope, unfolded the telegram inside, and read it aloud:

Mrs. Benson,

The Secretary of War desires me to express his deep regret that the commanding general of the U.S. Army forces in the China-Burma-India area has reported your husband, Ensign James William Benson Jr., U.S. Navy Reserve, missing in action. Additional information will be sent when received.

W. Ulio,

Adjutant General

Washington, D.C.

"This says he's just missing in action!" she said hopefully. "It doesn't say he's dead!"

Irene placed her hand on Suzanne's.

Brad took a breath. "Where his plane went down, Suzanne, the mountains are at least ten thousand feet high. The temperature is forty below zero. There have been no radio transmissions since the plane went down some twenty hours ago and nobody has sighted any wreckage.

"They were flying over the Himalaya Mountains. They fly that route to carry supplies to China, since the Japanese control most of China. You might have read about it or seen it in the newsreels."

She nodded that she had.

"I wish I could be hopeful, Suzanne, but it's dangerous flying even on a good day. Over five hundred of our planes have been lost crossing those mountains. And nearly a thousand men.

"Bill was on a special mission to China," he added.

"China?"

"For the President."

"President Roosevelt?"

He nodded again.

"Bill took an earlier plane back to India. It disappeared in the Himalayas."

"What was this special mission?" she asked, trying not to be sarcastic.

"He was with a crew returning Madame Chiang Kai-shek to China. She had been visiting the White House and raising money for the Chinese to fight the Japanese."

"Why was *he* chosen?" she asked with growing irritation. "I don't understand why *Bill* had to go on this special mission."

"You know how much he wanted to get transferred out of here," Brad said patiently. "He wanted to be anything but a flight instructor. Two of his friends were going and they had connections, so they arranged for Bill to go with them."

"Do you know who the friends were?" she asked.

"Two buddies from flight school."

"Do you know their names?" she repeated.

"No. One was a Marine and the other a Navy pilot. I don't know their names."

"T.J. and Barry. Did they go down in the plane with Bill?" she asked dryly.

"No. The plane they flew to China in—the president's plane—couldn't return right away because of some mechanical problems and Bill was sent ahead on an Army transport."

"So, T.J. and Barry are still alive?" she asked.

"As far as I know."

"Brad, honey," Irene said to her husband, "why don't you check on the twins?"

Brad looked at his wife blankly for an instant.

"Would you mind, terribly?"

"Oh, sure! Excuse me."

Brad excused himself, walked into the boys' room and closed the door.

Irene moved into the chair where Brad had sat facing Suzanne. She reached over and took Suzanne's hands.

Suzanne sat silently for a few seconds and stood quickly and began pacing the room.

"Irene, I am so angry! I am so angry, I am ashamed of myself!" she said, flailing her arms as she talked. "I should be grieving, but I'm angry instead!

"I mean, you know how Bill and the other instructors are trying to wash out as many students as they can, because we're winning the war and we don't need as many pilots. So, the war is nearly over and Bill has to volunteer for this dumb trip to China to take Madame Chiang Kai-shek back home! Why Bill? Why did *he* have to go? Why? And the men who took him, they sent him on ahead, and they're still alive."

Irene stood and faced Suzanne.

"War is a game to men, Suzanne." she said calmly. "It's something I'm afraid we women don't understand. Brad would have left flight school, too, to get into action. He was promised he'd make commander if he stayed here, so he stayed."

She placed her hand on Suzanne's arm.

"Don't be angry at Bill, Suzanne. He was the sweetest, finest man I've ever known. I would never want Brad to know it, but Bill was, in every way, I sincerely believe, head and shoulders above the lot of them.

"But, he was a man and men...well, this is the sort of things men do."

Suzanne stood, glaring at her friend.

"Brad had offered to kill the orders, Suzanne. He told Bill that, but Bill really wanted to go."

Suzanne's eyes and mouth opened suddenly.

"He told me that, too," she said, looking into Irene's eyes. "He told me he wouldn't go if I really didn't want him to.

"Oh, Irene! I could have stopped him. I'm the one to blame."

Suzanne's hands went to her face and she began to weep.

Irene put her arms around her tightly as Suzanne's heart broke.

*   *   *

SUZANNE HESITATED AS SHE LIFTED the heavy, black receiver and pressed it against her ear.

"Hello," she said.

"Suzanne?"

"Yes. Hello, Edna."

"I hope I'm not bothering you," Edna said, "but I just wanted to see if you had changed your mind about coming down tomorrow for Billy's memorial service."

"Oh, Edna, I just don't think I could do it twice. I would be like a zombie. And, you know, with all the gas rationing and getting packed up. I just don't think I could handle it."

"We understand. I couldn't do it twice, either. I'm not sure I can do it once."

Edna closed her eyes and blew out her breath in an effort to control her emotions.

"Well, come on down when you can. The girls are over at Sally's now, getting her spare bedroom ready for you and the boys," Edna said.

"Brad and Irene have been a big help," Suzanne said. "I'm going to aim for early next week. I think the sooner the better. The Navy will ship whatever I can't get into the car. Just about all the furniture belongs to the Navy."

She suddenly broke into tears and placed the telephone on the desk as she pulled a handkerchief from the pocket of her dress.

She blew her nose and picked up the telephone again.

"I'm sorry. I do that a lot. I'm sorry."

"We're the same down here. Maybe it'll get better," Edna said.

"I hope so. I never realized I had such a supply of tears. Are all of you going to be all right?"

"Oh, Suzanne," Edna said, "Billy's Uncle John is really taking this hard. Grace says he hasn't eaten since we found out. And he just walks around like he's lost. He's not doing well at all."

"I know how much Bill loved him. He'll come around, eventually. He just needs time."

"I hope so. But the rest of us are staying busy. That helps. I hope everything goes well at your service up there. We'll be thinking of you. Call us any time if you need us for anything."

"Thank you, Edna. I will. Say hello to everybody."

"Are the boys okay?" Edna asked, not wanting to end the conversation.

"Oh, sure."

"How about you?" Edna asked. "Are you all right?"

"Well, like you, I guess. I'm working on it."

"It isn't easy, is it?" Edna asked.

"No, it isn't. It certainly isn't."

*   *   *

BRAD AND IRENE CAME BY FOR SUZANNE the next afternoon, three days after Suzanne had received the telegram. One of the neighbor's girls was going to keep the boys while the three were at the memorial service.

Suzanne wore a Navy blue suit and a matching hat with a veil. She wore the single strand of pearls Billy had given her on their first wedding anniversary and the smaller gold Navy wings pin on the left side of her jacket. Suzanne knew Edna would be wearing hers, too.

The base band, in dress blues, and an honor guard of Marines and Naval personnel stood outside the chapel on either side of the walk when they arrived.

Present...Harms!

The band members and honor guard came to attention.

Suzanne looked at the chapel as they approached it. She had never cared for its architecture: gray-shingled, like the other buildings on the base; squat and temporary looking, with barely a pitch to its roof, and a tiny cross at the apex. *And why did they have to name it Livermore Chapel?* she wondered. *Such an ugly name for such an ugly building.*

As Brad and Irene walked into the chapel, following Suzanne, the large gathering of friends, most of them in uniform, stood quietly.

Chaplain Weber, wearing a dark surplice with a stole that reached the front hem, walked quickly up the aisle to greet her and embrace her lightly. Mary Pavlick, in her dress blues stepped from her pew and embraced Suzanne. She joined Suzanne and the Kendricks and fell in behind the chaplain who led them to seats in the second row of pews.

Seated behind Suzanne and the Kendricks were several nurses from the base hospital, all wearing their dress blues. Suzanne gave them a nod and a slight smile. They all looked different. She realized she had never seen most of them in anything except their white nurses' uniforms.

Instructors from the flight school sat in the pew behind them.

Cadets in their dress blues were in other pews throughout the chapel.

Brad had cancelled all classes and flights that morning.

The band outside began the *Star-Spangled Banner* as the congregation remained at attention, facing the flag on the dais.

The congregation sat as Chaplain Weber mounted the podium.

He paused as he looked out over the assembly and then at Suzanne.

"We have a difficult task before us this morning."

He paused and pressed his lips together.

"This is never easy. Never. Especially when the person to whom we must bid farewell is someone whom we all truly loved and cherished and admired."

He paused again.

"We have all gathered here today to give thanks for the life of our dear friend, Ensign Bill Benson, to commend his soul to Almighty God, and to seek His comfort for all who mourn. We particularly pray for God's restoring peace and loving presence with Bill's wife, Suzanne, his sons, his parents and family, and all of us assembled here.

"Would you please stand and join in singing the Navy Hymn? The words are in your program."

The band outside was cued and played an introduction to the hymn and continued as the mourners sang.

Eternal Father, strong to save,
Whose arm hath bound the restless wave,

Who bidd'st the mighty ocean deep
Its own appointed limits keep;
Oh, hear us when we cry to Thee,
For those in peril on the sea!

Lord, guard and guide the men who fly
Through the great spaces in the sky.
Be with them always in the air,
In darkening storms or sunlight fair,
Oh, hear us when we lift our prayer,
For those in peril in the air.

Following the song, Chaplain Weber asked the congregation to be seated again.

Once more, he looked out into the faces of the congregation, as if gathering strength to continue. He announced that he would read from the thirteenth chapter of First Corinthians, which begins:

Though I speak with the tongues of men and of angels, and have not love, I am become as sounding brass, or a tinkling cymbal...and ends with:

And now abideth faith, hope, love, these three, but the greatest of these is love.

"I suppose I need not tell you why I chose that familiar passage about love," he said, closing his Bible.

"In the military, I'm afraid our masculine pride and," he smiled, "the Uniform Code of Military Justice, prevent our ever saying outright to our mates, 'I love you.'"

"But I think we in the military show our friends in other ways that we do love them.

"It could be in the way we greet each other and look at each other as we speak, or invite friends over for a meal, or go fishing together.

"As for our good friend, Bill Benson, I believe, I sincerely believe each person gathered here today would have to truthfully say that, if we somehow had the opportunity to say to Bill that we loved him, we would, and we could, without embarrassment.

"When you think about it, we are saying that now, by our presence here. We are telling Suzanne how much we loved Bill when he was with us. That we love him still, and we are showing her the very high regard in which we held him.

"But, I am also confident Bill knew how we felt about him. He loved us, too, and showed it every day by being the good, decent human being that he was. Bill was, in my opinion, the living realization of that beautiful passage I just read, describing love. He was all those things. He was a loving, lovely, decent person, easy to love and respect. I believe Bill was as Christ-like as any man I have ever known, and that includes some very fine clergymen and military men.

"In my opening remarks, I mentioned my difficulty with having to bid farewell to Bill, or any number of our friends, as we have had to do so often in this time of war.

"Please consider this, however: it may be farewell here," he said, tapping his finger on the podium, "where we are. But we have to believe—because we believe Jesus' words that we would live again with Him in heaven—we have to believe that what is Farewell for us on Earth, is Welcome for Bill.

"I believe that. I sincerely do," he said placing one hand over the other over his heart. "I have no doubt that Bill is basking in the light of the Son of God at this very moment.

"He would not want us to grieve for him, but to rejoice with him that he has gone home to the Father.

He looked directly at Suzanne.

"Suzanne, I want you to believe that, too. I want you to believe that Bill is in a place of indescribable beauty, and is happy and fervently waiting for us to join him."

He lifted his gaze and addressed the congregation.

"Don't anyone misunderstand me. We are all going to miss Bill and we will grieve over our great, great loss.

"I am not ashamed to say I have wept bitterly over the news. I miss him, terribly, already.

"And, Suzanne, we are going to miss you, too. I wish there were some way we could keep you and the boys here, but I know that is not the case.

"These are long and sad days for you. We will all pray for you, that your time of grieving will end soon. And, please know, there will come a day when you can smile and laugh and remember the precious, but all too brief, time that you and Bill were together.

"Please take with you our love for you and Bill and our thanks for such wonderful memories during our short time here together."

A tear rolled down his cheek. He wiped it with his fingers and he paused.

"Would all of you bow your heads, please?

"Our Heavenly Father, we give thanks to You this morning for the life of our dear friend and brother in Christ, Bill Benson. We thank You, O Father, for Bill's strong sense of family, his service, and his devotion to his country, his love for You, and for his commendable spirit.

"We thank You, O Father, for the way he touched the lives of all of us here—his students, his fellow officers, his staff members, his wife Suzanne, his sons, and his family.

"We give thanks for all those qualities that endeared him to us, Holy Father; for his patience, his strengths, his wit, and his commitment to living a Christian life.

"We pray, especially, for our sister, Suzanne, Father, that you would console her and assure her that her husband and our brother, Bill, is with You and Your Son in Paradise.

"We pray these things in the name of Jesus.

"Amen."

He lifted a folded handkerchief from his podium and wiped his eyes before continuing.

"Before the choir sings," he said, "I would like to read a short passage from William Shakespeare, from *Hamlet*, that I feel ties in with our service, that I have altered slightly for this occasion.

These lines were spoken by Hamlet's friend Laertes at the end of the play, when Hamlet lay dead after being killed by a poisoned sword."

The chaplain lifted a black, leather-bound notebook and read in a strong voice:

Let four captains
Bear him, like a warrior, to the stage,

For he was likely, had he been put on,
To have proved most royally and, for his passage,
The sailors' music and rites of war
Speak loudly for him.

Now crack noble hearts.
Good night, sweet prince.
Farewell, our good friend Bill.
And flights of angels sing thee to thy rest!

The choir, which was made up of service personnel and their families, stood to sing a new anthem, written just that year: essentially rising and falling musical thirds and bold dissonances, mystical and mysterious, hovering ethereally over sustained droning by the basses:

Alleluia!
May flights of angels sing thee to thy rest.
Remember me, O Lord, when You come into Your kingdom.
Give rest, O Lord, to Your servant, who has fallen asleep.
The choir of saints have found the well-spring of life, and door
of paradise,
Life: a shadow and a dream.
Weeping at the grave creates the song:
Alleluia.
Come, enjoy rewards and crowns I have prepared for you.

When the song ended, Chaplain Weber returned to the podium.

"There is a poem with which I am sure you are familiar: 'High Flight.'

"It was written by a young American, John Gillespie Magee Jr., who joined the Canadian Air Force in 1940. He wrote the poem and sent a copy to his parents shortly before he was killed in England in an air accident in 1941. He was only nineteen years old.

Oh, I have slipped the surly bonds of earth
And danced the skies on laughter-silvered wings:
Sunward I've climbed, and joined the tumbling mirth

Of sun-split clouds — and done a hundred things
You have not dreamed of — wheeled and soared and swung
High in the sunlit silence. Hov'ring there
I've chased the shouting wind along, and flung
My eager craft through footless halls of air.
Up, up the long delirious, burning blue,
I've topped the windswept heights with easy grace
Where never lark, or even eagle flew —
And, while with silent lifting mind I've trod,
The high unsurpassed sanctity of space,
Put out my hand and touched the face of God.

Chaplain Weber paused and looked over the congregation.

He then asked, "Will you please stand and bow your heads for the commendation, and remain standing until 'Taps' is played?"

He shut his eyes, raised his hand, and held it out over the heads of the standing congregants.

"Let us commend our brother Bill to the mercy of God, our Maker and Redeemer.

"Bill, our companion in faith and brother in Christ, we entrust you to God.

"Go forth from this world in the love of the Father, who created you,

"In the mercy and grace of Jesus Christ, who died for you,

"In the power of the Holy Spirit, who strengthens you.

"At one with all the faithful, living and departed, may you rest in peace and

"Rise in glory, where grief and misery are banished and light and joy evermore abide.

"In the name of Jesus, we pray, Amen."

A bugler outside began playing Taps.

When he sounded the third note, however, Suzanne turned to Mary and buried her face in her shoulder.

As the clarion call wafted through the chapel, all those gathered there—the pilot officers, the nurse officers, the cadets, the minister, the civilians—all wept bitterly for the friend they would see no more in this life, for there is nothing so final, so absolute, so permanent, so irrevocable, so irreversible, so heart-breaking at a military funeral or memorial service, as the fleeting melancholy notes of *Taps*.

Each time the sad refrain fades away into infinity, the fallen, ephemeral hero is no more; enduring only as a spirit, a memory, living on, however, as long as those who knew him or learn about him, survive.

*   *   *

SUZANNE HAD FOUND IT IMPOSSIBLE to control her thought processes as she prepared to leave Millington. Over and over, she had played and replayed her conversation with Billy as they washed dishes their last weekend together:

I could have stopped him.

I could have stopped him.

The drive to Riverton provided some relief, in that the narrow highway and heavy traffic demanded that she concentrate on her driving.

She went first to the Benson's house, driving to the back, where her arrival was met by the entire extended family, pouring out the back door, down the wooden steps, and swarming around her, tearfully hugging her and the boys and taking them into the living room through the back of the house.

She was relieved that the ensuing talk was positive and upbeat, not moribund or depressing. The Bensons were spiritual people, optimistic, and cheerful. Discussions of Billy were buoyant and upbeat. Suzanne was thankful she now could talk about him without dissolving into tears.

She noted that the banner in the window now displayed a gold star in the place of the blue one.

Sally Moore was summoned to join them for a hearty, popular wartime supper of chicken and dumplings, which could be stretched to feed the crew of a battleship, if necessary, and home-grown vegetables and a spice cake Velma had made without eggs or sugar.

At Sally's house, where Suzanne would remain until she could decide her next move, Suzanne tucked the boys into the baby crib that Edna had sent over from Billy's room, until the Navy shipment arrived. Suzanne would share the room with them, sleeping in a single bed.

Sally was in the swing on the front porch when Suzanne closed the screen door quietly and sat in the rattan chair near the door.

Behind her, hanging in the window, was a small banner with a blue star for Sally's husband, Eddie, an enlisted sailor stationed at Pearl Harbor, Hawaii.

"I never thought anything like this would ever happen," Suzanne said. "I feel a bit like one of those displaced persons I see pictures of in the newspaper."

"You're welcome here for as long as you want to stay."

"Thank you, Sally. I appreciate everything all of you are doing for us.

"Right now, though, I'm just, I don't know, *confused*, I suppose, is the word.

"Everything was so ideal at Millington. Even if it was temporary. But Bill came home every night, unless he had the duty. Everything was right there on the base for us. I knew the pilots and their wives and children. Exchange, chapel, everything. Everything taken care of. It was, I suppose, too neat. It was just too good to last.

"And, now, here I am, without a husband, without a home, with no present means of support. No plans for the future."

"Don't think you have to have all the answers right now," Sally said. "Give yourself some time."

"I know. Time. The great leveler. The great healer."

"What were you going to do after the war?" Sally asked.

"Bill wanted to stay in the Navy, if he could do something besides being a flight instructor," she said, with a quiet laugh. "He really hated doing that. He never complained that much about it to me, but I knew. He felt something would open up for him after the war.

"How about you? When the war ends, I mean," Suzanne asked.

"Eddie's still in Hawaii. I don't think he'll stay in the service, though, even with all that good aviation mechanic training. I can teach school anywhere, so, when his enlistment is up, we'll talk about it. I'm flexible. I don't care. Riverton. Pearl Harbor. I don't care."

She wanted to add; "I don't care as long as we're together," but she kept that to herself.

*   *   *

"A SPECIAL DELIVERY LETTER just came for you, Suzanne!" Sally said excitedly, as she entered the bedroom a few days after Suzanne's arrival.

Suzanne, who had just finished feeding the boys, looked up from the crib.

"Really?"

"Look!" Sally said, pointing to the return address on the envelope. "It's from the White House!"

"The White House?" Suzanne asked, reaching for the envelope.

She tapped the edge of the envelope with her hand, tore off the edge, and removed the letter.

"My Dear Mrs. Benson,

"Accept heartfelt condolences from Mrs. Roosevelt and myself upon the death of your husband, Lieutenant, junior grade, James William Benson Jr., of the United States Navy.

"As you know, Lieutenant, j.g., Benson was one of several special crewmembers I asked to fly Madame Chiang Kai-chek to China, in my personal airplane.

"Every mission in this war is fraught with dangers and I am particularly grateful for the selfless devotion to duty that has characterized our country's young men and women.

"I take no pleasure in being the Commander-in-Chief who has to send so many of our fine young military personnel into harm's way. But please be assured that Mrs. Roosevelt and I are parents of servicemen and we know the fears each family shares.

"Please do not be of the opinion that your husband's sacrifice is unappreciated, for it is that very spirit that is winning the war.

"With every good wish, we remain

"Sincerely,

"And the letter is signed:

"Franklin D. Roosevelt,

439

"President of the United States

"Eleanor Roosevelt,

"First Lady of the United States

"Isn't that amazing?" Suzanne asked. "I know he doesn't do that for everybody. I'm really honored. I know the Bensons will be proud to see it, too. He had Billy's rank wrong, though. He was only an ensign."

A Western Union messenger arrived on a bicycle that afternoon, to deliver a telegram to Suzanne.

She took the envelope in her hands. Her name and address appeared through the cellophane window.

She went inside the house and walked to the kitchen where Sally was peeling potatoes.

"A telegram. At least I don't have to dread opening it," she said, referring to the black-edged telegrams that indicated a serviceman's death.

She sat at the kitchen table and tore open the envelope.

Sally turned from the sink to face her.

A smile crossed Suzanne's face. She looked up, brandishing the telegram.

"Heavenly days! This is from Madame Chiang Kai-shek."

"Really? What does she say?"

"Mrs. Benson,

"Had pleasure of knowing your husband. Fine Southern gentleman. My deepest sympathy.

"Mayling-Soong

"(Mme.) Chiang Kai-shek

"This is overwhelming," Suzanne said, wiping her eyes. "I had heard how words from people can comfort people who are grieving, but I had no idea how much difference it really makes.

"I always thought Bill was special. It's gratifying to know so many others, like Madame Chiang Kai-shek…"

"And President and Mrs. Roosevelt," Sally interjected.

"Yes. Well, I really can't claim any credit for all this praise," she said as she folded the telegram and slipped it back into its envelope. "That goes to the Bensons. They're the ones who are responsible for what he became."

Further gratification arrived two days later when a Navy officer called Suzanne and asked if he could come by the house to present a posthumous award.

When the lieutenant arrived, accompanied by a young enlisted sailor who seemed over-laden with a canvas knapsack hanging from his shoulder and a large flash camera in his hand, the two entered a living room filled with Billy's parents, sisters, and Velma, Robert, Ollie, and Buddy.

The officer introduced himself as Lieutenant Chapman, and the young sailor as Matt Blake, a photographer's mate.

"I hope you don't mind," Suzanne explained, "I asked Bill's family to be here."

The officer smiled. "Not at all. I think is it altogether appropriate."

He pulled a flat, hard, Navy-blue presentation box from his coat pocket and turned to face the gathering.

"Would you stand beside me, Mrs. Benson?" Mr. Chapman asked Suzanne, indicating his left side.

Suzanne complied and then said, "Edna and Jim, why don't you come stand on the other side of Mr. Chapman?"

The two approached shyly and took their places, Edna's hand gently holding Jim's arm.

The photographer, holding his Speed Graphic press camera before his face with both hands, moved directly in front of the four and took pictures throughout the award ceremony. Edna flinched each time the bright light quickly and brilliantly flashed.

Chapman removed an envelope from his inside breast pocket, pulled out a folded piece of paper and read:

"Lieutenant, j.g., James William Benson Jr., United States Navy Reserve, distinguished himself by performing exceptionally meritorious services to the Government of the United States, as a Naval Officer, as a Naval Flight Instructor, and in carrying out the direct orders of the President of the United States.

"Lieutenant, j.g., Benson Jr., was an exemplary leader of his men in his role as a Naval Aviator. He made significant suggestions for improving flight instruction procedures in his capacity as Flight

Instructor at NAS, Memphis, Tennessee. Those suggestions were made policy, resulting in greater efficiency in the training of cadet pilots.

"In his tenure as Flight Instructor, Lieutenant, j.g., Benson Jr., flew more than seven hundred hours instructing his students, without a single mishap.

"On his final mission, as a member of a flight crew selected by the President of the United States, to return Madame Chiang Kai-shek to China in the President's personal airplane, Lieutenant, j.g., Benson Jr., disregarded the inherent dangers the assignment presented, including an attack by enemy fighter planes, and demonstrated, characteristically, great loyalty in carrying out his orders, to the President, the citizens of the United States, and the people of China.

"It is, therefore, fitting that the United States Government recognize the invaluable contributions to the war effort of Lieutenant, j.g., William Benson by awarding him, posthumously, the Navy Distinguished Service Medal.

"Henry L. Stimson,
"Secretary of War"

Suzanne resisted the temptation to challenge the incorrect rank noted in the commendation.

The lieutenant opened the case and presented it to Suzanne.

She stepped behind the officer and slipped in between Edna and Jim, holding the case for them to admire the medal: a wide, Navy-blue ribbon with a gold stripe down the center, below which hung a small star, bearing a bas-relief anchor, and beneath that, a large bronze disk, displaying an eagle with open wings, trimmed with a Navy-blue circle, resting regally on the dark, plush lining of the case.

She handed the case to Jim to hold as she put her arms around the waists of her adopted parents. The three continued to look lovingly at the medal, tears streaming down their faces.

The rest of the family gathered around quietly, in awe of the award.

Lieutenant Chapman pulled another folded sheet of paper from his breast pocket.

"Here is the address of a company that sells display cases, if you want to mount his medals."

Suzanne blotted her eyes with a handkerchief and took the paper. "Thank you," she said.

"Now, I have another presentation for you," Mr. Chapman said.

Suzanne looked at him curiously. She and Billy's family were already overwhelmed by all the attention Billy had received.

Mr. Chapman pulled a small, black presentation box from his coat pocket.

"You may have noticed in the letter from the President that your husband had the rank, 'lieutenant, junior grade,' after his name."

"Yes, I had," she confessed.

"I am pleased to tell you it is the wish of President Roosevelt that the Navy promote Ensign James William Benson Jr., posthumously, to the rank of Lieutenant, junior grade. Here are his silver bars."

He opened the box and handed it to Suzanne.

Suzanne's eyes filled with tears again as she took the opened box into her trembling hands and looked at the pair of silver collar devices.

She shook her head slowly and handed the box to Jim.

Suzanne wiped her eyes.

"Thank you, Mr. Chapman," she said. "I appreciate this so much. I know Bill would be so proud. And thank you for bringing the medal. It is beautiful and it really means a lot to all of us."

"Here is President Roosevelt's personally signed order for the promotion," Lieutenant Chapman said, handing her an envelope.

"We'll send you some pictures we took today, and a write-up to the news media," the lieutenant added.

He and photographer excused themselves and left.

After the Bensons returned home through the back door, Suzanne wondered aloud to Sally if there might be further tributes.

Later that afternoon the telephone rang. It was T.J. Macintosh.

Suzanne knew T.J. would contact her eventually, but she had been unsure of what her response to him might be.

"Suzanne, I arrived in the States only this morning," he said. "I'm in Virginia now and wanted to talk to you."

He paused.

She wasn't certain what he expected her to say, so she said nothing.

"I have so much to say to you and I don't know how to go about it. First of all, I want to know how are you doing." he asked.

"It hasn't been easy, T.J." she said matter-of-factly, "but I think I'm doing as well as can be expected."

"Suzanne, I can't tell you how painful all this has been to me. I-I feel responsible and it has been a heavy burden for me to bear."

She didn't reply.

"I called the Bensons just now, since I didn't know where you were. I told them I wanted to visit them. And you. I owe all of you...I don't know...apologies...explanations. But I have to talk to all of you, face to face.

"I have some leave time built up I'm going to try to get a hop to Millington and take the train down there. The Bensons are going to pick me up at the station."

"When are you coming?" she asked, trying not to sound cold.

"I'm going to leave in the morning and hope to get down by afternoon. I really won't know, since I'm flying Space 'A'. Anyway, as soon as possible."

Space 'A' is flying on military aircraft if there is space available.

"Okay, T.J. Thank you for calling."

She hung up and stood beside the telephone table in the hall.

T.J. was not her enemy. Bill had made his own decision to fly to China. She had no one to blame, but she still felt uncharitable toward T.J.

T.J. was alive.

T.J. was home.

Billy was neither.

*   *   *

T.J. LOOKED FIT IN HIS MARINE green uniform. The Bensons were holding photographs T.J. was showing and narrating, when Suzanne entered through the back way.

He stood and walked to her.

"Hello, T.J."

"Suzanne, I-I can't tell you how sorry I am the way this turned out."

"I know."

"If I had it all to do again, I would have gladly taken Bill's place. Believe me, I would have, but he had been told to return to the States since we didn't know if it would be days or weeks before we could get the plane repaired."

"I don't blame you, T.J.," she said, smiling gently at him and placing her hand on his arm.

Tears ran down his face.

"I don't blame you," she repeated, placing her arms around him, letting him embrace her.

"Thank you," he said, wiping his eyes with his handkerchief.

As she stepped away from him, he asked, "Did you bring the boys?"

"No, they're taking their naps."

"Could I see them? And I have some pictures to give you."

"Sure. Come on over to Sally's with me."

The two excused themselves and walked out the back way across the alley and into Sally's kitchen, where she stood at the sink.

"Hello, Sally," he said.

"Hi, T.J.," she responded, drying her hands to return his hug.

"I've come to see the boys."

"Don't you dare wake them," she said with mock sternness.

"Aye, aye, ma'am!"

Suzanne and T.J. walked quietly into the darkened bedroom, where the twins lay sleeping soundly.

He bent over them and observed their blond, Billy Benson features. He patted each lightly on his shoulder and followed Suzanne from the room.

She walked to the living room and sat in the overstuffed mohair-covered chair and motioned for him to sit on the matching sofa next to her.

He laid three envelopes on the cushion beside him.

"Suzanne, I know how much you and Bill loved each other. I really loved him, too. I don't know anyone who didn't. He was a lovely chap and me best mate.

"I know."

"Just a little background on why we didn't leave together.

"We were attacked by a Jap Zero on the way to China and our wing was shot up. Barry and I had to stay back and work on our plane but Bill's orders were to return on the next flight.

"When I found out that his plane had gone down, I-I was really beside meself. I wanted to scream. I wanted to yell. I wanted to blame everything and everybody, but I had only meself to blame. I was the one who talked Barry into including Bill on the flight."

Tears were streaming from his eyes.

"That's why I had to come down here. I had to get forgiveness from you and the Bensons for what I did."

He reached into his inside breast pocket and pulled out a crumpled piece of paper and handed it to Suzanne.

"I took this off Barry's desk. They were all over the deck."

She looked at the sheet of stationery.

At the top was a date and below it were the words, "Dear Suzanne."

"That's as far as he got with any of them.

"I brought it to show you, in case you've wondered why you haven't heard from him. He's in the same agony I've been in."

Suzanne leaned toward him and placed her hand on his, that was gripping the arm of the sofa.

"T.J., believe me, I don't blame you or Barry. I really would like to be able to blame somebody, but I can't. I know Bill did this because he wanted to. He told me he could refuse the orders if I really wanted him to. But I knew how much it meant to him to get away, so I didn't stop him.

"I'm as much to blame as anyone. But I think we're making a big mistake if we play the blame game. No one is to blame. This is just the way it all worked out."

"Thank you," he said, wiping the tears from his face, "And now, if I could just convince meself.

"I came down here for atonement, Suzanne. I have been in such torment. I knew I could never forgive meself if you and the Bensons couldn't."

"There are no sins to atone for, T.J."

"Thank you. That makes me feel a little better," he said, smiling with relief.

Me, too, Suzanne thought.

He picked up one of the envelopes from the sofa and pulled out three eight-inch-by-ten-inch black and white photographs.

"An Army photographer met us at the airport in China. Here's a group picture for you."

She studied the photograph of the plane's crew, standing behind Generalissimo and Madame Chiang and Madame Chiang's aides with the president's plane in the background.

"And here is one Madame Chiang asked to be made."

Suzanne's face lighted up as she observed Billy's happy face, Madame Chiang, with her arm draped over his and her husband's.

"And here's one she didn't ask for," T.J. said with a smile.

Billy was kissing Madame Chiang's cheek. He held a small black box in his hand.

"She had given Bill a gift for you. That's what's in his hand."

"Thank you, T.J. I'll have these framed."

He handed her a smaller envelope.

"These are some snapshots we made in China."

She looked through the pictures.

"Thank you, T.J."

"There are a couple of other things I wanted to talk to you about," he said. "I'll have to set them up just right, though, so you won't throw me out of the house."

She looked at him.

"I know Bill took out the maximum life insurance on himself, but I know how much things cost and the money won't last forever.

"As the boys grow up and start to school, there will be expenses, and I don't want them to miss anything for lack of money."

"T.J.," she said.

"Let me finish," he said, raising his palm toward her.

"There's their schooling. And college. It'll come before you know it. And it won't be cheap.

"So, here's what I've done. Don't get mad. I've opened a savings account for each of the boys. You can write checks for anything on them any time you want."

"No, T.J. I couldn't let you do that."

"Suzanne, it's part of me atonement package. I've got to do something, don't you see? I couldn't sleep at night if I thought the boys couldn't have a good education because Bill isn't here to provide it for them, and I can. Let me do that, at least."

"It's sweet of you to offer, T.J., but I just wouldn't feel right letting you."

"Let me do it for Bill. For the twins."

She looked at her hands in her lap.

"There's already money in the account," he said. "And here are your checks."

"T.J."

"For the boys. For Bill."

She smiled. "I don't know if I'll ever use them, but okay."

He nodded and smiled as he handed the envelope to her.

"Thanks. Now there's something else.

"I never told Bill about me family. He knew that me mum was from Virginia, but I've never told a soul the rest of me story."

"What's that?" she asked with growing interest.

"Me mum was a Lee," he began.

"The Lees. Do you mean the Lees of Virginia?" she asked incredulously.

"Right, FFV, the first families of Virginia," he continued, in his broad Australian accent. "All dignified and conservative types, except for me mum. She was one of those free spirits, you know. Up and ran away Down Under, where she met me dad, but they didn't get married until I was well on the way. Her family were still big on proper introductions and all that. You can just imagine how news about me set with the Lees of Virginia."

She laughed aloud and then remembered the sleeping boys.

"Anyway, after me dad died and me mum and I moved to Hawaii, well, the family eased up on her a bit, but she's never gone back to see 'em. Her choice, not theirs. But they don't have any grudge against me, I'm proud to say.

"Since I've been in the States, I've gone up several times to the old plantation in Hampton, to meet me American family."

"How did that go?" she asked.

"Smashing! Let me tell you, Suzanne. They still live on what's left of the family plantation. Some twenty acres or so of prime real estate. Quite nice. Lovely landscaping, fountains. The main house, built in eighteen hundred and something, is a large, red brick mansion. It's not only large. Let's face it. It's huge! And then, there's the widow's cottage…"

"What's that?"

"In the olden days, when primogeniture was in flower, so to speak, whenever the master died, the oldest son took over everything, and his mum, the widow, was bumped out of the big house—they call it a hoose—and moved out into a little house with one or two rooms, away from the big house. In this case, two rooms."

"Compassionate, weren't they?"

"Well, this one is fixed up quite nicely now. They've added a little galley, a little head. As a matter of fact, they've turned it completely over to me to use whenever I want to get away from the base.

"And there's the house where me two maiden aunts lived until a year or so ago. They've moved into the big house with me uncle. He's a widower and his son—my cousin, whom I never met—was sent off to Europe and never been heard from again. Missing in action, you know."

"Oh, I'm sorry."

"Right. His only son. The last limb on that branch of the family tree. There's a daughter, but she's happily married to a bloke in Washington, and, so, I've sort of been adopted by the Lees of Stanton."

"Good for you, T.J."

"Oh, there's more. Me Uncle Jack wants me to take over the family business when the war's over."

"What's the family business?" she asked.

"The Coca-Cola bottling plant in Norfolk."

"I'll bet those thirsty sailors keep him in business."

Then she added, "I went to nurses' training in Norfolk."

"Oh, I didn't know."

"Well, anyway, since I've been received and am now a part of the family, I sort of, uh, positioned them to, uh, make an offer."

She waited.

"For you."

"For me?"

"Right. Hang on, now. Don't hit me."

She laughed again.

"Hit you? For what?"

"I told them about you and Bill and the boys, and how things are with you now, and what a fine man Bill was and how I feel responsible and all, and before I even got around to asking, me aunts said, 'Why don't you ask Suzanne if she'd like to live in our house?'"

He stopped and looked at her.

"They *what*?"

"They want you to live in the house they moved out of. They're getting old, Suzanne, and with both children gone, it's too quiet. They want some young folks around.

"It's a rather elegant house, at that...the house where they lived before they moved into the big house, I mean. It's got a living room, dining room, kitchen, and a nice screened-in back porch downstairs, three big bedrooms upstairs, and a sleeping porch, a garage. Everything. You can use their furniture—all fine antiques, you know, with Oriental rugs on the floors, or you could bring your own. They even have a live-in maid who'll clean your house and wash your dishes, too."

Suzanne laughed quietly again.

"T.J., you are too much.

"Why don't *you* move into their house?" she asked.

"Oh, I'm quite happy in the widow's cottage. It's just right for me tastes.

"Look, you can't stay here with Sally forever. Her husband will be coming home when the war's over and you'll have to go somewhere. Why not to old Virginny?"

"No. No. Thank you, T.J., but that's totally out of the question."

"The house is yours, whenever you want it, for as long as you like. No strings attached.

"Oh, and there are several hospitals in the area," he added. "And don't forget the big naval hospital at Norfolk. There are probably some doctors and nurses there that you know."

"Married nurses' children have to be at least seventeen years old," she reminded him.

"That's just for Navy nurses. There aren't any conditions like that for civilian nurses."

"You've been a busy little beaver, haven't you?"

"I told you. I need atonement."

"No, T.J. Please thank your aunts for me. That's really sweet of them, but tell them I don't think I'll be able to accept their kind and generous offer."

T.J. reached into his wallet.

"I'm going to leave me telephone number with you."

"Okay, T.J., but don't expect me to call you any time soon about your offer."

"Keep all options open," he said.

"Now, that we're having this truth session, there's something I want to talk to you about," she said, nervously twisting her diamond ring.

"Okay," he said.

"Would you tell me all you know about the plane that Bill was on when he went down?"

He took a deep breath.

"Four Jap Zeroes attacked us in the Himalayas on the way into China. One of them shot us up and we had some wing damage, like I said. Flight control cables. That was why we had to stay over."

She nodded.

"Bill couldn't wait around for us to locate the parts we needed and then fly them in. We didn't know how long it would take to get the plane repaired. It turned out to be nearly a week before we could leave. He had the Army personnel office to ask Washington what he should do and he was told to return."

She nodded.

"We saw Bill off on a transport that was going back to India, stopping along the way to pick up some wounded GIs.

"A few hours after he left, one of our crew overheard some of the Army guys talking about a plane that had radioed a 'Mayday' as it was losing altitude. He told us about it, so we went to the flight control office to see if it was Bill's plane, and it was.

"They said the radio contact was broken up pretty badly because of poor reception. You can imagine that the mountains make for poor radio transmissions.

"Anyway, all they knew was that the pilot kept saying they were losing altitude. He didn't say why. It could have been engine problems, icing, or any number of things.

"We just don't know, Suzanne."

She nodded absently.

"I guess we'll never know," she said.

*   *   *

THE DAY AFTER T.J. LEFT, Suzanne received a telephone call from Mrs. Watson.

"Oh, yes, Mrs. Watson. How are you?"

"Oh, I'm fine," she replied, "but my question to you is, 'How are you?'"

"I suppose I'm doing as well as could be expected. We're all getting by."

"I would like to drive over and pay my respects," Mrs. Watson said.

"Of course. Any time you like."

"How about now?" she asked.

"That would be just fine."

Suzanne was waiting in the living room when Mrs. Watson's big black LaSalle parked at the curb. Suzanne walked down the sidewalk to meet her guest.

Marcus, in a black suit and chauffeur's cap, held the back door for Mrs. Watson and helped her step onto the curb where Suzanne was standing. Mrs. Watson was wearing a long black dress with matching hat and gloves, and a long silver fox scarf that hung from her neck to below her waist. She steadied herself with a walking stick topped by a silver handle.

"I am so glad to see you again," Suzanne said, taking Mrs. Watson's outstretched hand.

"Do you remember Marcus?"

"Of course. How are you today, Marcus?"

Marcus removed his cap as he shook Suzanne's hand.

"Both of you, come on inside," Suzanne suggested.

The three walked slowly up the sidewalk, across the porch, and into the living room.

"Could I see the twins before we talk?"

"Of course. Come on in here."

She led them into the room where the boys were sleeping.

Mrs. Watson stood over them and smiled.

She looked at Suzanne.

"They look just like Billy. A blessing and a curse, I suspect"

Suzanne nodded.

They returned to the living room.

"Please, have a seat."

Marcus helped Mrs. Watson sit on the sofa, handed her the rolled up papers he had been carrying, and then pointed to the kitchen.

"You're welcome to stay in here," Suzanne said.

Marcus smiled shyly and shook his head.

Billy had told Suzanne of Marcus aversion to speaking.

"Okay. There are some Cokes in the refrigerator. Help yourself."

Marcus nodded and walked to the kitchen.

Suzanne sat in the large chair beside the sofa.

"Would you like anything?" Mrs. Watson.

"No, thank you. I can't stay long."

"First of all, my dear," Mrs. Watson began, "there is nothing I could say that could help you right now. I've lived so long, I've said goodbye to nearly everybody in my family.

"I've seen too many people wallow in their grief and anger and I believe that just isn't healthy. We have to get on with our lives."

Suzanne nodded agreement.

"I'm sure you know how much everybody loved Billy," Mrs. Watson said, "and if tears could bring him back, he'd be here now. He was one of the finest people I have ever known."

Suzanne smiled and nodded again. "Thank you."

Mrs. Watson handed Suzanne the paper cylinder.

"I'd like for you to look at this and tell me what you think," she said, removing her gloves.

Suzanne unrolled the paper. It was a design for a stained glass window.

A soaring Yellow Peril, surrounded by blue skies and fleecy, white clouds took up the top two thirds of the drawing.

Underneath was the inscription:

James William Benson Jr.
"Billy"
Ensign, USNR
1922-1944

"I would like to donate this to Billy's church in his memory. I don't know if they have stained windows or not, but I'll pay whatever it takes to have it installed.

"It's beautiful, Mrs. Watson," she said, as she studied the rendering.

"I believe a military theme is inappropriate in a house of worship," Mrs. Watson explained. "I thought just Billy's name and dates and that little yellow airplane he loved so much would be enough. I think simplicity befits his memory."

"I think so, too, Mrs. Watson. Except he was promoted to Lieutenant, junior grade. Could you make that change?

"Of course!"

"Well, I think it's perfect. And so sweet of you to think of it."

"I'll talk to Billy's father," Mrs. Watson said, "so he can take the design to their elders. I do hope they'll like it."

"Oh, Mrs. Watson. I know they will. Thank you again."

*   *   *

A RAPID ESCALATION OF EVENTS in 1945 led up to the end of World War II:

General Douglas MacArthur returned to the Philippines in early February and began offensive action to drive the Japanese back to the land of the rising sun.

In mid-March, the Marines took control of Japanese-held Iwo Jima in the bloodiest battle of the Pacific.

The months of April and May saw a rapid capitulation of events involving world leaders: President Roosevelt suffered a cerebral hemorrhage and died April 12. Just days later, Russian troops captured Berlin. Benito Mussolini, his mistress, and his cabinet were captured and executed on April 28. Adolph Hitler committed suicide on April 30, and Germany surrendered unconditionally May 7.

On August 6, the U.S. B-29 Superfortress, *Enola Gay*, dropped an atomic bomb on the Japanese industrial city of Hiroshima. On August 9, a second bomb was dropped on Nagasaki.

The Japanese were defeated.

President Truman declared August 14 as the day to celebrate Victory over Japan, or V-J day.

The Japanese surrendered unconditionally September 2, 1945, on the U.S. battleship *Missouri*, "the Mighty Mo."

The war in which over 55,000,000 people had died was over.

The long night was ended at last.

No more warriors would have to die.

No more death notices would have to be delivered to mothers or wives.

No more planes would have to fly the Hump.

The war was over and the combatants of every country would begin wending their ways homeward.

Billy Benson would not be in that number.

Eddie Moore would.

*   *   *

"HE'S COMING HOME! HE'S COMING HOME!" Sally was shouting over and over as she came running across the back yard, up the steps, and into the Benson home.

Everybody ran into the kitchen where Sally, shedding tears of joy, passed around the telegram she had just received.

"He's coming home in three weeks!"

Suzanne hugged Sally and wept with her.

Her husband was coming home.

Suzanne now had to face her future.

She felt it was time to start her life again.

That evening, she sat at Sally's telephone bench in the hall and called the officers' quarters at Norfolk to leave a message for T.J.

MANORLEE, Hampton, Virginia. Used by permission.

Chapter Nine
Hampton, Virginia

SUZANNE WAS PLEASED ALICE had volunteered to travel with her to Virginia, since she didn't relish the prospects of having to tend to the twins and drive alone through four states. Too, Suzanne had observed with some amusement, how Alice still gazed at T.J. with stars in her eyes each time he stayed at the Bensons. She was certain Alice had an innocent, yet, ulterior motive for offering to be a travel companion.

Jim Benson had taken the Buick to Darby's Standard Oil service station in downtown Riverton to have the oil changed and the hoses and belts checked and the gas tank filled. The family helped carry the luggage and personal effects to the car. It was stuffed so full, Edna assured Suzanne, she was certain the car could not possibly turn over.

Velma and Ollie had fried chicken and apple turnovers and baked homemade yeast rolls and packed fresh fruit for them.

After a tearful farewell, the women settled the boys in the back seat and drove away, waving as they left the Bensons' home, Buddy joyfully chasing them up the street, barking as he ran.

T.J. had drawn and mailed a detailed map for Suzanne to follow. They alternated driving and navigating as they headed east, carefully observing the 50 mile-per-hour speed limit. The narrow, single-lane state roads and the climb over the Appalachian Mountains slowed them considerably. They stayed at depressing motor courts, stopped at greasy roadside cafes after the chicken was eaten, and looked forward, with great anticipation, to arriving in Hampton.

Four days after leaving Riverton, they spotted the wooden sign announcing MANORLEE, and turned at the road bordered on either side by Milky Way Farms fences: extended, white wooden rectangles with two inserted crosspieces, making long, wide, horizontal, white 'X's.'

The main house at the end of the road was a two-story, red brick Georgian structure with a slate roof and large chimneys on either end, behind neatly trimmed boxwoods.

As soon as they turned onto the U-shaped pea-gravel driveway, two large brick-colored dogs emerged from the side yard, barking as a warning to whoever had entered their territory.

The heavy, white front door of the house swung open and two elderly women emerged.

"That's enough, Bruno, Cleo," one of the women said to the dogs, who immediately sat on the grass and watched the scene with wagging tails and broad smiles on their faces.

Suzanne and Susie opened their doors and stood.

"The dogs won't bother you," one of the women assured them as they descended the stone steps.

"Hi, I'm Suzanne Benson," Suzanne said, "and that is Alice Benson, Bill's sister."

"Welcome to Virginia, one of the women said. "I'm Annie Lee. Everybody calls me Miss Annie, and this is my sister, Lula."

Suzanne walked around the car to greet their hostesses.

Miss Annie and Miss Lula swept her up into their arms.

"We're so glad you're here," Miss Lula said.

"And you, too, Alice," Miss Lula added, hugging Alice.

Miss Annie followed suit.

"And where are the boys?" she asked.

"In the back seat. Here, we'll get them out for you."

"This is Grant," Suzanne said.

"And this is John." Alice said.

"Oh, my! Aren't you a fine-looking boy?" Miss Annie said, taking John's hand lightly in hers. Would you let me hold you?" she asked.

John looked intently at the old lady's face and reached for her pince-nez.

"Let's don't do that, John, honey," Suzanne said, reaching for Bobby's hand.

"Oh, let him. They're on a chain," she said, as she took him from his mother.

"Could I hold you, Grant?" Miss Lula asked.

Grant laughed and lifted his hands toward her.

"Come here, you sweet thing."

The two older women smothered the boys with kisses and chirped to them so lyrically, they were totally captivated.

"Let's go on inside," Miss Annie said.

"William will help you bring in whatever you need."

Suzanne and Alice followed the women inside the spacious, high-ceilinged central hall. Bruno and Cleo trotted in behind them, their toenails clicking on the random-width hardwood floor.

The hallway extended the entire length of the house. A large staircase at the far end rose from the left side went across the back and up the right side of the hall. A tall, imposing grandfather clock stood on the landing.

"Um, it smells so nice in here," Suzanne said.

"That's our potpourri," Miss Annie said. "We make it ourselves. I'm glad you like it."

"Let's go into the living room," Miss Lula said, leading them into a large, bright, formal room.

"Oh, you probably want to wash up," Miss Annie said. "I know you've had a long trip."

Miss Annie pulled a tassel on the bottom of a wide tapestry band hanging beside the door.

"Ophelia will be here in a minute. She'll show you to the bathrooms."

"Have a seat," Miss Lula said, as she and her sister continued entertaining the boys. "I thought we could get acquainted and then we'll have William take you to your hoose."

"T.J. won't be here to meet you, I'm afraid," Miss Annie said. "He was called out on a flight somewhere. He won't be in until next week."

Alice looked disappointed.

A black maid wearing a white dress and white shoes appeared at the door.

"Yes, ma'am?"

"Oh, Ophelia. Miss Suzanne and Miss Alice need to freshen up. Would you take them upstairs and show them the bathrooms?"

"Yes, ma'am."

"Hello, Ophelia. I'm Suzanne Benson, and this is my sister-in-law, Alice."

"I'm pleased to meet you," Ophelia said, returning their smiles. "Come on with me. I'll take you upstairs."

*   *   *

SUZANNE AND ALICE FOLLOWED WILLIAM, who was driving a black Ford pickup truck, to a house a hundred yards from the Lee's house. The women each picked up one of the twins as William led them up the brick steps to the porch of the large wooden house.

"We've aired the house out for you. It may still smell a little stuffy, but after you've lived in it for a few days, it'll be fine."

He unlocked the front door and held it open as the women went inside to a small foyer where the aroma of sweet spices lingered lightly in the air.

"It smells good over here, too," Suzanne said.

"That's Miss Annie and Miss Lula's potpourri."

"Here's the living room," William said, leading them into a long, low-ceilinged room with one exposed beam running its length. It was furnished with an antique camelback sofa, matching wing chairs, a desk, and a large fireplace with an elaborate mantle. A thick oriental rug covered the polished, wooden floor of random-width boards. A mirror hung over the fireplace and paintings of stern-faced ancestors hung from the walls.

Suzanne looked around at the room approvingly.

"The kitchen is over here," William said, crossing another hallway to a small kitchen. "There's a small bathroom there," he pointed out.

"And in here, the dining room."

"Very nice."

"And back there is a little sitting room with a screened porch off it," William continued.

"Heavenly days!" Suzanne said with a broad smile. "This isn't anything like our little apartment in Millington."

William took them upstairs to walk through the bedrooms.

"We put fresh linen on all the beds. All you got to do is just slip between the sheets and saw them logs."

Suzanne and Alice laughed.

"I'm sure we will. Thanks, William."

He took them to the sleeping porch where they could see the river through the trees beyond the edge of the property.

"And that little house down by the river," he said, pointing, "is where Mist' T.J. stay when he come to visit."

"The widow's cottage," Suzanne said, almost to herself.

"That's right. Where the old misses used to have to go when they husbands die.

"Now, I'm going to start bringing your things in. You can go ahead and start making yourself to home, Miss Suzanne," William said, disappearing down the stairs.

"Alice, I feel like I've won the Irish sweepstakes," Suzanne said, easing Robby onto a bed.

"It really is nice," Alice said.

"It's almost too good to be true. Oh, how I wish…" She caught herself before she finished what she had started to say, and forced herself not to cry.

*   *   *

SUZANNE FELT better after taking a bath and changing clothes. She and Alice and the boys returned to the main house for dinner, accompanied by Bruno and Cleo, who had run to greet them as they drove up in Suzanne's car.

Suzanne rapped on the door with the heavy metal knocker.

Miss Annie opened the door. She had changed into a long dress and a jeweled choker.

"Suzanne and Alice, come on in, but let that be the last time you knock on the door, Suzanne. This is your hoose now. Just call to us when you come inside. There's always somebody here."

"Here, let me take the boys into the study. Ophelia's daughter is going to watch after them and feed them while we eat."

"Well, there you are," a man's voice with a thick Virginia accent boomed from the stairway.

A tall, middle-aged, balding man in a three-piece blue pinstripe suit came toward them.

"I'm Jack Lee," he said, holding out his hand.

"I'm Suzanne, Uncle Jack," Suzanne said.

"Uncle Jack! Good for you, Suzanne," he said, giving her a gentle hug.

"And who is this lovely young lady?"

"This is my sister-in-law, Alice."

"Welcome to Virginia, Alice," he said, giving her a hug also.

"Come on into the living room," he said. "Let's get better acquainted."

He led them into the comfortable room and invited them to sit.

"Can I get you anything to drink?" he asked, walking to a bar against the wall.

Suzanne looked at Alice.

"Well, if you have some wine or sherry," Suzanne replied.

"How about you, Alice?"

"Do you have any fruit juice?"

"Of course," he said, tugging on the call bell.

*   *   *

DINNER WAS SERVED in the large, formal dining room. The table had been set with china, sparkling crystal, and polished silverware, all carefully laid out, with lighted candles in massive, ornate, silver candelabras at both ends.

Jack sat at the head of the table, his back to the kitchen door. His sisters sat on either side of him and Suzanne and Alice sat beside each of them.

"Let's say grace," Jack said, as he took the hands of his sisters. They, in turn, held Suzanne and Alice's hands.

"Our heavenly Father.

"We offer You our thanks for this day and for the food You have provided us.

"Bless our guests and our loved ones with us still and those with You.

"In the name of Jesus we pray.

"Amen

Miss Lula picked up a small, silver bell beside her plate and shook it by the slender handle.

Miss Annie unfolded her linen napkin and laid it in her lap.

Suzanne and Alice followed her cue.

The door from the kitchen opened as Ophelia backed in, carrying a silver platter with a large ham surrounded by sweet potatoes still in their skins.

She had changed to a black dress with white apron, cuffs, and a lacy white headband.

"Ah, wonderful, Ophelia," Jack said. "Right here," he said, lifting the silver carving fork and knife that had been laid out in front of his plate.

She returned with a white, fluted, ceramic bowl on a heavy pad. "This is hot, ladies. Be careful," she said, as she placed it beside Miss Lula.

"Oh, my! Look at that spoonbread!" Miss Lula said. "Ophelia makes the best spoonbread in Virginia."

"That's the truth," Miss Annie said.

Ophelia pushed through the door once again, carrying two silver bowls: one with cooked apple slices and the other with green beans, topped by lightly browned, slivered almonds.

She then walked to the mahogany sideboard for a silver pitcher to fill each water glass.

When she had finished, Jack said, "Thank you, Ophelia. It looks delicious."

"It certainly does," Suzanne echoed.

"Thank you," Ophelia said, as she returned to the kitchen.

"Pass your plates, girls. I know you're hungry after that long drive," as he began slicing the rich, salty ham.

Suzanne and Alice were introduced that night to classic Virginia cuisine: paper-thin slices of Smithfield ham; light, steaming spoonbread; baked sweet potatoes, split and drenched with real butter; fried Shenandoah Valley apples and green beans seasoned with salt pork.

Suzanne and Alice savored the food as they carried on a pleasant and spirited conversation with the Lees.

"Oh, my!" Suzanne said. "That was one of the best meals I've ever had in my life!" pressing her napkin to her lips.

"Me, too," Alice said.

"I apologize for eating so much. I didn't realize how hungry I was," Suzanne added. "And you're right about the spoonbread. It was the best I've ever had!"

"It was the first I'd ever had," Alice confessed.

"Did you like it?" Uncle Jack asked.

"Oh, yes. It was delicious. Everything was," she responded.

"Well, we wanted to make a good impression. We want you to be happy here," Jack said.

"I couldn't do this very often, though," Suzanne laughed. "I would gain a hundred pounds in no time."

Uncle Jack rose to walk to the sideboard, where he pulled a cigar from a wooden humidor and picked up a long, narrow, crystal ash-tray.

"Would you ladies object if I smoke?"

"Not at all," they assured him and watched as he clipped the cigar and lit it.

Miss Lula rang the little bell again and Ophelia came in and began to clear the table.

"Does anybody want coffee?" she asked.

"None for me, thanks," Suzanne said.

Alice shook her head.

"I guess not, Ophelia," Jack said.

"But I want to thank you for cooking all that wonderful food for us," Suzanne said.

"Me, too," Alice said.

"You're quite welcome," Ophelia said. "I'm glad you liked it."

After Ophelia left the room, Miss Annie spoke: "Ophelia and William usually don't work this late. She normally leaves the meal cooked and Lula and I serve it and clean up afterward.

"But this was special. We do so want you to be happy here, Suzanne."

Miss Annie took Suzanne's hand.

"We know what you and Alice have had to go through," she said. "I'm sure T.J. told you that we've been there, too."

Suzanne nodded her head.

"Are those your husband's wings?" Miss Lula asked.

Suzanne's hand went to the pin on the left side of her dress.

"Yes. Billy gave one of these to his mother and one to me."

"Wars never prove anything, do they?" Miss Annie said. "They change everything forever, but they all end the same. Just like the Great War. Lula and I both lost our fiancés there. I hope this is the last war we'll ever see."

"And the last one you'll ever see," Miss Lula said.

"So do I," Suzanne said. "And let me say again how much I appreciate what all of you have done. I just didn't know what I was going to do. Your offer of a house was literally a Godsend. Thank you again."

"Our pleasure," Uncle Jack said. "We need to hear some children laughing and running through the hoose again.

"By the way, Suzanne," he continued, "I took the liberty of calling all the local hospitals to ask them to send some applications. I'll give them to you before you leave"

"Thank you, Uncle Jack. I appreciate that."

"Not at all. There's a typewriter in the sitting room at your hoose. Also a fountain pen in case you don't like having to get the type lined up on the forms."

"I think the pen will be a lot easier."

"Feel free to use my sisters and me as references. A lot of people know us and it might help you."

"I certainly will. Thank you."

"And William drives me to work every morning. When you get the applications mailed out and you're ready to start interviewing, he can drive you around after he lets me off at the bottling plant, if you'd like."

She laughed.

"I think I'll decline that offer, Uncle Jack. I might give the wrong impression if I showed up for a job interview in a chauffeur-driven limousine. Somebody might think I don't really need a job."

Uncle Jack smiled broadly and nodded his head.

"I think you have a point there. Well, if you need driving directions or a phone call or anything, just feel free to ask."

"Thank you, Uncle Jack. I certainly will."

*   *   *

THE BOYS HAD BEEN PUT TO BED. Alice was brushing her

teeth as Suzanne changed for bed.

She sat at her vanity and began brushing her hair.

A framed picture of Billy in his Navy uniform stood on one side of the table and one of them on their wedding day was on the other.

She dreamily pulled the brush through her hair as she studied the photographs.

How different everything was. She had moved three times since marrying Billy. Would this move be longer lasting? She craved direction in her life. She wanted a stable home life for the boys. She wanted them to have friends.

Uncle Jack could be the father figure they needed and his sisters would certainly give them love.

She quietly longed for Billy.

How strange life is, she thought. *It isn't so much about going along your own way as it is responding and reacting to the forces and obstacles and people encountered along the way.*

Alice appeared in the doorway.

Suzanne turned to face her.

"I'm going to bed now. I don't think I'll have any trouble sleeping," Alice said.

Suzanne smiled. "Neither will I."

"It's been a good day, hasn't it?"

"Yes, it has. The Lees seem to be very fine people."

"I'm glad it's worked out for you. I know how much you miss Billy. This should help get you started again."

"I think it will. I hope so, anyway."

"Well, good night."

"Good night."

Suzanne turned back to face the mirror. She looked at Billy's photograph in his uniform. She laid the brush aside and picked up the photograph and kissed his lips.

And good night to you, too, my sweet Bill.

*   *   *

ON THE FOLLOWING SUNDAY EVENING, the telephone rang at Suzanne's house.

"Hello?"

"Suzanne?"

"Oh, hi, T.J."

"Well, how are you doing in your new digs?"

"I'm afraid I'm going to wake up and find out it was all just a dream"

"No, it's real, all right."

"Aunt Annie and Aunt Lula and Uncle Jack and Ophelia and William have been just wonderful."

"My thoughts exactly. Remember, I was a stranger there meself just a few months ago. Anyway, I'm back on base, but I'll be heading out your way in a little while and wanted to know if I could stop by."

"Of course. We'd be glad to see you. Alice is here, you know."

"No, I didn't know, but I'll be glad to see her, too."

An hour later, they heard the crunching of an approaching car and the barking of Bruno and Cleo.

A car door slammed shut, steps were heard climbing the front steps and walking across the wooden porch. The doorbell rang.

"Come in, T.J.," Suzanne said, opening the door.

T.J. walked in, removing his wool fore-and-aft cap as he did, and gave Suzanne a light hug.

Alice came bounding down the stairs and approached T.J., who greeted and hugged her, too.

"Where are the boys?" he asked.

"Upstairs. Do you want to see them?" Suzanne asked.

"Of course!"

He followed the women up the stairs and into the boys' room, where they were in their beds watching a wind-up musical display of small airplanes slowly rotating over their heads.

He walked to the cribs and spoke to the boys and caressed their heads affectionately.

The scene was bittersweet. Suzanne, of course, remembered the same sort of homecoming each evening in Memphis. T.J., too, was aware of the twist of fate in all of their lives.

"Well, you seem to have made this old house a home again," he said after they had left the boys' room.

"Everything was already set up. All I had to do was hang up my clothes. Come on downstairs. I'll make us some coffee."

The three sat in the living room, drinking coffee and talking.

"Did you stop by your uncle's house?"

"Right. I always pop in to say 'hello', especially when I plan to stay over."

"How long will you be here?" Alice asked.

"I'll have to go back to the base Tuesday morning."

"That's when I'm going back to Riverton," she said.

"I can drop you off at the train station, if you'd like," he offered.

"Sure," she said happily. "Is that okay with you, Suzanne?"

"It would be a great help. Taking the boys out, whether for a short or long period of time, is always a major maneuver."

T.J. stood.

"Well, I'm pretty tired from that long flight. I need to get me beauty sleep. Oh, would you like to see me wee cottage?"

"I'll have to take a rain check on that, T.J. I need to feed the boys."

"How about you, Alice?"

"Yes, I'd like to see it."

"Good. I'll see you tomorrow, Suzanne."

She stood and walked with them to the front door.

"Good night, T.J."

"Good night, Suzanne."

"I'll try not to wake you, Suzanne." Alice said.

"Okay. Good night."

*   *   *

SUZANNE WASN'T SURPRISED THAT a romance sprang up between T.J. and Alice. He told Suzanne casually that they had exchanged a few letters after she returned to Riverton.

Suzanne, meanwhile, interviewed for three hospital jobs: two civilian and one at the Navy base. She was offered a position as an operating room nurse at Hampton Memorial, which worked well for her. Since surgeries were scheduled during the day, she had no night shifts or emergency room duties.

She took the boys to the main house each morning as she left for work. After returning home in the afternoons, she retrieved the boys, took them to their house, where she changed clothes and cooked supper for herself and the boys. She and the boys ate dinner at the Lees Saturday and Sunday evenings.

With the boys so lovingly and well cared for, rewarding work at the hospital, along with making new friends there, and a pleasant home to come home to, Suzanne settled into her new routine and quickly felt content in Virginia.

T.J. was released from the Navy three months after her arrival. He moved into the cottage permanently and began accompanying his uncle to the bottling plant, both of them sitting in the rear seat of the black Lincoln Continental sedan as William drove.

It wasn't long before T.J. began driving himself in a second-hand Chrysler he bought, since he often had to stay late to finish his paper work and learn all the operations of the plant.

Suzanne saw him at dinner with the Lees on weekends, where he filled them in on the demise of his short-lived romance with Alice. Alice, it seems, discovered long-distance relationships required a great deal of letter writing, which she didn't particularly enjoy, and telephone calls were too expensive. Anyway, her boyfriend in Riverton had once again become more attentive to the point that he proposed marriage to her.

As Suzanne came upon the first anniversary of Billy's death, she grew quiet and withdrawn.

The Lees respected her privacy. Each of them had faced the same unhappy mileposts in two world wars themselves.

The depression lingered. Suzanne soon found herself despondent, despite efforts to mask her mood.

T.J. asked if he could visit her one Sunday night after dinner at the Lees.

They talked quietly in her living room as the boys entertained themselves in the upstairs nursery.

"I know you're still grieving, Suzanne. I've been suffering along with you," he said. "Of course, me own suffering is still mostly conscience and even though you and the Bensons have forgiven me, I haven't forgiven meself. I don't think I ever will."

"I know. It's hard to do, T.J. But you know we hold no hard feelings. In my case, I just miss Bill. And it isn't getting any better.

"Every time I pick up the boys or look at them while they sleep, I see him, since they're carbon copies of him. It's impossible for me to forget him or let him go."

"How long has it been since you've been out?" he asked.

"Too long, I guess," she said.

"Why don't we go to the movies next weekend?"

"Oh, I don't know, T.J."

"There's a drive-in theatre on the way to the base," he said. "We could put the boys in the back seat."

"We wouldn't be able to enjoy the movie."

"I'll ask me aunts if they would mind keeping them."

"Okay, but I don't want to see anything depressing. I'm down enough as it is."

"Does that rule out *Gilda*?"

"Who's in it?"

"Glen Ford."

"Who else?"

"Rita Hayworth."

"Rita Hayworth. Oh, yes. I see now," she teased.

"Caught me," he said. "I'll see what else is playing. So, it's a date?"

"Let's not call it a date. How about an evening out?"

"Fine! It's an evening out."

She noticed that she seemed to be feeling better already.

"How long has it been since you've been out?" she asked.

"I can't remember," he responded. "Uncle Jack and the plant keep me too busy."

The following Saturday, Suzanne took the twins to the Lees and awaited the arrival of T.J.

They drove to a drive-in restaurant where they had barbecue sandwiches and milk shakes brought to their car by a waitress on roller skates and served from a tray hung on the outside of the car door.

"This is like high school," she said cheerfully, as they ate their meal, listened to the outside speakers blaring *Delicado, By a Sleepy Lagoon* and other popular songs, and watched as the waitresses whizzed by.

Afterward they drove to a theater to see *It's a Wonderful Life*.

"I thought that movie was going to go downhill all the way," Suzanne said, as they drove home, "but the ending really made me feel good.

"I guess it's true that we really can measure a person's worth by how many friends he has," she said.

They both thought immediately of Bill and his capacity for making friends, but neither spoke of it.

"I agree, "T.J. said. "Especially if you're all alone."

"Like me," she added.

"And me."

"Right. If it weren't for you and the Lees, I don't know what would have happened to the boys and me."

*   *   *

THE TWO CONTINUED SEEING EACH OTHER occasionally until it became apparent to Suzanne that she was beginning to care for T.J.—for his thoughtfulness, for his patience, for his stability, for his humor, and for his devotion to her boys.

She wasn't certain she should or could let anything romantic develop.

And then one evening as he was at her front door about to leave, he took her lightly by the shoulders and looked into her eyes. He bent over to kiss her. She turned her head slightly. He kissed her on the cheek.

"Good night, T.J."

"Good night, Suzanne."

She locked the door, waited until she heard him shut his car door before turning off the porch light and the lights downstairs and walking up to her room.

She had felt a rush when she felt his lips on her face: his warm, moist lips, the stubble of his beard on her cheek, and the slight aroma of Mennen's after-shave. She touched her cheek and smelled her fingers to see if any of his aroma lingered.

It's been only fourteen months since Bill died, she thought. *This isn't right.*

But she continued seeing T.J., looking forward to their outings, now thinking of them as dates.

And she let him kiss her on the mouth.

She had backed away immediately afterward the first time and told him good night.

And the next time she didn't back away.

"I think we need to talk," she eventually told him.

They returned to the living room. She sat in a chair, and motioned for him to sit on the sofa.

"This is going to be extremely complicated," she said.

She paused.

"You're becoming more than just a friend, T.J., but how I feel about you doesn't diminish my love for Bill. I don't know how this is supposed to work, but I just don't think I should be in love with two men at the same time."

He nodded that he understood but said nothing.

"I feel like I'm cheating on Bill."

"I understand."

"I don't think I'll ever stop loving him."

"I wouldn't expect you to."

"But a woman should love only one man."

"I know."

She took a sharp breath and closed her eyes.

She let out the air and looked at him.

"I'm in a tight spot," she said.

"Time will make a difference," he suggested.

"Yes, but how long do we have?" she asked him. "I've got enough love for Bill stored up to last two or three lifetimes."

"I know."

"Let's just go slow, T.J. I've got a lot of things to sort out."

"Right. Slow."

A week later, Suzanne called Edna Benson in Riverton.

After filling Edna in on the latest accomplishments of the twins and news about her work, Edna announced with grandmotherly pride that Sally Moore "was expecting," since the word "pregnant" was still considered too shocking and vulgar for polite society to use.

After a few more exchanges, Suzanne broached the subject:

"Edna, T.J. and I are dating."

"I'm not surprised, Suzanne. He's a fine man."

"I agree with you, but that doesn't help me any."

"Because of the way both of you feel about Billy?"

"Yes, but also because I feel, in dating T.J., or thinking about any possible future between us, I'll have to be unfaithful to Bill."

"It isn't going to be easy, is it?"

"No, because I think I love Bill more now than when he was alive."

"I doubt that, Suzanne. You couldn't have possible loved him more then. All of us knew that."

"How am I going to love T.J. and love Bill, too?"

"I guess by facing the painfully obvious, Suzanne. T.J. is living and Billy isn't."

"I know that, and I've tried to make myself accept it, but I just can't do it. The last thing Bill told me when he left that morning was a promise that he would come back. And I can't get it out of my head, Edna. I believed him and I still want to believe that he'll somehow return."

"Suzanne," Edna began, "I've never told anybody this, but I've gone through every possible plot I can think of to convince myself that Billy wasn't even *in* that airplane. And then I've played with the notion that he's still alive in the plane, eating all the provisions they had stored away; or that he would somehow be able to just walk down off that mountain. Of course, none of that could be true."

She took a deep breath. "So, I always come back to the truth: That Billy was in the plane and was killed and won't ever come back."

She paused before continuing.

"And, as far as you and T.J. are concerned, you can love him and not be unfaithful to Billy. You really have to let him go, Suzanne. Accept the fact, deep in your heart, that he's gone. He's…he's dead. He isn't coming back."

Suzanne sat quietly with the telephone still to her ear.

After a few seconds, she spoke.

"I know you're right, Edna. I appreciate your being so wise and loving. I told Sally that Billy owes—owed everything he was to you and Jim. He was a wonderful man because he had such wonderful parents."

"Thank you, Suzanne. And all of us felt he deserved you. We'll always love you and never question your judgment. We love T.J., too. And Billy loved him. Jim and I would be proud to think of him as our—what? Son-in-law, once removed?"

Suzanne laughed. "No, I don't think it works that way, but I'm glad you think so highly of him."

"Oh, we do. And whatever you two decide to do will be fine with us."

"Thank you, Edna. Goodbye."

"'Good luck. Let us hear what you decide."

*   *   *

SUZANNE AND T.J. LEFT FOR THEIR HONEYMOON 18 months after Billy's plane was reported missing.

The ceremony had taken place in the living room of Manorlee, with the Lee's Anglican minister reading the vows. Suzanne wore a lime-green suit and carried a colorful nosegay. T.J. wore a double-breasted, Navy-blue pinstripe suit.

A reception in the dining room followed and then a rice and tin can sendoff, with Bruno and Cleo chasing them until the car turned onto the main road and disappeared from sight.

T.J. had rented a secluded cottage at Virginia Beach only yards from the rolling waves of the Atlantic.

They drove to a nearby country club for dinner with champagne and dancing to the music of a small band.

Driving back to their cottage, Suzanne became quiet. By the time they arrived, she was stone-faced and literally trembling.

T.J. made no mention of it.

While Suzanne was changing in the bathroom, T.J. slipped into the only pair of pajamas he owned, purchased exclusively for this night.

Suzanne emerged slowly, wearing a pastel pink linen negligee and peignoir.

T.J. walked to her and embraced her.

Her arms hung limply at her sides.

"T.J."

"Yes?"

"T.J., I don't think I can do this."

He held her tighter.

"Do you hate me?" she asked.

"Hate you? No! Never!"

"I know this isn't what you had in mind, but let's talk."

He led her to the table on their balcony overlooking the moonlit ocean. He pulled a chair out for her and then sat across the table.

The waves rolled onto the beach, breaking in long, white, hissing parabolic arches in the moonlight. Foghorns and bells could be heard over the sounds of the surf.

The breeze played gently with her hair.

It was a perfect setting for a honeymoon.

"I don't know what to say," she began.

He looked at her face in the light of the moon.

"There are three of us in there," she said, nodding toward the bedroom.

He nodded.

"Can you forgive me?"

"There's nothing to forgive," he said quietly, taking her hand.

"I'm trying to work through this. I really am."

"I know you are," he said. "We can still be happy together. I can be your friend for as long as it takes, and hope someday to be your lover."

"Thank you, T.J."

T.J. slept on a bed in another room for the next three nights, but during their time together, sightseeing, eating in restaurants, they held hands, smiled and laughed, and chatted amicably as any honeymooning couple would.

They were both happy to return to the plantation, happy to see the boys and the Lees.

At their house, they lived as any normal, happy married couple would, except at night, when Suzanne went to bed alone and T.J. retired to the sleeping porch with a briefcase of reports and papers from the bottling plant that he read in bed.

Three weeks after returning from Virginia Beach, the same dream came to her four nights in a row:

Billy, dressed in flying togs—leather jacket with a fur collar, tall boots that came to just below his knees, leather aviator's cap with the goggles pushed onto his forehead, and a long, white, billowing scarf around his neck—stood on the crest of a dark hill, against a brightly lighted pink and gold background. He smiled and waved to Suzanne. She tried to wave to him and go to him.

He lifted his arm and waved again, still smiling happily. He turned and vanished in the bright illumination on the other side of the hill.

Each time she had the dream, she woke up in a sweat.

The fourth night, however, she cried out to him, again and again, but he disappeared, nonetheless.

She awoke, hearing T.J. repeating her name as he shook her by the shoulder.

He had heard her calling, hurriedly gotten out of his bed, pulled on a pair of shorts and gone to her.

"Suzanne! Suzanne! Wake up. You're having a nightmare."

She sat up in wild-eyed alarm. She was lost. She couldn't acclimate herself.

"It's all right, now. It was just a bad dream," he said.

She looked at him, still in a panic.

"Let me get a cloth for you."

He went to the bathroom and wet a face cloth, filled a water glass, returned, and sat on the edge of her bed to wipe her face.

"Do you feel better now?"

She smiled.

"Yes. Thanks."

He offered her the water.

She drank some of it and handed him the glass.

"Thank you, T.J."

"You're welcome."

He began to stand.

"No, wait. Don't go."

He sat on the edge of the bed again, set the glass on her bedside table and laid the cloth across the top of the glass.

"It was Bill, T.J. He was waving goodbye.

"I've dreamed it for four nights. The same dream, over and over. He was dressed in his aviator's gear and he smiled and waved at me. And then he turned and disappeared over a hill."

"What do you make of it?" T.J. asked.

"He was smiling each time. You know, that wonderful, happy smile he had. He was smiling as he waved goodbye and walked away."

Suzanne took T.J.'s hand.

"I think he was telling me that you and I are okay. That he was releasing me."

T.J. smiled gently at her.

"Can you release him?" he asked.

She leaned forward and took T.J.'s arm with her hands. She leaned her face against it.

"You are one of the sweetest, dearest men I have ever known, T.J. There aren't a lot of men who would have put up with me the way you have."

He laid his hand on her head and lightly stroked her hair.

"You're worth waiting for."

"Thank you."

He stood again and reached for the glass and cloth.

"No. Don't go," she said.

He sat on the bed as he looked at her.

They sat, unmoving, gazing intently into each other's eyes in the dimly lighted room.

He placed his hand against the side of her face. She grasped it lightly with her hand and kissed his palm.

He leaned forward and kissed her on her lips. She returned the kiss, feeling the heat in her body rising.

He embraced her with both arms, pulling her close to him.

She breathed in his aroma and pulled him tightly to her.

He released her, stood, and pulled her to her feet. He held her close and kissed her passionately.

"Are we alone?" he asked.

She ran her hands slowly down his chest to his waist and unsnapped his shorts, letting them fall to the floor.

"Yes."

He pulled her gown gently over her head, tossed it aside and drew her against him again.

"Oh, Suzanne. How I love you."

READ ON FOR AN EXCERPT FROM
BILLY BENSON
THE SEQUEL TO *FLIGHTS OF ANGELS*
AVAILABLE IN 2007

Two old women, one black and one white, filled their supper plates at the kitchen stove and carried them to either end of a wooden drop-leaf table in the center of the room. They pulled their chairs to the table in short, scraping jerks and bowed their heads.

The white woman said grace: "Bless these gifts from Thy bounty that we are about to receive, O Lord. Bless our loved ones who still live and the memory of those who are with You. In the name of Jesus we pray, Amen."

"Amen," the black woman repeated.

"I always think of Billy when we have this supper," the white woman said. "He loved salmon croquettes and turnip greens and cornbread better than anybody I ever knew."

"Better than any white boy, that's for sure," the black woman laughed.

The telephone rang.

"Wouldn't you know?" the black woman said.

"I'll get it," the white woman said, turning in her chair to rise stiffly and walk the three steps to the sink, where the telephone hung from the end of a cabinet.

"Hello?"

"Edna? Hi, this is Suzanne. Turn on CNN and I'll call you back later."

Edna returned the receiver and switched on the small color television set on the counter across from the table.

"That was Suzanne," she said as she sat. "There's something on the news she wants us to see."

... and, as shown by these pictures shot from the air earlier today, the tail section of the airplane is clearly visible sticking out of the glacier.

Tibetan hunters stumbled upon the plane two days ago and this morning CNN's correspondent in India filed the report.

The markings on the craft are American and it is highly probable the plane is one of the more than five hundred U.S. transport planes that crashed into the Himalayan Mountains during World War Two, while flying supplies from India to China.

A team from the Army Central Identification Laboratory is awaiting permission from the Chinese government to explore the wreckage. The identification laboratory was established in nineteen seventy-three in Thailand by the U.S. to locate and identify the remains of combatants in the Vietnam War.

In other news, President Ronald Reagan sent gifts of his favorite jellybeans to orphanages in his home state of California ...

Edna turned off the television set and sat back in her chair.

"What do you make of that, Velma?" she asked.

"Do you reckon Suzanne thinks that might be Billy's plane?" Velma asked.

"I don't know," Edna said. She placed her hand on the Navy aviator's pin on her dress and pressed it gently, as if to confirm its presence.

"But wasn't it odd that we were just talking about him when she called?"

"It's just going to get you all worked up and then there won't be anything to it," Velma said bluntly.

"The strange thing is that I'm not sure how I'd feel about it if it does turn out to be his plane."

She placed her elbow on the edge of the table, shut her eyes and rested her head on the tips of her fingers.

The telephone rang again.

"Let me get it," Velma said, sliding her chair back and walking to the phone.

"Hello?"

"Velma? It's Suzanne. Did Edna watch that report?"

"Yes, but it ain't done nothin' but upset her."

"Will she talk to me?"

"She wants to talk to you," Velma said, handing the telephone to Edna.

"Suzanne?"

"I didn't mean to upset you, Edna, but I have had the most bizarre day. I haven't been able to get Bill out of my mind, and then when this came on, I just had the strongest feeling that maybe this is going to lead to something. Something with an ending, you know."

"Velma and I were talking about him when you called. We're having salmon croquettes and turnip greens and cornbread, and you remember how he loved them."

"Of course I remember. Velma taught me to cook them. Well, I won't bother you any more tonight. Try not to get upset over this. I'll call you tomorrow. Maybe there'll be an update."

"All right. Goodbye."

Edna handed the receiver to Velma, who had waited, disapprovingly, for her to finish the conversation.

"Are you going to be okay?" Velma asked as she returned to her chair.

Edna dropped her hands to her lap and shook her head. "I've lost my appetite."

"Eat a piece of the salmon."

She shook her head again. "I'm sorry, Velma. You went to so much trouble and I was really looking forward to it, but I just don't think I can eat."

Her companion looked at her and gave her a smile and nod of understanding.

"I think I want to go up to his room for awhile. Maybe I'll feel more like eating later," Edna said.

GENERAL BIBLIOGRAPHY

"Air Force One: A History." The History Channel video, 1966.

Barin Field reunion commemorative.

Brain, Marshall, "How Stuff Works: How Airplanes Work." Printed from Website:http //www.howstuffworks.com/airplane.htm, 2002.

Crohn, Arnold E., "A History of the V-5 Cadet Program: The First Twelve Years." Unpublished History for Fourth Reunion of Carrier Air Group 153/15, Virginia Beach, Virginia, 1989.

"Carrier on the Prairie: The Story of the U.S. Naval Station, Ottumwa, Iowa," U.S. Navy, et al.

"Flight Manual for the B-24 Liberator." Government Publication, 1942. Printed from Website: http://www/kensmen.com/b24how.html.

Boeing-Stearman's Pilot's Handbook for Model N2S-3.

"Flight Training," June, 1943. Naval Aviation, United States Naval Institute, Annapolis, Maryland, pp. 28-29.

"Flying the Piper Cub," printed from Website http://www.santapaulaairport.com/pipercub1.htm, 2002

Gelfand, H. Michael, "Tomorrow We Fly: A History of the United States Navy Pre-Flight School on the Campus of the University of Georgia, Athens, Georgia." Unpublished Masters Thesis, University of Georgia, 1994.

Herrod, Thomas E., "Hump Pilot." Self-published memoir.

Hynes, Samuel, "Flights of Passage." Savannah, Ga.: F.C. Beil, Publisher, 1988.

Lawson, Robert, and Tillman, Barrett, "U.S. Navy Air Combat, 1939-1946," MBI Publishing, 2000.

McMackin, Roland N., "The Life of a Boy from Hollow Rick, Tennessee." Unpublished autobiography, 1994.

Moser, Don, "China-Burma-India." World War II Time-Life Books, 1978.

"Naval Support Activity, Mid-South 2001." Welcome Aboard Publication for Naval Personnel, Millington, Tennessee. MARCOA Publishing, San Diego, CA.

"Student Flight Checkout. Primary Flight Instruction - Stearman N2-S." U.S. Navy training film. Procured from Historic Aviation.

"Student Flight Checkout. Intermediate Flight Instruction - SNJ." U.S. Navy training film. Procured from Historic Aviation.

"Pilot's Flight Operating Instructions for Army Model BT-13A Airplanes, Navy Model SNV-1 Airplanes," (Vultee BT-13). Replica of manual published by Flying Books, Publishers and Wholesalers, 1995.

"Pilot Procurement," Naval Aviation, June, 1943, pp. 24-25.

"Primary Training: Instructors Produce Navy Fliers for Combat." July 1, 1943, No. 244. Naval Aviation News, Navy Department, Washington, D.C., pp. 18-29.

"The Story of the Texan," Foreword by Leo J. Kohn. (History and Flight Manual.) Aviation Publications, 1975

Timberlake, Lewis, "Time of War and a Time of Peace." New York: Ballantine Books, 1986.

"The U.S. Naval College for Primary Flight Instructors," Pictorial Edition, published by Naval Air Station, New Orleans, La.

"The United States Navy Flight Preparatory Schools: Meet the N2S." (Pictures and text from Bureau of Aeronautics Training Film, "The Pilot Meets the N2S.") Published by the Jam Handy Corporation.

Wainwright, P.D., "An End of an Era: Park Field to Naval Support Activity." Unpublished history of NAS Millington, Tennessee.

Werner, David M., "Journal of a Student Naval Aviator." (Internet Diary.)Website: http://members.aol.com/DaveUF96/Journal.htm